THE ECONOMIC GEOGRAPHY
OF CHINA

THE ECONOMIC GEOGRAPHY OF CHINA

Editor: Sun Jingzhi

HONG KONG
OXFORD UNIVERSITY PRESS
OXFORD NEW YORK
1988

Oxford University Press

Oxford   New York   Toronto
Delhi   Bombay   Calcutta   Madras   Karachi
Petaling Jaya   Singapore   Hong Kong   Tokyo
Nairobi   Dar es Salaam   Cape Town
Melbourne   Auckland

and associated companies in
Berlin   Ibadan

This edition © Oxford University Press 1988
First published under the title
中國經濟地理概論
by Commercial Press, Beijing, 1984
This edition first published, by arrangement with Commercial Press,
by Oxford University Press 1988

Published in the United States
by Oxford University Press Inc., New York

ISBN 0 19 584079 8

OXFORD is a trade mark of Oxford University Press

British Library
Cataloguing-in-Publication Data
available

Library of Congress
Cataloging-in-Publication Data
available

Printed in Hong Kong by Liang Yu Printing Fty. Ltd.
Published by Oxford University Press, Warwick House, Hong Kong

Preface

ECONOMIC geography is the study of the distribution of the forces of production as determined by the mode of social production. It is only when enterprises and production departments are distributed rationally, in accordance with geographical factors, that social production is able to achieve maximum economic returns at the national level. Maximum economic returns are those requiring a minimum of manpower, material, and financial resources.

Rational distribution of the forces of production is a basic requirement of the socialist economy if it is to achieve planned and balanced development of the national economy. China's territory of 9.6 million square kilometres is abundant in natural resources and its natural conditions are also favourable. Its one billion people are industrious, with a history of civilization of thousands of years. A socialist system, when combined with such conditions, makes possible such rational distribution of the forces of production.

Since 1949, great advances have been made in industrial and agricultural production in China. The process of rationalization is continuous, however, and there is still much to be done if the country is to develop and exploit fully its tremendous natural advantages.

The distribution of production in China affects all aspects of socialist construction. Of prime concern, therefore, is collaboration between departments. Economic geography – the study of the laws governing the distribution of production – will hence play a greater role in the future restructuring of industry and agriculture as part of the process of rationalization.

The Economic Geography of China describes the historical evolution of China's present system of production. It analyzes the factors that have contributed to changes in the system, particularly since the founding of the People's Republic of China in 1949, and examines the major achievements and problems that have occurred since 1949 in economic construction and in the distribution of the forces of production. It also probes the fundamental concerns associated with continued reconstruction of the economy in the future.

Each of the five sections in the book analyzes a specific sector of production, and regional overviews identify the basic characteristics of production as well as the similarities and differences between various parts of the country.

Efforts have been made in the writing of the book to assimilate the results of scientific research carried out in China as well as to suggest new areas for study. As a study of regional economic geography, the emphasis has been on description and analysis, rather than on the basic theories of economic geography (which nevertheless are interwoven with the text, being the basis upon which analysis has been carried out). Some of the viewpoints put forward remain to be put to the practical test.

The book has been compiled jointly by Liu Zaixing, Wu Yuwen, and Lian Yitong of the China People's University and the South China Teachers'

University, who have for many years taught and conducted research in the field of economic geography.

The compilers and the editor received support from the Society for Research and Teaching on China's Economic Geography and from the Commercial Press. We also wish to express our sincere gratitude to those experts and scholars in the field of economic geography who made valuable suggestions during the writing of this book.

In recent years, large numbers of books, theses, reports, and, in particular, yearbooks have been published on the subject of China's economic development. These publications have furnished the compilers of this book with solid, reliable, and systematic data for the purposes of discussion, analysis, and comparison. Any errors are therefore our own.

SUN JINGZHI
October 1982
Beijing

Editor's Note

CHINA'S 5th Five-year Plan, which ended in 1980, had as its long-term aim the quadrupling of the gross national industrial and agricultural output by the year 2000, based on the 1980 level of production. The material and data on China's economy used in this book are thus dated, for the most part, up to and including 1980.

In order to provide readers with information on changes in China's economic targets, figures relating to China's basic production situation in 1981 have been tabulated and appear as an appendix at the back of the book. Statistics on the national economy do not include Taiwan, Hong Kong, or Macau.

In the process of compiling this book, reference was made to many books, articles, and news reports. Space limitations mean that not all of them can be listed here. However, the main references appear in the Bibliography at the back of the book.

The writing of the book was done as follows. Parts I and II were written by Liu Zaixing; Part III was written by Wu Yuwen; Part IV was written by Lian Yitong; and Part V was written by Liu Zaixing and Lian Yitong. The figures were prepared by Wang Jianqin and Luo Shoumei.

October 1982

Contents

Part IV   Transport and Communications

Tables

Appendix: China's Production
Statistics, 1981

Figures

Part I: The Development of Production

1. Introduction

Geography

The People's Republic of China ('the PRC') is the third largest country in the world, extending 5,200 kilometres from east to west and 5,500 kilometres from north to south. The northernmost point is the Heilong Jiang (Heilong river), north of Mohe in Heilongjiang province; the southernmost point is Zengmu Shoal in the Nansha Islands in the South China Sea. The total area is 9.6 million square kilometres.

China's land border of 22,800 kilometres is shared with Korea in the north-east; the Soviet Union in the north-east and north-west; Mongolia in the north; Afghanistan and Pakistan in the west; India, Nepal, Sikkim, and Bhutan in the south-west; and Burma, Laos, and Vietnam in the south. To the east and south-east, it faces Japan, the Philippines, Malaysia, Brunei, and Indonesia.

Population

China has the world's biggest population, with more than a billion people. The Hans make up 94 per cent of the population; the balance is made up of 55 minority nationalities. Despite differences in their numbers and their levels of economic and cultural development, these various nationalities have influenced each other throughout history and have together created China's unique civilization.

Historical Development

Civilization began in China in the 21st century BC. In the intervening 4,000 years, China has contributed a great deal to the scientific knowledge and culture of mankind. During the Tang and Song dynasties (7th–13th centuries), China led the world in economic and cultural development. During the 16th, 17th, and 18th centuries, however, a new period in world history began with the development of Western European countries from feudal to capitalist societies.

Although in the West the new capitalist system encouraged the development of large-scale production, society in China was still largely feudal; a small-scale peasant economy was controlled by a feudal land system which was closed, stagnant, and self-supporting. Feudalism resisted the concentration of capital, the socialization and division of labour, and improvements in the tools of production. It made impossible the large-scale use of natural resources and modern science and technology. As a result, China lagged far behind the newly emerged capitalist countries in terms of its forces of production and level of output.

China was defeated by Britain in the First Opium War (1839–42) and the doors of the Qing dynasty were forcibly opened to the West. This foreign interference affected China's self-supporting economic structure and changed the character of Chinese society. For more than 100 years, social, economic, scientific, and technological development was impeded and China became a semi-feudal, semi-colonial country. What little modern industry, communications, and transportation did exist developed very slowly. Agriculture — the main occupation of the country's labour force — was in a state of regression, and economic development varied considerably from area to area. There was little co-operation between the cities and the countryside. In short, the country was in a state of chaos and near-collapse. In 1911, a popular democratic revolution finally resulted in the fall of the Qing dynasty and the establishment of the Chinese Republic in 1912. The May Fourth Movement of 1919, led by the Communist Party of China, found great popular support which eventually led to the establishment of the People's Republic of China in 1949.

Since 1949, the economy of China has been built up through an independent industrial-agricultural economic system. Science and technology have expanded and the standard of living has improved. Production in formerly advanced areas has been expanded and new industries have been established and developed in the backward areas. New production bases, transport lines, and towns have been built in the interior and in the minority nationality areas. However, the post-1949 period has also seen a period of lowered economic effectiveness and other difficulties caused by mistakes in national economic construction policies and the distribution of production. New approaches in recent years, however, have effected considerable improvements in the country's economic situation. Continued adjustment of the economic structure, consolidation of existing enterprises, and reorganization of the distribution of production — fast, efficient, and well-planned development — will ensure China's place amongst the comparatively economically advanced countries by the 1990s.

Administration

China is a socialist country, based on a worker-peasant alliance. Its government is a people's democratic dictatorship. The country is divided into provinces, autonomous regions, and municipalities under the direct control of the central government (Fig. 1.1). Provinces and autonomous regions are divided into autonomous *zhou* (prefectures), counties, autonomous counties, and cities. Counties and autonomous counties are divided into *xiang* and townships. Large cities and municipalities are divided into districts and counties. Autonomous *zhou* are divided into counties, autonomous counties, and cities. Autonomous regions, *zhou*, and counties have national autonomy. The minority nationalities manage their own internal and local affairs under the leadership of the Communist Party and the government. Special administrative zones have also been established by the central government to suit special needs (Table 1.1 and Fig. 1.2).

Fig. 1.1 China's Administrative System

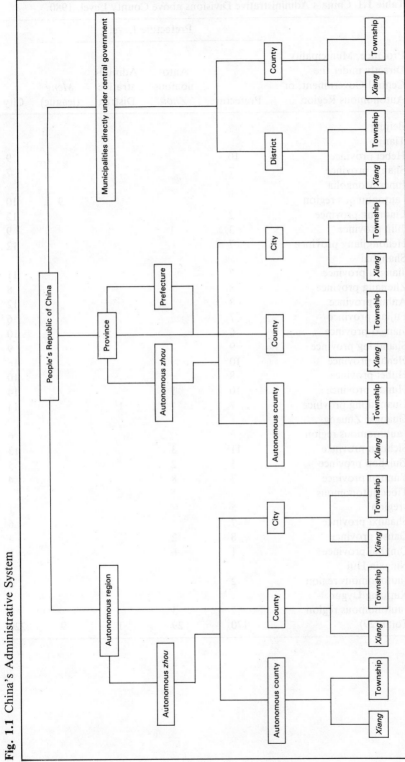

Table 1.1 China's Administrative Divisions above County Level, 1980

Province, Municipality Directly under the Central Government, or Autonomous Region	Prefecture Level				
	Prefecture	Auto-nomous *Zhou*	Admini-strative District	*Meng* (league)	City
Beijing					
Tianjin					
Hebei province	10				9
Shanxi province	7				7
Inner Mongolia autonomous region				9	10
Liaoning province	2				12
Jilin province	3	1			9
Heilongjiang province	7				12
Shanghai					
Jiangsu province	7				11
Zhejiang province	8				8
Anhui province	8				12
Fujian province	7				6
Jiangxi province	6				10
Shandong province	9				9
Henan province	10				16
Hubei province	8				10
Hunan province	10	1			14
Guangdong province	7	1	1[1]		14
Guangxi Zhuang autonomous region	8				6
Sichuan province	11	3			13
Guizhou province	5	2			5
Yunnan province	7	8			4
Tibet autonomous region	5				1
Shaanxi province	7				6
Gansu province	8	2			4
Qinghai province	1	6			2
Ningxia Hui autonomous region	2				2
Xinjiang Uygur autonomous region	7	5			8
Total (29)	170	29	1	9	220

				County Level				
County	Autonomous County	Qi (banner)	Autonomous Qi	Special Region	Industrial and Agricultural Districts	Forest District	Mountains	Township
9								
5								
137	2							
101								
22		54	3					
43	2							
35	2							
63	1							
10								
64								
65								
70								
62								
80							1[5]	
106								
111								
70	2					1[4]		
86	4							
92	3							
72	8							
177	2				3[3]			
66	9			4[2]				
102	19							1[6]
71								
91								
66	7							
32	5							
16								
74	6							
1,998	72	54	3	4	3	1	1	1

Table 1.1 *continued*

Province, Municipality Directly under the Central Government, or Autonomous Region	Land Area (km²)	Population (10,000)	Capital
Beijing	1.68 m.	886	
Tianjin	over 1.1 m.	751	
Hebei province	19 m.	5,168	Shijiazhuang
Shanxi province	over 15 m.	2,476	Taiyuan
Inner Mongolia autonomous region	over 110 m.	1,877	Hohhot
Liaoning province	over 15 m.	3,487	Shenyang
Jilin province	over 18 m.	2,211	Changchun
Heilongjiang province	over 46 m.	3,204	Harbin
Shanghai	5,800	1,146	
Jiangsu province	over 10 m.	5,938	Nanjing
Zhejiang province	over 10 m.	3,827	Hangzhou
Anhui province	over 13 m.	4,893	Hefei
Fujian province	over 12 m.	2,524	Fuzhou
Jiangxi province	over 16 m.	3,270	Nanchang
Shandong province	over 15 m.	7,296	Jinan
Henan province	over 16 m.	7,286	Zhengzhou
Hubei province	over 18 m.	4,684	Wuhan
Hunan province	over 21 m.	5,281	Changsha
Guangdong province	over 22 m.	5,780	Guangzhou
Guangxi Zhuang autonomous region	over 23 m.	3,538	Nanning
Sichuan province	over 56 m.	9,820	Chengdu
Guizhou province	over 17 m.	2,777	Guiyang
Yunnan province	over 38 m.	3,173	Kunming
Tibet autonomous region	over 120 m.	185	Lhasa
Shaanxi province	over 19 m.	2,831	Xi'an
Gansu province	over 39 m.	1,918	Lanzhou
Qinghai province	over 72 m.	377	Xining
Ningxia Hui autonomous region	over 6.6 m.	374	Yinchuan
Xinjiang Uygur autonomous region	over 160 m.	1,283	Ürümqi
Total (29)			

Notes: 1. Hainan administrative area.
2. Shuicheng, Liuzhi, Panxian, and Wanshan special districts.
3. Jinkouhe, Huayun, and Baisha industrial and agricultural districts.
4. Shennongjia forest district.
5. Jinggang Shan.
6. Wanting town.

Fig. 1.2 China's Administrative District Divisions

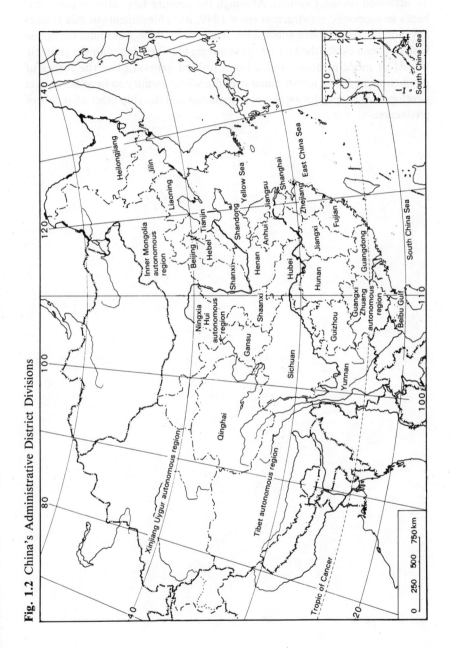

Development Prospects

China's long history, its large land area and population, and its varied natural environments and rich natural resources are factors which can be used to create an advanced socialist system. Although the country has suffered some set-backs in economic construction since 1949, its achievements in this respect have, on the whole, been substantial. A relatively wide and sound economic base has been established on which to advance. In keeping with the strategic targets of modernization, and using a unified general plan, the forces of production are being redistributed over the whole country so as to best effect development in specific areas and to maintain and develop other elements of production.

2. Factors Affecting Production

THE location of production bases and the level of development of production are determined by a number of factors. The location of these bases is known as the 'spatial distribution' of production. Different countries may have different modes of production, or similar modes which vary in accordance with the particular requirements of each country.

This does not prevent the same economic basis from showing infinite variations and gradations in its appearance, even though its principal conditions are everywhere the same. This is due to innumerable outside circumstances, natural environment, race peculiarities, outside historical influences, and so forth, all of which must be ascertained by careful analysis.[1]

China is a socialist country, based on public ownership. The socialist mode of production has enabled China to begin to transform the irrational distribution of production of the pre-1949 era into a new, rational distribution of production. This has been achieved in a number of stages according to an overall plan. Within the framework of the socialist mode, however, account has been taken of other factors which determine the distribution and development of production. Natural conditions, natural resources, population, and regional economic and technical levels all influence production to some extent.

Natural Conditions

China occupies one-quarter of the land area of Asia and 6.4 per cent of the world's land area. It is almost the size of Europe. In terms of available land in which to distribute enterprises, it therefore has a large area in which to manoeuvre and many areas from which to choose. Although a large expanse of land provides many natural resources, it also has a great variety of natural conditions, some of which will be more favourable to production and its distribution than others.

Although China's absolute land resource is enormous, the country's huge population means that each person has only 15 *mu* (or one hectare), compared with the world average of 49.5 *mu*. This per-capita figure is further reduced when the mountainous regions (33 per cent of the total area), plateaux (26 per cent), and hills (10 per cent) are taken into account; China's plains constitute only 12 per cent of the total land area. Land above 1,000 metres above sea level constitutes 65 per cent of the total land; west of the Lanzhou–Kunming line, most of the land is mountainous, with some areas at 3,500 metres.

1. Karl Marx, *Capital* (Beijing, People's Publishing House, 1975), Vol. 3, p. 892.

Most of China's mountains run from west to east. In addition to being important sources of minerals, they act on air currents to produce rainfall, they prevent the passage of cold air masses from the north, and their forests provide plants and animals. However, most of the land in the mountainous areas cannot be used productively. High altitudes and low temperatures provide only a short growing season, and hilly terrain and a thin soil cover make farming difficult. Irrational use of such land causes water loss and soil erosion. Some mountainous areas are completely unsuitable for cultivation or any other type of enterprise.

Because of the high proportion of unusable mountain and hill land, and because of the large expanses of desert (more than 1.51 billion *mu*), China's land utilization ratio is low and there are very few suitable areas still to be developed. Of the total land area, 10.4 per cent (1,800 million *mu*) is under cultivation. Forests cover 1,800 million *mu* (12.7 per cent) and pastures cover 5,300 million *mu*, although most are dry or semi-dry with a low productive efficiency for agriculture. Land suitable for opening up in the future to agriculture, forestry, and animal husbandry has been estimated at only 1,880 million *mu*. Much of this, however, is suitable only for growing trees or for breeding stock. Only 500 million *mu* is suitable for farming or for building artificial pastures.

At the same time as there exists a severe shortage of new land suitable for cultivation or production, some suitable land is being used unscientifically or is not being used at all because of the irrational agricultural production structure and land use in the past. These factors have reduced the level of production below that which the amount of suitable and available land makes possible. Therefore, there is wide scope for the future development of agriculture, forestry, animal husbandry, and aquaculture if the structure of production is adjusted through rational planning and if land is used according to local conditions.

China from north to south encompasses five climatic zones — cold-temperate, temperate, warm-temperate, subtropical, and torrid. Most of the country is in the temperate and subtropical zones. With the exception of most of the Qinghai–Tibet plateau, only 26.7 per cent of the country is in high altitudes with a cold climate; another 1.2 per cent is in the cold-temperate zone.

The annual accumulated temperature from north to south is 2,000–9,000°C. The frost-free period ranges from 120 days to year round. The total hours of sunshine (with the exception of the Sichuan basin, the Guizhou plateau, the hilly areas south of the Chang Jiang (Yangtze river), and some of the south-eastern areas of Tibet) exceed 2,000. In north-west China and most of the Qinghai–Tibet plateau, the annual hours of sunshine exceed 3,000. The total annual radiation volume of the sun throughout the country is 80–200 kcal. per square metre, with the Qinghai–Tibet plateau and the north-western regions receiving the most radiation volume. These favourable conditions are ideal for crop cultivation.

China has distinctive monsoon and continental climates from east to west. The eastern parts of the country are humid or semi-humid, with a high rainfall. Although they comprise only 48 per cent of the country's total area, these areas record 80 per cent of the total rainfall and 90 per cent of the total river run-off volume. More than 80 per cent of the rainfall occurs during the hot crop-growing period and these summer monsoons moderate temperatures in north and south China for nearly half the year. Because northern China is warmer than regions at the same latitude in other parts of the world, annual warm-weather plants can be cultivated. However, a monsoon climate is unstable and the volume of rainfall and run-off vary considerably from season to season and from year to year, causing both floods and droughts.

Western China (52 per cent of the total land area) has a continental climate and is divided into arid and semi-arid regions. The volume of rainfall is small and other water resources are poor. Crops are grown in the semi-arid regions without irrigation, except near the mountains where there is water from melted snow or in oases where underground water can be tapped.

The absolute volume of China's water resources is large. The average annual precipitation is 630 millimetres and the average river run-off is 2,660 billion cubic metres (the sixth highest in the world). However, the volume of water per unit of area is lower than in most other countries. It is also 315 millimetres lower than that of the average run-off of the world's total land area. The volume average per capita is even smaller (2,700 cubic metres), being one-quarter of the world average.

Approximately 800 million cubic metres of underground water is available for use every year and deep ground water, snow on the high mountains, and glaciers are large water reserves, though as yet undeveloped.

The distribution of water resources in China is uneven, with wide variations between the coastal and inland areas and between the north and the south. Fujian, most of Guangdong, Jiangxi, and Hunan, and part of Guangxi, Sichuan, Yunnan, and Tibet have rich water resources. In normal years, their run-off depth is more than 1,000 millimetres. The broad middle and lower reaches of the Chang Jiang south of the Hai He (Hai river) and the Hanshui river, Yunnan, Guangdong, the major part of Sichuan, and the Changbai Shan (Changbai mountain) area in the north-east have the next richest water resources. In normal years, their run-off depth is between 300 and 1,000 millimetres. The North China Plain, Shaanxi, most of the areas north-east of the Huai He (Huai river) and the Hanshui river, southern Gansu, western Sichuan, and eastern Tibet have a run-off depth of between 50 and 300 millimetres in normal years. The poorest water resources are in the pastoral areas in Inner Mongolia, the upper reaches of the Huang He (Yellow river), western Tibet, the Tian Shan (Tian mountain) area, and the Altay mountain area in Xinjiang. Their average run-off depth is 10–50 millimetres. That of the arid areas of Inner Mongolia, Ningxia, Gansu, the desert area in Xinjiang, and the barren lands in Tibet is less than 10 millimetres.

The Chang Jiang and Zhu Jiang (Pearl river) valleys in the south comprise only 24 per cent of the country's total area, but their surface run-off covers as much as 52 per cent of the total area. By comparison, the Huang He, Huai He, and Hai He valleys in the north cover 14 per cent of the country's total area, but their surface run-off covers only 4.9 per cent of the total area.

The distribution of water resources is also affected by monsoons, which concentrate much of the annual rainfall in a short rainy season. At that time, the run-off is large, but it may be seriously inadequate during the dry seasons. The inadequate number of water conservation projects means that even during times of abundant run-off, much of it is wasted. The uneven distribution of water resources in China has a direct impact on agriculture, industry, and urban facilities.

Topographical and climatic conditions and varied human activities create distinct regional differences in soil types. On the Qinghai-Tibet plateau and in the mountainous areas of the north-west, the soil is mainly alpine. In the arid north-west are desert and saline-alkaline soils, with steppe soil in the semi-dry areas. In the humid areas of the east, soils are of the forest type. From north to south, brown conifer forest soil gives way to dark brown, light brown, yellow, and red soils. Soils also vary in their content of organic matter. Dry desert soil, with only 0.15–0.5 per cent organic matter, has a humus layer 20–30 centimetres thick. The chestnut soil of the steppes in the semi-dry regions has 30–80 centimetres of humus and 1.5–3.8 per cent organic matter. Black earth has 3–4 per cent organic matter (6–10 per cent in some areas); the brown forest soil in the humid areas contains 2–9 per cent; yellow soil has 5–10 per cent; red soil has 1–4 per cent; and laterite soil has 8–10 per cent organic matter.

China's geographical conditions affect the distribution of its animal and plant resources. The eastern regions have a monsoon climate with high rainfall (400–2,000 millimetres), most of which falls in the summer; both floods and droughts are common because of the uneven distribution of rainfall. These areas account for 92 per cent of the country's cultivated and forest land as well as 95 per cent of the total farm population, which produces 95 per cent of China's total agricultural output. Livestock breeding is also important in these areas.

The continental dry and semi-dry areas in the north-west consist mostly of desert and saline-alkaline soils which provide poor support for vegetation. In the south-west, the high elevation and low temperatures make the land difficult to utilize.

The subtropical and torrid regions in the south, with abundant rainfall and warm temperatures, grow two or three crops a year on the available land. The slightly acidic soil is well suited to cultivation and livestock breeding.

North China has vast areas of flat land and a warm-temperate climate which is suitable for crop cultivation. However, the lack of forests and an unreliable water supply can turn the soil to saline-alkaline and can cause floods and droughts. The loess plateau in the north has warm temperatures but low rainfall; the soil is loose and deep and the terrain is hilly, creating sparse vegetation cover and serious soil erosion. The per-unit yield of crops is low.

The huge North-east China Plain has fertile soil and good rainfall, and there are many forests. Temperatures are low, however, and the growing period is short (usually only one crop a year).

Natural conditions such as topography, climate, and soil fertility therefore vary considerably from one part of China to another, affecting their suitability for agricultural production.

Mineral Resources

To date, more than 140 minerals have been found in China and the reserves of 132, including 50 metals, have been verified. The reserves of tungsten, antimony, zinc, rare earth, and lithium are the largest in the world, and those of tin, mercury, vanadium, titanium, molybdenum, lead, aluminium, copper, nickel, manganese, and iron are amongst the world's largest. Of the 80 non-metals, troilite, magnesite, and boron reserves are the largest in the world; phosphate reserves are the second largest; and the reserves of coal, asbestos, gypsum, graphite, fluorite, alum, rock salt, and arsenic rank amongst the largest. Rare, high-quality non-metal minerals include piezo-electric crystal, diamonds, rezhikite, and Iceland spar.

China's rich energy resources are of great importance in production and in the overall development of the country's economy. The reserves of usable water resources are the largest in the world and there are good supplies of oil and natural gas. A number of factors determine the use of these mineral reserves, such as their quality, the presence of associated deposits, and their availability, distribution, and accessibility.

Most of China's iron resources are medium-grade or lean ore which requires special dressing; high-grade ore accounts for less than 5 per cent and its widely scattered deposits hinder concentrated exploitation. Less than 10 per cent of the country's copper deposits have a copper content exceeding 2 per cent. Compared with the copper content of deposits in Zambia and Zaire, China's average copper grade is very low. Similarly, only a very small percentage of phosphorus ore deposits are of a high grade. Bauxite deposits are mainly boehmite, containing a higher percentage of silicon, and the ratio of aluminium to silicon is lower than gibbsite. Low-grade ore requires complex separation and smelting procedures, resulting in high production costs.

Iron deposits found on the middle and lower reaches of the Chang Jiang and in Hebei, Shandong, and Shanxi provinces are often associated with copper, cobalt, and sulphur. Those in Guangdong and Fujian are linked with tin, antimony, lead, and zinc. In Bayan Obo, iron ore contains large amounts of rare earth, niobium, and fluorite and in the Panxi area and Damiao, it is associated with vanadium, titanium, nickel, and cobalt.

China has large reserves of vanadium, but only 9 per cent has a high content; the remainder is scattered in other mineral deposits. Copper ore deposits on the middle and lower reaches of the Chang Jiang are often associated with molybdenum, cobalt, gold, silver or tungsten, and tin. In the north-west and south-west, it is often associated with lead, zinc, gold, silver, cadmium, indium, and selenium. The lead-zinc ore in Hunan, Guangdong, Jiangxi, Sichuan, Guizhou, Qinghai, Xinjiang, and Shaanxi is associated with cadmium, germanium, gallium, and indium. Some non-metallic mineral deposits, such as phosphorus, are associated with rare earth, uranium, iron, vanadium, and titanium. Although deposits of combined ores provide varied resources, they can be difficult to separate and smelt and so have a low recovery rate.

Some minerals are largely unavailable. China has low reserves of chromium, beryllium, zirconium, hafnium, gallium, and cesium. To date, sylvite (an important potash fertilizer used in agriculture) has been found in only a dozen places. The country's reserves of potassium chloride are only one-thousandth of the world's total supply of sylvite, and sufficient only to produce 250,000–500,000 tonnes of potash fertilizer a year.

The distribution of China's main mineral resources also varies. For example, iron, copper, coal, phosphorus, and some other minerals are found in more than 20 provinces and autonomous regions. A dozen provinces and regions have reserves of wolfram, bauxite, stibium, and asbestos, and diamonds have been found only in Shandong and Liaoning. The varied distribution of these resources contributes to the development of different sized industries. Transportation over long distances is a problem, however, because of the often remote or inaccessible locations of deposits. For example, chromium is found mainly in Xinjiang, Inner Mongolia, and Tibet. Water resources are found mainly in the south-west, far from the industrial centres which require large quantities of energy. The rich oil and natural gas fields are located mainly in the desert areas in north-western China, where population is sparse, transportation is difficult, and water supplies are inadequate.

Some areas rich in resources do not co-operate with one another. For example, Liaoning province has large deposits of iron ore and manganese ore, but most of it is of a low quality and it has to import high-quality ores from other areas. Liaoning also has insufficient deposits of coking coal and hard refractory clay for its needs, and no deposits of chromium, vanadium, or titanium ore, which also have to be imported. Heilongjiang is rich in coking coal, but lacks iron ore; Jiangsu has large deposits of iron ore, but insufficient coal.

Accessibility also affects the use of verified reserves. In some cases, geological conditions and the difficulties of separating the ores prevent their exploitation. One-quarter of China's iron ore reserves are inaccessible for exploitation at present.

Population

China has long had the world's largest population. Several times between 1954 and 1957 and between 1962 and 1971, the population reached a peak and its increase was essentially out of control. Between 1949 and 1980, the population increased by 650 million (the net increase was 440 million). At present, China accounts for 22 per cent of the world's population.

A large population is an important factor in production. It provides large labour resources and a large domestic market. Purchasing power has increased in recent years, along with the per-capita income. The total volume of retail sales in 1980 was 214.6 billion *Renminbi* (hereafter, the Chinese currency is referred to as RMB), an increase of RMB34 billion over the 1979 total. A further RMB20.4 billion increase over the previous year was recorded in 1981. Such a huge market favours the development of production, but it also poses some problems.

A large population reduces the per-capita volume of natural resources. The average per capita of natural resources in China is lower than the world average. Although it has the world's largest water power reserves, the per-capita average per year of power is only 1,964 kwh. (the world average is 2,330 kwh. per year). The country's rivers have a total run-off volume of 266 million cubic metres, which is sixth in the world, but the per-capita average is one-quarter of the world average. China is the world's third largest country, but the average area per person is only 31 per cent of the world average. Cultivated land is 31.25 per cent, forest is 11.87 per cent, and grassland is 50 per cent of the world average.

A large population also slows the country's accumulation. Demographers have calculated that RMB1,600 is needed to raise a child to 16 years of age in the rural areas; RMB4,800 is needed in the small and medium-sized cities, and RMB6,900 is necessary in the large cities. Since 1949, 600 million people have been born. It has been estimated that RMB1 billion has been spent by the state, collectives, and families on raising those people. One-third of state and collective accumulation funds have been spent in this manner, and social material wealth and state accumulation have been affected as a result.

A further problem is the standard of education of the population. Investment in education has not kept pace with the rapid increase in population. The number of technical personnel and student enrolments in universities per 10,000 people is lower than in some other developing countries. Of the country's 800 million peasants, 30 per cent are illiterate and 40 per cent have been educated only to primary school level. The declining standard of education affects the growth of technology and production.

Since 1949, China's national economy has developed rapidly. The effects of increased material wealth on the standard of living have been offset, however, by the rapid increase in population. Between 1952 and 1978, the national consumption fund increased 2.9-fold. The average annual increase was 5.4 per cent. During the same period, the population increased by 66.7 per cent. As a result, the average consumption per person increased only 1.3-fold and the average annual increase against population was 3.2 per cent. This meant that 60 per cent of the accumulation fund was spent each year on the population increase. The net increase per capita was therefore very slow and, at times, it decreased. Problems occurred in the provision of employment, communications, transport, and housing.

China has a rural-based population. More than 80 per cent of the population are peasants and 70 per cent of the total labour force is engaged in agriculture. The rural nature of the population is greater even than in India or Brazil (Table 2.1). The difficulties involved in harnessing 800 million peasants to carry out China's construction are of great importance in terms of the country's production system.

China's population is also young. The average population growth rate since 1949 is 20 per cent (25.95 per cent in 1970, after which it decreased to 11.66 per cent in 1979). During that time, 600 million people have been born and the age structure is young: 65 per cent are under 30, 50 per cent are under 21, and less than 5 per cent are over 65. The median age is 21, compared with the world average of 22.9. The natural population growth is expected to increase in the near future because of the large numbers of people born during the 1950s and 1960s (peak population growth decades) who are

Table 2.1 Agricultural Population in the Total Labour Force in China and Other Countries, 1978 (%)

Country	Percentage of Agricultural Population in the Total Population	Percentage of Agri-cultural Power in the Social Labour Force
China	84.6	73.8
United States	3.7	5.0
Soviet Union	18.1	18.1
Japan	12.2	12.5
France	9.5	9.5
Great Britain	2.2	2.2
Federal Republic of Germany	4.6	4.6
Hungary	19.3	17.3
Romania	49.0	49.0
Yugoslavia	39.8	39.8
India	64.6	64.6
Brazil	39.7	39.7
World Total	46.9	46.2

Source: *China's Agricultural Yearbook, 1980* (Agricultural Publishing House, Beijing, 1981).

now of marriageable age. If the average birth rate can be controlled at 1.5, then 15 million people will be born each year (a net increase of 10 million), resulting in a population of 1.2 billion by the year 2000. The country's total labour force will be 600 million and there will be 5–6 million people unemployed.

Although family planning methods could be used to control China's population growth, of more importance is the need to develop production and a thriving economy. The aim of China's national economic construction, as determined by the 12th Party Congress in 1982, is a fourfold increase in the total national industrial and agricultural output value by the end of the century, to be achieved through continued improvements in economic effectiveness. The average yearly increase of 7.2 per cent will mean an output value of RMB2,800 billion. The national income will be increased at the same speed as industrial and agricultural production, to RMB1,400 billion. The per-capita income in urban and rural areas will be doubled and living standards will be much improved.

China is a unified country of many nationalities. The most populous nationality is the Han and the largest minority nationality is the Zhuang, with more than 13 million people. The smallest minority is the Hezhe, with only 1,500 people. Although they are small in number, the minority nationalities are scattered over 50–60 per cent of the country in the five large autonomous regions and in compact communities in the three north-eastern provinces; in Gansu and Qinghai in the north; Sichuan, Yunnan, and Guizhou in the south; Hubei, Hunan, and Guangdong in central and south China;

Hebei in the north; and Fujian in the east. There are also 10 million minority nationals living amongst the Hans in communities throughout the country.

The minority nationality areas abound in natural resources. The Hetao plain in Ningxia and Inner Mongolia is one of China's main commercial grain bases. Xinjiang is China's largest producer of long staple cotton. Guangxi yields abundant sugar-cane; and Yunnan, Guangdong, and Hainan Island produce coffee, rubber, and other tropical crops. China's largest natural pastures and forests also lie in the minority nationality areas. These have rich resources and deposits of coal, oil, iron, tin, bauxite, rare earth, copper, zinc, potassium, salt, and asbestos.

The main compact communities of the minority nationalities are in the border regions. Their economic and cultural development is uneven and behind that of areas in which the Hans live. Development of the economy and culture in the minority nationality areas would enable China's natural resources to be exploited in a planned way. It would also unify and strengthen the country and provide secure border regions.

The uneven distribution of population also affects production. Although China's average population density is more than 100 people per square kilometre, the distribution of population over the total area is uneven. Some 90 per cent of the country's population is concentrated in the areas east of a line between the Da Hinggan mountains and Tengchong county. Of these, 80 per cent are in the North China Plain, the middle and lower Chang Jiang plain, the Zhu Jiang delta, the Chengdu plain, and other low-lying areas. Very high densities occur in Jiangsu (580 people per square kilometre), Shandong (482), and Henan (499), and very low densities occur in the western provinces, such as Xinjiang (8 people per square kilometre), Qinghai (less than 5), and Tibet (less than 2). The mountainous regions have very few inhabitants.

Since 1949, the western regions have developed as production, and especially industry, has shifted away from the coastal centres. The population has increased faster in the western regions than in other parts of the country, including the densely populated areas in the east. By 1979, China's population had increased by 80 per cent over its 1949 total. Shanghai's increase was 50 per cent; in Hunan, Anhui, and Henan it was 70–80 per cent; and in Jiangsu, Hebei, and Shandong it was 60–70 per cent. However, in Ningxia, Gansu, Xinjiang, Qinghai, western Sichuan, Yunnan, and Tibet, as well as in Heilongjiang and Inner Mongolia, the increase in population was 140–50 per cent. Up to one-third of the population increase was due to in-migration from other parts of China. Today, these areas constitute 13.2 per cent of the total population, compared with 10.1 per cent in the early 1950s.

The change in the distribution of population has been an important factor in the opening up of the more remote areas and in the redistribution of production. Nevertheless, cultural and economic development has not kept pace with the more densely populated areas and western China continues to have limited appeal to enterprises and individuals.

Because of the relatively low rate of production in western China, there has as yet been no shortage of labour. However, the rich natural resources which exist in the sparsely populated areas could be developed with sufficient high-quality labour forces. The lack of technology is also an obstacle to development in these areas. Technical personnel, skilled workers, and enterprise managers are in short supply compared with densely populated eastern China which has a surplus of labour power.

A relatively even distribution of production would improve the distribution of population, and a better distribution of population would promote a more rational distribution of production.

Economic Factors

Prior to 1949, China was one of the world's poorest and most backward countries. Since 1949, large-scale capital construction has been carried out using funds diverted from non-productive capital investment items such as food, clothing, and housing. The development of the national economy has been rapid, and China now has a considerable economic base, with production forces at a fairly high level of development. There are 400,000 industrial and communications enterprises, RMB800 billion in fixed assets and floating capital, 100 million staff and workers, 300 million agricultural workers, an annual energy output of 620 million tonnes of standard coal, and 2.6 million machine tools. The outputs of grain, cotton, coal, and cloth rank amongst the highest in the world. For a long time after 1949, however, production was neglected in favour of capital construction. High accumulation and low efficiency, plus the irrational economic structure and the unbalanced main sectors of the economy, contributed to the low social wealth and the low standard of living.

China has a comparatively low labour productivity and agriculture (more than 70 per cent of the total labour force) is the lowest sector. An agricultural labourer in China produces far less than his counterpart in many other countries (Table 2.2).

The commodity rate of agricultural products is therefore also low. The output value of commodity agricultural products is about 30 per cent of the total agricultural output value (compared with more than 80 per cent in advanced capitalist countries). Commodity grain accounts for only 13–15 per cent. This means that of a total annual grain output of 325 million tonnes, only 45 million tonnes have a commodity value. If the value of sideline products is taken into account, the total annual output will still only be RMB50 billion (RMB70 a year for each agricultural labourer). Low labour productivity means that the requirements of industry and the needs of the people living in the cities cannot be met to any appreciable extent.

China's per-capita income is amongst the world's lowest (Table 2.3). During the First Five-year Plan (1st FYP) period (1953-7), the national income increased annually by 8.9 per cent. In subsequent plan periods, there was a constant decrease in the rate of acceleration of the national income, with the exception of the period 1963–5, during which the increase was 14.5 per cent compared with 3.1 per cent during the 2nd FYP period (1958–62). In recent years, however, there has been some improvement. In 1981, the national income was RMB388 billion, compared with RMB315 billion in

Table 2.2 Agricultural Productivity in China and Other Countries, 1978 (*jin* per person)

Country	Grain	Cotton	Edible Oils	Sugar	Meat	Dairy Products	Eggs	Fruit	Aquatic Products	Number of People Supported by One Agricultural Labourer
China	2,162	15	37	17	59	7	14	48	32	3.26
United States	166,523	1,198	1,782	2,665	12,766	28,076	2,010	29,954	1,782	55.40
Japan	4,998		18	168	697	1,655	532	1,485	2,917	15.60
France	43,502		655	3,747	4,221	27,585	700	11,454	737	24.60
Federal Republic of Germany	39,847		490	4,542	6,550	35,557	1,374	4,719	626	46.80
Great Britain	66,786		507	3,968	10,214	56,571	2,929	1,482	3,750	
Hungary	30,326		761	1,198	3,217	5,174	609	4,100	65	11.60
India	1,871	15	101	188	9.2	102	1	31	29	4.00
Brazil	4,926	62	44	1,068	514	1,602	70	1,208	115	8.00

Source: China's Agricultural Yearbook, 1980 (Agricultural Publishing House, Beijing, 1981).

Table 2.3 The World's Richest and Poorest Countries, 1980 (published by the World Bank, the gross national product per person, in US$)

Richest Countries			Poorest Countries		
Country	1980*	1979	Country	1980*	1979
United Arab			Bhutan	80	80
Emirates	30,070	23,410	Bangladesh	120	110
Qatar	26,080	20,020	Chad	120	120
Kuwait	22,840	20,520	Nepal	140	120
Switzerland	16,440	15,360	Ethiopia	140	120
Luxembourg	14,500	13,260	Guinea (Bissau)	160	170
Federal Republic			Upper Volta	190	180
of Germany	13,590	12,220	Mali	190	180
Sweden	13,520	12,250	Rwanda	200	190
Denmark	12,950	12,030	Burundi	200	190
Norway	12,650	11,230	Zaire	220	210
Belgium	12,180	11,020	Malawi	230	220
Brunei	11,890	10,220	India	240	210
France	11,730	10,650	Gambia	250	220
The Netherlands	11,470	10,490	Maldives	260	220
United States	11,360	10,610	Tanzania	260	250
Iceland	11,330	10,360	Sri Lanka	270	230
Saudi Arabia	11,260	9,960	Mozambique	270	250
Bermuda	11,050	9,820	Haiti	270	230
The Faroe Islands	10,620	9,740	Sierra Leone	270	250
Austria	10,230	9,130	Uganda	280	290
Canada	10,130	9,410	China	290	260
Japan	9,890	8,730	Guinea	290	260

Note: The 1980 figures are preliminary figures.
Source: World Economic Herald, 12 April 1982.

1978. Even so, the per-capita income was less than half the world average. Some 80 per cent of the increased national income was spent on increased consumption. There was minimal net accumulation and the accumulation ability of the peasants was even lower. On average, one *mu* of land accumulated at best RMB10 a year in 1980. The average annual accumulation for a production brigade was about RMB10,000 and, for an able-bodied labourer, several dozen *yuan*.

China's per-capita consumption of consumer goods is one of the world's lowest (Table 2.4). Since 1978, there has been a considerable increase in the production of consumer goods and the volume of consumer goods owned and consumed per capita has also increased substantially. However, the average consumption level — standard of living — is low. In 1980, the average consumption of grain was 427.6 *jin* (two *jin* equals one kilogram); that of vegetable oil was 4.6 *jin*; of pork, 33.3 *jin*; of sugar, 7.7 *jin*; and of cloth (including chemical fibres), 10.4 metres. The average per-capita share of consumer funds was RMB224.

Table 2.4 The Average Consumption of Consumer Goods per capita, 1978 (*jin*)

Country	Grain	Cotton	Vegetable Oil	Sugar	Meat	Dairy Products	Eggs	Fruit	Aquatic Products
China	636	4.5	11.0	4.7	17.0	2	7.5*	13.7	9.7
United States	3,005	22.0	32.0	48.0	230.0	507	36.0	541.0	32.0
Japan	314		1.2	11.0	45.0	106	34.0	95.0	187.0
France	1,771		27.0	153.0	172.0	1,123	29.0	466.0	30.0
Federal Republic of									
Germany	851		10.0	97.0	140.0	760	29.0	101.0	13.0
Great Britain	668		5.1	40.0	102.0	566	29.0	15.0	38.0
Hungary	2,610		65.0	103.0	277.0	445	52.0	353.0	5.0
India	468	3.8	25.0	47.0	2.3	25	0.3	8.0	7.0
Brazil	616	7.7	5.0	137.0	64.0	200	8.7	151.0	14.0

Note: Average possession of non-agricultural population.
Source: China's Agricultural Yearbook, 1980 (Agriculture Publishing House, Beijing, 1981).

The uneven development of production in China can be attributed to the physical size of the country, variations in its geographical conditions and natural resources, the distribution of its population, and economic and political factors. Regional differences are reflected in the rate and scale of development. The eastern coastal areas are comparatively advanced in economic and social development, with large populations. Shanxi, Shaanxi, Henan, Hubei, Hunan, and eastern Sichuan provinces in central China are comparatively backward. Further west and north, economic and cultural development is even lower, and the population is sparse. Even in the coastal areas, the level of development varies between provinces. Since 1949, efforts have been made, and with some effect, to rationalize the distribution of the forces of production. However, the basic regional differences in distribution remain.

China has a huge population, with enormous labour power. Educational levels are generally low, however, and science and technology are backward. Despite China's abundant natural resources, the per-capita volume of resources is small. After centuries of exploitation, the country's economic foundation is poor and uneven. The relatively rapid economic development in the last 30 years has failed to achieve a high level of production. If the country is to raise its economic effectiveness, it must develop a rational strategy which is based on the factors affecting production, and adopt the steps and measures necessary for its success.

3. Achievements in Production since 1949

SINCE 1949, the socialist system in China has made possible the planned and rational exploitation of the country's rich natural and human resources in order to develop the national economy and to increase the standard of living of its people.

Advances in Technology

The speed of economic growth in China since 1949 is an indication of the country's vigour and of the effectiveness of its production methods. In pre-1949 semi-feudal, semi-colonial China, the speed of economic growth was very slow and the level of productivity low. Agriculture developed only from 1936, industry from 1942–3, and railway construction and freight facilities from 1932–7. Nevertheless, the level of production remained low throughout the period of the Sino-Japanese War and up to 1949 (Table 3.1), and well below the level of advanced countries (Table 3.2).

China occupies 6.4 per cent of the world's total land area; in 1949, its population accounted for one-quarter of the world's population. The country's industrial output value, however, represented less than 1 per cent of the world total. Since 1949, China's economy has increased more rapidly than that of most other countries, despite some fluctuations (Table 3.3). By 1980, its production of cotton yarn, cotton cloth, bicycles, and sewing machines was first in the world; tobacco was second in the world; coal was third; steel, iron ore, clocks, and watches were fifth; electricity was seventh; and oil was ninth in the world. In agricultural production, tobacco, pork, horses, mules, sheep, and rabbits were first; grain, rape seed, silk cocoons, and tea were second; and aquatic products were third in the world. The output of freshwater fish was also the highest of any country.

Production technology has improved significantly since 1949. By 1980, the fixed assets of state-owned industrial enterprises had increased 30-fold over the value in 1952, and although there were six times the number of employees, the average value of fixed assets per worker had increased fourfold over that period. Based on the industrial output value, worker efficiency had increased 1.9-fold. Established industries have diversified their range of products, and quality has improved through the introduction of better technology and highly skilled workers. New industrial sectors such as petrochemicals, atomic energy, electronics, and sensitization materials have been created or expanded since 1949.

On the whole, 36 years of construction have brought about an industrial system and economy of considerable production scale and technological level, enabling China to emerge from the backward state it was in before 1949.

Table 3.1 The Development of Productive Forces before 1949

Item	Unit	Highest Annual Output		Output in 1949	
		Year	Output	Absolute Amount	Percentage of Highest Annual Output
Agriculture					
Grain	10,000 tonnes	1936	15,000.0	11,318.0	75.5
Cotton	10,000 tonnes	1936	84.9	44.4	52.3
Peanuts	10,000 tonnes	1933	317.1	126.8	40.0
Rape seed	10,000 tonnes	1934	190.1	73.4	38.5
Sesame	10,000 tonnes	1933	99.1	32.6	32.9
Jute and dogbane	10,000 tonnes	1945	10.9	3.7	33.9
Silkworm cocoon	10,000 tonnes	1931	22.1	3.1	14.0
Tussah cocoon	10,000 tonnes	1921	9.4	1.2	12.8
Tea	10,000 tonnes	1932	22.5	4.1	18.2
Sugar-cane	10,000 tonnes	1940	565.2	264.2	46.7
Sugar-beet	10,000 tonnes	1939	32.9	19.1	58.1
Flue-cured tobacco	10,000 tonnes	1948	17.9	4.3	24.0
Draught animals	10,000 head	1935	7,151.0	5,977.6	83.6
Pigs	10,000 head	1934	7,853.0	5,775.0	73.5
Sheep	10,000 head	1937	6,252.0	4,235.0	67.7
Aquatic products	10,000 tonnes	1936	150.0	45.0	30.0

Industry	Unit	Year			
Cotton yarn	10,000 tonnes	1933	44.5	32.7	73.5
Cotton cloth	100 million metres	1936	27.9	18.9	67.7
Crude salt	10,000 tonnes	1943	392.0	299.0	76.3
Sugar	10,000 tonnes	1936	41.0	20.0	48.8
Cigarettes	10,000 boxes	1947	236.0	160.0	67.8
Coal	100 million tonnes	1942	0.62	0.32	51.6
Crude oil	10,000 tonnes	1943	32.0	12.0	37.5
Electric energy	100 million kWh	1941	60.0	43.0	71.7
Steel	10,000 tonnes	1943	92.3	15.8	17.1
Pig iron	10,000 tonnes	1943	180.0	25.0	13.9
Cement	10,000 tonnes	1942	229.0	66.0	28.8
Sulphuric acid	10,000 tonnes	1942	18.0	4.0	22.2
Soda ash	10,000 tonnes	1940	10.3	8.8	85.4
Caustic soda	10,000 tonnes	1941	1.2	1.5	125.0
Metal-cutting machine tools	10,000 tonnes	1941	0.54	0.16	29.6
Modernized transport volume					
Rail freight	10,000 tonnes		13,665.0	5,589.0	40.9
Truck freight	10,000 tonnes		819.0	597.0	70.7
Boat and barge freight	10,000 tonnes		1,264.0	543.0	43.0

Note: Draught animals include cows, horses, donkeys, and mules.
Sources: China's Economic Yearbook, 1981 (Economic Management, 1981) and State Statistical Bureau, *The Great Decade* (People's Publishing House, Beijing, 1959).

Table 3.2 China's Output of Major Products Compared with Other Countries, 1949 (10,000 tonnes)

Item	China	United States	Soviet Union	Japan	Federal Republic of Germany	Great Britain	France	India	China's Percentage of Total Output of Foreign Countries	China's World Ranking
Steel	15.8	7,074.0	2,329	311.0	916.0[1]	1,580.0	915.0	137.0	0.10	26
Pig iron	25.0	4,982.0	1,639	160.0	717.0[1]	968.0	841.0	164.0	0.22	23
Cement	66.0	3,594.0	815	328.0	846.0[1]	936.0	688.0	214.0	0.57	—
Coal	3,243.0	43,597.0	23,500	3,974.0	11,740.0	21,861.0	5,304.0	3,220.0	1.98	9
Crude oil	12.0	24,892.0	3,344	19.0	84.0	16.0	8.0	25.0	0.02	—
Electric energy (100 m. kWh)	43.0	3,451.0	783	410.0	357.0	506.0	303.0	49.0	0.51	25
Chemical fertilizers[2]	0.6	398.0		62.0	158.0	62.0	155.0	2.0	0.43	—
Sulphuric acid	4.0	1,037.0	220	161.0	114.0	169.0	115.0	10.0	—	—
Cotton yarn	32.7	171.0	61	16.0	23.0	37.0	23.0	62.0	—	—
Cotton cloth	18.9	76.8	36	8.2	8.7	18.3	10.9	34.6	—	—
Sugar	20.0	199.0	222	3.0	61.0	52.0	88.0	118.0	0.69	—
Paper	22.8	939.0	100	51.0	89.0	163.0	87.0	9.0	—	—
Rail freight volume	5,589.0	111,300.0	73,506	12,800.0	20,100.0	28,400.0	16,100.0	7,100.0	—	—

Notes: 1. Output does not include Saarland.
  2. Output is calculated from 1 July 1948 to the end of June 1949, except in the case of China and the Soviet Union.
Sources: *China's Economic Yearbook, 1981 (Economic Management,* 1981), State Statistical Bureau, *The Great Decade* (People's Publishing House, Beijing, 1959), and Chinese Academy of Social Sciences, *The World Economic Statistics Handbook* (Chinese Academy of Social Sciences, Beijing, 1981).

Table 3.3 China's Rate of Economic Growth Compared with Other Countries[1]

Item	China	USSR	USA	Japan	Germany	Britain	France	India	The World
Annual rate of increase of total agricultural value of output[2]	4.40	3.50	2.10	2.40	1.80	2.00	2.20	2.70	—
Annual rate of increase of total industrial value of output	13.20	9.83	4.66	12.46	6.94	2.57	5.32	6.26	—
Annual rate of increase of output of major industrial and agricultural products									
Grain	3.54		2.60	0.10	2.10	2.10	2.30	3.20	3.00
Cotton	3.66	4.00	-1.40					3.10	2.00
Three major oil crops	0.95							0.00	2.21
Jute and dogbane	9.10								1.39
Sugar-cane	4.83		5.30	12.10				4.50	5.60
Sugar-beet	9.47	6.30	3.30	10.50	5.30	1.60	3.80		2.40
Mulberry silk[3]	4.30			0.20				3.90	2.10
Tobacco[3]	11.50[5]		0.10	2.50				1.80	3.10
Tea	4.32			4.10				2.60	
Pigs	5.52		decrease	10.50	4.00	3.60	2.10	3.10	2.70
Sheep	4.91		decrease		decrease	1.50	1.20	1.10	
Aquatic products[4]	7.71		1.04	4.08				3.73	4.34
Steel	19.25	6.66	1.95	12.79	5.32	0.87	3.20	7.07	5.04
Pig iron	17.56	6.82	1.63	14.45	5.07	0.57	2.88	6.33	5.22

Table 3.3 continued

Item	China	USSR	USA	Japan	Germany	Britain	France	India	The World
Rolled steel	18.52								
Iron ore	18.46	6.81	decrease	decrease	decrease	decrease	0.25	8.87	4.56
Raw coal	9.99	3.95	1.10	decrease	1.98	decrease	decrease	4.16	2.04
Electric energy production	14.67	9.87	6.74	9.46	8.22	6.93	7.12	10.99	7.74
Crude oil	24.42	10.29	1.90	3.67	6.39	22.18	9.53	14.03	6.53
Machine tools	15.38	4.56	2.79	10.80					
Chemical fertilizer	27.89		5.61	4.38	3.65	3.41	3.90	18.38	7.23
Cement	16.73	10.00	2.41	11.87	4.85	1.85	4.98	7.94	6.45
Timber	7.51		0.84	decrease	decrease	decrease	0.62	5.66	3.65
Cotton yarn	7.33	3.40	decrease	3.63	decrease	decrease	decrease	1.33	—
Cotton cloth	6.50	2.30	decrease	3.65	0.34	decrease	decrease	decrease	
Machine-made paper	10.71	8.03	6.45	12.73	7.30	3.27	6.18	9.01	6.47
Sugar	8.60	5.08	3.32	11.00	5.61	2.65	5.41	6.68	4.03
Volume of goods transported by train	10.13	5.75	0.44	0.10	1.31	decrease	1.11	4.27	

Notes: 1. China's rate of economic growth is calculated from 1949 to 1980, with the exception of mulberry silk and tobacco. Figures for other countries are calculated from 1949 to 1978, unless otherwise indicated.
2. 1950–78, with the exception of China.
3. 1954–78.
4. 1950–78, with the exception of China.
5. For China, flue-cured tobacco.

Sources: China: State Statistical Bureau, *The Great Decade* (People's Publishing House, Beijing, 1959). Other countries: *China's Agricultural Yearbook, 1980* (Agriculture Publishing House, Beijing, 1981) (agriculture) and Chinese Academy of Social Sciences, *The World Economic Statistics Handbook* (Chinese Academy of Social Sciences, Beijing, 1981) (industry and transportation).

The Development of an Industrial-agricultural Economy

Agriculture and light and heavy industry are the bases of the production economy. The relationship between these sectors directly determines China's overall industrial structure. The development of production alters that structure, which in turn determines future growth. A rational industrial structure is necessary if production is to increase and the economy to grow.

In 1949, China's industrial structure was characterized by backward industry and agriculture, with a small-scale peasant economy. The development of production since that time has been achieved at different rates in different sectors, creating changing relationships between agriculture, light industry, and heavy industry within the overall industrial structure (Tables 3.4 and 3.5).

Between 1949 and 1957, agriculture declined as light and heavy industry expanded, although agriculture still accounted for the largest proportion of the country's total output value. After 1957, however, heavy industry developed faster than the other sectors, and by 1978, it had surpassed light industry and agriculture in proportion to its contribution to the total output value. Thus, within two decades, the balance of China's industrial and agricultural structure had been reversed. During this period, the proportion of heavy industry increased by 16.06 per cent; light industry increased by 1.66 per cent; and agriculture declined by 17.72 per cent. Further economic adjustment during the following three years increased the proportion of agriculture by 5.29 per cent and light industry by 3.79 per cent, and decreased the proportion of heavy industry by 9.08 per cent. Although this trend resulted in a more reasonably balanced economic structure, the decline in heavy industry was somewhat excessive. The change in the ratio of agriculture, light industry, and heavy industry (1 : 0.32 : 0.11 in 1949, 1 : 1.44 : 1.63 in 1980, and 1 : 1.56 : 1.47 in 1981) is significant in that it shows the emergence of China over the space of little more than 30 years from a backward, agriculture-dominated country to one with an industrial-agricultural economy, based on modern industry.

During the period of change in the relative contribution of these sectors to China's total output value, their internal structures also changed. In agriculture, the proportion of farming decreased as forestry, animal husbandry, sideline production, and aquaculture increased. Sideline production experienced the greatest growth due to the emergence during this period of rural enterprises. In light industry, the sectors dependent upon agricultural raw materials declined as the emphasis changed to non-agricultural raw materials. Manufacturing increased in the heavy industrial sector, supplanting the production of raw and semi-finished materials. These changes were indicative of a strengthened manufacturing and processing capacity, better use of industrial resources, and increased social wealth, while at the same time they contributed to a shortage of raw and processed materials and energy. The processing and machinery manufacturing industries were, as a result, unable to operate at full capacity.

Changes have also occurred in transport. The volume of rail freight has steadily increased; that of inland water transport has decreased (although the volume of ocean-going transport has risen rapidly); and air transport has

Table 3.4 Differences in the Rate of Economic Growth of Different Areas of Production (%)

Department	1949–57	1953–7	1958–78	1979–80	1949–80	1952–80
Total industrial and agricultural value of output						
Agriculture	12.73	9.20	6.91	7.86	8.45	7.38
Light industry	8.02	4.53	2.94	5.61	4.40	3.41
Heavy industry	17.80	12.86	8.72	13.93	11.38	9.82
	35.97	25.45	10.60	4.50	16.23	12.66
In agricultural value of output						
Crop growing	7.70	3.89	2.10	2.85	3.57	2.47
Forestry	23.03	24.83	5.44	7.32	10.08	9.05
Animal husbandry	8.55	6.96	3.06	9.53	4.86	4.19
Sideline occupations	8.01	4.04	9.11	14.29	9.15	8.55
Fishery	21.07	15.76	8.11	1.65	10.87	8.96
In light industrial value of output						
Taking agricultural products as raw materials		11.29	7.82	13.94		7.09
Taking non-agricultural products as raw materials		21.94	11.55	13.91		13.51
In heavy industrial value of output						
Mining		21.61	10.16	10.09		11.43
Raw and semi-finished materials industries		23.45	10.03	7.86		12.16

Manufacturing industry	13.44	2.94	11.13	28.58
Total volume of goods transported				
Railway	9.22			
Highway	10.15			
Water transport	7.79			
Pipeline	9.57			
Civil aviation	just beginning			
	4.57			
Turnover amount of goods				
Railway	13.07			
Highway	11.72			
Water transport	11.75			
Pipeline	15.18			
Civil aviation	just beginning			
	6.34			

Sources: State Statistical Bureau, *The Great Decade* (People's Publishing House, Beijing, 1959), *China's Economic Yearbook, 1981* (*Economic Management*, 1981), and *China's Agricultural Yearbook, 1980* (Agriculture Publishing House, Beijing, 1981).

Table 3.5 Changes in Production, 1949–81

Item	1949	1952	1957	1978	1980	1981
Agriculture and light and heavy industry[1]						
Agriculture	79.80	58.50	43.3	25.58	24.58	24.80
Light industry	15.50	26.73	30.1	31.76	35.41	38.70
Heavy industry	4.70	14.77	26.6	42.66	40.01	36.50
Agriculture[1]						
Crop growing	82.50	83.10	80.6	67.80	64.30	64.10
Forestry	0.60	0.70	1.7	3.00	3.10	3.00
Animal husbandry	12.40	11.50	12.9	13.20	14.20	14.30
Sideline occupations	4.30	4.40	4.3	14.60	17.10	17.30
Aquaculture	0.20	0.30	0.5	1.40	1.30	1.30
Light industry[1]						
Taking agricultural products as raw materials		87.50	81.6		68.41	
Taking non-agricultural products as raw materials		12.50	18.4		31.59	
Heavy industry[1]						
Mining		15.30	13.1		11.28	
Raw and semi-finished materials industries		42.80	39.5		37.81	
Manufacturing industry		41.90	47.4		50.91	
Transport services[2]						
Railway	34.72		34.1		46.27	46.50
Highway	49.47		46.7		31.61	30.90
Water transport	15.80		19.2		17.74	17.90
Pipeline					4.37	4.70
Civil aviation	0.01				0.01	
Transport services[3]						
Railway	72.02		74.4		49.65	49.17
Highway	3.19		2.6		2.21	2.19
Water transport	24.71		23.0		43.87	44.34
Pipeline					4.26	4.29
Civil aviation	0.08				0.01	0.01

Notes: 1. Taking the gross value of production as 100.
2. Taking the total volume of goods transported as 100.
3. Taking the turnover amount of goods as 100.
Sources: State Statistical Bureau, *The Great Decade* (People's Publishing House, Beijing, 1959), *China's Economic Yearbook, 1981* (*Economic Management*, 1981), *China's Agricultural Yearbook, 1980* (Agriculture Publishing House, Beijing, 1981), *Statistics*, 1982, No. 3, and Ma Hong and Sun Shanqing, *The Economic Structure of China* (People's Publishing House, Beijing, 1981), Vol. 1.

developed rapidly, although it still accounts for only a small proportion of the total volume. The potential of the inland waterways network remains to be realized. On the whole, and despite significant internal problems which set back economic development, significant advances have been made in the development of the economy in China since 1949.

Rationalization of the Distribution of Production

One of the most important policies in China's post-1949 development has been the redistribution of production. The distribution of the country's industry and agriculture in 1949 was unbalanced, irrational, and counter-productive to the requirements of a socialist society. Since 1949, much headway has been gained in distributing production in accordance with the country's production requirements and local conditions.

Changes in Regional Distribution

Significant advances have been made in the development of the backward areas over the past three decades. The ratio of investment in the coastal[1] and inland areas in the period was 1 : 1.43. The emphasis in the large regions[2] has changed over the period, although the cumulative total of investment of the five-year plans to date has been relatively equally distributed amongst them. Central-south and east China received the most investment, equally apportioned; north and north-east China received similar amounts of investment, as did the south-west and north-west which were the lowest areas of investment. The ratio of investment between the three groups of areas between 1949 and 1980 was 1 : 1.21 : 1.40 ('1' being the south-west and north-west). Twelve provinces and one municipality (Sichuan, Liaoning, Heilongjiang, Hubei, Henan, Beijing, Hebei, Shaanxi, Gansu, Shandong, Guangdong, Shanxi, and Hunan) accounted during the same period for 61 per cent of the total investment. Of these, one-third are coastal areas and two-thirds inland areas.

The regional distribution of investment determines the scale and speed of capital construction in those areas through the expansion of fixed assets. In turn, it determines the speed of social change and growth. The ratio of investment between 1949 and 1980 is based on the further development of industry, agriculture, transport, and urban construction in the developed eastern regions and the expansion of production westward.

A number of new industrial bases have been established in the former backward inland and frontier regions of Shaanxi, Gansu, Ningxia, Qinghai,

1. The coastal areas include the municipalities of Beijing, Tianjin, and Shanghai, and the provinces of Liaoning, Hebei, Shandong, Jiangsu, Zhejiang, Anhui, Fujian, Guangdong, and Guangxi.
2. The lge regions are north China (Beijing, Tianjin, Hebei, Shanxi, and Inner Mongolia), the north-east (Liaoning, Jilin, and Heilongjiang), east China (Shanghai, Jiangsu, Zhejiang, Anhui, Fujian, Jiangxi, and Shandong), central-south China (Henan, Hubei, Hunan, Guangdong, and Guangxi), the south-west (Sichuan, Guizhou, Yunnan, and Tibet), and north-west China (Shaanxi, Gansu, Qinghai, Ningxia, and Xinjiang).

Inner Mongolia, Xinjiang, Yunnan, and Guizhou. Modern industry has expanded at the same time as new agricultural areas and transport systems have been developed. Production in the new industrial cities and industrial and mining areas has expanded rapidly so that its rate of growth now exceeds that of the coastal areas. The rate of growth of transport also exceeds that of the eastern regions.

From 1949 to 1980, the national average annual growth rate of industrial output value was 13.16 per cent. In Gansu, Ningxia, and Qinghai, the rate was 15.3–17.5 per cent; in Inner Mongolia and Shanxi, it was 14.44–16.21 per cent; and in Shanghai, Jiangsu, Shandong, Tianjin, Liaoning, and Guangdong (where industry was well established), it was 11–13.4 per cent. The national average annual growth rate of rail freight volume between 1952 and 1980 was 7.11 per cent, compared with 8.5–11.14 per cent in Yunnan, Shaanxi, Henan, Hubei, Hunan, and Shanxi. Considerable rail transport capacity was developed where virtually none existed in Ningxia, Qinghai, and Xinjiang, whereas in Liaoning and Hebei, which before 1952 had the largest rail freight volume in the country, the growth rate was only 4.7–5.6 per cent.

The contribution of the industrial output value of the north-west to the national total increased by 1.34 per cent between 1949 and 1980. In Henan, Hubei, and Hunan, the contribution increased by 4.5 per cent, and that of Shanxi and Inner Mongolia increased by 1.28 per cent. At the same time, the contribution of formerly advanced areas such as Shanghai and Jiangsu dropped by 10.31 per cent. Tianjin, Guangdong, and Shandong also contributed less to the total output value of industry over this period. The south-west increased its percentage of total rail freight volume by 6.09 per cent; in the north-west, the increase was 4.82 per cent; in Henan, Hubei, and Hunan, it was 4.81 per cent; in Shanxi and Inner Mongolia, it was 3.94 per cent; and a decrease of 17.68 per cent occurred in Liaoning and Hebei.

The comparatively rapid growth of the economy in the western areas has corrected to a significant extent the over-concentration of production in a few areas in the east. It has also expanded the exploitation and utilization of resources, strengthened the national economy, and raised the country's defence capacity.

The Development of the Minority Nationality Areas

The areas inhabited by national minorities constitute 63 per cent of the total land area of China. Grasslands in these areas account for 89 per cent of the total grasslands; forests account for 37.8 per cent; water resources account for more than 50 per cent; and coal, iron, and many non-ferrous metals deposits constitute a very large proportion of the total resources. Despite the abundance of such resources, however, these areas have long been sparsely populated and economically backward.

Since 1949, the development of the minority nationality areas has been a point of principle. State funding has enabled the economy of these formerly undeveloped areas to develop rapidly. Within the space of 30 years, their total industrial and agricultural output value has increased eight-fold; the industrial output value alone has increased 40-fold. Improvements in farming techniques and irrigation have increased the per-unit yield of grain 1.87-fold and that of cotton, 4.56-fold (although the total cultivated area has not expanded significantly). Animal husbandry, a traditional land use in these areas, has also developed. The number of draft animals has increased 1.36-fold and that of sheep has increased 4.9-fold. The outputs of major industrial products (pig iron, coal, crude oil, electricity, wood, and cotton cloth) have increased between 5.8- and 226-fold; the output of steel has increased from zero to 1.5 million tonnes; rail service mileage has increased 2.3-fold; and highway service mileage increased 17.5-fold between 1952 and 1979.

Today, the minority nationality areas have reasonably well developed economic bases, which make a significant contribution to the national economy (Table 3.6). In addition, their economic development has reduced the inequalities between nationalities, strengthened national unity, and consolidated China's frontiers.

Table 3.6 Changes in the Economic Importance of the Minority Nationality Areas, 1949–79 (%)

Item	1949	1979
Total agricultural output value	9.57	10.60
Total industrial output value	3.80	4.80
Output of major products		
Steel	—	4.50
Pig iron	0.30	
Raw coal	2.68	9.00
Crude oil	11.92	5.90
Electric power	1.11	6.40
Timber	20.80	
Cotton cloth	0.91	3.30
Grain	10.69	10.00
Draught animals	27.42	41.10
Sheep	39.94	53.80
Transport		
Rail service mileage	15.96	22.50
Highway service mileage	14.11	24.10

Source: *China's Economic Yearbook, 1981* (*Economic Management*, 1981).

The Development of Rural Enterprises

China has a huge amount of rural land, with a large labour force, sizeable quantities of exploitable natural resources for industry and agriculture, and a vast market. For many years, however, the rural areas were dominated by a single-activity economy. Most were engaged in agriculture and there were few industrial enterprises or trades. Rural transport, communications systems, banking services, and commercial and service trades were undeveloped.

In 1958, industry-dominated rural enterprises began to be developed on the basis of the people's communes in order to eliminate the poverty and backwardness of the rural areas, to invigorate the economy of rural collectives, and to integrate local industry and agriculture. By 1981, there were 1.43 million rural enterprises in the country (767,000 of which were industrial), employing 30 million people, or 10 per cent of the rural labour force. The value of their fixed assets was RMB32.7 billion (32 per cent of the combined production team, brigade, and commune assets). Their annual income was RMB61.4 billion (34 per cent of that of production teams, brigades, and communes combined). The industrial output value of RMB52.7 billion was 10 per cent of the national total and RMB18.3 billion more than the national total in 1953. The rural areas produced RMB2.3 billion worth of products for export (8 per cent of the national total); their annual net profit was in excess of RMB10 billion; and they paid RMB2.6 billion in taxes to the state.

Rural enterprises include industry, agriculture, transport, construction, and commerce. Industry includes metallurgy (particularly the mining of iron and non-ferrous metal ores), electricity (produced by small hydroelectric power stations), coal mining, petroleum, chemicals production (especially phosphate fertilizer and the extraction of chemical deposits), machinery, building materials, forestry, food processing, textiles, weaving, and embroidery. In general, the structure of rural enterprises follows that of the country's industry (Table 3.7). Some products account for a significant proportion of the country's total output. In agriculture, tea accounts for 33 per cent, fruits account for 30 per cent, aquatic products account for 16 per cent, and silkworm cocoons account for 10 per cent of the national total. In industry, coal accounts for 17 per cent, gold accounts for 31 per cent, sulphur accounts for 36 per cent, phosphate fertilizer accounts for 37 per cent, wood and bamboo account for 8 per cent, cement accounts for 8 per cent, machine-made paper and paperboard account for 15 per cent, crude salt accounts for 11 per cent, silk fabrics account for 14 per cent, small and medium-sized farming tools account for 7 per cent, food products account for 7 per cent, and bricks, tiles, lime, sand, and stones account for 75–90 per cent of the national total output. Drawnwork, embroidery, and bamboo, palm, and straw-weaving account for 80 per cent of that produced each year.

Rural enterprises, which are scattered over a large area, have become an important part of provincial and regional industry. The output values of rural

Table 3.7 The Structure of Rural Enterprises, 1980 (%)

Section	Number of Enterprises	Number of Employees	Amount of Profit
Industry	51.8	62.5	76.3
Construction	3.3	10.3	7.5
Transport	5.6	4.0	4.1
Farming and breeding	30.0	18.2	6.5
Commercial services	9.3	5.0	5.6

Source: *China's Economic Yearbook, 1981* (*Economic Management*, 1981).

enterprises in Henan, Hunan, Guangxi, Guangdong, Jiangsu, Zhejiang, Fujian, Jiangxi, Shandong, Hebei, and Shanxi account for more than 9 per cent of the provincial total. In Sichuan, Yunnan, Guizhou, Shaanxi, Hubei, and Anhui, the contribution of rural enterprises to the provincial total output value is between 5 and 9 per cent. In Qinghai, Gansu, Ningxia, Xinjiang, Shanghai, Beijing, Tianjin, Inner Mongolia, Liaoning, Jilin, and Heilongjiang, it is less than 5 per cent of the total.

Rural enterprises account for a large proportion of the total output value in provinces in which industry and agriculture are well developed and where there is a dense rural population. Their significance is less in provinces in which industry and agriculture are backward and population is sparse, and in the large cities where industry is well developed but where agriculture contributes little to the economy.

The degree of development of agricultural production and the extent of the rural population in an area are directly related to the development of rural enterprises. The availability of raw materials and of labour is essential for the production of goods that will be sold locally and whose production is combined with agriculture. The growth of rural enterprises (particularly of industrial enterprises) has broadened the rural economic base. It has helped to bridge the gap between industry and agriculture, expanded employment opportunities, improved the utilization of rural resources, and increased the income of the state, collective, and individual. The economies of the rural and urban areas are as a result more closely linked, to their mutual benefit.

4. The Problems of Development and Distribution of Production

SINCE 1949, China has undergone considerable development and redistribution of its forces of production. The measures employed to achieve this transformation were, however, often hasty and ill-conceived and reflected a lack of understanding of the factors which had previously determined the regional distribution of production. These measures created problems in terms of the level of investment in capital construction, the structure of production, the utilization of natural resources, and the effect of production on the environment.

Investment in Capital Construction

For many years, China's investment in capital construction was out of proportion to the country's capability. Because the scale of construction was too large for the country's resources, production and consumption had to be curtailed. It has become apparent that the distribution of construction must match local conditions, that the construction cycle needs to be shortened, and the results of investment increased. Raw materials and funds are better utilized in improving the production capability of the existing 400,000 industrial enterprises. The proportion of investment in the developed coastal areas and in the developing western areas also needs to be readjusted.

In the past, insufficient attention was paid to exploiting the accumulated production power in the developed areas; the difficulties of developing the backward areas were also underestimated. Rash measures were implemented in order to achieve immediate results. Strategic factors outweighed practical and economic considerations, and the proportion of investment in the backward areas was, for a long time, too high. Many industries were moved to the west for strategic reasons and capital construction was too widely dispersed. Investment was concentrated in heavy and national defence industries, new industries, and capital construction. As a result of these factors, the economic return on investment was poor.

The situation has not improved to any real extent, and the western regions remain backward in economic terms. Yunnan and Guizhou provinces accounted for only 2.79 per cent of the national gross value of industrial and agricultural production in 1980; Gansu and Qinghai provinces, Ningxia, and Xinjiang accounted for only 3.04 per cent. Of the 10 provinces, municipalities, and autonomous regions which each yielded less than 2 per cent of the national gross value of industrial and agricultural production, eight were in the west and remote regions. Their combined gross value of industrial and agricultural production was only 7.5 per cent of the nation's total. This was less than Shanghai (9.83 per cent), Jiangsu province (9.13 per cent), and Liaoning province (7.76 per cent).

Since 1949, accumulated investment has been evenly distributed over the country, but the production levels of industry and agriculture vary greatly from region to region (Table 4.1). One of the most fundamental problems relating to the distribution of production in China is the relationship between the developed regions and the backward regions. Investment in different regions needs to be rationally apportioned and a balance achieved through careful planning. The gap in economic and technical levels, and in the per-capita income between the advanced and backward regions needs to be closed. This is best achieved through the gradual modernizing influence of the advanced regions on the backward regions. The balanced development of the different regions is necessary if China is to achieve a balanced socialist economy on a national level.

The strategic goals of the distribution of production in China are the

Table 4.1 A Comparison of Regional Agricultural Production Levels, 1980

Regions	Density of Output Value (RMB10,000/km²)	Per-capita Agricultural and Industrial Output Value (RMB/person)
Regions of 1st category: Shanghai, Beijing, Tianjin, and Liaoning	101.420	2,586.80
Of which: Shanghai	1,084.800	5,678.18
Regions of 2nd category: Jiangsu, Heilongjiang, and Jilin	14.070	934.38
Of which: Jiangsu	58.720	1,018.50
Regions of 3rd category: All other provinces and regions	4.530	488.20
Of which: Inner Mongolia, Qinghai, Xinjiang, and Tibet	0.346	443.80
Yunnan, Sichuan, and Guizhou	6.730	479.24
Average in the country	6.900	673.70
Ratio of 1st and 2nd categories	7.2:1	2.77:1
Ratio of 1st and 3rd categories	2.32:1	5.3:1
Ratio of Shanghai to Inner Mongolia, Xinjiang, Qinghai, and Tibet	3,135.26:1	12.97:1
Ratio of Shanghai to Sichuan, Guizhou, and Yunnan	161.2:1	11.85:1

Source: China's Economic Yearbook, 1981 (Economic Management, 1981).

encouragement of mutual support, the advancement and prosperity of all regions and nationalities, the development and consolidation of the strategic rear areas, and the reinforcement of national defence. Attainment of these goals is possible using the socialist system, the country's natural resources, and its production potential. One of the main tasks is to consider and make rational use of local conditions and production capabilities, and to adopt effective measures in order to achieve an appropriate balance of development throughout China.

Eastern China is superior to the western regions in terms of its natural conditions, economic development, and culture. Despite a deficiency of raw materials, it is densely populated and has a high concentration of large industries. There are, however, problems of overcrowding in the larger cities. Western China is backward in terms of economic and cultural development, particularly in the ethnic minority areas. However, it is rich in natural resources and it constitutes an expanding and important market for products developed in the east. The west also requires the economic and technical support of the east so as to better utilize its abundant resources. The socialist system and its principle of production distribution also requires the mutual support of the Han regions in the east and the ethnic minority areas in the west in order to strengthen national unity and to create a developed and prosperous national economy.

If these goals are to be achieved, investment in the western regions will need to be concentrated in the building of new backbone industries to exploit raw materials, in renovating and reforming existing enterprises, and in improving transport conditions. Secondly, technical and managerial levels in the west need to be raised through the intervention of the developed areas. Scientific study and research also need to be conducted in the east in order to provide a scientific base for the further exploitation of the western regions. Specialized personnel need to be trained from amongst the ethnic minority nationalities. Finally, national economic organizations need to be established as a means of integrating the superior economy and technological facilities of the east with the natural resources in the west and to provide mutual support.

The Structure of Production

Changes in the structure of industrial and agricultural production in China since 1949 have met with some success. However, there are some major problems. In agriculture, the needs of construction have not been met by grain production, which has increased slowly. During the period 1953–80, the annual speed of increase was only 0.8 per cent higher than the growth of the population. Also, large fluctuations in the total output of grain meant that the per-capita allocation was unstable. In addition, the structure of agriculture was irrational. Whilst the ratio of farming and cultivation was as high as 44.3 per cent, forestry, animal husbandry, sideline production, and aquaculture were only 35.7 per cent of the total. The proportion of forestry, animal husbandry, and aquaculture was 3.1, 14.2, and 1.3 per cent respectively.

Light industry has also developed slowly and the supply of main products cannot meet the demand. The national purchasing power in 1980 was RMB10 billion more than the value of the available commodities. Too much emphasis has been placed in the past on heavy industry, particularly the iron and steel and machine-building industries. The building materials and timber industries were underdeveloped. The structure of heavy industry was irrational in that it was unable to contribute to the development of agriculture and light industry. It also contributed to serious shortages of energy reserves. The output of the iron and steel industries was high in quantity, but the products were poor in quality and variety. There was also a surplus of particular products and insufficient supplies of others; the output of these industries did little to meet market demands. The machine-building industry was also unable to satisfy the demands of the market.

Industry and agriculture generally were unable to meet the requirements of economic development. This kind of production structure does not coincide with the Marxist theory of social reproduction. Marxism holds that, in the final analysis, the production of the departments of the first category serve the departments of the second category. Their speed and scale of development are conditioned by the development of the departments of the second category. However, for many years in China, too much emphasis was placed on the production and development of the means of production, which divorced it from the needs of agriculture and light industry. Such a system of development is unsuitable in China where 80 per cent of the population is peasantry, and where agricultural production is mainly by manual labour, with a consequent low level of productivity. A large investment in heavy industry in an agricultural country requires diversion of the accumulation of agriculture and, hence, a slowing down of its development. If agriculture fails to progress, the rural per-capita income will remain at a very low level, which will affect purchasing power and, in turn, the development of light industry. The resulting nation-wide imbalance between agriculture and industry reduces the speed of development of the national economy and the people's standard of living.

From 1949 to 1957, heavy industry was developed in China simultaneously with agriculture and light industry. During this period of balanced investment and growth, the national economy grew rapidly and there was a corresponding increase in the standard of living. The gross output value of industry and agriculture increased at that time by an average of 14.6 per cent annually; the national income grew on average by 12.6 per cent each year. The actual average annual growth of per-capita income was 5.5 per cent. However, after 1958 (excluding the readjustment period, 1963–5), the country's production structure became progressively more irrational. The rate of growth of the national economy and of the standard of living dropped. Between 1958 and 1978, the average annual decrease in the gross output value of industry and agriculture was 7.6 per cent; the national income decreased on average by 5.1 per cent; and wages decreased by 0.1 per cent.

The solution to this problem is the incorporation of agriculture and light industry into national economic and strategic policies. Future economic development will require acceleration of the speed of development of these

two sectors, the development of energy resources, and a more rational investment of funds and labour resources.

Although the production of consumer commodities should not be emphasized at the expense of the development of heavy industry, the speed of its
development needs to be slowed and based more closely upon agricultural and
light industrial production. The orientation of heavy industry also needs to be
changed from self-service and service to capital construction, to service to
agriculture, light industry, and export. An expansion of the scope of heavy
industry will check the trend towards a too rapid decrease in heavy industrial
production and, in the process, will invigorate this sector.

The general situation in China requires a readjustment of the production
structure and the selection of key industries to be developed, taking into
consideration not only strategic policies, but also local conditions. The
closed, self-servicing industrial structure of the past needs to be refashioned
under a unified state plan which will create a rational regional distribution of
the forces of production, based on the country's regional differences. China's
experience in the past has pointed to the irrationality of disregarding local
conditions when building an industrial structure based on either heavy or light
industry. The country's vast territory and its pronounced regional differences
are crucial determinants of its local industrial structures. A single model
cannot be adopted for the whole country. The industrial structure in a
particular region should be determined by local characteristics and requirements. Only through a rational composition of light and heavy industrial
structure at this level can China achieve a rational national industrial
structure.

At present in China, heavy industry is still predominant. However, at the
local level there is considerable variation in emphasis. Some areas are
predominantly heavy industry-based, with abundant raw materials and
developed facilities. Some areas have a spread of heavy and light industry and
agriculture, but few raw materials and facilities. Others are rich in resources,
but have undeveloped industrial and agricultural production. North-east China
has a strong foundation of heavy industry. It plays an important role in the
national economy and it has guaranteed supplies of raw materials. Since
1949, the north-east has become a key heavy industrial base in China.
Production is concentrated in Shenyang, Fushun, Anshan, Benxi, and Dalian,
and the new industrial centres of Qiqihar, Harbin, Changchun, Jilin, and
Liaoyang, as well as the oilfields in Daqing, Fuyu, and the Liao He (Liao
river) basin. Development has included the reformation of the Anshan Iron
and Steel Company and the strengthening of the machine-building industry
(which produces mainly heavy machinery, generating equipment, and transport machinery) and the petroleum, petrochemical, and coal-chemical
industries. The production of coal, electricity, non-ferrous metals, timber,
cement, paper, and synthetic fibres and textiles has also been expanded. North-
east China has a complete heavy industrial structure, based on steel,
petroleum, chemical products, and timber.

The industrial output value of the region in 1980 was 81.7 per cent of the
gross industrial and agricultural output value; agriculture accounted for 18.3
per cent. (In Liaoning province, the ratio was 87.5 per cent industry and 12.5

per cent agriculture.) Heavy industry accounted for 70 per cent of the gross industrial output value. (In Liaoning, heavy industry was 73 per cent.) The ratio of agricultural, light, and heavy industries was 1 : 1.34 : 3.13, compared with 1 : 1.89 : 5.11 in Liaoning and 1 : 1.24 : 1.66 in the country as a whole.

The output value of the north-east's heavy industries comprised 21 per cent of the total output value of heavy industry in China. Many of its heavy industrial products occupy an important place in the national industrial structure. These heavy industries were developed for the most part on the basis of local resources. Of the gross output value of heavy industry, mining constituted 16.4 per cent (the average contribution of the excavation industry in China was 11.45 per cent). The raw materials industry constituted 43.18 per cent (compared with the national average of 36.93 per cent) and manufacturing industry accounted for 40.35 per cent of the gross output value (compared with the average of 51.62 per cent). The north-east is therefore of great importance as a heavy industrial base which will support the modernization of agriculture and of the weak textile and light industries.

Heavy industry-based industrial structures of this kind are often, however, self-servicing. For many years, this orientation of the service of heavy industry was a serious problem in the north-east, particularly in Liaoning province which produced an average of eight million tonnes of steel and five million tonnes of steel products each year. Light industry required only 170,000 tonnes of steel annually, or 3 per cent of that produced, but it had to rely on imported steel for about one-third of its requirements. The output value of the machine-building industry in Liaoning exceeded RMB10 billion, but less than 1 per cent of this was used to service light industry.

It is essential that the product structure of heavy industry in the north-east be readjusted so that it supplies local agriculture with a greater variety of and better quality farm machinery, fertilizers, insecticides, plastic products, and trucks and its local light and textile industries with more equipment and raw materials. There is also a need for more products for daily use.

Heavy industry in the north-east has depleted some of its essential resources, and the volume of new reserves is growing only slowly. The supply of coal and electricity is inadequate. It is imperative, therefore, that heavy industry in this region be allocated a proportion of energy and financial reserves which will allow sufficient for other needs to be met. For example, these resources are needed for the construction of grain and soya bean-producing bases in the San Jiang (San river), Songhua, and Run river basins and in the central part of Liaoning province, as well as for the development of such products as sugar-beet, flax, and tussah silk, and light and textile industries which use industrial products as their raw materials. Only in this way can the imbalance between the means of production and the production of consumer goods be corrected.

The second type of industrial structure, which has few raw materials and facilities to supply its light and heavy industries and agriculture, includes such areas in China as the coastal provinces and cities south of the Great Wall, especially Shanghai, Tianjin, Beijing, and the provinces of Jiangsu, Zhejiang, Guangdong, and Hebei. Before 1949, these areas were characterized by intensive farming, a high commodity rate, and a heavy concentration of light and textile industries. Since 1949, heavy industries have also been developed on a large scale and agriculture and light industries have become highly developed (Table 4.2).

In these areas, the output value of both industry and agriculture is high and a wide variety of high-quality goods are produced. For many years, products of the light and textile industries have been very competitive on the international market and have sold well in Hong Kong, Macau, and South-east Asia. However, these same areas have severe shortages of energy resources. The high productivity of the light and textile industries has also contributed to a relative shortage of farm raw materials.

The problem in areas with this kind of industrial profile is the better utilization of funds and technology as well as an increase in the unit and gross output of grain and silk, sugar-cane, rape-seed oil, tea, and aquatic products. Emphasis should be placed on the upgrading of processing technology and the expansion of exports so as to form an industrial structure with a balanced distribution of light and heavy industries, producing a great variety of high-quality products.

In the national production structure, these areas are best suited to functioning as bases for technology that produces quality precision and new industrial products and export commodities. Based on a sound heavy industrial foundation and a readjusted commodity structure, they are able to supply equipment for the renewal of light and textile industries and to exploit new raw material sources in order to raise the output, quality, and variety of products of those industries. At the same time, they can supply equipment for the exploitation of new energy sources and the renovation of communications and transport. They will also help to expand exports by enabling more heavy industrial products to enter the international market.

Areas that are superior in resources but which have undeveloped industrial and agricultural production include the newly exploited regions of western Inner Mongolia, Shanxi, Henan, Hubei, Hunan, Shaanxi, Gansu, Qinghai, Sichuan, Yunnan, and Guizhou provinces and the Ningxia Hui Autonomous Region. These areas have rich reserves of mineral resources and a large proportion of the country's total energy, ferrous metals, non-ferrous metals, and certain chemical industry raw materials such as phosphorus and sylvite resources. They produce a great variety and quantity of agricultural raw materials such as cotton, flax, rape-seed, sesame, and tobacco. They also possess a large proportion of the country's agricultural resources, such as vast tracts of cultivable virgin soil and mountains and grassland suitable for afforestation, only a small part of which has been reclaimed and utilized.

The production structure in these areas is characterized by a low proportion of agriculture. Heavy industry (particularly machine building) dominates the industrial structure, whilst the proportion of light industry is lower than in the coastal areas and the country as a whole. This is particularly the case in Gansu, Shanxi, and Qinghai provinces and in the Ninxia Hui autonomous region (Table 4.3).

This type of industrial structure has many problems. Economic results are often unsatisfactory, as in Sichuan, Yunnan, Guizhou, Shaanxi, Gansu,

Table 4.2 The Production Structures of Shanghai, Jiangsu, Zhejiang, Guangdong, Tianjin, Beijing, and Hebei, 1980

Item	Shanghai	Jiangsu	Zhejiang	Guangdong	Tianjin	Beijing	Hebei
In gross industrial and agricultural output value							
Proportion of industry (%)	96.20	73.20	63.30	71.80	93.40	94.1	68.70
Proportion of agriculture (%)	3.80	26.80	36.70	28.20	6.60	5.9	31.30
In gross industrial output value							
Proportion of heavy industry (%)	50.69	50.66	40.57	42.81	50.52	46.8	58.44
Proportion of light industry (%)	49.31	49.34	59.43	57.19	49.48	35.2	41.56

Source: China's Economic Yearbook, 1981 (Economic Management, 1981).

Qinghai, and Ningxia. The amount of capital invested constitutes 20.21 per cent of the national total, but profits and taxes are only 11 per cent (56.78 per cent of that of Shanghai). Other problems are a shortage of light industrial products and textiles and a low local financial income. Despite the considerable industrial foundation that has been built up in recent years, poverty has not been eliminated and the task of readjusting the local industrial structure is therefore all the more arduous and complex.

In the short term, one of the main tasks in these areas is to readjust the production and commodity structure so as to shift it from a closed to an open-type industrial structure. Normal industrial production needs to become more integrated with the munitions industry, which is the focus of production. Civil industry would both support and expand the defence-related industries so that production would satisfy the needs of the military as well as supply consumer goods. At the same time, local industry (especially the light and textile industries) needs to upgrade its processing technology through the application of the superior technology available to the heavy and munitions industries. This modernization would also raise the utilization rate of equipment in these industries as well as lower production costs and generally invigorate all sectors. The economic results of existing industry would also improve through the collaboration of these areas with the coastal areas with respect to the supply of mineral resources and agricultural raw materials from the east where they are more plentiful.

The production of the means of subsistence in these areas is still low and most areas are unable to be self-sufficient in terms of food supplies. Light industrial products and textiles are also far from meeting local needs in terms of quantity or quality. The situation requires an intensification of local agricultural and light industrial production. Although most of the land in these areas is unproductive, there are nevertheless large tracts of plains, basins, valleys, and oases suitable for growing food and industrial crops. Larger tracts of grassland and mountainous areas are suitable for afforestation, and virgin soil can be cultivated. The structure of agricultural production should be readjusted in accordance with the local conditions. Existing grasslands and forests must be protected to prevent upsetting the ecological balance, especially on the loess plateaux and in agricultural and pastoral areas. The comprehensive development of agriculture, forestry, and animal husbandry in areas with this kind of industrial structure, with the support of heavy industry, would make possible the more rapid development of light industry and a more balanced industrial base.

In the long term, the rich mineral resources of these areas should be more fully exploited through the construction of large coal-mines in Shanxi, northern Shaanxi, western Hunan, Helan Shan (Helan mountain), western Guizhou, and eastern Yunnan. Emphasis should also be placed on exploiting the rich hydroelectric power potential of the upper reaches of the Huang He, the main tributaries along the middle and lower reaches of the Chang Jiang, and the waterways of the south-west and Xijiang in order to develop the non-ferrous metals, rare metals, and chemical industries. In the process, in addition to speeding up the development of those industries, it would solve the

Table 4.3 The Production Structures of Gansu, Shanxi, Ningxia, Inner Mongolia, Yunnan, Guizhou, and Sichuan, 1980

Item	Gansu	Shanxi	Ningxia	Qinghai	Inner Mongolia	Yunnan	Guizhou	Sichuan
In industrial and agricultural output value								
Proportion of industry (%)	77.90	75.00	73.80	71.20	77.00	58.10	59.20	65.10
Proportion of agriculture (%)	22.10	25.00	26.20	28.80	23.00	41.90	40.80	34.90
In industrial output value								
Proportion of heavy industry (%)	81.74	71.65	71.73	70.84	66.45	57.04	67.02	58.35
Proportion of light industry (%)	18.26	28.35	28.27	29.16	33.55	42.96	32.98	41.65

Source: *China's Economic Yearbook, 1981 (Economic Management,* 1981).

problem of China's present energy shortage, help transform these backward areas, and improve the country's industrial distribution as a whole.

The Utilization of Natural Resources

Land is the basic means of production in agriculture. It is also indispensable to other sections of the economy, trades, and professions. For this reason, the rational use of land, which ensures sufficient for the needs of urban and industrial development and for communications without destroying or appropriating vast amounts of farm land or damaging the environment, is of crucial importance. Although China has a huge land area, only a small amount of it is usable and much of that is poor in quality. Very little suitable land has not already been developed. This relative land shortage therefore makes rational utilization all the more important.

As agriculture's primary natural resource, land must be considered along with climate, geomorphology, soil, vegetation, and hydrology. Its basic characteristics are productivity and regional features. The quality of land being relative, its assessment, development, and utilization must be suited to local conditions. If land is used rationally, its productivity and output will increase steadily; if it is used unwisely, the result will be depletion of its fertility and destruction of the ecological balance. The problem in China, therefore, is not so much the relatively small amount and poor quality of the land, but its manner of development and use.

China's long history as an agricultural society has led to the innovation of many high-yield cultivation methods and unique procedures. Since 1949, many projects have been implemented to conserve farm land, grasslands, forests, and water sources. At the same time, however, the misuse and waste of land resources has been widespread. For many years, the principle of adaptability to local conditions in the overall arrangement of agriculture was violated because the structure of agricultural production and land use was irrational. Grain production was emphasized in spite of the unsuitability of many areas for this type of agriculture. Also, it led to the destruction of forests, the abandonment of animal husbandry, and the reclamation of land from lakes. This emphasis on utilization to the neglect of conservation increased the output of grain and other farm products in a short time through the expansion of the area under cultivation, but at great cost to other sectors of the agricultural economy. Another consequence of heavy cultivation was the reduction of organic matter in the soil.

The unscrupulous felling of trees in the forests and the failure to reafforest resulted in a decline in coverage in some of the densely forested areas and a consumption that was greater than could be supplied. In Yunnan, coverage dropped from 50 per cent in 1949 to 24 per cent in 1980; in Sichuan, it dropped from 20 per cent to 13 per cent; and in the Da Hinggan mountains, forested areas were reduced from 71 per cent to 57 per cent. Overgrazing in the grasslands also led to the degeneration of vegetation. By 1976, an estimated 770 million *mu* had been affected in this way. Similar wasteful practices were also emphasized in aquaculture.

Because of the destruction of large areas of forests and grasslands, the amount of land which has been reduced to sand has increased from 1.6 billion *mu* in 1949 to 1.9 billion *mu* in 1980. Eroded soil areas totalled 1.5 million square kilometres in 1980. Some 26 million tonnes of silt are carried each year by rivers to the sea and silt build-up in reservoirs built since 1949 has decreased their capacity by an estimated 400 billion cubic metres. The average soil loss throughout the country is 50 million tonnes a year and the loss of soil nutrients is equivalent to 40 million tonnes of chemical fertilizers.

Various construction projects not associated with agriculture have provided the technical and material conditions for boosting the utilization rate and productivity of the land. However, wasteful practices and the encroachment on large amounts of farm land of other forms of production has to a certain extent offset these gains. Between 1957 and 1977, more than 236 million *mu* of cultivated land was occupied and used for other purposes. Cultivated lands were thus reduced by 22 million *mu* every year (equivalent to all the cultivated land in Fujian province).

Unless changes in land utilization methods occur, a cycle of deterioration will ensue. Environmental deterioration will result in a drop in land productivity and a reduction in the amount of land that can be used productively, which in turn will accelerate environmental deterioration and disruption of the ecological system as a whole. The adjustment of the structure and distribution of agriculture and the development and utilization of different kinds of land resources according to local conditions are urgently indicated if the situation is to be remedied.

Grain production is a necessary focus of agricultural production in China as a whole. At the same time, however, a diversified economy should be developed, including the production of cotton, oil-bearing crops, and sugar crops. At present, 100 million hectares of China's cultivated land grow food crops. Any expansion of this amount of land under cultivation should have as its focus crops other than grain so as to establish a rational structure of agricultural production. The utilization and economic value of different land types would thereby be improved. It is imperative that agriculture be developed in the light of local conditions if its distribution is to be rational within the overall orientation of development.

China's vast territory creates a wide variety of natural, economic, and technical conditions in various parts of the country. Variations occur between localities, between the plains and hilly or mountainous areas, and even within single provinces or counties. An all-embracing agricultural structure that takes no account of the characteristics of different regions and which stresses self-sufficiency will be tied to the growing of multifarious crops, the scattering of cultivated lands, and a generally irrational system, with poor economic results. The development of agriculture on a large scale and along socialist lines requires the analysis of natural resources and the socio-economic conditions of agriculture, taking into account the regional differences and specific local conditions. On this basis, the focal points of agricultural development and the diversified economy of different regions can be fixed and the various regional production structures, each with its own characteristics, set up. At the regional level, bases of agricultural production can then be established according to the requirements of the different sectors and crops.

The country can be divided into four types of agricultural economic zones based on specification and individual characteristics. The first type of zone includes areas around the large cities, coastal areas, and in the Chang Jiang and Zhu Jiang delta areas where agricultural production structures are characterized by the integration of agriculture, industry, and commerce. Such areas function mainly as producers of commercialized farm products to serve the needs of the cities and of export trade.

The second zone includes the plains of the north and north-east, the middle and lower reaches of the Chang Jiang, and the Guangdong and Sichuan basins. In these areas, bases for growing grain, cotton, hemp, and sugar, such as the sugar bases in Guangdong, Fujian, Guangxi, and Sichuan basins; grain and cotton bases in the Chang Jiang delta; soya bean and beet bases in the north-east; peanut bases in Shandong; and cotton and wheat bases in the north are appropriate land uses. In these large regions, agricultural production structures characterized by the integration of agriculture, forestry, and stock breeding may be established around the individual specialized sectors.

In the third type of zone, the stock-breeding areas, agricultural production structures should emphasize stock breeding integrated with agriculture and forestry. The main focus of these areas is the provision of animals and animal products to the state and the establishment of pasture and fodder areas. There is no attempt to achieve self-sufficiency in food and grain.

In the areas in which agriculture and animal husbandry are mingled, the situation is more complicated. The orientation of agricultural development in these areas has long been unstable, sometimes emphasizing one or the other, or both simultaneously. The natural and economic conditions in these areas favour animal husbandry (rather than agriculture, which is the present emphasis) and the orientation needs to be shifted. Pasture and fodder areas need to be developed as part of the improvement of animal husbandry. Forestry in these areas should also serve the needs of animal husbandry and pasture formation. Taking into account the distribution of mountains, water, forests, farm lands, roads, and residential areas, the agricultural production structure should emphasize animal husbandry integrated with agriculture and forestry.

In the mountainous and hilly zones, forestry and animal husbandry are the most appropriate orientation, with some production of goods of a local character. In the tropical and subtropical hilly areas in the south, forestry has a strategic focus in addition to the provision of fuel, timber, and water. Animal husbandry and agriculture, particularly the cultivation of grains, should also be a focus in suitable areas.

At the same time as the structure and distribution of agricultural production are being adjusted, the more rational use of land for other construction projects needs to be emphasized. Urban planning, which concentrates similar functions in designated areas and which in other ways rationalizes the utilization of land in cities, is an important tool in this regard. One effective method of maximizing land use in cities is the construction of high-rise buildings which create vertical land-use zones, thereby economizing on horizontal land use. New settlements are best based around existing villages and constructed according to local conditions. Other land-saving methods are the planned use of vacant and open spaces between buildings, roads, and villages, the reduction of caving and dumping practices, and reduction of the width of the land-consuming rail networks.

The utilization of mineral resources also needs to be nationalized. Mineral resources are the material foundation of China's modernization drive. The growth of modern industries creates an increasing demand for mineral resources, and the rational development and utilization of these resources is therefore a prerequisite for economic development. Much progress has been made in the mining industry in China since 1949, but an inadequate understanding of the characteristics of the country's mineral resources has caused many problems in their development and utilization.

Most of China's mineral reserves occur in mixed deposits; single-mineral deposits are rare. China also has many associated minerals, which compounds the problem of comprehensive prospecting and assessment. A major problem continues to be separate prospecting procedures by individual departments who discard minerals other than those required, with the result of duplication of work and diseconomies of time and investment. Comprehensive prospecting and assessment would correct this problem and create conditions for their comprehensive development and utilization. Dressing and smelting processes need to be modernized through the introduction of new technology. In this way, waste would be reduced and the value of intergrowth minerals, which is often greater than that of the main minerals, realized. In Bayan Obo, for example, iron ore reserves have a niobium and rare earth content which is 20 times more valuable than the iron ore. Multiple utilization in Baotou, Panzhihua, and Jinchuan has not only added many minerals, including cobaltite, molybdenum, titanium, and rare earth, but has increased the output of gold, sulphuric acid, and nickel. Recovery of these intergrowth minerals in the smelting process reduces the amount of slag and waste produced, the amount of farm land used for mining, and pollution.

Although China has rich deposits of many minerals — enough to meet domestic demands and to provide large amounts for export — backward dressing and smelting techniques have kept China out of the world market. Tungsten deposits, for example, are the largest in the world, but the standard set by the world market for the concentrate is 70 per cent, which China cannot yet reach. Lower grade oxide tungsten is exported and high-quality tungsten filament, costing as much as 100 times more, has to be imported. The price of one tonne of rare earth metal on the world market is as much as US$700,000 but because separation in China is impure, its exported rare earth is valued at no more than US$100,000 a tonne. The present need for foreign exchange makes it necessary to export some mineral resources, but in the long term, the export of processed products should be emphasized to increase foreign exchange earnings.

The practice in China is to exploit rich mines before poor mines. However, some of the country's mineral reserves are found mainly in poor mines. This makes it necessary for a certain quantity of rich ores to be imported until such time as resources of high-grade ores which are of strategic importance are found. At the same time, higher grade ores could be produced from poor mines with concentrated reserves if access to transport and other facilities for exploitation and separation was developed to a greater extent. In this way, the country's industrial production would be placed on a more solid domestic natural resources footing.

The verified deposits of some minerals, such as potassium salt, are also very small. However, there are many rock salt mines, and as basins forming the salt further evaporate and concentrate, potassium salt is likely to emerge. A problem in discovering potassium salt is the absence of surface indications of deposits and the fact that it is very active and easily destroyed.

Other minerals in short supply, and where there is little possibility of reserves being found or developed, may have to be imported. At the same time, research should be carried out into the use of substitutes, with the aim of establishing an alloy industrial system based on the characteristics of China's natural resources.

Minerals are formed and distributed unevenly over the earth's crust. This creates regional characteristics where, in a given area, certain minerals may be concentrated, whilst others are scattered or non-existent. In east China, for example, the superior minerals are tungsten, silver, tantalum, alumstone, fluorite, and gypsum; the inferior minerals include manganese, vanadium, mercury, and antimony. In the central-south, the predominant minerals are manganese, zinc, tungsten, tin, antimony, gallium, indium, bismuth, tantalum, ochre, cadmium phosphorus, ferrous sulphur, and oil shale, whilst the inferior minerals are vanadium, nickel, mercury, and coal. In the south-west, the predominant minerals are iron, vanadium, titanium, copper, lead, zinc, tin, mercury, manganese, chromium, phosphate, rock salt, and asbestos, whilst the inferior minerals are tungsten, bismuth, beryllium, magnesite, potassium, and boron. In the north-west, nickel, cobaltite, molybdenum, beryllium, niobium, tantalum, potassium salt, boron, asbestos, magnesium, and chromium are superior, whilst the inferior minerals include iron, manganese, tungsten, ferrous sulphur, coal, and oil shale.

This varying distribution of superior and inferior mineral resources should be taken into account when the geographical distribution of national economic construction is centrally planned. The characteristics of the distribution of these resources in different zones must be considered when defining the main focus, scope, and speed of development in each zone. The situation in China requires the establishment of regional mineral production bases and the construction of related industries if the resource advantages of different zones are to be fully utilized. In this way, each region's needs can be met through a national system of integration and balance.

It is futile for a region to set goals of self-sufficiency in mineral production without taking into account the actual distribution of reserves. In the past, planning errors occurred through such attempts to create large, all-embracing, closed economic structures. Factories were established and plans were formulated before reserves were even verified. The exploitation of mineral resources must be rationalized if advantage is to be taken of China's resources and their present distribution. Changes in the relative worth of certain minerals on the world market is another consideration when planning comprehensive exploitation of the available reserves.

Environmental Impact

Population growth and the steady utilization of natural resources is destroying the environment. The laws of economics are usually at odds with the laws of nature and the practice of dumping industrial waste into rivers, for example, creates problems of contaminated water, blocked river channels, damage to the fishing industry, and navigation and flooding difficulties. Air pollution is another equally serious problem, as is visual pollution when factories are built in scenic areas such as Guilin, Hangzhou, and Suzhou with no thought to their effect on the environment.

Industrial construction and production are still emphasized in China, and there is little planning for the protection of the environment. The annual discharge of industrial waste water is many billions of tonnes, only about 10 per cent of which is treated. Also, millions of tonnes of harmful waste gases are discharged into the air and only about 20 per cent of the several hundred million tonnes of slag produced each year is utilized. Because most of China's industries are concentrated in the medium-sized and large cities, the problem of pollution exists to some degree everywhere. It is even more serious in cities where industries with greater pollution potential, such as chemical plants, are concentrated.

In the rural areas, the ecological balance has been disrupted by the destruction of forests and grasslands and by land reclamation. Erosion and the formation of sandy wastes have been caused by such practices. Existing cultivated land has also been used without thought being given to natural side-effects. For example, the cultivation of single crops without compensatory or balanced cropping systems has depleted soil fertility and resulted in a drop in productivity. Water conservation projects have tended to concentrate on irrigation rather than drainage, and salination of the soil has become a problem. In the development of mineral resources, there is also a tendency to exploit reserves irresponsibly, to destroy the ore body, and to waste resources.

Environmental protection is necessary if natural processes are to be allowed to continue to provide the resources that are necessary for production and a healthy living environment. Comprehensive planning is required during economic development in order to reduce the impact of man's endeavours on the environment and to allow for the means of production to continue.

In industrial distribution, the impact on the environment can best be reduced through a combination of concentration of development and its rational dispersal. Analysis and assessment of the impact of new industries must be carried out in the early planning stages and anti-pollution devices should be installed when construction commences. Natural resources should be developed and utilized in accordance with unified planning and a rational approach to local characteristics, the distribution of production, and the function of the ecological system.

Natural resources may be either ecological, biological, or mineral resources. Ecological resources, such as solar radiation, atmospheric temperature, and moisture content, have a distinctly regional character, are renewable (as opposed to non-renewable) resources, and operate outside human control. Biological resources, such as forests, grasslands, aquatic products, animals, and soil, can be renewed and require a balance of protection and development. Protection of these resources controls their use and ensures that they do not exceed their productive capacity. Over-exploitation, such as irresponsible reclamation, tree-felling, and over-fishing, is a serious problem in this respect. Distinctions need to be made between water-source forests and fuel forests, and between agriculture and a diversified economy, if resources are not to be seriously depleted. Regeneration and development of these resources ensures that they continue to be available for proper use.

Mineral resources are found in unevenly distributed, limited deposits and, as such, are non-renewable. Care must be exercised in their development and utilization so as to prevent waste and to maximize their potential. Waste products from industrial processes (over 900 million tonnes each year) are harmful pollutants, yet with proper planning they can be used to produce silicates and other valuable by-products.

The relationship between environmental protection and economic development must be balanced. The environment provides the means for economic development and a healthy living environment, but it is easily damaged by excessive economic development. Pollution control measures should be planned and implemented at all levels of industry, and particular key industries (such as metallurgy, energy, chemicals, and paper-making) should be especially concerned about pollution control. Areas where concentrations of polluting industries occur, such as in the large cities and industrial zones around the Bohai Sea and those areas drained by the Huang He and the Chang Jiang, need to emphasize control measures and where possible to adopt new science and technology in order to reduce the number of pollutants caused by industrial processes. At the same time, comprehensive utilization and the economic conversion of waste should be practised.

Environmental planning is, in essence, national territory planning. The country's 9.6 million square kilometres of land and water resources need to be attended to by means of state guidance in environmental planning, comprehensive plans for the development and utilization of the national territories, the study of the relationship between the consumption of the nation's natural resources and their regeneration and replenishment, and the study of the relationship between the development of resources and ecological balance. Such considerations must be basic to any consideration of the overall distribution of production.

The scope, function, and development of cities should also be carried out in the light of environmental considerations. Regional and city planning should concentrate on the rational distribution of like functions within a city. The amount of land under plant cover should be expanded through the building of parks and gardens. In this way, environmental protection can be combined with innovative planning and the rational distribution of the city's installations.

Part II: Industrial Geography

5. The Development and Distribution of Industry, 1840–1949

Factors Affecting Industrial Distribution

In the century between the First Opium War (1839–42) and the founding of the People's Republic of China in 1949, there was very little modern industrial develop-ment in China. What little industry existed was controlled by the foreign powers. In 1936, foreign investment in China totalled RMB4.5 billion. Foreign-owned factories and enterprises produced 99 per cent of China's output of iron, 60 per cent of its cotton cloth, and more than 55 per cent of its coal, electricity, and tobacco products. During the Sino-Japanese War of 1937–45, foreign capital increased to RMB9.7 billion, further monopolizing China's industrial production.

Foreign interest in China at this time was largely self-serving. Britain, Germany, Russia, Japan, and the United States had three main purposes in developing China's industries. First, China's rich mineral resources could be exploited as raw materials for foreign industries, and its agricultural products could be processed and sold at a high profit on the world market. Secondly, strategic military bases were established as part of the drive to divide and control China. Also, domination of China's huge domestic market through the exploitation of its resources and cheap labour was profitable. Factories were set up for these purposes in the cities and ports along the east coast and in other areas where the foreign powers were influential.

China's political and economic weaknesses at this time meant that manu-facturing was dominated by the foreign powers. Chinese industrialists were reliant upon imported foreign machinery and funds. This tended to concentrate Chinese-owned enterprises in the coastal cities where protection could also be sought from the foreign powers against the political strife that was disrupting the country. Although the relationship between the Chinese- and foreign-owned enterprises was unequal, these economic and political bonds strength-ened the concentration of manufacturing in the coastal areas.

Changes in Industrial Distribution

The distribution of industry during the period 1840–1949 can be divided into four main stages. From the time of the First Opium War in 1839 to the start of the first Sino-Japanese War in 1894, industrial enterprises were largely concentrated in south-east China. At this time, foreign interest in China was focused on exploiting the country's raw materials and capturing the Chinese market. Foreign-owned businesses were not permitted to open mines or to build railways in China and their business activities were limited to a few coastal cities. There were very few Chinese-owned enterprises, apart from those processing agricultural products in the south-east.

In 1842, the Treaty of Nanjing opened the ports of Guangzhou, Fuzhou, Xiamen, Ningbo, and Shanghai on the south-east coast to foreign economic activities. The Treaty of Tianjin in 1858 opened a further 10 ports, eight of which (Tainan, Danshui, Chaozhou, Qiongzhou, Hankou, Jiujiang, Nanjing, and Zhenjiang) were also in the south-east. The south-east area of China had at this time a comparatively developed economy and a variety of commercial activities. It was the centre of China's tea, silk, and sugar-cane industries. Transport by river and sea was convenient. The foreign powers were able to exploit the natural resources of the region and to establish commercial relationships with local industrialists and entrepreneurs. They were also able to enjoy privileges stipulated in the 'unequal treaties' and their profits were protected. The cities along the south-east coast were for these reasons convenient for the development of processing of agricultural products and for the import of machinery. Chinese businesses were drawn to the south-east for the market they represented and for the convenience they afforded in the import of machinery and technical equipment.

The agricultural processing and Chinese-owned textile industries were concentrated mainly in Shanghai, Guangzhou, and Wuhan. These were China's first industrial centres and accounted for 64 per cent of the country's factories. There was very little industry elsewhere (Fig. 5.1).

The second stage in the growth of industry extended from 1895 to the First World War. Industries in the south-east expanded and heavy industry developed in the north of China (Fig. 5.2). Foreign imperialism during this period had as its main focus the export of capital from China. The Treaty of Shimonoseki confirmed the right of the foreign powers to establish factories and their influence was further consolidated by the reliance of the Qing dynasty government on foreign assistance in suppressing for a time what became the Chinese Revolution of 1911. This reliance opened the door even wider for foreign capital to flow into China. The right to build railways was granted, which was soon followed by the right to open mines. This expanded the spheres of influence of the foreign powers and made possible the exploitation and export of mineral resources and the expansion of manufacturing industries.

The spheres of foreign influence had a direct impact during this second stage of industrial growth on the distribution of China's industries. British influence was centred around Shanghai where the light and textile industries were based. Coal-mining was also developed in Shanxi, Hebei, and Henan provinces on the middle and lower reaches of the Huang He. Coal-mines were also opened up using German capital in Shandong province, based around Qingdao. Russia and Japan were dominant in north-east China, where they established flour mills, oil extraction and other light industrial factories, lumber yards, and coal-mines (Table 5.1).

The influx of foreign capital into Shanghai, Guangzhou, and the other large cities had the effect of squeezing out Chinese-owned enterprises into cities near the main foreign-controlled centres. Whilst Shanghai, Guangzhou, and Wuhan still accounted for 57 per cent of China's total industrial production, a number of smaller industrial centres emerged, particularly in the

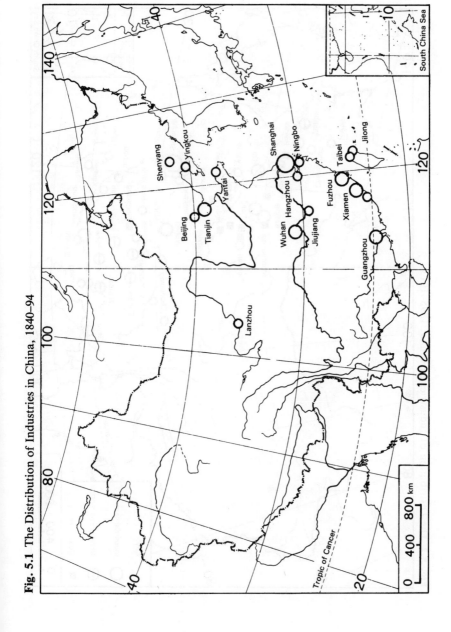

Fig. 5.1 The Distribution of Industries in China, 1840–94

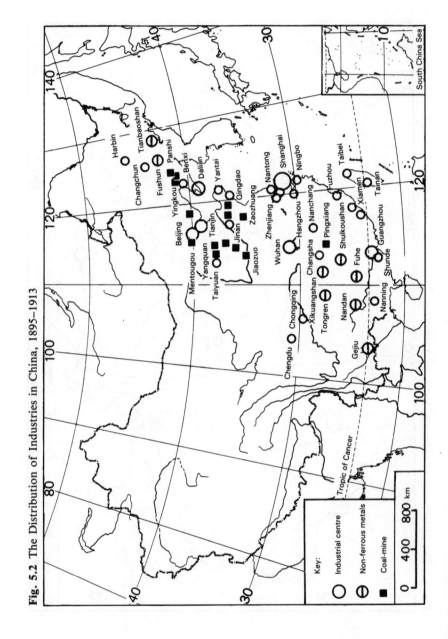

Fig. 5.2 The Distribution of Industries in China, 1895–1913

Table 5.1 District Factories and Mines, 1895–1913 (%)

District	% of Country's Total Factories and Mines
South-eastern regions	57.22
Shanghai	17.84
Jiangsu	10.48
Wuxi	1.69
Zhenjiang	1.55
Suzhou	1.20
Nantong	1.20
Zhejiang	4.10
Fujian	2.80
Anhui	2.80
Hubei	6.94
Wuhan	5.60
Guangdong	12.26
Shunde	7.36
Guangzhou	2.26
Northern regions	27.84
North-east	14.54
Liaoning	7.64
Hebei	9.48
Beijing ⎫	
Tianjin ⎬	6.23
Tangshan ⎭	
Shandong	3.82
Others	14.94

Source: Chen Zhen and Yao Luo, *A History of Modern Industry* (Sanlian Bookstore, Beijing, 1957).

north-east. Harbin and Dalian developed as manufacturing centres and coal mining was established in Fushun and Benxi, as well as in Shandong, Kailuan, and Jingxing. Beijing, Hebei, Tianjin, Jinan, and Yantai expanded their light industrial bases. These changes in industrial distribution occurred slowly, however, and apart from the coal industry, manufacturing in the north was on a small scale. China's industrial base remained for the most part in the south-east, where it was increasingly monopolized by foreign-owned industries.

From 1914 to 1936, industry began to develop in a number of cities situated in the Chang Jiang delta. In the north-east, Tianjin and Qingdao became important industrial centres. Events during the post-First World War period had an important influence on the growth of industrial production in China. The fall of the Russian Tsarist government led to the withdrawal of Russian capital from China. European and American attention was occupied with domestic rehabilitation. By the terms of the Sino-German treaty of 1921, Germany gave up its special rights and privileges in China. The May Fourth Movement in 1919 was an expression of Chinese nationalistic sentiment. These changes allowed China's industries to grow, particularly in Shanghai where textiles and flour mills expanded.

Japan's influence in China during this period was steadily increasing. It expanded its control of the textile industries in Shanghai in an attempt to supplant England as the leading foreign capital investor in China and in order to weaken Chinese industries which had developed during the war. Textiles became Shanghai's main industry and the Japanese domination of the industry once again led to the situation where Chinese-owned industries moved to smaller cities near Shanghai. Production bases for cotton textiles were established in Nantong and Changzhou; cotton textiles, silk weaving, and flour processing were developed in Wuxi; and Suzhou became a silk-weaving base. Together with Shanghai, these cities formed an industrial region based on light and textile industries.

At the same time as Chinese-owned enterprises were being redistributed around Shanghai, where Japan dominated production, the Japanese also began to shift their investment north. With the intention of colonizing the area and establishing a military base inside China for the purpose of further expanding its sphere of influence, heavy industries were established in the north-east. Iron and steel industries were built up around the region's coal and iron ore deposits; chemicals and engineering industries were developed for military purposes; and energy industries were established to provide cheap power. There was no heavy industrial base in China other than in this region.

Japanese aggression in China had as its main aim possession of the north-east. Its second target was the economic expansion of north China, but the area's political instability and the huge investment in north-east China slowed development. Japan exploited the north-east's cotton, coal, salt, and iron ore resources and built mines and chemical industries. It annexed Chinese-owned enterprises and developed the textile and mining industries in Qingdao and Tianjin, which by 1937, along with Shanghai, had become China's largest industrial centres.

This third stage in China's changing industrial distribution saw the expansion of heavy manufacturing in the north-east and the growth of Qingdao and Tianjin as large industrial bases. In the south-east, Hubei, Guangdong, and Fujian provinces were relatively stagnant in industrial development. Japan was the most monopolistic of the foreign powers involved in production in China (Fig. 5.3).

The final stage of industrial development and redistribution in China before 1949 was the period of the second Sino-Japanese War. Complex changes occurred during this period. Heavy industries expanded in the north-east and began to develop in the north; there was a decline in production in the south-east and some development in the west. Japan's war against China saw the occupation of its main industrial centres and the confiscation of the assets of other foreign enterprises. Japanese investment replaced all other sources of foreign capital and, in the occupied areas, the majority of industries were under the direct control of the Japanese.

Japan's economic aggression against China was closely associated with its military aggression. Its military aim was the annexation of north-east China

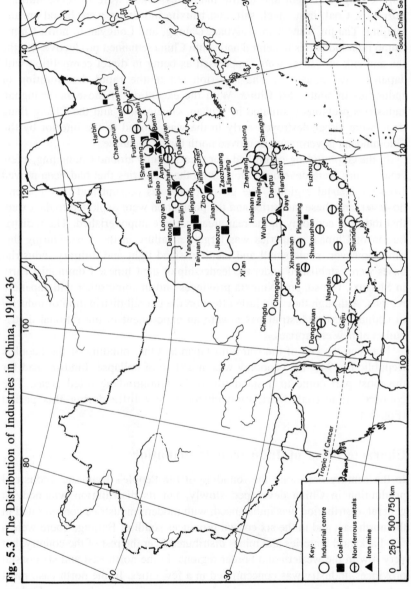

Fig. 5.3 The Distribution of Industries in China, 1914–36

and the reduction of the rest of China to a colony dependent upon, and with the function of supplying raw materials to, north-east China. Whilst Japan's military, engineering, and precision industries were to be based in Japan, the cities of Anshan, Fushun, Benxi, Dalian, and Shenyang in north-east China were to become production bases for the power, mining, smelting, partial engineering, and light and textile industries which were to serve military purposes. Coal, iron, steel, salt, and bauxite industries were based around Beijing, Tianjin, Tangshan, Taiyuan, Datong, and Longyan in north China. Some light industries in central and south China remained productive, but the tea and silk industries were suppressed as being in direct competition with Japan's own industries. The situation led to the rapid deterioration of industries in south-east China. With the exception of those in Shanghai, industries previously situated in Wuhan, Guangzhou, and the Chang Jiang delta were either destroyed early in the war, moved to the interior by the Guomindang government, or moved north by the Japanese.

In the Guomindang-controlled rear areas, mainly around Chongqing, a few small mines were developed along with the industries that had been moved from the coastal regions. The government was corrupt and incompetent, however, and these industries and the population were exploited to the extent that the rural economy in the rear areas became impoverished. The redistribution of China's industries was largely a failure in the west. During this time, however, some small and medium-sized light and military industrial bases were established under the leadership of the Chinese Communist Party in Shaanxi, Gansu, and Ningxia provinces and in some other anti-Japanese regions. Although they had little effect on the overall distribution of industry in China, these industrial bases were an experiment in the rational distribution of new enterprises.

Between the end of the war with Japan and the founding of the People's Republic in 1949, the economy was in a state of collapse. Industry had for the most part come to a standstill in the Guomindang-ruled areas. The country's industrial distribution changed very little during this period (Fig. 5.4).

Characteristics of Industrial Distribution

In the century preceding the founding of the People's Republic, industrial production in China developed slowly, but its distribution widened. In general, distribution was imbalanced, with modern industries concentrated in the north-east and in the six coastal provinces south of Beijing. There were a few backward factories and mines distributed over the rest of the country, but very few in the western and border regions. In the north-east and six coastal provinces, industry was concentrated in a few cities. In the north-east, most industrial production was centred in Liaoning province, in Shenyang, Fushun, Anshan, Benxi, and Dalian. South of the Great Wall, Shanghai, Nanjing, Wuxi, Tianjin, Beijing, Qingdao, and Guangzhou accounted for the bulk of the area's production. There was very little industry in Zhejiang, Fujian, Hebei, Shandong, Jiangsu, and Guangdong provinces. The few industries in

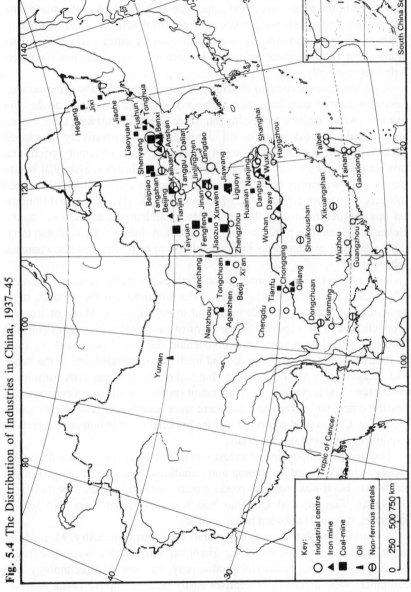

Fig. 5.4 The Distribution of Industries in China, 1937–45

the interior and border regions were largely confined to Taiyuan, Wuhan, and Chongqing and their productivity was much lower than that of the coastal cities.

In addition to its uneven distribution, China's industrial production developed at an uneven pace. Whilst industries expanded in some provinces and cities, those in others stagnated or declined. For example, industry developed in the north-east at the same time as it declined in the south-east. Cities with a relatively long history of industrial activity, such as Fuzhou, Xiamen, Ningbo, and Anqing, were overtaken by cities such as Qingdao, Dalian, and Tianjin, where industry was more recently established but where it developed rapidly.

A second characteristic of distribution during this period was the remoteness of industrial sites from their sources of raw materials. In Shanghai, for example, where China's processing industries were concentrated, there was no local supply of coal, iron, or oil. Jiangsu had comparatively developed agriculture, but was unable to supply Shanghai with sufficient agricultural raw materials for its well-developed processing industries. Shanghai had to import a large quantity of its raw materials, particularly wool and flue-cured tobacco, from more distant areas. Mines were also largely dissociated from the set-ups required to process their products. Coal, bauxite, and salt in Shanxi, Hebei, and Shandong provinces; iron in Hubei, Anhui, and Guangdong; tungsten in Jiangxi; and antimony in Hunan all had to be transported elsewhere for processing.

Some of the heavy industries in the north-east were far removed from the source of their raw materials. Most of the raw materials for its iron, steel, cement, acid, and textile industries had to be imported. Many of its own products had to be exported in the form of raw materials or semi-finished products, including magnesite, molybdenum ore, paper pulp, and pig iron.

In addition, many of the small and medium-sized industries in the south had access to rich natural resources but lacked the raw materials for mining production. The region produced abundant supplies of silkworm cocoons, oil-bearing crops, and sugar-cane, but there were insufficient related processing industries. Cotton production fell and the important textile industry lacked the required quantities of raw materials.

Thirdly, the composition of industry in different areas was often irrational. Heavy industry, based on mining and munitions, was well developed in the north-east, but it was unable to produce many necessary articles for daily use. Shanghai, Tianjin, and Qingdao had well-developed light and textile industries, but very backward heavy industry.

A fourth characteristic was the overall weakness of industry. Most of the large industrial centres, including Shanghai and Tianjin, were essentially commercial centres. Industrial productivity was low and technology and equipment were outdated. Enterprises easily became impoverished. Another problem in the distribution of industry was the vulnerability in the case of war of much of the country's industry, most of which was located on the north-east border.

Finally, the industrial centres and the rural areas were sharply opposed. The isolated industrial centres had a strong colonial character and tended to exploit the rural areas to provide agricultural resources and cheap labour for their own purposes. The prosperity of the cities was based on this exploitation and, in turn, the rural areas became dependent upon them. This relationship did not, however, modernize agricultural production in the rural hinterland. Very few cities produced agricultural machinery, tending to concentrate mainly on the production, repair, and assembly of armaments. During this period, there was not one factory in China producing tractors, nor were irrigation and drainage equipment or modern farm tools manufactured. There were only two chemical fertilizer plants (in Nanjing and Dalian), producing 227,000 tonnes of ammonium sulphate annually. The 57 hydroelectric power stations scattered throughout the country had a total capacity of 5,000 kilowatts. Even in the relatively developed areas, agriculture was poorly equipped.

A number of conclusions can be drawn from these characteristics of industrial distribution in China before 1949. First, a rational industrial distribution must be based on a rational social system. Despite its large territory and population and the country's rich resources, China's status during this period as a semi-feudal, semi-colonial state prevented the exploitation for its own benefit of these resources. The result was a serious imbalance in the country's industrial distribution, requiring fundamental changes in China's social system if the situation was to be remedied. Attempts to disperse industries to the interior were largely unsuccessful. For more than a century, the country's industrial distribution could not be rationalized. It would appear, therefore, that the distribution, characteristics, and development of industry in China were the result of the social system and relative mode of production before 1949. Other factors influencing industrial production were of secondary importance. It also became obvious that the spontaneously developed distribution of production of pre-1949 China could not meet the needs of a socialist China. Change had to be based on the existing structure, however; reforms were needed in order to adapt established industries to serve new purposes.

Thirdly, pre-socialist China's industrial distribution exhibited characteristics of both capitalist and colonial or semi-colonial countries. As in capitalist countries, it had an unbalanced distribution of production; production was divorced from raw materials; the structure within industrial centres was irrational; and a poor relationship existed between the industrial cities and the countryside. Like colonial countries, its industry was backward, concentrated in the coastal areas, and it provided insufficient support to agriculture.

The overall situation in 1949 was a difficult one to remedy. New industrial centres needed to be established at the same time as existing industries were renovated and strengthened. There were problems as to the priorities of the distribution of labour, materials, and funds between the old and new industries. The low labour productivity of the agricultural areas created the danger of excessive rural-urban migration, with its problems of overcrowding and food shortages. A further problem was the unsuitability for redevelopment of many of the industries in the north-east border areas.

6. The Development and Distribution of Industry since 1949

Changes in the Industrial Structure

Prior to the founding of the People's Republic in 1949, China's industry was poorly developed and unbalanced. The textile industry dominated the industrial scene; heavy industry and machine building were backward, with outdated equipment and technology, and they were low in self-sufficiency and manufacturing capacity. Heavy industry was unable to provide a sound base for economic development.

The 1st FYP attempted to transform this situation, which was the legacy of industrial development and distribution up to 1949. The plan focused on further development of the traditional sectors and the establishment of new industries to fill the gaps in the industrial structure. A more broadly based and comparatively independent and integrated system began to develop during this period (Fig. 6.1). Changes also occurred in the rate of development of the various sectors (Tables 6.1 and 6.2).

Tables 6.1 and 6.2 indicate the relative strength of the food-processing and textile industries in the years immediately after 1949. These two sectors together accounted for 51.6 per cent of the gross industrial output value.

Table 6.1 The Rate of Development of the Industrial Sectors, 1953–79 (%)

Sector	1953–7	1958–62	1963–5	1966–70	1971–5	1953–79
Gross industrial value	18.0	3.8	17.9	11.7	9.1	11.6
Metallurgy	29.1	7.4	20.4	8.8	5.3	13.2
Electric power	20.4	20.7	12.8	11.5	10.9	15.1
Coal	17.1	11.8	0.1	8.8	5.4	9.3
Petroleum	32.7	22.2	27.4	18.5	14.6	21.6
Chemical industry	31.2	14.4	23.9	17.3	10.4	8.2
Fertilizers and insecticides	44.6	43.1	22.2	13.7	11.6	27.3
Machinery	29.6	7.6	21.8	15.8	13.6	16.4
Agricultural machinery	34.1	23.5	20.9	29.5	16.1	23.3
Building materials	20.0	−4.5	30.1	9.4	11.5	12.1
Timber	13.7	−4.9	8.1	−1.8	7.5	4.8
Food	13.2	−1.7	11.4	2.4	8.4	6.7
Textiles	8.6	−3.3	21.8	8.0	4.2	7.3
Paper	19.1	2.5	12.1	3.3	6.5	8.8

Source: China's Economic Yearbook, 1981 (Economic Management, 1981).

Table 6.2 Changes in the Industrial Structure, 1952–79 (%)

Sector	1952	1957	1965	1975	1979
Gross industrial value	100.0	100.0	100.0	100.0	100.0
Metallurgy	5.9	8.5	10.7	9.0	8.9
Electric power	1.3	1.7	3.1	3.9	3.8
Coal	2.4	2.9	2.6	2.8	2.6
Petroleum	0.5	1.1	3.2	5.6	5.4
Chemical industry	4.8	6.8	12.9	11.3	12.2
Fertilizers and insecticides	0.1	0.2	1.9	1.9	2.3
Machinery	11.4	16.9	22.3	27.7	27.1
Agricultural machinery	0.3	0.4	1.0	2.6	2.4
Building materials	3.0	3.2	2.8	3.1	3.6
Timber industry	6.5	5.8	2.9	1.9	1.8
Foodstuffs	24.1	19.7	12.6	12.0	11.3
Textile industry	27.5	20.4	15.8	12.3	12.9
Paper making	2.2	2.2	1.8	1.3	1.3

Source: China's Economic Yearbook, 1981 (Economic Management, 1981).

During the period of the 1st FYP, their speed of development slowed, and that of the metallurgy, power, petroleum, chemicals, machine-building, and timber industries increased at a rate greater than that of industry as a whole. By 1957, the textile and food-processing industries accounted for only 40 per cent of the gross output value of industry.

In the period after 1958 (excluding the years 1960–2), heavy industry was emphasized and the proportion of investment in light industry compared with heavy industry dropped steadily. By 1979, the industrial structure had changed to the extent that heavy industry was the strongest sector. This rapid development of heavy industry laid firm foundations for production in other sectors by means of improved equipment and technology. Light industry and agriculture have improved their production methods and have developed rapidly in the 1980s.

The transformation of China's industrial structure since 1949 has not been achieved, however, without some problems. First, light industry was neglected in favour of heavy industry to the degree that it created a disproportionate distribution of labour. In addition to this imbalance between heavy and light industry, the growth of the various heavy industrial sectors was unbalanced. The iron and steel and machine-building industries were stressed, whilst the development of the coal and building materials industries slowed after 1957. Between 1953 and 1979, the annual average speed of growth of the coal industry was only 9.3 per cent. This rate of growth was much less than that of the other heavy industrial sectors and of industry as a whole.

A third problem was the unbalanced development within individual heavy industrial sectors. In metallurgy, for example, the iron and steel industries grew, whilst the non-ferrous metals industry remained backward. Furthermore, within the iron and steel industry itself, steel was emphasized, but there were

Fig. 6.1 The Structure of China's Industrial Sectors

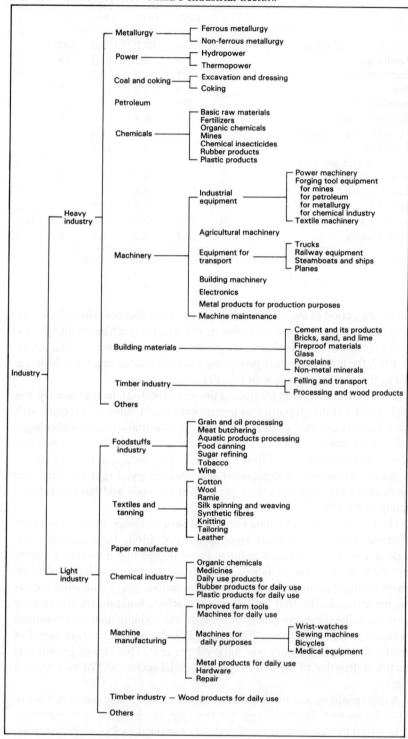

insufficient mines and rolling capacity. In the power industry, thermal power was emphasized and hydroelectric power was undeveloped. In the machine-building industry, ordinary products were over-produced, whilst there were inadequate supplies of new and precision products. In the chemical industry, there were insufficient raw materials sources to meet the processing capacity of the industry.

Finally, heavy industry tended to be self-servicing rather than capable of servicing agriculture and light industry. Despite increases in the production of farm machinery, chemical fertilizers, and insecticides, heavy industry was unable to provide the required tractors, electricity, diesel oil and petroleum, agricultural steel, and machinery maintenance. This low level of technology in agriculture remains a problem today. Similarly, the supply of raw materials, fuel, power, and technical equipment to light industry is still below required levels. The greatest proportion of raw materials for light industry remains farm products and crops. Power supplies necessary for light industrial development are depleted by heavy industry, which consumes 80–90 per cent of available power each year.

China's industrial structure has become significantly more rational since the end of the 1st FYP period. The proportion of light industry increased from 42.7 per cent in 1978 to 51.29 per cent in 1981. The production of cotton yarn increased by 33.2 per cent between 1978 and 1981; that of cotton cloth increased by 29.4 per cent, paper and paper board by 23 per cent, sugar by 39.7 per cent, bicycles by 105.4 per cent, sewing machines by 113.6 per cent, watches by 112.6 per cent, and television sets by 943.3 per cent (a conspicuous improvement in market supply).

During the same period, heavy industry expanded its service base and the output of main products increased (for example, the volume of electricity increased by 20.5 per cent; cement by 28.8 per cent, and chemical fertilizers by 42.6 per cent). Although the trend in heavy industry has been towards a more rational structure, many heavy industrial sectors (such as machine building) have experienced an alarming decrease in pro-duction output. Coal-mining and petroleum are two sectors which must increase production through the location of new reserves. The machine-building industry must also be invigorated as part of the readjustment of the service orientation of heavy industry.

Changes in Industrial Distribution

Rationalization of China's industrial distribution is one of the main tasks in the planned development of the country's economy. The distribution of the forces of production needs to be based on local conditions and requirements, unified planning in relation to national defence and the overall development of the national economy, and the integration of industry with agriculture and the cities with the rural areas. The large-scale industrial construction that has occurred since 1949 has been planned to achieve this rationalization of distribution.

The Development of the Hinterland Areas

One of the main problems of industrial distribution in pre-1949 China was the underdevelopment of the hinterland areas. Some 70 per cent of industries were concentrated in the thin coastal strip from Liaoning province in the north to Guangdong province in the south. There was very little modern industry in the hinterland and remote areas, and vast areas had no industry of any kind. The economy for the most part was based on agriculture and handicrafts. Some of the minority nationality areas were still practising slash-and-burn-type cultivation.

The redistribution of industry would require the opening up of vast areas of land in the interior and border regions, the relocation of key national defence industries in the hinterland, and the gradual establishment of new industrial bases in these regions according to national plans. The hinterland areas were poor, however, and the environment and conditions were hardly conducive to building up modern industries and bases. If a production capability similar to that of the coastal regions was to be built up, huge investments in time and funds would be required as well as the support of the existing bases of production.

The coastal belt was a more suitable choice for development, in some respects, because of the existing industries, transport facilities, technical forces, and public utilities. Industrial construction there would require a smaller investment and would provide faster results. However, the over-concentration of industry along the coast was irrational because of the serious shortages of raw materials, the outdated equipment, backward processing technology, and the low productivity of the area. If the country's industrial development as a whole was to be rationalized and accelerated, better utilization methods in and the reform and development of the coastal industrial bases were equally as important as the development of the hinter-land areas, with their raw materials and strategic importance. At the same time as the old industrial bases would be reinforced and upgraded to form the foundation of the country's industrial structure, new bases would be established in hitherto undeveloped areas as part of the overall redistribution plan. In this way, the coastal and hinterland areas would be mutually supportive, with a common goal of rationally distributed industrial bases.

This approach has been taken since 1949. The 1st FYP period saw the focus of construction begin to shift to the interior. Heavy industrial bases were built in the north-east, based around the Anshan iron and steel complex; coastal cities had their industries modernized; a number of new industrial bases (such as the Baotou and Wuhan iron and steel works) were built in north and central-south China; and construction started in north-west and south-west China. During the period of this plan, the regional allocation of national investment was 41.8 per cent for the coastal areas and 47.8 per cent for the hinterland.

During the 2nd FYP period, the industrial bases in the north-east were further strengthened, and industry in north, east, and central China and in the coastal cities was fully utilized. Emphasis was placed on the development of the iron and steel industry, non-ferrous metals industry, and the hydroelectric power industry in the south-west, north-west, and around the Sanmen gorge of the Huang He. Construction in the petroleum and non-ferrous metals industry in Xinjiang continued and Tibet was surveyed for development. The development of the hinterland remained the main emphasis.

During the 3rd FYP period (1966–70), south-west China was developed. Several trunk rail lines were built and a new industrial base was centred around the Panzhihua iron and steel works. In the north-west, hydroelectric power stations were built on the Huang He and a number of non-ferrous metal industrial bases were established. During this period, investment in the hinterland rose dramatically to 2.16 times the investment in the coastal areas.

Western Hunan, Henan, and Hubei provinces were a focus for construction and development during the 4th FYP period (1971–5). At the same time, new oilfields were opened up in the vicinity of Beijing, Tianjin, Shanghai, and Shandong and Jiangsu provinces. Large petrochemical complexes were built and the harbours expanded.

In the period up to the end of the 4th FYP, investment in the hinterland exceeded investment in the coastal regions. The country's large iron and steel complexes, alloy-steel plants, machine-building projects, chemical factories, hydroelectric power bases, thermal power stations, wool and cotton textile mills, non-ferrous metals bases, and coal-mining bases were located in the hinterland. A number of large industrial bases took shape.

On average, industry in the hinterland developed at a rate faster than that of the coastal areas and of the country as a whole. The ratio of fixed assets, the number of workers and staff, and the total industrial output value of state-owned industry was higher in the hinterland areas than in the coastal areas. The output of coal, electricity, oil, and cement was also higher in the hinterland.

The industrial development of the hinterland invigorated and strengthened the country's industrial base. The scale of exploration and utilization of natural resources expanded. Transport and communications facilities were developed and urban construction was accelerated so that economic and cultural levels rose significantly. Industrial development in the hinterland areas not only gave new force to the strategic rear regions of China and raised the self-sufficiency rate of industrial commodities, but it also eased the pressure on the coastal industrial bases, freeing them for the production of high-grade precision and new products. At the same time, the interior provided the established centres with large quantities of coal, crude oil, non-ferrous metals, timber, and other raw materials which made possible their continued development.

The distribution of industry in the hinterland areas was uneven, however, and placed heavy demands on national defence. The hasty establishment of new bases away from the coast diverted emphasis away from the consolidation and upgrading of the existing bases, which had been an important part of the overall rationalization process. From the period of the 3rd FYP, the investment in the hinterland areas was larger than could be absorbed; many projects were suspended because of insufficient supplies of food, light, and textile industrial products and inadequate public utilities. The situation called for a reduction in the level of investment in the hinterland and in the general scale of construction. An increase in the ratio of investment in the coastal areas was required in order to update equipment and technology, to consolidate existing industries, and to upgrade bases producing raw materials such as fuel. The diversion of investment away from the coastal areas, rather than a redistribution of the limited investment capital between the coastal and hinterland areas, had jeopardized the main task of the existing industrial bases which was to manufacture top-grade precision and new products for export.

The importance of the coastal areas is such that they cannot be discounted in order to divert funds and investment to open up the western areas. However, in the long term, the resources in the west are crucial to the development of industry along the coast. A more balanced development of the economy of the whole of China is necessary. The situation at present requires that full use be made of the existing economic bases in the hinterland and border regions, that important resources be exploited, transport facilities expanded, and specialized personnel trained. Long-term construction projects need to be initiated now with a mind to the steady industrialization of the west. Although state investment in the hinterland areas will continue, economic and technical collaboration between the west and the advanced areas will be encouraged as a means of exploiting the resources of the west whilst importing funds, manpower, and advanced technology to quicken the economic development of the backward regions.

Decentralization of Industrial Sites and Enterprises

Modern industry requires adequate concentration of industrial enterprises so as to fully utilize public utilities, manpower, resources, technical expertise, and to facilitate production and distribution. It also restricts the uninhibited spread of industrial sites in cities. However, the overall distribution of industrial enterprises should be dispersed to avoid the over-concentration in large cities of large and medium-sized enterprises. The rational distribution of industry has as one of its characteristics the linking of dispersed industrial sites by well-developed transport networks such as railways and waterways.

Since 1949, a number of provinces and municipalities have been selected as key areas for industrial construction. Large and medium-sized enterprises have been distributed amongst these centres. At the same time, improvements in transport networks, the discovery of new mineral resources, increased supplies of agricultural raw materials, and the development of power supplies have seen the growth of industry in medium-sized and small cities and in the mineral and agricultural raw material-producing areas. As a result, industry is no longer over-concentrated in large cities; a network of industrial bases of various sizes has been formed over the whole country with the effect of strengthening the country's industrial base as a whole.

In 1949, on the basis of 1970 constant prices, only Shanghai and Jiangsu and Liaoning provinces were close to RMB1 billion in industrial output value. Today, 65 cities in 25 provinces, municipalities, and autonomous regions have reached or exceeded RMB10 billion in industrial output value. The proportion of industrial output value of the large administrative regions in the national industrial output value has also changed (Table 6.3).

Table 6.3 Changes in Local Industrial Output Value in the Total Industrial Output Value, 1952–80 (%)

Region	1952	1980
North China	14.1	16.09
North-east China	22.5	16.22
East China	40.7	37.65
Central-south China	13.3	17.57
South-west China	6.6	7.47
North-west China	2.8	5.00

Source: China's Economic Yearbook, 1981 (Economic Management, 1981).

Table 6.3 indicates that there are still significant differences in industrial development in different parts of China. East China is the most industrialized region; central-south, north-east, and north China are developed to a similar level; and south-west and north-west China are the least industrialized areas. The backward regions have developed at a faster rate than the advanced areas, however, in terms of their output value. In all regions, the industrial capability has exceeded the gross industrial output of China in 1949.

The nation-wide distribution of industrial sites facilitates the exploitation of natural resources and bridges the gap between large-scale industrial production bases and the raw material- and fuel-producing areas and markets. This decentralization of industry promotes regional co-operation in terms of production, transportation, and markets; it promotes co-operation between industry and agriculture; and it strengthens the mutual support of the urban and rural areas. It is also of strategic importance in the event of war.

The course of decentralization of industrial bases since 1949 has not been smooth, however. During the first three years of the 2nd FYP, the expansion of industry in medium-sized and small cities and in the vast rural areas was over-emphasized in order to reduce the dichotomies between industry and agriculture, between the urban and rural areas, and between physical and mental labour. This policy was implemented without due regard to manpower, raw materials, and financial resources; the conditions essential for the construction of local industry; or the characteristics of the enterprises and their distribution requirements. Industries were scattered all over the country. Some 10,000 new industrial sites were built, but many projects were halted in mid-construction when economic and technical problems became apparent. Many completed projects relied on state subsidies to overcome location-induced production problems.

By the 1970s, five small industrial bases centred on the iron and steel, coal, chemical fertilizer, cement, and machine-building industries had been developed to meet the country's needs. There was no consideration of economic returns. As a result, industrial distribution was too thinly spread. In the hinterland areas, especially, too much emphasis was placed on national defence-related production. Factories were located in inaccessible areas, causing difficulties in transport and supply. Long-term capital construction projects were initiated, with no prospects of production capability in the short term. Once in operation, these projects were plagued by the difficulties stemming from their location and there were long periods of unproductivity.

In 1977, small-scale light and textile industrial enterprises began to be decentralized without consideration for the supply of raw materials, fuel, and power supplies, and with no regard to the technical and managerial levels available or even the suitability of products to market demands. Raw materials and power were in short supply and many well-equipped factories were under-productive, whilst ill-equipped new and small enterprises used quality raw materials to produce high-priced products of poor quality. At the same time as small industries were being excessively decentralized, the country's large industries were becoming over-concentrated. New projects continued to be located in the industrially concentrated large cities instead of in the medium-sized and small cities.

The overall situation was one of confusion and uneconomic distribution. The policies of the period were counter-productive. The decentralization of small industries created insoluble transport problems and hindered technical and economic co-operation. There was no unified plan to concentrate capital construction and industrial production in a way that would promote industrial development and economic growth.

The over-concentration of large industries in the established industrial centres also caused problems at this time. Such cities became overcrowded, with the concomitant problems of insufficient water supply, housing shortages, traffic congestion, poor living conditions, and pollution. They also competed with agriculture for available land. As such, the over-concentration of industry is as much an uneconomic mode of production as is the excessive decentralization of small industries.

The solution to these problems appears to lie in the readjustment of the layout of construction of medium-sized and small cities and towns, correction of the tendency in the past to emphasize the development of large cities whilst neglecting the construction of small cities and towns, and a shift in emphasis to the gradual construction of small industrial centres. In this way, the distribution of small industries can be readjusted and concentrated around suitably sized bases. It will encourage specialization, flexibility, co-operation with nearby large and medium-sized enterprises, improvements in technology, and the development of precision industries based around a solid economic base. Cities of this type would also offer attractive living environments and conditions for investment which would ease the over-concentration of industry and population in the large cities.

Regional Specialization

China's centuries-old system of small-scale production, combined with certain state economic policies aimed at the country's overall development, the branding of regional division as capitalist and revisionist, the weaknesses of the managerial system, and the tendency to disregard local conditions and to focus on iron and steel production, created an irrational distribution of production where regions and industrial systems sought self-sufficiency.

Production at this time was uneconomic and overly decentralized, with little of the co-ordination and co-operation apparent in a structure based on regional specialization.

It is uneconomic for a region to attempt to be self-sufficient in industrial production by developing all industrial sectors and producing all the commodities it requires. Modern methods of production, and large-scale production particularly, require a degree of regional specialization. The needs of different regions for industrial goods varies, as do the natural, economic, technical, and labour resources and the characteristics of historical development. Even within one industrial sector, there is a great diversity of production methods and products. Processing techniques differ for different raw materials required to produce even one product. The economic production of goods varies considerably on a regional basis. The mining industry, for example, is limited to areas in which its resources are distributed. Apart from the availability of raw materials, there exist regional differences in the level of investment in capital construction, productivity levels, the costs of production, transport facilities, and so on.

Economic production is based on the large-scale production of appropriate goods which will be sufficient to supply local needs and to export to other regions, whilst at the same time importing goods from other regions to make up deficits in locally required products which cannot be produced in sufficient quantity or at all. China's vast territory and pronounced regional differences require its industrial base to be specialized to a degree on a regional level. State planning of production has enabled industrial development to proceed with regard to these regional differences and to co-ordinate production in the light of surpluses and deficits. Socialist planning makes possible a co-operative national industrial system aimed at the economic development of the country as a whole.

Regional specialization relies on the rational utilization of resources and infrastructure in order to produce large quantities of high-quality, cheap products for the domestic market. Rational utilization implies that a particular region is able to produce its specialized range of products quickly, in large quantities, with a small investment and low production costs. Raw materials, labour, and investment are more economically used in the development of regional specialities, but at the same time, production sectors which complement the specialized sectors, as well as the basic infrastructure, consumer items, and self-sufficient sideline products, should be developed in a comprehensive way to ensure a diversified economic base centred on specialized production.

Since 1949, regional specialization has been an important component of China's rationalization policies. It has been based on the country's requirements and local conditions favouring various modes of production. At the same time, the over-specialization of some regions in the past has been balanced by the establishment of new industries to broaden the economic base. For example, the mining and munitions industries were dominant in the industrial structure of north-east China, but the synthetics and textile industries and machine building for civil purposes were very weak. In recent years, the machine-building, petroleum, and petrochemicals industries and some sectors of light industry have been built up. In north China, raw materials production, especially coal, iron, and salt, was well developed, but the associated processing industries were very backward. Today, the iron and steel, machine-building, salt, soda chemicals, and coking chemicals industries have been developed to complement the region's raw materials production. Large petrochemical industrial bases have also been built to process oil from the new oilfields.

In east China, the light, textile, and processing industries were strong, whilst heavy industry and the production of raw materials were weak. In recent years, the machine-building and chemicals industries have been developed along with the production of coal, iron, machinery, petroleum, pulp, and electric power.

Central China was also weak in heavy industry, although light industry and mining were well developed. Today, the iron and steel, non-ferrous metals, coal-mining, electric power, and chemicals industries are important sectors in this region's economic base. South-west China's industrial base was disorderly and unsystematic in 1949, following the Sino-Japanese War, and north-west China had a very poorly developed petroleum industry. In both of these regions, there has been a rapid development of the metallurgy, machine-building, coal-mining, electric power, and chemicals industries. The large administrative regions have also tended to diversify their industrial structure further as well as to strengthen the specialized sectors.

The Development of the Raw Materials- and Fuel-producing Areas

One of the main problems resulting from the distribution of production in China has been the distance between the centres of production and the fuel- and raw materials-producing areas and markets. This situation has overtaxed transport facilities, prolonged the circulation of raw materials and commodities, and wasted labour resources. The redistribution of industry in order to bring production closer to raw materials, power supplies, and consumers is an important component of the rationalization of production. In addition to reducing the number of links in the production chain, thereby creating savings in investment and manpower, it eliminates the transport problem, raises productivity, and generally enables capital to be circulated at a faster rate with significant effects on the growth of the national economy. It also contributes to the development of a wider product base. Further, redistribution in this way promotes the comprehensive and economic use of raw materials and fuel and the development of areas producing those resources.

Since 1949, industry has moved west from the coastal areas. The expansion of industrial enterprises and the comprehensive development of regional industry have created favourable conditions for bringing industrial production closer to the raw materials- and fuel-producing areas. The geological surveying and exploitation of mineral and water resources have developed and a number of mineral-producing and hydroelectric power bases have been built or expanded. The mining and raw materials industries have developed in some remote areas. The result has been an increase in the output value of heavy industry in every region.

The redistribution of production has also affected agricultural production and distribution. A number of agricultural raw materials bases have been established or expanded, resulting in increased output of farm raw materials and expansion of the area under cultivation.

New sources of raw materials have been explored and opened up, including the comprehensive utilization of mineral resources and raw materials for the textiles and light industries. In 1980, 31.54 per cent of the country's output value of light and textiles industries used non-farm products as raw materials. In north-east China, 34.7 per cent of the output value used non-farm products, and the north-west and south-west regions used 23.89 and 22.35 per cent respectively of non-farm products as a proportion of their output value of these industries. The situation over the country as a whole reveals increased utilization of non-farm raw materials compared with 1949. At the same time as these areas have been opened up and their resources exploited, China's industrial production has moved closer to these more remote regions. The country's processing industries in particular are less reliant on imported raw materials and fuel to sustain production than was previously the case.

Although the situation has improved to a great extent, there are still some problems relating to the distribution of production and the distribution of raw materials and fuel. The total consumption of raw materials and fuel exceeds that produced. The production of these resources needs to be accelerated in preference to the further development of the processing industries. Also, many of the raw materials and fuel resources are not transportable. This requires that the production of these resources be as close as possible to existing processing industries. The extent and speed of their exploitation depends, however, on the regional distribution of these resources and on other environmental conditions. The scale and speed of the production of farm raw materials and their regional distribution are limited not only by agricultural natural resources but by the relationship between the development of farm raw materials and other agricultural sectors and crops.

In the past, the difficulties involved in the development of these resources were underestimated. Some processing enterprises were distributed before their resources were verified; others expanded their facilities despite declining reserves. The main problem at present in China in this respect is the distance of the energy-producing industries from the energy-consuming industries. Coal, electricity, petroleum, and gas are produced mainly in the western regions, whilst the energy-consuming industries are concentrated for the most part in the eastern coastal areas. There is an energy surplus in the west and a shortage of energy in the east. The long distance between them creates a shortage of transport capability.

From the point of view of the rationalization of production in the raw materials- and fuel-producing areas, the processing industries in areas where raw materials and fuel are in short supply need to have their expansion curtailed, whilst the potential for further exploitation of reserves is explored in order to raise these areas to a level of self-suffiency. Heavy industries with high energy consumption need to be located close to abundant energy resources. Areas rich in fuel and raw materials resources need to be developed in a systematic way so as to best utilize their potential.

7. The Energy Industry

ENERGY supply is a crucial factor in the development of China's economy. Since 1949, utilization of the country's energy resources has been based on an assessment of production and demand, analysis of its resources, as well as technological, natural, and economic factors.

China's Energy Resources

The scale, structure, and distribution of the energy industry is influenced by the distribution of its resources. China has abundant coal, water, oil, and natural gas reserves. In 1980, verified coal reserves totalled 640 billion tonnes, ranking third in the world after the Soviet Union and the United States. Oil and gas reserves are found in geological conditions similar to those in the United States. Surveys have located more than 300 sedimentary basins suitable for prospecting, covering 4.5 million square kilometres, as well as 1.2 million square kilometres of offshore areas. Petroleum reserves have been estimated at between 30 and 60 billion tonnes, although some estimates have put the total as high as 100 billion tonnes.[1]

The main reservoir structure in China is continental sedimentary rock. The areas of oil-bearing basins contain many faults, however, and are unequal in quality and often inaccessible. In the western areas of China, the development of oilfields is complicated by the terrain, which is mostly mountains and deserts. The marine sedimentary rock found in these areas is also easily destroyed. As a result, only about 20 per cent of the petroleum and gas areas in China have been prospected. Large-scale offshore prospecting has only recently been undertaken. For these reasons, despite its abundant reserves, China's operating reserves amount to a mere several billion tonnes. This is much less than the total operating reserve in the United States, though China still ranks eighth in the world. Natural gas reserves rank sixteenth.

Verified petroleum and gas reserves are inadequate to meet the demand. This is a result not of a shortage of reserves or depletion by exploitation, but of insufficient prospecting. No new petroleum or gas reserves have been discovered since the 1970s, although great potential exists for the discovery of further reserves.

China is rich in hydropower resources, with an estimated 680 million kW in reserves and an estimated annual generation of 5,900 billion kWh. The actual exploitable reserves are, however, 370 million kW and annual generation is 1,900 billion kWh. China ranks first in the world in this regard, accounting for 25 per cent of the world total.

When converted into standard coal for the purposes of calculation, China's verified coal, oil, gas, and water reserves account for 10 per cent of the world total. Its energy resource density, or average reserve per square kilometre, is

1. *People's Daily*, 16 April 1982.

higher than the world average. However, the country's huge population means that the per-capita energy reserve is only half the world average (one-tenth that of the United States and one-seventh of the per-capita figure in the Soviet Union). The situation requires acceleration of prospecting to locate additional reserves for large-scale exploitation as well as the economic use of existing resources so as to avoid waste.

Petroleum and gas are high in thermal power and easy to utilize. However, verified petroleum and gas reserves account for only 4 per cent of China's mineral reserves; coal accounts for 96 per cent. (In the Soviet Union, this ratio is 25 : 75.) In general, China's energy resources are of a high quality. Of the country's coal resources, the proportion of brown coal, which is low in thermal content, is lower than the world average. However, coking coal, for which there is a great demand world-wide, constitutes a considerable proportion of the country's coal reserves. There is a large amount of crude oil of low light-quality oil content, but paraffin and sulphur contents are high. The oil produced offshore and in north-west China is also of a high quality.

The distribution of energy resources throughout the country is uneven. More than 85 per cent of coal reserves are located in areas north of the Qin Ling (Qin ranges) and the Huai He; more than 60 per cent is in north China. Less than 2 per cent of the total reserves of coal are located south of the Chang Jiang. More than half of the total petroleum reserves are located in the north-east. Natural gas is located mainly in Sichuan, Guizhou, Liaoning, Hebei, Shandong, and Qinghai provinces; Sichuan and Guizhou account for a major part of the national total. The exploitation of water resources in the south-west accounts for 71 per cent of the national total.

Most areas of China have abundant reserves of one kind of energy resources but are deficient in others. The north-east, for example, is rich in oil, but has few coal, water, and gas reserves. The north lacks water resources, but has very rich coal and oil deposits. The north-west has abundant water, oil, gas, and especially coal reserves. In the south-west, water, gas, and coal reserves are plentiful, but there is a shortage of petroleum. In all these areas, energy resources of one kind or another are abundant. In the central-south and east, however, water is the only plentiful energy resource. This problem is exacerbated by the fact that these areas are densely populated. If the national per-capita average amount of energy resources is 100, the average figure in the north is 416; in the south-west and north-west, it is 167 and 146 respectively; and in the north-east, east, and central-south, the figures are a very low 40, 22, and 19 respectively.

China's energy resources are obviously adequate to meet the demands of economic development and modernization. The failure to prospect for further reserves, however, and the uneven distribution of energy resources pose two major problems in the development of the energy industry. First, the reserves of all energy resources (with the exception of water) are inadequate. Oil and gas reserves in particular will not increase significantly in the near future and will decline over time. Secondly, the rational distribution of the energy industry is made even more difficult by the intensifying regional contradiction between supply and demand and by the steady increase in the absolute amount of energy resources needed in different regions. The contradiction between supply and demand is most apparent in the transportation of coal. Coal has long been shipped to the south from the north. It is now also transported from the west to the east. Thermal electric power is also planned to be transmitted from north to south and hydroelectric power from west to east. At present, petroleum (including crude oil and oil products in the north and oil products in the east) is transported to the south and west. In the future, crude oil will be transported from the west to the east and possibly to the centre of the country from both east and west. Such movement of energy resources will greatly increase transport expenditure and investment.

The Structure of the Industry

The structure of China's energy resources industry can be measured using three methods. First, water resources can be calculated according to annual generated electricity capacity, and coal (excluding a quantity not for use by the power industry), oil, and gas are calculated according to their recoverable reserves. By this calculation method, coal accounts for 98.7 per cent of total energy resources, oil accounts for 0.8 per cent, gas accounts for 0.1 per cent, and water accounts for 0.4 per cent. (However, as a renewable energy resource, water has a much more dominant position than is indicated by this calculation method.)

Secondly, water resources can be calculated according to generated electricity capacity for a number of years, while coal, oil, and gas are measured by their recoverable reserves. When water resources are calculated in periods of 100 and 300 years, coal accounts for 60.6 and 34.39 per cent of the total; oil accounts for 1.1 and 0.6 per cent; natural gas accounts for 0.1 and 0.06 per cent; and water accounts for 38.2 and 64.95 per cent. The proportion of water resources is much higher using this calculation method because undiscovered reserves of coal, oil, and gas are not taken into consideration.

Thirdly, when water resources are calculated according to the total electricity generated in 300 years, and coal, oil, and gas are measured in terms of their estimated reserves, coal accounts for 90.58 per cent of the total, oil accounts for 2.34 per cent, gas accounts for 0.84 per cent, and water accounts for 6.23 per cent. This third calculation method provides a more realistic estimation of the relative importance of each kind of energy resource. It also reflects the character of China's energy resources structure. That is, China has abundant reserves of coal and water resources but is deficient in oil and gas reserves. Priority therefore needs to be given to the full exploitation of coal and water resources for energy production. The structure of energy production in China is presently as follows: coal accounts for 70.7 per cent of the total, oil accounts for 23.3 per cent, gas accounts for 2.9 per cent, and water accounts for 3.1 per cent. The importance of coal in energy production is in accord with available coal reserves. However, the high proportions of oil and gas in the total production do not accord with available reserves of these energy resources. At the same time, the proportion of hydropower in production is low because of the low utilization rate of water resources (2.5 per cent). Some hundreds of millions of tonnes of water are wasted each year in run-off. The situation requires that coal continue to be developed as the most

86   THE ECONOMIC GEOGRAPHY OF CHINA

important source of energy production and that the exploitation of water
resources be accelerated so as to increase the proportion of hydropower in the
total energy output.

The development of hydropower production in China has caused some con-
troversy. During the period of the 1st FYP, thermal power was emphasized in
the development of the energy industry and a number of hydropower stations
were constructed in sites with accessible water resources. A considerable
amount of survey work on water resources was also carried out. As a result,
the proportion of hydropower increased steadily. In 1958, 30 large and
medium-sized hydropower stations with a capacity of 10 million kW were
under construction in accordance with the policy to emphasize hydropower
first and thermal power second.

During the 1960–2 period of readjustment of the economy, all of the
projects with the exception of those at Liujiaxia and Xinanjiang were
suspended. Although it was then decided to develop both hydropower and
thermal power simultaneously, thermal power projects were emphasized in
practice. This policy continued for a number of years with the result that, up
until 1978, the proportion of hydropower in the national total remained
basically unchanged despite minor fluctuations. The main cause of this
stagnation was the greater time and investment required for the building of
hydropower projects than for thermal ones. The country's increasing energy
requirements had the effect of emphasizing thermal power and of lowering the
proportion of investment in hydropower projects.

When all of the factors are considered, however, the investment per kWh of
electricity for hydropower and thermal power projects is similar. For example,
the investment for large power stations where conditions for using water
resources are favourable (such as at Liujia Xia, Danjiangkou, Gongzui, Xin'-
anjiang, Duoxi, Yanguoxia, Xinfengjiang, and Xijin) is 10 per cent less than
for thermal power stations with the same capacity. Moreover, the annual cost
of operation per kWh of electricity of a hydropower station is lower than for a
thermal power station, and the accumulation funds a hydropower station
provides to the state are twice those provided by an equivalent thermal power
station. Despite their higher initial investment costs, hydropower stations
have a lower annual expense and a shorter cost recoupment period than
thermal power stations. (For example, the initial investment in the Liujia Xia
power station was recovered in six years.) Although the time required to build
a hydropower station is longer than for a thermal power station, the latter
requires a related coal-mine, which may require 10 years to build. Nevertheless, the construction of hydropower stations has the associated problems of
inundation of farmland, the relocation of population, and seasonal fluctuations
in river level. During the wet season, the generated electricity capacity is
approximately twice that of the dry season.

China's plans for the development of its energy industry include acceleration of the exploitation of the country's water resources and the elevation of
hydropower to a more prominent position in the energy production structure.
Although thermal power projects will be de-emphasized, their absolute
amount of growth will still exceed that of hydropower projects.

Coal is expected to retain its present proportion of total energy production;

oil will rank second, although its proportion will be less than at present; and hydropower will rank third, with a marked increase in its proportion of the total. Development plans for the industry also emphasize a varied industrial structure, based on the local characteristics of energy resources and modernization.

The Utilization of Resources

The structure of the energy industry can be varied by changing the way in which China now utilizes its energy resources. The rural areas consume 300 million tonnes of organic energy sources each year, most of which is burned directly. Only about 10 per cent of the potential thermal energy is used by this method, with the result that there are great shortages of fuel. Better planning would enable organic substances such as straw and night soil to be converted by burning or fermentation into methane, with a considerable increase in the utilization rate of thermal energy. It is estimated that 300 million tonnes of straw, night soil, and other waste materials can be converted to 100 billion cubic metres of methane — sufficient fuel for the country's entire rural population. A small methane-generating pit can provide fuel for a family of five, saving from one to one and a half tonnes of organic fuel a year. Surplus methane can be converted to mechanical and electric energy to compensate for the rural shortage of oil and power. One cubic metre of methane is sufficient to produce 1.5–2 kWh of electricity. A group of methane-generating pits totalling 100–200 cubic metres in a production team of from 30 to 50 families can power a small diesel engine using methane with diesel oil. In turn, a diesel engine can power a small generator, thereby reducing the power supply problem and saving 70 per cent on diesel oil.

The number of such methane-generating pits in China has reached 7 million. A large number of communes and brigades in Sichuan, Zhejiang, Jiangsu, and Guangdong provinces and Shanghai have built small power stations, making possible the use of threshers and other machines to process grain, tea, and fodder, as well as for cooking and lighting.

This readjustment of the energy structure in the rural areas has led not only to a considerable increase in the utilization ratio, but also to a fuller utilization of organic energy resources. In addition, after fermentation, straw can be used as organic manure because of its rich humus, nitrogen, phosphorus, and potassium content. Methane-generating pits require little investment and a short time to build. (A 10-cubic-metre pit costs only a few dozen yuan.) The cost of 1 kW of electricity produced by this means is less than half that produced by a small hydropower station and much less than that produced by a wind, tidal, or solar energy station. Furthermore, the raw materials required to produce methane are readily available and renewable. This method of energy production is especially suited to south China, where the climate favours a prolonged generating period.

In addition to this manner of energy production in the rural areas, small hydropower stations and coal-mines are being encouraged and forests are being planted for fuel where conditions are favourable. The planting of fuel forests is particularly important where mineral resources are scarce. Fast-growing tree varieties can be used as a fuel source within three to five years of planting. Barren mountain areas and wasteland in farming areas are ideal for the planting of fuel trees. This source of energy has the potential to become one of the major energy resources in the rural areas.

It is apparent, therefore, that one solution to the energy problem lies in varying the structure of energy resources and adapting their utilization to local conditions. Variations in the rural areas also assist in the restructuring of energy resources throughout the whole country.

New Resources

Wind, tidal, solar, geothermal, and nuclear energy resources have been utilized in China on only a small scale. The construction of nuclear power stations has helped to modernize the structure of China's energy resources and to economize on non-renewable energy resources. Nuclear power stations are not restricted in their location by the distribution of energy resources as are other types of power stations, with the effect that energy production and marketing are able to be more evenly balanced.

However, nuclear power requires a higher initial investment. The country's first Chinese-designed 300,000-kW pressurized-water nuclear power station is under construction in Qinshan in Zhejiang province. The power station will enable the accelerated development of China's nuclear technology and energy industries. Additional planned nuclear power stations are expected to further ease the shortages of energy resources in east, north-east, and south China.

Energy Production and Consumption

China's energy output and consumption have increased rapidly since 1949. Between 1949 and 1980, coal output rose from 32.43 million tonnes to 620 million tonnes (a 19.1-fold increase); crude oil output increased from 120,000 tonnes to 105.95 million tonnes (an 882.9-fold increase); natural gas output rose from 11 million to 14.29 billion cubic metres (a 1,297.3-fold increase); electric power output rose from 4.3 billion kWh to 300.6 billion kWh (a 69.9-fold increase); and hydroelectric power rose from 700 million kWh to 58.2 billion kWh (an 83.1-fold increase). The country's gross direct-use energy output, when converted into standard coal for the purposes of calculation, rose from 23.75 million tonnes in 1949 to 637.21 million tonnes in 1980 (approximately 6 per cent of the world total and slightly lower than that of the United States and the Soviet Union). The consumption of energy during the same period was 585.88 million tonnes (6 per cent of the world total and again lower than that of the United States — 2,636 million tonnes — and the Soviet Union — 1,529 million tonnes).

Between 1953 and 1978, the annual growth rate of the consumption of energy resources was 10.7 per cent, while that of industrial output value and gross output value of industry and agriculture was 11.3 and 8.2 per cent respectively. Compared with the growth rate of industrial output value and of gross output value of industry and agriculture, the coefficient of consumption of energy resources was 0.95 and 1.3 respectively. Although the growth rate of consumption of energy resources is higher in China than in other countries, the coefficient is equivalent to the figure in the early and middle industrialization periods of the leading industrial countries.

Although it has the largest population in the world, China's annual consumption per capita of standard coal (0.6 tonnes) is lower than that of other industrial countries (12.2 tonnes in the United States, 5.9 tonnes in the Soviet Union, 5.6 tonnes in the Federal Republic of Germany, and 4.4 tonnes in Japan). Because of backward industrial equipment and technology, imperfect economic management, and an irrational industrial structure, the consumption per-unit output value in China surpasses that of the leading industrial countries. (The consumption of energy per US$10,000 of output value costs 28.58 tonnes of standard coal in China compared with 12.76 tonnes in the United States, 11.95 tonnes in the Soviet Union, 7.07 tonnes in Japan, and 5.35 tonnes in the Federal Republic of Germany.) For these reasons, China's energy output is in extremely short supply. In 1978 alone, the country produced 40 billion kWh of electricity less than was required by industry, with the result that 20–30 per cent of the productive capacity of enterprises could not go into operation, resulting in a loss of output value equivalent to RMB70 billion. In the rural areas, fuel for home use is in great demand in addition to that required for farm production. Although the state allocates more than 20 million tonnes of coal to the rural areas each year and some 40 million tonnes are produced by small local coal-mines, the available fuel supply is far from meeting requirements. As a result, most rural families use straw as a substitute for coal.

The annual straw output is 450 million tonnes. Of this, 230 million tonnes are used as fodder and for processing raw materials. The remaining 220 million tonnes are inadequate to meet annual fuel requirements, which are estimated to be 600 million tonnes of straw. Consequently, of the 170 million rural households in China, 70 million are fuel-deficient. Furthermore, state-supplied diesel oil does not meet the needs of China's 200 million horsepower of farm machinery.

There is a marked imbalance between the production of and demand for energy in various regions. Direct-use energy production basically meets the demand (with a slightly higher output than demand) in the north-west and south-west. Its proportion of the total energy output is also higher than that of national energy consumption in north and north-east China. Large quantities of coal and oil produced in north China are transported to other parts of the country, while in the north-east, oil is exported and coal is imported. The proportion of energy consumption in east and central-south China is higher than that of energy output in the national total. This imbalance between production and consumption is particularly marked in the nine provinces south of the Chang Jiang. A similar situation exists in Liaoning, Hubei, Jiangsu, Guangdong, Zhejiang, and Gansu provinces, and in Shanghai, Beijing, and Tianjin. In Shanghai and Liaoning province, there is an annual deficit of about 20 million tonnes of standard coal. These developed provinces and municipalities account for half of the total national industrial output value; energy shortages there will consequently affect economic activities throughout the country.

Energy shortages affect daily life and production and retard economic development. Attention needs to be focused not only on the conservation and economic use of energy, but also on the further exploitation and regional distribution of energy resources. The redistribution of the energy industry requires the controlled development of industrial enterprises that consume large quantities of energy located in the coastal areas, especially south of the Chang Jiang, and their gradual relocation in west China where energy resources are abundant. Such measures will ensure that China's energy resources are able to meet energy production and consumption needs and that the transportation over long distances of energy resources, especially coal, is reduced.

Primary Energy Resources

The exploitation of energy resources is determined not only by their distribution and quality, the amount of available reserves, and the practical means of exploitation and utilization, but also by the distribution and changing requirements of energy consumption areas, the facilities for energy transportation, and the co-operation of related departments. In broad terms, it requires a national regional division of labour and development of the locational advantages, with increased overall economic results. This requires consideration not only of investment, the period of construction, and the cost of production, but also of the amount of investment in related enterprises, of circulation costs, including transport, and the reduction of total labour consumption in capital construction and in the process of reproduction.

Coal

China's first modern coal-mine was built at Kaiping in northern Hebei province in 1878. It was not until 1913, however, that the country's annual coal output exceeded 10 million tonnes. By 1942, it had reached 61.87 million tonnes, but by 1949 the output had dropped to 32 million tonnes. It is only since 1949 that coal resources have been exploited on a large scale. Although the industry developed comparatively slowly, it has today become a large-scale industry in China.

Between 1950 and 1980, 517 mines and 12 open-cut coal-mines were built, with a designated output capacity of 363 million tonnes. By 1980, there were 2,456 coal enterprises, with an annual output of 620 million tonnes (an 18-fold increase over 1949). In the early 1950s, there were only two coal-mines, at Fushun and Kailuan, each producing only 5 million tonnes annually. Today, there are 12 coal-mines with an annual output of 10 million tonnes, and coal bases are distributed throughout the country (Fig. 7.1). Since 1949, two mines at Kailuan and Datong in the north have been reconstructed and expanded on a large scale. They are now the country's largest coal bases. In 1985, each base produced approximately 25 million tonnes. The Kailuan mine produces rich coal, while that at Datong produces fine-quality coal for the energy industry. Both mines have abundant reserves

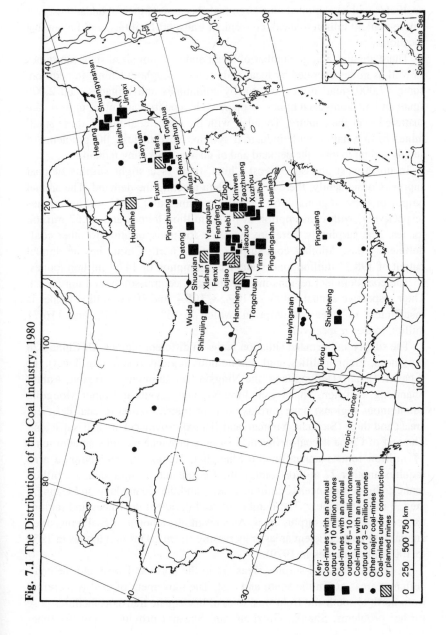

Fig. 7.1 The Distribution of the Coal Industry, 1980

despite 70–100 years of extraction; Datong in particular has considerable untapped potential.

The more recently established large coal bases at Pingdingshan in the central-south and Huaibei in the east (both coal-deficient areas) are the closest coal bases to the Wuhan-Daye and Chang Jiang delta industrial areas. These coalfields will be exploited on a large scale because of their abundant reserves (more than 30 billion tonnes), convenient transport facilities, and favourable location.

There are also a large number of small and medium-sized state-run mines as well as mines operated by local authorities throughout China. In addition, some 17,000 small mines are run by communes and brigades, and 2,000 small and medium-sized mines — operated by counties and other units — are scattered over the country. Together with the major coal-mines, these small mines form a nation-wide industrial system. Nevertheless, the problems of supply failing to meet the demand and of uneven marketing remain.

In north-west and south-west China, there is a slight surplus of coal supply. Consequently, there is no problem meeting the demand. The annual output of these regions is 68.32 million tonnes and 49.41 million tonnes respectively, with consumption at 65.88 million tonnes and 45.62 million tonnes. The surplus is therefore available for transportation to other coal-deficient areas. Another coal-surplus region, north China, has an annual output of 198.23 million tonnes and a consumption of 147.3 million tonnes.

The coal-deficient regions include the east, central-south, and north-east. Their respective annual output of 109.58, 105.4, and 104.6 million tonnes is insufficient to meet consumption, which is 128.65, 113.78, and 116.71 million tonnes respectively.[2]

The supply and demand situation varies in different regions. Of China's 28 provinces, municipalities, and autonomous regions (excluding Tibet), 11 (Shanxi, Henan, Heilongjiang, the Ningxia Hui autonomous region, Anhui, Shandong, Guizhou, Shaanxi, and the Xinjiang Uygur and Inner Mongolia autonomous regions) have surplus coal for transportation to coal-deficient areas, and three (Sichuan, Yunnan, and Jiangxi provinces) are self-sufficient. The rest of China is coal-deficient. Liaoning province requires an additional 17 million tonnes annually; the Shanghai, Hangzhou, and Ningbo area requires another 27 million tonnes; the Beijing and Tianjin area, 20 million tonnes; Hubei province, 12 million tonnes; and the Guangdong and Guangxi area, 7 million tonnes.[3] The number of coal-deficient provinces and regions exceeds that of coal-surplus areas. As a result, the amount of coal transported annually to coal-deficient areas is increasing (from 20 million tonnes in 1957 to 100 million tonnes in 1979).

In general, the coal-surplus areas are in the north and west and the coal-deficient areas are in the south and east. The movement of coal is therefore from north to south and from west to east. Inadequate transport facilities pose further problems. Shanxi, Guizhou, and Shaanxi provinces and the Inner

2. Li Dazheng, 'Expanding the Exploitation of Coal to Meet the Requirements of the Four Modernizations', *Energy*, 1981, No. 2.
3. Ibid.

Mongolia and Ningxia Hui autonomous regions have difficulties in transporting surplus coal to other areas. In Shanxi, over 10 million tonnes of coal
are kept in stock each year, while Guizhou, Shaanxi, and the two autonomous
regions have reduced their production to conform with their transport capacity.
A further problem in the coal-deficient areas is that production is affected not
only by a shortage of coal but also by an inadequate power supply.

There are a number of reasons for this imbalance between coal production
and marketing. First, the distribution of coal resources is uneven in different
areas. Coal resources are scattered mainly in the north and west. Coal reserves
in north China (above the Qin Ling and Dabie mountains) account for 85 per
cent of the national total. Those in Shanxi and Inner Mongolia account for
61.4 per cent. Coal reserves in south China, including south Jiangsu
province, account for a mere 1.8 per cent of the national total. From another
point of view, the 11 eastern provinces account for only 8 per cent and the
western areas for 87.7 per cent of the national total.

Secondly, industrial distribution is not appropriate to the location of
energy resources. Prior to 1949, industry was concentrated in the coastal areas
which lacked coal supplies. After 1949, the rapid growth in these areas of iron
and steel plants, thermal power plants, and the chemicals industry using coal
as a raw material intensified the contradiction between coal production and
consumption. For example, coal resources in Liaoning province account for
only 1.5 per cent of the national total, yet its steel output accounts for 26.7
per cent and its thermal electric power for 11.5 per cent of the national total.
In the nine southern provinces, which produce only 1.8 per cent of the
national total coal output, the output value of industry and agriculture
accounts for 40 per cent of the national total; the output value of steel
accounts for 36.6 per cent; and that of thermal electric power accounts for 29
per cent.

A third reason for the imbalance between coal production and marketing is
the poor utilization of coal resources in the past. During the 1st FYP period,
emphasis was placed on the development of coalfields in the north and north-
east at the same time as a number of old coal bases in the coal-deficient east
were reconstructed and new bases were built in the north-west. This rational
distribution of coal exploitation took into account the location of the
country's coal resources and production and marketing facilities. During the
3rd FYP period, emphasis was placed on the opening of new coalfields in
the south-west in order to promote construction in the remote areas. At the
same time, however, the development of the old coal bases was neglected.
During the 4th FYP period, coal exploitation in areas south of the Chang
Jiang was emphasized in order to reduce the transportation of coal from the
north, but coal exploitation in the north was then ignored. The 5th FYP
period (1976–80) saw a move in emphasis to the north-east and eastern Inner
Mongolia, but construction of a coal base in Shanxi province was still not a
priority. The emphasis on coal exploitation in the south-west was important
to guarantee the construction of the Panzhihua iron and steel base in Sichuan
province, but the productive capacity of coalfields there could not be fully
exploited because of the continuing problem of coal transportation. Although
the development of coal exploitation south of the Chang Jiang went some

way towards meeting the urgent demand for coal in the south, some of the mines built during the period were small in scale or had their construction suspended because of the limited coal resources and the unfavourable conditions for extraction.

The mistakes of the past 36 years have not only delayed development of the coal industry by at least five years, but have also caused coal to be in extremely short supply in China as a whole. The disparity between verified reserves and coal production, as well as the lack of accord between coal production and transportation, and between production and marketing, remain major problems. Verified coal reserves in Jilin, Liaoning, Hebei, Shandong, Jiangsu, Anhui, Hubei, Hunan, and Jiangxi provinces account for 14 per cent of the national total, but the coal output in those provinces is about half the national total. Other areas, with abundant coal reserves, remain undeveloped.

Because of the distribution of coal resources and industry, coal will continue for the present to be transported from north to south and from west to east. The immediate emphasis is on achieving a balance between production and marketing in the country as a whole in the shortest possible time. Within that overall aim, consideration will be given to the achievement of a balance between coal production and marketing in different areas and a reduction in the amount of long-distance coal shipment with consequent savings in transport costs and related investment.

The coalfields in Shanxi and Shaanxi provinces and in the southern part of Inner Mongolia are the most suitable for immediate further exploitation. The largest coalfields are concentrated in these areas, the verified coal reserves of which account for more than half the national total. Moreover, these areas have favourable conditions and the varieties of coal found there are fine in quality, simple in structure, and the coal-bearing seams are stable and shallow. Coal in Shanxi province is low in ash, sulphur, and phosphorus content and high in thermal quantity. Coal for the power industry in Datong, anthracite in Yangquan and Jincheng, and coking coal in Xishan are in great demand in the international market. A second reason for emphasizing further exploitation of these areas is the fact that their exploitation is economical. The investment per tonne of productive power (RMB63) and per tonne of production cost (RMB14.36) in Shanxi is much lower than the national average (RMB103 and RMB17.8 respectively). The period of construction is half that in other areas of China and, consequently, higher economic results are obtained more quickly.

Thirdly, these areas are conveniently located, with adequate transport facilities. They are linked with coal-deficient Beijing, Tianjin, and Liaoning by the Beijing–Baotou, Beijing–Taiyuan, Beijing–Shenyang, and Beijing–Tonghua rail lines and with such other coal-deficient areas as Shanghai and Jiangsu by the Shijiazhuang–Taiyuan, Dezhou–Shijiazhuang, Jinan–Qingdao, Lianyungang–Lanzhou, and Tianjin–Shanghai railways. They are also linked with the three main port cities of Qinghuangdao, Shijiu, and Lianyungang. Coastal navigation lines provide transport to coal-deficient areas such as Liaoning in the north, east China, and the central-south. When fully exploited, the large coal-mines in Shanxi, Shaanxi, and southern Inner Mongolia will be able to support the four main coal-deficient areas of

Liaoning, the Beijing–Tianjin area, Jiangsu, and Shanghai, as well as the south-eastern coastal provinces. In addition, the export of coal will be able to be expanded.

The key coal-mining areas under construction or planned for the near future in these areas include Datong, Yangquan, Xishan, Gujiao, and Huoxian in Shanxi, Hancheng in Shaanxi, as well as open-pit mines in Pingshuo in Shanxi and Junggar in Xinjiang. Simultaneously, geological and hydrological prospecting are underway and the existing transport lines and a number of harbours are being renovated and upgraded. By the year 2000, these areas are expected to account for most of the country's increased coal output.

Large coalfields in a number of other areas are also planned to be more fully exploited. One such area includes the Yanzhou, Xuzhou, and Huaiyin regions, especially the Huaibei, Huainan, Xupei, Zaoteng, and Yanji mines. The largest coal-producing areas in east China are located in Xuzhou and northern and southern Anhui province; each has an annual coal output in excess of 10 million tonnes. Based on old coal-mining areas, seven large and medium-sized coal pits, with a total designed capacity of 14 million tonnes, are under construction in northern and southern Anhui province. New large mines are being built in Fengxian, Peixian, and Tongshan, adjacent to the old coal-mining areas in Xuzhou. The construction of new mines, including those in Yanzhou and Zaoteng in Yanzhou, began in 1966, and Yanzhou has achieved a productive power of 2.2 million tonnes. Another four pairs of pits with a total designed capacity of 11 million tonnes are also under construction. In addition, the construction of mines in Jiangzhuang and Chaili in Zaoteng is underway. These fields have stable beds and produce a complete variety of high-quality coal. Their location in western Shandong, northern Jiangsu, and the northern Anhui plains, where agriculture is well developed, has the added advantage of rich water resources and convenient inland and water communications. Transport costs to the nearby largest coal-deficient area in China are therefore able to be reduced.

The disadvantage of this area is that reserves are very deep underground. Exploitation is complicated, requiring a large investment per unit of productive power, a long construction period, and highly intensive exploitation. In addition, their unexploited reserves are insufficient to meet the needs of economic development in east China. These coal-producing areas can therefore only be developed to supplement rather than to fulfil the coal requirements of east China.

A second area planned for further exploitation is western Guizhou province, where large coalfields in Lupanshui, Zhijin, and Nayong have rich deposits, concentrated distribution, stable beds, and a complete variety of good quality coal. Reserves in these areas are much higher than indicated by their present output and great potential exists for further exploitation. When fully exploited, the western Guizhou area will be able to supply the nearby provinces of Sichuan, Yunnan, and Guizhou itself, as well as provide supplies to coal-deficient Guangdong province and the Guangxi Zhuang autonomous region.

For the present, however, coal transportation in this area is limited. Only one main rail line — the Guiyang-Kunming line — runs through the area in addition to three local railways in the eastern part of the province. The terrain further limits the transportation of coal to the east. Future plans include the construction of a conveyance system at the Lupanshui coalfield so as to raise its productive power, and the gradual renovation of the existing rail line. The construction of Fangcheng port will further improve transport conditions, as well as the construction of the Nanning–Fangcheng and Kunming–Nanning railways. The hydropower resources of the Xi Jiang (Xi river) system are to be comprehensively developed, the Xi Jiang dredged, and connections opened with port facilities in Guangxi province. The connecting up of Yunnan, Guizhou, Guangdong, and Guangxi provinces will solve the problem of transporting coal to the east and create conditions conducive to the fuller exploitation of coal resources in the south-west.

A third area of China suitable for further exploitation is the western part of Henan province, including the coalfields in Pingdingshan, Xinmi, Yima, Jiaozuo, and Hebi. Coal beds in this area are of a high quality and conditions for exploitation are superior to those in the Xuzhou and Huaiyin areas. Coal-deficient Hubei province is nearby and the Beijing–Guangzhou and Jiaozuo–Zhicheng rail lines provide better transport conditions than those in western Guizhou. Compared with Shanxi province, there is less pressure on transportation. Such advantages indicate high economic returns from this coal-producing area in the near future. Its main focus will be to support Hubei province, thereby reducing the quantity of coal transported to the south from Shanxi.

Finally, the eastern parts of Heilongjiang province and Inner Mongolia, including Jixi, Hegang, Shuangya, and Qitaihe, are the principal coal-producing bases in the north-east, providing coking coal to the iron and steel bases in Anshan and Benxi. However, their comprehensive utilization means that their potential for further development is small. Although the coal-mining areas of the Helin and Yimin rivers and Mount Yuanbao in eastern Inner Mongolia produce brown coal of poor quality and low thermal content, the thick beds are close to the surface and can easily be converted to open-pit mines. One such mine with a designed capacity of 20 million tonnes is under construction in the Helin river area which has a 12.9-billion-tonne reserve. These areas are close to coal-deficient Liaoning province and established transport facilities are able to avoid the route monopolized by Shanxi province in transporting its coal to other parts of the country. They are therefore important supplementary bases which to some extent mitigate the problem of coal shortages in the north-east.

Coal resources located south of the Chang Jiang are also of importance, although, compared with the north, they are generally inferior. Deposits are small and sparsely distributed; beds are thin, with large volumes of underground water; associated gas complicates exploitation; and investment per tonne of productive power and per tonne of production cost is high. However, coalfields with favourable resources have been discovered and a number of key pits with advantageous conditions have been built. Some sites with favourable conditions still await exploitation. If priority is given to such areas, higher economic results are possible.

Although the coal produced in the south is generally poor in quality (with a high content of sulphur and gas) and is unsuitable for industrial purposes, it can be used to generate electricity at local power plants. Of greater importance is the superior geographic location and transport facilities in the south. The savings in transport costs offset the high investment and cost of locally produced coal. The supply of coal in China is insufficient to meet the needs of the national economy. State-allocated supplies transported from the north to the south cannot meet the needs of small local industries or of daily life. Locally produced coal is therefore of importance in the south in making up the deficit, even if profits are minimal at the local level.

Coal exploitation in China is faced with a number of problems which await solution. For many years, the price of coal has been low compared with that of oil and electricity. It is consequently a low-profit industry (5.4 per cent profit rate, compared with the national average for industry of 16 per cent). Many coal-producing areas are therefore unwilling to exploit new mines even if conditions are favourable. In order to approach the national average profit rate, the price of coal would need to be raised, but this would produce too great an impact on the economy. Other economic measures are therefore needed, one of which is state subsidies. Other measures are combining fixed prices (for coal supplied by planned quota) with negotiated prices and encouraging joint ventures between coal-producing areas and coal-deficient and industrially developed areas.

A second problem is the sheer bulk of coal, which poses transportation problems. Coal-mining bases need to be planned around transport trunk lines. Thirdly, the coal processing industry needs to be developed more comprehensively, with development of the associated coal-washing, thermal power generation, chemicals, and building materials industries. In this way, coal resources will be used more economically, economic benefits will be raised, and at the same time, freight volume will be decreased and pressure on transport facilities will be reduced. Comprehensive development in this way is also conducive to the co-ordinated development of the local economy.

Finally, the economic structure of the main coal-producing areas is usually based on heavy industry. These areas are comparatively backward in agriculture and light industry, which places a strain on the supply of daily necessities and consumer goods. In addition to raising the level of agriculture and light industry, trans-regional economic contacts need to be reinforced so as to enable these areas to exchange coal for other commodities such as grain, oil, and light industrial consumer goods.

Hydropower

The distribution of hydropower resources in China, although concentrated, is comparatively more balanced and widespread than coal, oil, and gas resources. The most abundant hydropower resources are located in the south-west, followed by the central-south and north-west, and north China. The Chang Jiang system accounts for 53.7 per cent of total resources; the Yarlung Zangbo river and the international river system in the south-west account for 15.8 and 12.2 per cent respectively; and the Huang He and Zhu Jiang systems account for 6 and 5.2 per cent respectively. The river systems along the south-east coast, in the north-east, and in the hinterland in the north, as well as the international rivers, account for 2–2.7 per cent each. Hydropower resources are most scarce along the Huai He and Hai He, with only 0.1–2 per cent each of the total.

China's hydropower resources are concentrated mainly along the upper and middle reaches of rivers in the west. Economic results from such resources in these areas are high and the area inundated by reservoirs is small, with a consequent low level of disruption to the region. However, these areas are sparsely populated, with inconvenient communications and transport conditions and a backward economy; and they are also remote from power consumers. In addition, the larger the river, the more sophisticated and expensive the techniques and equipment required to utilize the water resources.

East China is poor in hydropower resources. Hydropower projects result in the inundation of large areas, with consequent relocation of large numbers of people. However, they are close to power consumption centres, are economically well developed, and the technical conditions for exploitation are favourable.

The absolute volume of hydropower resources in China is large. After 1949, emphasis was mainly on exploiting the hydropower resources of the coastal areas, such as Zhejiang, Fujian, and Guangdong provinces. The focus then shifted to the middle and upper reaches of the Huang He and to some tributaries of the Chang Jiang. The focus for exploitation of hydropower resources in the future will continue to move to the upper reaches of the Huang He, the upper and middle reaches of the Chang Jiang, the upper and middle reaches of the Xi Jiang, and some of the international river systems in the south-west.

Significant achievements have been made in the development of the hydropower industry in China since 1949. By 1980, China's installed capacity of hydropower and generating capacity had grown 100-fold and 80-fold respectively over 1949 figures. Nine provinces and autonomous regions, including Gansu, Sichuan, Yunnan, Hebei, Hunan, Guangxi, Guangdong, Zhejiang, and Fujian, possess an installed capacity of over one million kW each. Guizhou, Jiangxi, Liaoning, and Jilin exceed 500,000 kW in installed capacity. That of Sichuan, Yunnan, Tibet, Gansu, Ningxia, Hunan, Guangxi, Guangdong, Hubei, Zhejiang, and Fujian constitutes more than 50 per cent of the total installed capacity in their respective areas. There are more than 2,000 hydropower stations with a generating capacity of 500 kW throughout the country. In addition, 18 large hydropower stations with a generating capacity of more than 250,000 kW have been built on rivers in the south-west, central-south, north-east, and along the eastern and southern coast (Fig. 7.2). Their combined installed capacity totals 8.7 million kW. All but two have been built since 1949.

There are more than 85,000 small hydropower stations with a generating capacity of less than 500 kW and a combined installed capacity of 7.57 million kW (one-third of the total national installed capacity). These small stations are distributed amongst 1,500 counties. Approximately half of these counties have their electricity needs fully met from this source.

The widespread production and consumption of hydropower in the rural

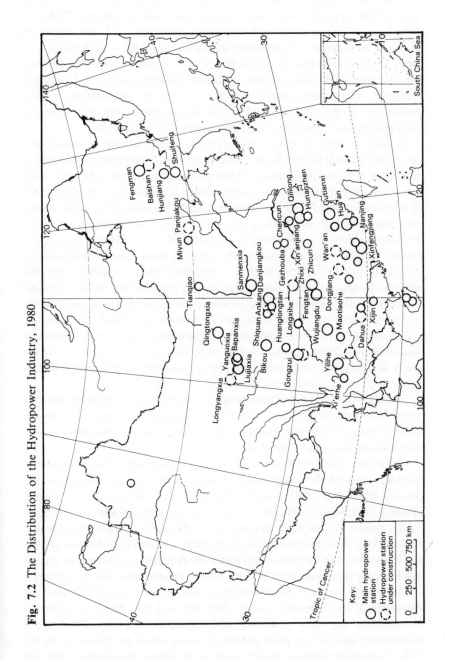

Fig. 7.2 The Distribution of the Hydropower Industry, 1980

areas has changed considerably the distribution of the hydropower industry, although construction is still limited in scale compared with available resources and the country's needs. For example, the rate of exploitation of hydropower is still low — only 3.06 per cent of the available resources, and only 5.49 per cent in terms of the country's total installed capacity. This is a very low rate when compared with other countries. The proportion of hydropower within the entire energy industry is also low — 30.8 per cent in terms of installed capacity and 9.36 per cent of the country's generating capacity. Most hydropower stations are small, whereas available resources and conditions favour the construction of a number of large stations with a generating capacity of 2 million kW. The largest power station in China, at Liujia gorge, has a generating capacity of only 1.22 million kW.

In order to meet the energy requirements of the national economy, and taking into account the structural characteristics of China's energy resources, a number of large and medium-sized hydropower resources are to be more fully developed. Priority will be given to the staged construction by the year 2000 of a hydroelectric base on the upper reaches of the Huang He in the north-west, the Yalong, Dadu, Lancang, and Wujiang river bases in the south-west, the Nanpan–Hongshui river base in the mid-south, a west Hunan base, and a Fujian–Zhejiang–Jiangxi base in the east. In most cases, inundation of cultivated land and relocation of the population will be minimal compared with the losses and disruption caused by the construction in the 1950s of hydropower stations in the densely populated coastal areas. The planned power stations are located for the most part in sparsely populated mountains in valley areas with very little cultivated land. Near these bases are also abundant deposits of non-ferrous and rare metals and certain industrial chemicals which could be developed into a profitable electrometallurgy and electrochemicals industrial system centred on hydropower.

In addition to these bases, hydropower resources in the north and north-east are to be more fully exploited. The Baishan hydropower station is presently under construction on the Songhua river as well as the Panjiakou power station on the Luan He (Luan river).

China has considerable potential for the development of its hydropower resources through the construction of small power stations throughout the country. More than 1,040 of the 2,000 counties have the potential to produce between 10,000 and 30,000 kW, and in some cases 60,000 kW, of electricity by this means. Although the per-unit cost is higher than that of large power stations, they have the advantage of simplicity, a short construction period, and local sources of investment and materials. Benefits can therefore be gained much sooner than from large power stations, thereby relieving the country's serious energy shortage. Small projects of this type are suitable for meeting the needs of local farming and of daily life and they have the effect of invigorating the rural economy and increasing income. Small-scale hydropower stations are most suitable in areas which are distant from the large hydropower centres, in areas south of the Chang Jiang where coal and energy resources are scarce, where large and medium-sized hydropower resources have been exhausted, and where energy resources other than electricity are prohibitively expensive.

Petroleum and Natural Gas

Between 1949 and the early 1960s, the country's petroleum and natural gas output centres were concentrated in the north-west. With the discovery of the Daqing oilfield in 1959 and a number of other fields, such as those at Fuyu, Liaohe, Huabei, Shengli, and Jianghan, the area of concentrated exploitation spread from the north-west through the Songliao plain in the north-east to the Bohai Gulf. From the early 1960s to the early 1970s, the petroleum industry developed rapidly.

Since 1978, China's annual oil output has exceeded 100 million tonnes. The structure of the industry has also changed. In the early 1950s, three small oilfields in Gansu, Shaanxi, and Xinjiang produced natural petroleum and two shale oil factories in Liaoning produced artificial petroleum. Two gas fields, at Shengdengshan and Shiyougou in Sichuan province, produced natural gas. Today, more than 250 gas fields have been discovered (128 of which are being exploited) in 22 provinces, and 16 provinces, municipalities, and regions are producing natural petroleum. Oilfields with 10-million-tonne annual output are located at Daqing in the north-east, Renqiu in the north, and Shengli in the east. Other oilfields are located at Liaohe, Karamay, Dagang, Nanyiang, Fuyu, Changqing, Jianghan, Yumen, Lenghu, Dongpu, and Subei.

The number of provinces, municipalities, and regions producing natural gas has increased to 13. Those with an annual output of one billion cubic metres are Sichuan, Heilongjiang, Liaoning, and Shandong. Many oilfields also produce natural gas. The main gas fields are located in Sichuan province and, of the 59 fields that have been discovered, 53 have gone into production. Their annual output accounts for 44 per cent of the national total. The eastern Sichuan gas field produces 2 billion cubic metres annually of natural gas, the largest in the country.

More than 50 oil refineries have been constructed in 21 provinces, municipalities, and regions. The total amount of crude oil refined each year is 90 million tonnes. The main refineries are located in Beijing, Daqing, Shengli, Shanghai, Nanjing, Lanzhou, and Dalian. Approximately 9,700 kilometres of petroleum and gas pipeline have been built to connect the main oil and gas fields, refineries, and petroleum-exporting ports (Fig. 7.3).

Since 1949, the annual output of crude oil has increased on average by 25 per cent. The total tax revenue from the oil industry is 3.2 times the total state investment. The country has been self-sufficient in oil since 1983 and crude and processed oil have been exported since 1973. Between 1973 and 1979, some 61.26 million tonnes of crude oil and 18.43 million tonnes of processed oil were exported, earning US$7.4 billion in foreign exchange.

The oil industry today has a high development rate, realizing good returns on investment. Moreover, despite its wide dispersal over the country, it forms an integrated and well co-ordinated system from exploration through to transportation. In recent years, however, the oil industry has not maintained its steady increase in output. One reason for this is the backwardness of its prospecting. Other reasons are the lack of oil reserves, the imbalance between reserves and production, and depletion of the old oilfields.

China's oil reserves are distributed over the continental shelf, the eastern

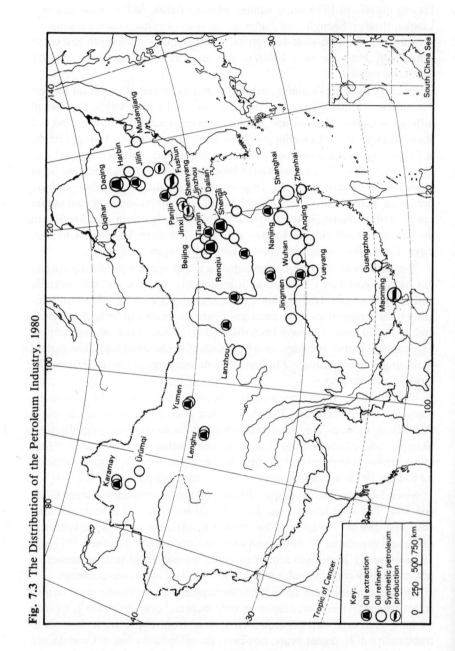

Fig. 7.3 The Distribution of the Petroleum Industry, 1980

upland area, the middle region (from Inner Mongolia, Shaanxi, Gansu, Ningxia, and Sichuan to Yunnan, Guizhou, and Guangxi), and the western areas of Gansu, Qinghai, Xinjiang, and Tibet. Although the oilfields in the north-east, north, and east can be developed further, it is necessary to discover new fields near or between the present oil-producing areas so as to utilize fully the existing industrial and transport facilities in those areas. These areas are also close to the main oil-consumption areas and export ports. The construction of long pipelines would therefore be unnecessary and a strong technical labour force is available, thus keeping unit investment and costs low.

Although the level of prospecting in these areas is high, the verified reserves are located only in shallow structures. Potential still exists, therefore, for discovering new deep deposits. Prospecting should take into consideration both oil and gas as well as shallow and deep deposits, although the most viable deposits should be developed initially. For example, the estimated reserve in the Songliao basin is approximately 45 billion tonnes, which is much greater than the already verified geological reserves. The Shengli oilfield develops small deposits while continuing its prospecting for new reserves in new areas and structures. In both areas, a number of small but rich oilfields have been discovered as a result, and their reserves have expanded. In addition, new types of oil deposits have been discovered in eight new areas through this process, and three major areas have been designated for exploitation in the near future. More than 40 oil strata have been found on both the eastern and western edges of the Renqiu oilfield, 85 per cent of which are major oil-bearing structures. Oil deposits have also been found in the north, around Beijing and Tangshan, and exploitable gas deposits suitable for extraction have been found in a dozen locations on the periphery of the old Daqing oilfield and in north Dagang. The potential for locating additional reserves in the east upland oilfields is therefore good.

China has a broad, shallow continental shelf, covering one million square kilometres. The East China Sea is potentially the most promising of the offshore areas, followed by the South China Sea. The Bohai Sea also has potential for further prospecting because of its shallow depth. Six resources of oil gas discovered in the Bohai Sea, the Yellow Sea, the East China Sea, the Yingge Sea in the South China Sea, the Beibu Gulf, and the Zhu Jiang basin have thick deposits, diversified structures, good conditions for oil production, and further potential. Furthermore, they are linked with the main continental oilfields. The Bohai basin, for example, which contains large reserves, is part of the Dagang, Shengli, and Liaohe oilfields complex. A number of test wells in the Bohai Sea and Beibu Gulf have yielded oil. In the East China Sea, test drilling has also discovered multiple layers of high-pressure gas.

The costs of prospecting and sinking wells in marine areas are higher than for continental fields, however, because of the dangerous conditions, complex technology, and longer construction period. Nevertheless, costs are lower than for continental fields in the west because of their closer proximity to the large economic centres with their developed transport facilities, technology, and funds. The offshore areas are also economically viable for exploitation because of their high yield per unit of area and their high-quality oil with low sulphur and wax content.

Also suitable for further prospecting are the western continental fields. Ten of the basins are larger than 100,000 square kilometres and three of these are located in Xinjiang and Qinghai. The Tarim basin, covering approximately 610,000 square kilometres, is the largest sedimentary basin in China. The main sedimentary rock of the Junggar basin, 13,000 metres thick, is the thickest in China; that of the Tarim and Qaidam basins is 10,000 metres thick. These three basins have considerable potential because of their large reserves and good structures. Test wells indicate that conditions are especially suitable for production on the south-west periphery of the Tarim basin. The oil layer in the area is under high pressure, producing a large daily output of high-quality oil.

Further prospecting of these western fields is hampered, however, by their remoteness from the major economic centres, poor transport facilities, inhospitable terrain and climate, low population, and the lack of water resources. Although prospecting costs are high as a result, there is potential for viable production. The expansion of China's oil industry is dependent upon further exploitation of the existing main areas whose potential for further reserves has been established.

Secondary Energy

Secondary energy is energy produced directly or indirectly from primary energy resources. It includes petrol, coking coal, marsh gas, surplus heat, and electricity. Different kinds of primary energy produce different kinds of electricity. Thermal power is the most widely used form of power in the world today. Its exploitation involves the integration of primary and secondary energy.

Thermal power constitutes most of the electricity industry in China. At the end of 1980, there were 2,870 power stations with a generating capacity of more than 500 kW, 1,340 of which were thermal power plants. Although they are fewer in number than hydropower stations, they account for 70 per cent of the country's gross installed capacity of 63.02 million kW. In terms of generating capacity, the ratio of thermal power to hydropower stations is even higher. There are 56 large thermal power plants with installed capacities of more than 250,000 kW, 16 of which have more than 500,000 kW generating capacity. The Qinghe power plant in Kaiyuan, the largest of its kind in China, has a capacity of 1.1 million kW. Smaller thermal power stations with a capacity of less than 250,000 kW are scattered throughout the country (Fig. 7.4).

Some 275,000 kilometres of transmission lines connecting thermal and hydropower stations and substations form 12 large power grid systems, each with a capacity of more than one million kW. There are also a number of regional grids, including five trans-provincial grids, each with a capacity of more than 3 million kW. The total combined capacity of these grids is almost 30 million kW (Fig. 7.5).

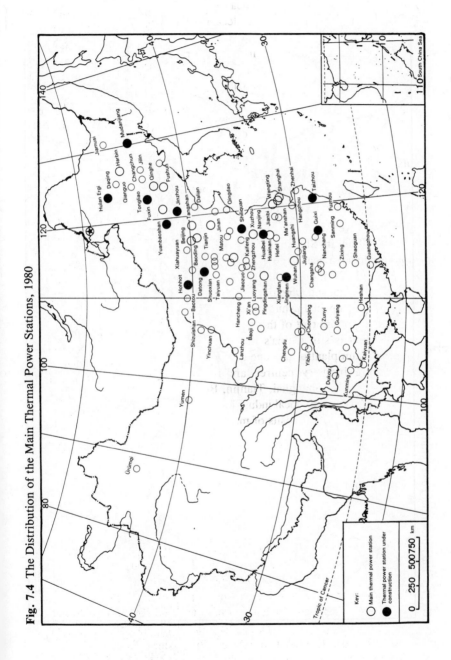

Fig. 7.4 The Distribution of the Main Thermal Power Stations, 1980

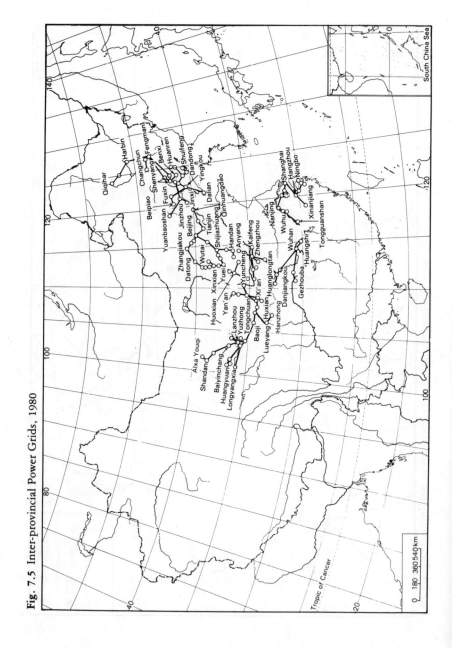

Fig. 7.5 Inter-provincial Power Grids, 1980

The distribution of thermal power plants is more flexible than that of hydropower stations. Load capacity and the distribution of fuel-producing bases are the most important locational factors; other factors are water supply and transport facilities. Many of the large and medium-sized thermal power plants built in China since 1949 are located near power loading centres (that is, large power-consuming cities). Because of their convenient transport facilities, fuel from other areas can easily be transported to these centres. Their main advantage is their proximity to power consumers, which reduces the length of transmission lines. However, such power loading centres are usually located far from fuel-producing areas, resulting in higher coal costs. This cost in turn occupies a higher ratio in the power production cost. This is especially the case with power plants using coal instead of oil.

The second main locational factor is proximity to the fuel-producing bases. Most of China's thermal power plants use coal; very few use oil or gas. The advantage of being located near coal-mining or coal-dressing plants is the convenience of transporting coal, resulting in low transport and fuel costs. Other advantages are the savings on space and investment by not having to construct coal and cinder yards, the faster turnover of capital, and the better co-ordination with coal-mines. Coal of low heat, which is unsuitable for long-distance transportation, can also be used efficiently.

The construction of power plants in coal-producing areas may reduce the over-concentration of industry in power loading centres and also enable coal bases to diversify their economy. However, the distance between power plants and power loading centres necessitates the construction of long transmission lines. The distance and capacity of transmission are limited by technical factors and voltage loads; in turn, the size of power plants is limited.

A third pattern of distribution of power plants is near both the power loading centre and the fuel-producing base, with all their locational advantages. Such plants can generate and transmit power more economically than plants distributed in other ways. However, power loading centres and fuel-producing bases are usually not integrated in this way. Other power plants are located near high-quality water sources connected to fuel bases by transport lines.

Northern China is rich in widely distributed coal reserves. The coal-mining industry is well developed and a number of mines are located near power loading centres. The large and medium-sized thermal power plants in Beijing, Douhe, Handan, Taiyuan, Datong, Baotou, and Yangchuan in the north; Fushun, Kaiyuan, Jinzhou, Hulan Ergi, Jiamusi, Mudanjiang, and Jilin in the north-east; Xi'an, Huxian, Shizuishan, Dawukou and Lanzhou in the north-west; Zhengzhou, Luoyang, and Pingdingshan in Henan; Xindian, Shilichuan, and Jining in Shandong, as well as the Huainan thermal power plant in Anhui province are located near both the fuel-producing areas and the power loading centres. The plants in areas south of the Chang Jiang where fuel is in short supply are located mainly near power loading centres and far from the fuel-producing bases.

On the whole, the majority of large and medium-sized thermal power plants are located near power loading centres because of the need for large amounts of power for industry (especially the iron and steel, chemical, petroleum products, paper, and sugar industries) and heating, and because of the limitations imposed on its supply by distance.

China's large power loading centres are areas of high concentration of industry. Power shortages are common. The solution lies not in the transportation of greater amounts of coal from the coal-producing areas to power-deficient areas — thereby placing an even greater burden on the already overloaded transport system — but in the expansion of power transmission by large power plants built near ample water sources in large coal-mining bases. Large thermal power plants of this type have been built in Datong, Shuoxian, Hexian, and Niangziguan in Shanxi province; Yanzhou and Xuhuai in Shandong, Jiangsu, and Anhui provinces; Pingdingshan and Jiaozuo in Henan; Huayin in Shaanxi; Lupanshui in Guizhou; and in eastern and southern Inner Mongolia. The construction of this type of thermal power plant must be based on an overall plan for coal and electric power production.

North, north-west, and south-west China's abundant energy resources have considerable potential for development. North-east, east, and central-south China are deficient in energy resources, while consuming more than 70 per cent of China's energy production. Deficiencies in these areas are made up by supplies from the energy-rich areas. This situation is expected to remain unchanged for some time.

The south-west is rich in water resources and Yunnan and Guizhou have rich coal reserves. The region is therefore suitable for the construction of hydropower plants and the transportation of coal to Sichuan province, which is coal-deficient and the biggest energy consumer in the region. Energy production in this region is sufficient to meet local needs and to supply some of the energy requirements of Guangdong province and Guangxi Zhuang autonomous region.

In north-west China, which is rich in coal reserves and water resources, thermal and hydropower plants can be constructed simultaneously, with a slightly higher proportion of hydropower projects, to satisfy local needs. The region's remote location and high transport costs restrict power transmission eastward to Shaanxi and Shanxi provinces.

North China has superior coal reserves, the exploitation of which is associated with the construction of coal-consuming thermal power plants planned to support east, north-east and central-south China.

Although central-south and east China have some coal reserves and water resources, energy is still in short supply and must be supplemented by the north and, to a degree, the south-west.

The north-east supplies oil to other parts of the country in exchange for coal. At present, the region has surplus energy. However, its oil supplies are limited, while its own demand for coal is expected to increase considerably. It will become dependent upon Shanxi province and Inner Mongolia to make up its deficiency.

8. The Metallurgy Industry

THE metallurgy industry is one of the most important branches of China's raw and semi-finished materials industry. It accounts for over 8 per cent of the total industrial output value and one-third of the output value of the mining and raw materials industries. Between 1949 and 1980, the industry produced some 300 million tonnes of rolled steel and a large amount of non-ferrous metals. The output values of ferrous and non-ferrous metals have a ratio of 7 : 3. The non-ferrous metallurgy industry is still relatively backward and if it is to meet the demands of the modernization drive, it must be developed rapidly.

China's rich and varied metal resources are distributed over a wide area, with a relative concentration of different ores. As such, conditions are favourable for the development of a metallurgy industrial system with a rational distribution. Since 1949, the metallurgy industry has developed mainly along the coast, with some development in the interior. Simultaneous with the construction of large key enterprises, many smaller enterprises were established throughout the country. A metallurgy industrial base of considerable proportions has been established as a result. The industry is most developed in east and north-east China, followed by the north and central-south; the south-west and north-west are the least developed. In the north and north-east, the ferrous metallurgy industry is predominant, whereas the non-ferrous metallurgy industry is predominant in the north-west and central-south. In the north-west, non-ferrous metals account for 60 per cent of the industry's total output value.

China's ferrous and non-ferrous production is distributed in four main ways. In Liaoning province and Shanghai, both ferrous and non-ferrous metallurgy industries are well developed. Liaoning's ferrous production accounts for one-fifth of the national total output value; its non-ferrous production accounts for one-eighth. Shanghai's production of ferrous metals is one-sixth of the national total output value, and its non-ferrous metals one-seventh. Liaoning accounts for one-fifth of the national gross output value of the metallurgy industry and Shanghai accounts for one-sixth.

Secondly, in provinces such as Gansu, Hunan, Yunnan, Guangdong, and Henan, the metallurgy industry accounts for a small proportion of the country's total metallurgy production. However, non-ferrous production dominates the local industry and occupies an important place in national production. Although the output value of the metallurgy industry in each of these provinces is only 2–3 per cent of the national total, that of non-ferrous metals is 4–8 per cent of the national total (55–85 per cent of the total metallurgy production within the provinces).

A third distribution pattern is dominated by ferrous production which occupies an important position in the country's total production. In Hubei, Sichuan, Beijing, Hebei, and Tianjin, for example, the output value of the metallurgy industry accounts for between 3.6 and 6.8 per cent of the national total. Ferrous production accounts for between 70 and 83 per cent of this output and between 4.2 and 8 per cent of the national total ferrous production.

Finally, in some areas (such as Shanxi, Inner Mongolia, Jilin, Heilongjiang, Shaanxi, Ningxia, Qinghai, Xinjiang, Shandong, Jiangsu, Zhejiang, Anhui, Jiangxi, Fujian, Guangxi, Guizhou, and Tibet), the metallurgy industry remains at a low level of development. The combined output value of the metallurgy industry in these areas accounts for less than 40 per cent of the national total (although ferrous production in Jiangsu, Shanxi, and Anhui, and non-ferrous production in Jiangxi and Shandong account for a fair proportion of the national production).

The distribution of the metallurgy industry is determined in part by the availability of resources. For example, Liaoning, Sichuan, Hubei, Hebei, and Anhui provinces are rich in coal or iron ore or both, which favours the development of the ferrous metallurgy industry. Abundant non-ferrous metals and good water power resources in Gansu, Hunan, and Guangdong provinces favour the development of non-ferrous production. In some regions with abundant resources, however, the metallurgy industry has not developed because of irrational production policies. Guangxi, Qinghai, and Jiangxi provinces, for example, have rich deposits of non-ferrous metals and abundant water power resources, but are deficient in coal and iron ore. Attention in the past was focused on the development of iron and steel production, at the expense of non-ferrous production, with the result that neither industry developed significantly. Similarly, Shanxi, Shandong, Guizhou, and Xinjiang have deposits of both ferrous and non-ferrous metals, but iron and steel production was emphasized.

The ferrous and non-ferrous metallurgy industries in China need to be developed, taking into account local conditions. The exchange of metals between regions would enable them more fully to meet the requirements of local development.

The Iron and Steel Industry

China is rich in iron reserves. Its iron and steel industry has long had priority in national industrial construction and remains today the principal part of its metallurgy industry. Confirmed reserves of iron ore are 44 billion tonnes, of which the deposits of industrial value account for about half (third in the world after the Soviet Union and Brazil). The grade of iron ore averages less than 34 per cent. Calculated at an ore-dressing rate of 85 per cent, 3.5 tonnes of ore are required to produce one tonne of iron. The grade of iron ore deposits in relation to the reserve means that considerable potential exists for the development of China's iron and steel industry.

A number of factors affect the utilization rate of confirmed reserves. The country's iron ore resources are concentrated, but in widely dispersed areas. Some 1,000 verified deposits are scattered in 27 provinces, autonomous regions, and municipalities, with the exception of Shanghai and Tianjin. The largest deposits are in Liaoning, followed by Sichuan, Hebei, Shanxi, Anhui, Hubei, Inner Mongolia, Shandong, and Yunnan. The deposits are concentrated mainly in Anben, Panxi, Jidong, Beijing, Wutai–Lanxian, Ningwu–Luzong, Exi, and Baobai, as well as in Handan, Xingtai, Laiwu, Xinyu, Edong, Shilu, Jiuquan, and Hongliuhe.

China is also rich in coking coal resources, which comprise one-third of the total coal reserve. Shanxi province alone accounts for more than half of the country's coking coal reserve and, with reserves in Anhui, Shandong, Inner Mongolia, Guizhou, Hebei, Xinjiang, Heilongjiang, Henan, Shaanxi, and Yunnan, comprises 90 per cent of the national total. Shanghai, Jiangsu, Zhejiang, Fujian, Jiangxi, Guangdong, Guangxi, Hubei, and Hunan in the south-east together account for only 1 per cent of the total. This concentrated but uneven distribution has largely determined the distribution of the iron and steel industry.

Gas coal accounts for 60 per cent of the country's coking coal; main coking coal accounts for 16 per cent; rich coal accounts for 13 per cent; and lean coal accounts for 11 per cent. In Shanxi and the south-west, all four types of coking coal are produced; in the north-east and east, gas coal accounts for 70–80 per cent of deposits. These proportions have led to difficulties in coal blending and the necessity for long-distance transportation. A further problem is the high dust content of coking coal which, after washing, produces inferior coke.

Some provinces, regions, and municipalities are rich in both coking coal and iron ore. Some (such as Liaoning, Beijing, Hubei, Sichuan, Guangdong, and Tibet) are rich in iron ore but deficient in coking coal; others (such as Shanxi, Guizhou, Qinghai, Ningxia, and Xinjiang) are rich in coking coal but deficient in iron ore.

The combining of coal, iron ore, and other reserves also poses problems. China has abundant ancillary raw materials necessary to the iron and steel industry, but their combinations differ in various localities. Limestone and refractory materials are accessible and close to the iron ore resources used by the Anshan, Benxi, Wuhan, Shoudu, Panzhihua, Baotou, Chongqing, and Taiyuan iron and steel industries. Manganese ores are distributed mainly in Hunan, Guizhou, and Guangxi, while Beijing, Tianjin, Shanghai, Liaoning, Hebei, and Anhui (where the iron and steel industry is fairly well developed) have only small reserves. Chromium ore, found only in remote areas such as Xinjiang and Tibet, is less of a problem because of the small quantities required.

Distribution

On the whole, China's resources provide favourable conditions for the development and distribution of the iron and steel industry. Iron and steel have been a priority in industrial construction since 1949, receiving the largest proportion of the total investment in industry. There are now nine major iron and steel bases (where 12 large enterprises each have an annual production capacity of more than one million tonnes of steel), more than 30 medium-sized iron and steel enterprises, a dozen special steel plants, and about 1,000 small iron and steel works and mines. Steel output has increased from 158,000 tonnes in 1949 to 37 million tonnes in 1980. Between 1958 and

1980, steel output increased by an annual average of 12.6 per cent (compared with 10.5 per cent in Japan).

The iron and steel industries along the eastern coast have been used successfully to extend the industry into the interior regions. During the 1st FYP period, more than half of the total investment in the iron and steel industry went into the Anshan iron and steel works, which served as a base for the expansion of the industry into other parts of the country.

During the 2nd FYP period, the Wuhan and Baotou iron and steel works were built as key projects, providing a base in the south-west. In east China, Shanghai's iron and steel enterprises formed the base for reconstructing, expanding, and building new enterprises to enlarge its base. A relatively evenly distributed iron and steel industrial system which took into account local conditions and requirements was built up. Enterprises included small and medium-sized iron and steel plants, independent steel works, steel rolling mills, and ferro-alloy plants.

The ratio of investment in the iron and steel industry between the coastal and interior regions is 6 : 4. Although the coastal industrial bases (such as Anben, Shanghai, Ma'anshan, Beijing, Tianjin, and Tangshan) have developed into major iron and steel bases, development in the interior regions has proceeded at an even faster rate. Since 1949, the industry has grown from nothing to its present large proportions. A considerable foundation for further development has been laid.

The new Baotou, Wuhan, and Panzhihua iron and steel works and the expanded Taiyuan iron and steel works are the main national iron and steel bases. A number of medium-sized complexes, such as those at Chongqing, Kunming, and Xiangtan, as well as special steel plants at Qiqihar, Daye, Chengdu, Jiangyou, Xi'an, and Xining, have been built or expanded, each with an annual capacity of over 100,000 tonnes.

Iron and steel products manufactured in the interior regions account for an increasing percentage of the national total. In 1949, for example, these regions produced only 13.9 per cent of the national total output of steel. In 1965, the proportion was 22.6 per cent; in 1980, it was 37 per cent. In the early post-1949 period, only six of the provinces, regions, and municipalities produced pig iron; eight produced steel and six produced rolled steel. These bases were located mainly in the coastal areas. Today, with nine major iron and steel bases as a framework, the industry has spread over the whole country, with the exception of Tibet.

The first large complex to be built after 1949 was the Anshan iron and steel works. It is China's largest, possessing several dozen major plants and mines, with 200,000 workers. In 1980, it produced 6.7 million tonnes of pig iron, 6.9 million tonnes of steel, and 4.2 million tonnes of rolled steel. Its four major mines — Dong'anshan, Qidashan, Gongchangling, and Dagushan — produce 25 million tonnes of ore annually. The nearby Benxi iron and steel works (which produces high-quality pig iron) and the Anshan company are together known as the Anben iron and steel base.

Shanghai has a dozen iron and steel enterprises, the most important being the Nos. 1, 3, and 5 companies, with 100,000 workers. In 1980, the city produced 5 million tonnes of steel and 4 million tonnes of rolled steel (second only to Anshan). Some 1,300 types of steel products and 20,000 specifications of rolled steel (more than any other base in the country) are produced. Because Shanghai produces only a small amount of pig iron, it depends mainly on Nanjing's Meishan iron and steel works and the Anhui iron and steel works.

Prior to 1949, the Ma'anshan iron and steel works mined ore and produced only a small quantity of pig iron. After 1949, it was expanded into an iron and steel base. It now produces large quantities of ore, pig iron, and more than a million tonnes of steel (although very little rolled steel).

The Beijing–Tianjin–Tangshan iron and steel companies form a base of small and medium-sized works. The Shoudu (Capital) Company is a large and complete iron and steel complex, producing (in 1980) 1.5 million tonnes of steel, 2 million tonnes of pig iron, and 500,000 tonnes of rolled steel. Its two major mines — Dashihe and Shuichang (in Qian'an, Hebei province) — produce 11 million tonnes of ore annually. The Tangshan iron and steel works and several enterprises in Tianjin specialize in small and medium-sized rolled steel production.

The Baotou, Wuhan, and Panzhihua iron and steel companies are the main bases built since 1949. Wuhan, the largest, produced 2.7 million tonnes of steel in 1980, 3.4 million tonnes of pig iron, and 1.8 million tonnes of rolled steel. Its Edong mining area produces 5 million tonnes of pig iron annually. When its new rolling mill goes into full production, Wuhan will be one of China's major bases for large rolled steel products.

In 1980, the Panzhihua and Baotou companies produced 1.6 and 1.2 million tonnes respectively of steel, 1.9 and 1.2 million tonnes of pig iron, and 1.1 and 0.3 million tonnes of rolled steel. The Panzhihua company possesses China's largest vanadium-titanium-magnetite mine. The Baotou company's ore is provided by the Bayan Obo mine, which has the country's largest deposits of iron, rare earth, and niobium. These associated minerals are extracted.

The Taiyuan and Chongqing iron and steel companies were reconstructed and expanded after 1949. They now have an important role in local rolled steel production.

The present distribution of the iron and steel industry has helped develop the backward areas in the interior and to improve distribution in the country as a whole (Fig. 8.1). However, per-unit capacity investment in the interior is much higher than for the coastal areas; the per-tonne comprehensive investment is three times that of the coastal areas. Further, the coefficient of return on investment and the ratio of profit-tax to funding[1] is higher in the coastal areas than in the interior. One reason for this is the fact that most of the iron and steel works in the interior regions are new and the investment in their ancillary projects, public utilities, and welfare facilities is therefore two or three times more than for the reconstruction or expansion of old enterprises. Other factors are faulty planning and improper siting. For example, poor

1. Ratio of profit-tax to funding = $\dfrac{\text{Profit + tax}}{\text{net fixed assets value + average amount of assigned circulating funds in use.}}$

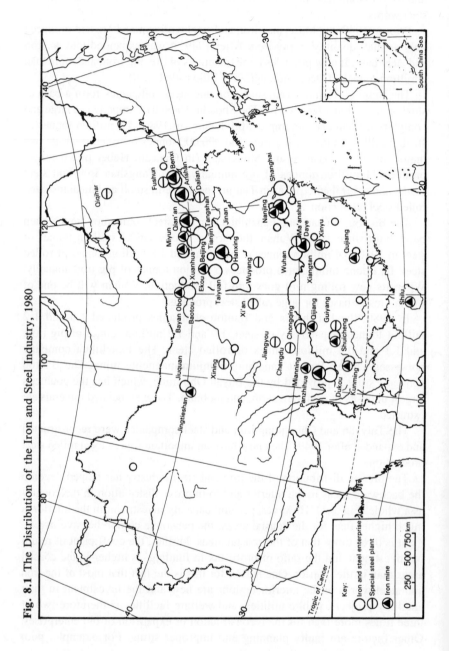

Fig. 8.1 The Distribution of the Iron and Steel Industry, 1980

factory sites required greater investment in capital construction. Ore-dressing, sintering, and smelting circuits did not fit the characteristics of resources, making dressing recovery rates and grades of concentrates low. The slow construction of mines resulted in low ore supplies and low blast furnace utilization ratios, thus increasing the cost of pig iron. Other problems resulted from poor co-ordination and management.

The rational distribution of China's iron and steel bases will require utilization of the original foundations and exploitation of existing bases; the parallel development of equipment manufacturing so as to maintain a balance in the industry; consideration of location, quality, and the conditions for exploitation of iron ore reserves when siting companies; and the solution of technological problems in mining and manufacturing. A balance between innovation, expansion, and new plants, and between coastal and inland locations needs to be maintained. The emphasis in the past on the inland areas in the allocation of investment produced poor economic results.

Today, the iron and steel industry is widely distributed and comprehensive in scale. Further development can therefore emphasize the renovation of old bases and enterprises which, compared with new mills, cost 50–60 per cent less in per-unit investment, and which have a 60 per cent faster rate of recovery of investment. It is necessary, however, to determine which of the existing bases and enterprises are suitable for renovation and expansion, and to what extent. The good economic results of the coastal iron and steel industry are due largely to the concentration of its mills. However, when concentration reaches a certain level, serious problems such as space limitations, shortages of energy resources, insufficient supplies of water and daily necessities, inadequate transport, and serious environmental pollution occur, with the result that economic results are lowered.

For these reasons, the technical reform of existing bases and enterprises should be emphasized in the redistribution of the industry. Technical innovation includes readjustment of the product structure so that the manufacture of products that are in short supply is increased. The achievement of an overall balance both within and between enterprises should also be emphasized, in addition to raising the range of productive capability, utilizing resources more comprehensively, using higher grades of iron ore, and raising recovery rates.

In the long-term, China's iron and steel industry needs to remedy the present situation where production is concentrated mainly in a few coastal areas. The conditions must be created to enable new iron and steel bases to be opened in the inland areas where the deposits of ore (especially high-grade iron ore and coking coal) are concentrated.

Structure

China's iron and steel industry is unbalanced in structure. Rolled steel capacity is low. There is a shortage of mill variety and difficulties in manufacturing complete equipment of some types. The output of iron is very low; large amounts of steel as well as a certain amount of high-grade ore have to be imported each year.

The structure of the industry is also unbalanced in different areas. In the mid-south (mainly Henan, Hubei, and Hunan provinces) and in the east (mainly Shanghai and Jiangsu and Shandong provinces), the mining of iron is low compared with the output of pig iron. The production of pig iron exceeds that of steel, but more than is needed is produced in the north-east, north, and mid-south. However, in the east, especially in Shanghai, insufficient pig iron is produced and almost all of Shanghai's requirements are imported. In the north, where there is an overall surplus of pig iron, Hebei province and Beijing have more than they require, while Tianjin and Tangshan have none at all. In the east, Shanghai's severe shortages of pig iron are in contrast to the surplus in Anhui and Shandong.

This unbalanced distribution of production results in high transportation costs. Ore must be transported from south to north and from east to west. Ore from Guangdong province is transported north in large quantities, and from Hebei to the west. Imported ore is transported west from the sea ports, while pig iron is transported from the north to the south and from the west to Shanghai, Tianjin, and Tangshan. This transportation not only raises production costs but also places a heavy burden on energy and transport facilities.

Steel plants need to be located in areas where there is a developed engineering industry and reliable power sources. The output and specifications of steel need to be adapted to local demands. Steel-making and steel-rolling capacities need to be balanced in order to avoid the transportation of semi-finished products and steel-rolling materials.

The restructuring of the iron and steel industries also needs to take into account the distribution of ores. Apart from in the north-west, the distribution of iron ore guarantees iron and steel industrial development. For example, Anshan, Benxi, western Panzhihua, and eastern Hebei province — half of the mining area — have large iron ore reserves. Their concentration enables them to meet the requirements of several large iron and steel enterprises. Daye and Shilu, which serve Wuhan, are also important mining areas. However, although the ore is of a high grade, the reserves are almost exhausted. In order to ensure the further development of the Wuhan iron and steel works, iron ore bases need to be expanded.

Shanghai produces more than 5 million tonnes of steel annually, using iron ore and pig iron mainly from Meishan and Ma'anshan. If, when completed, the Baoshan iron and steel works needs to use local ore, the problem of ore supply to Shanghai will become more severe. The need for new mining bases is therefore paramount.

Bayan Obo iron ore contains many associated minerals, including rare earth, niobium, manganese, fluorine, and phosphorus, and the rare earth content is very rich. The potential therefore exists for comprehensive exploitation to extract these associated minerals.

The Taigulan iron ore mining area in Shanxi province has large reserves, but is as yet largely unexploited. Shanxi's export of large amounts of coal monopolizes transport facilities, however, and further exploitation of this mining area is dependent upon the further development of the iron and steel industry in Shanxi itself.

Although the Handan and Xingtai iron mine has sufficient reserves of relatively high-grade ore, it is difficult to exploit on a large scale at present because of local hydrological and geological conditions. The Jiuquan iron mine, situated in high terrain, is difficult to exploit and its 'red ore' is of a low extraction value.

Anshan, Benxi, western Panzhihua, and eastern Hebei province are the key mining areas suitable for expansion. The Anshan and Benxi mines provide ore mainly for the Anshan and Benxi iron and steel works, but they have the capacity to supply ore to bases along the Chang Jiang which are deficient in ore. The Panzhihua mine provides not only the ore requirements for the Panzhihua and Shuicheng iron and steel works, but also supplies some of the requirements of Kunming and Chongqing and has the potential to supply new iron and steel works in the south-west. The eastern Hebei province mine supplies ore to the iron and steel works in Beijing, Tianjin, and Tangshan, and has the potential to meet the demands of a large iron and steel base.

Scale

The characteristics and development of China's iron and steel industry indicate that the concentrated distribution of large and medium-sized works is more economical than the construction of many small, dispersed, and techno-logically backward works.

During the 1st FYP period, investment in the iron and steel industry was comparatively concentrated. More than half of the total investment was directed to the Anshan iron and steel works; the balance was used to achieve satisfactory results in a dozen other key projects. During this plan period, the average annual increase in steel output was 31.7 per cent. Quality, consumption of raw materials, labour productivity, as well as other economic and technological indexes were also of a satisfactory standard. However, state policies in 1958 resulted in the establishment of many small iron and steel works which not only dispersed investment but also slowed the construction of the large enter-prises. The small works were inefficient and their economic efficiency was low because of backward techniques and equipment. As a result, the annual increase of steel output dropped to 4.5 per cent during the 2nd FYP period. Small works continued to be built throughout the 1960s and 1970s. Since 1978, the poor economic results of these works and China's iron and steel industry as a whole has resulted in the closure of several of these works. Nevertheless, small and medium-sized enterprises are necessary within the overall framework, with the provision that key construction is focused on the large enterprises.

China's iron resources are both widely distributed and highly concentrated. Verified deposits range from 10 billion tonnes to less than several 10 million tonnes. The comprehensive exploitation of these resources requires various sized mining enterprises as well as degrees of concentration and dispersion.

The larger the mining enterprise, the more superior its economic results and technology. The requirement for advanced technology creates problems of co-operation with other enterprises because of the large initial investment and the small number of workers required. Managers and employees also need to be highly skilled. There are also insufficient funds to import the most advanced technology and equipment needed to build complete bases that produce 6–10 million tonnes of iron and steel annually. China's large population, weak economic foundation, and backward technology exacerbate the problems of obtaining internal co-operation and complete equipment, with the result that the construction of new large-scale joint enterprises is not feasible at present.

The scale of iron and steel enterprises is restricted by many factors, which in turn results in different rational economic scales. China's present national conditions, energy resources, management levels, equipment manufacturing capacity, and technical forces make economical the construction of iron and steel enterprises of 1–3 million-tonne capacity. In some cases, conditions make feasible the construction of 5–6 million-tonne enterprises.

Medium-sized enterprises (of from 300,000 to 500,000-tonne capacity) are the backbone of China's iron and steel industry. For example, the Hangzhou iron and steel works is a medium-sized comprehensive enterprise with average equipment. Its economic effect is superior, however, because of available resources, a sound economic foundation, good management and administration, and an adequate technical level. In 1980, the ratio of its profit to funding was 34.3 per cent (making possible the recovery of investment in three years).

There are also many small, technologically backward blast furnaces in China, with a capacity of under 100 cubic metres, whose economic efficiency has been steadily raised. If distributed rationally, with guaranteed resources and transport, marketable products, efficient administration and management, and adequate technology and equipment, and if located in areas which have no large mines or iron and steel enterprises, such small enterprises are a necessary and economical alternative.

Locational Factors

A number of factors determine the location of iron and steel enterprises, including resources, energy and water supplies, transport facilities, economic foundations, conditions for co-operation, as well as topography, geology, hydrology, and meteorology. Different types of enterprises have different locational requirements. For example, enterprises producing alloy steel and other special kinds of steel need to be near energy supplies, consumer markets, and abundant supplies of scrap iron and steel. Independent steel rolling plants must be near commercial steel sources and markets. Both independent and complex enterprises that smelt iron depend on ore and need to be close to reserves.

Iron and steel complexes consume mainly ore and coking coal. Ideally, they should be located close to deposits of both. The Baotou iron and steel works, for example, has easy access to the ore of the Baobai iron mine and the coal of Baotou and Wuhai; the Taiyuan iron and steel works has access to Xishan and Fenxi coal and Ekou iron, and so on.

Most of China's key iron and steel complexes and independent iron smelters are close to iron ore, but transport coal from elsewhere. For example, the Panzhihua iron and steel works has easy access to the iron of

Panzhihua, but transports coal from Lupanshui in eastern Guizhou province. This type of enterprise is resource-based.

The iron and steel industries of Shanghai, Tianjin, and Tangshan produce mainly steel; iron smelting constitutes only a small part of production. Shanghai's smelting capacity is limited, but its steel and rolled steel capacity is immense. Each year, Shanghai imports several million tonnes of pig iron from Benxi, Ma'anshan, Wuhan, and Meishan, as well as all of its iron ore and coking coal requirements. Shanghai's iron and steel industries are of the distribution-based type.

A third type of enterprise is based on coastal shipping facilities. The new Baoshan works are of this type. High-grade coal is imported, as well as coking coal from the Yanzhou, Xuzhou, and Huai He areas. Large amounts of its products are exported. Yet other types of enterprises are market-based, with emphasis on proximity to local engineering industries. Some such enterprises (for example, in Dalian, Fushun, Chongqing, and Daye) are also close to pig iron-producing areas.

The Non-ferrous Metallurgy Industry

Non-ferrous metals can be classified as heavy (for example, copper, lead, and tin), light (aluminium, magnesium, sodium, potassium, and strontium), noble (gold, silver, and platinum), rare (tungsten, lithium, beryllium, and rare earth), and semi-metallic (boron, selenium, and arsenic). China has many non-ferrous metal areas or belts, including the Guizhou–Sichuan–Hunan–Guangxi mercury belt, the Hunan–Guizhou antimony belt, the Nanling tungsten and tin belt, and so on. The country's deposits of tungsten, antimony, rare earth, lithium, magnesite, tin, mercury, zinc, molybdenum, copper, lead, nickel, and titanium are amongst the largest in the world.

Although copper, lead, and zinc deposits are found in most provinces and regions, they are concentrated mainly in a few parts of the country. Copper is found mainly in Yunnan, Tibet, Sichuan, Gansu, Qinghai, Hubei, Guangdong, Jiangxi, Anhui, Shanxi, Inner Mongolia, Heilongjiang, and Jilin. Lead and zinc are concentrated in Yunnan, Gansu, Qinghai, Guangdong, Hunan, and Liaoning. There are large and concentrated deposits of tin, tungsten, antimony, molybdenum, and magnesium, which are widely used in industry but are unevenly distributed in the world. China is especially rich in deposits of rare earth, niobium, vanadium, and titanium, which are scarce in the world.

The areas that are rich in non-ferrous metal deposits are close to water resources and large coal-mines which provide cheap energy for smelting. However, some deposits are of a low grade or are in remote areas with poor transport facilities and conditions for exploitation. Therefore, despite the superior variety and distribution of non-ferrous metals reserves in China, backward ore dressing, smelting, and processing techniques prevent the comprehensive development of its resources.

The non-ferrous metallurgy industry is large and complex in structure. The 10 most commonly used non-ferrous metals are copper, aluminium, lead, zinc, nickel, tin, antimony, mercury, magnesium, and titanium. The outputs of copper, aluminium, lead, and zinc account for 90 per cent of the output of all non-ferrous metals. The outputs of high-grade ore containing tungsten and molybdenum are comparatively high. China's output of the 10 most commonly used non-ferrous metals is sixth in the world. The proportion of non-ferrous metals to iron and steel production is indicative of the level of economic development: the more developed the national economy, the greater the consumption of non-ferrous metals in proportion to the production of steel. The world average output of copper, aluminium, lead, and zinc in proportion to steel is 1 : 19.41; in China, the proportion is 1 : 33.48.

China's resources and its non-ferrous metals industry are unable to meet the demands of its developing economy. Since 1949, imports of the four main non-ferrous metals (copper, aluminium, lead, and zinc) have been a large proportion of its manufacturing output. Nickel, magnesium, and cobalt are also imported. Some non-ferrous metals are exported in large quantities (for example, tungsten, antimony, tin, and mercury). Since the 1960s, the volume of mining has also decreased significantly. The old mines are low in grade, conditions have deteriorated, yields are unbalanced, products are of a low quality, and processing depth is below standard. Moreover, the metallurgy industry's foundation is weak and the construction of new mines is slow. As a result, the competitive power of China's non-ferrous metals in the international market has been weakened, imports have increased, and exports decreased. Energy shortages have also slowed the development of some production bases.

Non-ferrous products are in high demand. Many non-ferrous metals are important for national defence purposes. The output value of the industry is large and the rate of profit and exchange is comparatively high. For these reasons, and having the advantage of rich resources, the development of China's non-ferrous metals industry should be accelerated. Further development could be achieved through the exploitation of potential reserves and the modernization of methods. Geological surveys of the areas adjacent to the present mines should be expanded, verified reserves should be enlarged, and the life of viable mines should be extended. Equipment needs to be manufactured for mining, ore dressing, and energy production if the range and quality of processing and production are to be expanded and the industry's competitive ability is to be increased.

With its superior non-ferrous metals reserves and energy resources, western China is well suited to planned exploitation and the creation of comprehensive non-ferrous metals bases as part of the redistribution of the industry.

The largest non-ferrous metals producers in China are Shanghai, Liaoning, Gansu, Hunan, and Yunnan. The output value of the non-ferrous metals industry in Shanghai is the highest in China. Its technical level and smelting capacity are high, and there is a large demand for its products. Nevertheless, its resources are limited and its energy supply is short. Liaoning, with the second highest output value, has abundant reserves and a sound foundation. Gansu, third in output value, not only has rich resources of non-ferrous metals, but also cheap water and electricity from the Huang He. It is the most important of the non-ferrous metals industrial bases built since 1949. Hunan and Yunnan, ranking fourth and fifth in output value, have a good foundation and abundant resources. Water and hydropower potential are also abundant. Their non-ferrous metals industry includes all major production processes, including mining, dressing, smelting, refining, and rolling. The distribution of the non-ferrous metals industries therefore varies according to their special requirements.

Heavy Non-ferrous Metals

Mining and mine construction account for 80 per cent of the total investment in the heavy non-ferrous metals industry. The construction of large integrated mining complexes at the site of rich natural deposits and in areas with good transport and communications facilities and fuel and energy supplies avoids high transport costs, accelerates construction, and enables a comprehensive utilization of energy and an easier solution of pollution problems. The best economic results are obtained by integrating a non-ferrous metals base with petrochemical and energy industries. In the absence of these conditions, some of the major production processes need to be separated. Because China's heavy non-ferrous metal ores are of a low grade, a large volume of ore is required to be transported between the mine and the dressing plant. Therefore, the lower the grade of ore, the closer the dressing plant should be to the mine.

After dressing, different metals have different grades. Ores with a low metal content can be crude-smelted near the dressing plant before being refined elsewhere using electrolysis. The amount of raw material on reaching the refinery is only slightly more than the amount of the refined product. Because it consumes large amounts of electricity, refining needs to be done in a power centre instead of near the crude smelting plant. If after dressing the metal content of the ore is rather low, crude smelting can be carried out in the fuel and power centre.

A comparatively high technical level is required in the rolling of pure metals and precious alloys. Because it is easier to transport metals and alloys than finished products, finishing can generally be separated from smelting and is best done in the major consuming area, especially near machinery industries. The co-ordination of the non-ferrous metals and machinery industries will enable production standards to be set according to the specifications required by the machinery industry. China's present distribution of the heavy non-ferrous metals industry is generally in line with these requirements (Fig. 8.2).

Copper, Lead, and Zinc

China's copper reserves are distributed mainly in the lower reaches of the Chang Jiang, in Yunnan, Gansu, and Shanxi provinces, and in the Changdu area. Lead and zinc are mined mostly in the Lingnan range and in the south-west and Gansu province. Because the copper, lead, and zinc ores are of a low grade, mining and dressing are closely related. Refining is carried out for the most part near electricity sources and medium-sized or large cities. Copper is refined mainly in Kunming, Baiyin, Luoyang, Shanghai, and Shenyang. Lead and zinc are refined mainly in Zhuzhou in Hunan province and Shaokuan in Guangdong province. Copper, lead, and zinc are also refined in Shenyang, lead

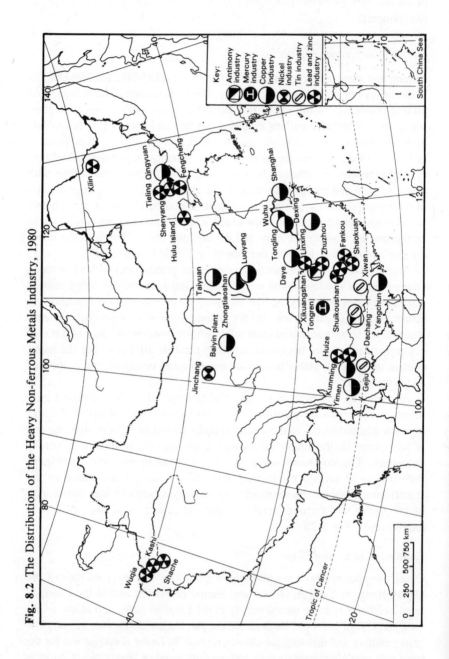

Fig. 8.2 The Distribution of the Heavy Non-ferrous Metals Industry, 1980

in Kunming, and zinc in Hulu Island. Copper processing is also carried out in the principal consuming centres of Shanghai, Luoyang, Shenyang, Beijing, Tianjin, Wuhan, Guangzhou, Chongqing, and Baiyin.

Tin

Gejiu country in Yunnan province is the largest and oldest tin producer in China. Its output is 70 per cent of the country's total output. Long exploitation, however, has reduced both the grade of its ore, and its output, and the output of associated minerals such as copper, lead, iron, manganese, and sulphur now exceeds that of tin in Gejiu. Recent surveys have discovered 17 mineral deposits in western Yunnan province, some of which are of a high grade which is rare in China. Conditions exist therefore for further expansion of the tin industry.

Antimony

The antimony industry centres mainly around Hunan province. Its output of antimony (obtained mainly from the tin mines) accounts for 80 per cent of the country's total output. The balance is mined in Guangxi, Gansu, Yunnan, and Guizhou provinces.

Nickel

The Jinchuan nickel mine in Jinchang is the largest nickel deposit in the world. It also ranks second in the world for sulphuric nickel. The reserve is large, the grade is high, and it is rich in associated minerals. Associated copper is one of the largest copper reserves in China. Other minerals include cobalt and platinum (both of which are the largest reserves in the country), palladium, osmium, iridium, rhodium, gold, and silver.

The large-scale exploitation of nickel in Jinchuan has ended China's dependence on imported nickel. New technological extraction processes for rare and precious metals have also raised the recovery rate of platinum from 49 to 75 per cent, that of palladium from 3 to around 50 per cent, and that of cobalt from 32 to 60 per cent, thereby making imports unnecessary.

Mercury

Guizhou province is China's largest producer of mercury; Hunan province is the second largest producer. The largest mines in Guizhou are the Wanshan special area and the Xinhuang mine.

Light Non-ferrous Metals

The main minerals of the light non-ferrous metals industry are aluminium and manganese. The industry is distributed close to electricity resources, and it requires comparatively high technology and conditions suitable for concentrated exploitation on a large scale. It is of considerable importance in national defence.

Deposits of bauxite are of a high grade (generally 40–50 per cent) and crude smelting, producing aluminium oxide, is usually done in the areas of bauxite reserves. However, one tonne of aluminium oxide requires 2.3 tonnes of ore, more than 2 tonnes of limestone, and 2–4 tonnes of coal. If limestone and coal are in short supply in bauxite areas, smelting is more economically done where supplies of these are abundant.

The production of aluminium by electrolysis consumes large amounts of electricity — 18,000 kWh per tonne. A plant producing 50,000 tonnes annually of aluminium therefore has an electricity requirement as high as 150,000 kW. A stable and reliable supply of electricity is a priority and plants need to be located near large-scale hydroelectric power stations and are often co-ordinated with thermal and hydroelectric power stations.

China's bauxite mines are widespread. Mines with verified reserves are distributed in 18 provinces and regions, with the largest deposits in Shanxi, Henan, Guizhou, and Guanxi provinces (Fig. 8.3). The best conditions for exploitation are at Xin'an in western Henan province, Xiaoyi and Yangquan in Shanxi province, Xiuwen and Qingzhen in Guizhou province, and Pingguo in Guangxi province. Other well-situated mines are in southern Liaoning, northern Shandong, Gansu, and Ningxia provinces, near large coalfields or hydroelectric power stations. China's three large aluminium oxide production bases (Zhangdian in Shandong, Zhengzhou in Henan, and Guiyang in Guizhou) are located near large bauxite mines with rich electricity resources.

The electrolysis industry has also developed. Aluminium plants at Lanzhou, Liancheng, and Qingtongxia rely on Huang He hydropower sources. A large plant set up in Fushun in Liaoning province during the 1st FYP period as an important part of the development of a heavy industrial base in north-east China is still China's largest electrolysis aluminium base. The Baotou aluminium plant is also one of China's largest. The main aluminium manu-facturing industry centres are in Harbin, western Gansu, and Chongqing. Plants in Shanghai, Tianjin, Beijing, Wuhan, Changsha, Xi'an, and Chengdu serve mainly local industries.

The country's largest deposits of magnesite are in the north-east and east, with the largest reserves at Dashiqiao in Liaoning province. The refining and production industries are concentrated in Fushun, where products manufacture is co-ordinated with the Fushun aluminium plant. An aluminium processing plant in western Gansu also produces magnesium materials.

Rare Metals

Deposits of rare metals (including tungsten, molybdenum, titanium, and vanadium) constitute half of the country's total non-ferrous metals reserves. China's reserves, output, and export volume of tungsten are first in the world. The main producer is the Nan Ling (Nan ranges) mining area, comprising southern Jiangxi, south-east Hunan, northern Guangdong, eastern Guangxi, and western Fujian provinces. The largest mines are at Dajishan (Quannan), Xihuashan (Dayu), Kuimeishan (Dingnan), eastern Hunan (Chaling), Taoyuan, Yaogangxian (Yizhang) in Hunan, and Shirenzhang (Shixing) in Guangdong province. Very large deposits have recently been verified at Shizhuyuan in Hunan province in addition to deposits of tin, molybdenum, bismuth, beryllium, copper, and niobium.

China has long been an exporter of tungsten. The country's present

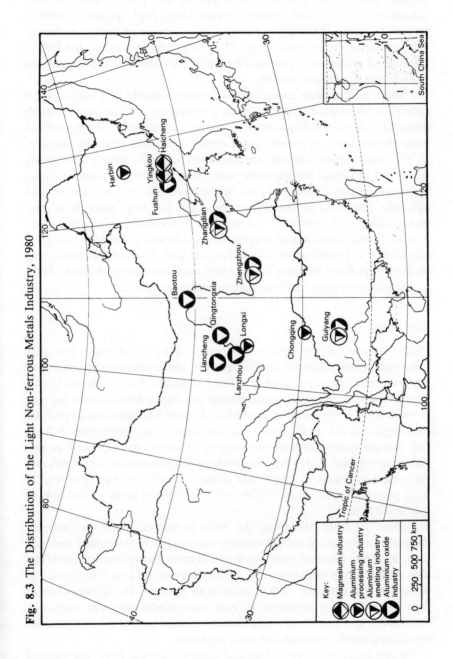

Fig. 8.3 The Distribution of the Light Non-ferrous Metals Industry, 1980

tungsten productive potential is equivalent to the total requirements of the international market and about half of the world consumption of tungsten concentrate comes from China. However, backward techniques mean that tungsten products in China are low in quantity and quality. Although large amounts of tungsten concentrate are exported each year, tungsten filament is imported in large quantities, requiring a great amount of foreign exchange. The raising of the technical level of the tungsten processing industry is therefore of utmost importance in developing the country's superior tungsten reserves and its tungsten industry.

China's molybdenum concentrate is produced mainly in Yangjiazhangzi (which is the oldest base, with the largest output) and Jinchengdui. Both mines have considerable potential for further development. The Luanchuan molybdenum mine, at present under construction, also produces tungsten.

The outputs of the titanium and vanadium industries (which are recently developed in China) are presently small, though with potential for future expansion. Some 80–90 per cent of the total reserves of titanium and vanadium are found in Panzhihua, which also has large deposits of iron, nickel, cobalt, and chromium. The country's first vanadium extracting plant, with an annual production of several thousand tonnes of vanadium dregs, is also located in Panzhihua. Its 45–48 per cent grade titanium concentrate can be used to produce titanium dregs, white titanium, sponge titanium, high-quality vanadium dregs, and high-grade vanadium pentoxide.

Rare Earth

China's reserves of rare earth are the richest in the world, with a complete variety of a good quality. Its verified reserves, which constitute 50 per cent of the world total, are located mainly in Inner Mongolia, Jiangxi, Hunan, Hubei, Guangdong, Guangxi, Sichuan, Shandong, and Gansu. More than 95 per cent of the country's reserves are in Bayan Obo in Inner Mongolia (the largest rare earth deposit in the world). Its average rare earth oxide content exceeds 5 per cent and the content of elements such as samarium and europium is also comparatively high. These deposits provide a solid foundation for China's rare earth industry which, although only recently established, has developed to large proportions. Its output in terms of oxide content ranks second only to the United States.

Baotou in Inner Mongolia, the main production base, has adopted comprehensive retrieval and ore-dressing technology which separates iron, rare earth, and other elements, resulting in iron of more than 60 per cent grade and high grades of rare earth elements. The recovery rate of iron is more than 80 per cent and that of rare earth is close to 40 per cent. The Baotou Chinese Rare Earth Company produces rare earth concentrate, rare earth oxide, rare earth alloys, and it separates single elements. Gansu and Jiangxi provinces are also comparatively important rare earth producers.

Despite its large rare earth deposits, superior technical forces are required for the exploitation and production if the industry is to develop significantly. At present, there is a low rate of utilization of resources, high product costs, and low product quality. Scientific research is required to widen the scope of application, to lower costs, and to raise quality. Utilization needs to be extended to the domestic production of iron, steel, petroleum, petrochemicals, glass, pottery, porcelain, electronics, pharmaceuticals, and daily use products. This is also a prime concern if China is to provide high-quality products for the international market.

9. The Engineering Industry

THE engineering industry provides technical equipment for different sectors of the national economy. The development of the industry is indicative of the level of industrialization in China. Before 1949, there was very little engineering industry apart from a few repair and assembly shops in the coastal cities. Approximately 80 per cent of the necessary machinery was imported. Today, the engineering industry has become one of China's most important industrial sectors. In 1980, there were 100,000 enterprises, with 12 million workers and an annual output value of RMB120 billion (about 25 per cent of the country's total industrial output value). Some 26,000 kinds of equipment were produced, supplying 80 per cent of the country's basic industries.

Development

The distribution of China's engineering industry has changed significantly since 1949. Solid machine-making industrial bases have been established in the middle and western parts of the country, beyond the Beijing–Guangzhou rail line. Between 1957 and 1980, the number of engineering enterprises in these areas increased from 13 to 38 per cent of the national total; fixed assets rose from 32 to 40 per cent of the total; machine tools rose from 23 to 32 per cent; and output value rose from 18 to 26 per cent of the national total. Many of these enterprises now have advanced equipment and systems which have resulted in a rapid increase in production. Several large and medium-sized engineering industrial bases have been established simultaneously with the construction in the eastern part of the country of a number of comprehensive engineering industrial bases with high technical levels. Many of these bases are renovated or expanded existing machine-making factories (Table 9.1). Most of the machine-making centres and engineering industrial districts in the central and western areas of the country were established after 1949 to balance the supply of equipment over the whole country (Fig. 9.1).

In 1952, 14 of China's 29 provinces, autonomous regions, and municipalities had virtually no modern engineering industry. Machine-making enterprises were concentrated mainly in Liaoning province and Shanghai. Since that time, the distribution of engineering industries of various sizes has changed significantly. Although its absolute output value is increasing, the percentage of the engineering industry in Liaoning and Shanghai against the national total has dropped considerably. Engineering industries have developed rapidly in Inner Mongolia, Shaanxi, Gansu, Ningxia, Qinghai, Xinjiang, Anhui, Zhejiang, Fujian, Jiangxi, Henan, Guangxi, Yunnan, and Guizhou provinces where in the past there was very little engineering industry. With the except of Tibet, every province, autonomous region, and municipality can today produce all the products of the engineering industry necessary to the building up of the regional economy. Such products include mining equipment, hoisting machinery, machine tools for metal-cutting, bearings,

Table 9.1 The Distribution of the Main Machine-making Districts, 1980

Machine-making District	Main Centre	Products
Middle and western		
Zhengahou-Luoyang	Zhengzhou, Luoyang, Shanmenxia, Lingbao	Bearings, emery wheels, mining machinery, tractors, textile machinery, hydraulic machinery
Taiyuan	Taiyuan, Yuci	Heavy machinery, machine tools, bearings, standard pieces, cast and forged pieces, power equipment, electric wire and cable, meters, electronics
Wuye	Wuhan, Huangshi, Echeng, Xishui	Heavy machinery, textile machinery, textile equipment
Western and northern Hubei	Shiyan, Xiangfan, Yichang, Shashi, Yidu	Automobiles, optical instruments, electronics, bearings, machine tools, petroleum machinery, textile machinery, electrical appliances and cable
Central Hunan	Changsha, Zhuzhou, Xiangtan, Liling, Shaoyang	Internal combustion engines, electric locomotives, power generating equipment, electro-ceramics, electric cable, electronics, textile machinery, machine tools
Hohhot and Baotou	Baotou, Hohhot	Heavy machinery, large containers, engineering vehicles, crane and transportation equipment, machine tools, electrical machinery, electrical appliances, electric wire
Guanzhong	Xi'an, Baoji, Xianyang, Qishan, Fengxiang, Weinan, Fuping, Luonan, Shangxian	Large power transmission equipment and transformers, building engineering machinery, petroleum machinery, textile machinery, automobiles, meters, electronics
Lantianningyin	Lanzhou, Tianshui, Xining, Yinchuan, Zhongwei, Wuzhong, Linxia, Longxi	Petrochemical machinery, metallurgy, prospecting machinery, machine tools, bearings, electric control equipment, material testing machines, optical equipment, electrical appliances and material, cast and forged pieces

Table 9.1 *continued*

Machine-making District	Main Centre	Products
Chengyu	Chengdu, Chongqing, Deyang, Ziyang, Zigong, Huayun industrial and agricultural district, Luzhou, Dazu, Nanchong, Mianzhu, Leshan	Large power generating equipment, metallurgical mining equipment, building engineering machinery, diesel locomotives, automobiles, electronics, meters and instruments, cutting and measuring tools, electrical appliances, electrical material
Kunming	Kunming, Anning, Malong	Machine tools, bearings, metallurgical mining machinery, forest machinery, cigarette and tea-roasting machinery, meters and instruments, electronics, machine tools
Guiyang-Zunyi	Guiyang, Zunyi, Qingzhen, Xifeng, Anshun, Huishui, Duyun, Kaili	Meters and instruments, electronics, motors and electrical appliances, machine tools, emery wheels, bearings, standard pieces
Harbin	Harbin, Acheng	Large power generating equipment, electrical appliances, electric material cutting and measuring tools, bearings, petroleum tank wagons, gas containers, tractors, forest machinery, meters and instruments, electronics
Jichang	Jilin, Changchun, Yushu, Huaide	Automobiles, tractors, locomotives, passenger trains, engineering machinery, diesel engines, material testing machines
Heidong	Jiamusi, Mudanjiang, Jixi, Yilan, Fujin	Electrical machinery, electrical wire, combines, coal-mine machinery, woodworking machinery, forest machinery

Machine-making District	Main Centre	Products
Eastern coastal		
Central and southern Liaoning	Shenyang, Fushun, Anshan, Benxi, Liaoyang, Yingkou, Dalian, Dandong	Heavy machinery, machine tools, bearings, cast and forge steel products, heavy automobiles, tractors, boats, and ships, internal combustion engines, textiles, paper making and leather machinery, power generating and transformer equipment, electrical appliances and materials, meters and instruments, electronics
Jing-Jin-Tang	Beijing, Tianjin, Tangshan	Machine tools, heavy machinery, light industrial and textile machinery, transportation machinery, tractors, combines, internal combustion engines, complete sets of power generating equipment, electrical appliances, electrical materials, meters, and instruments, electronics, bearings, machine tools
Along Jiao-Ji railway line	Jinan, Qingdao, Zibo, Weifang	Internal combustion engines, machine tools, tractors, transportation machinery, textile machinery, power-generating equipment, electronics, meters and instruments
Chang Jiang delta	Shanghai, Nanjing, Hangzhou, Wuxi, Suzhou, Changzhou	Every trade represented by electronics, meters and instruments, machines for civil use, power-generating equipment, automobiles, ships, and boats, light and textile industry
Zhu Jiang	Guangzhou, Jiangmen, Shenzhen	Electronics, optical equipment, navigation equipment, comprehensive electrical appliances, ships and boats, sugar-making machinery

Source: Directory of China's Industrial and Commercial Enterprises (Xinhua Publishing House, Beijing, 1961).

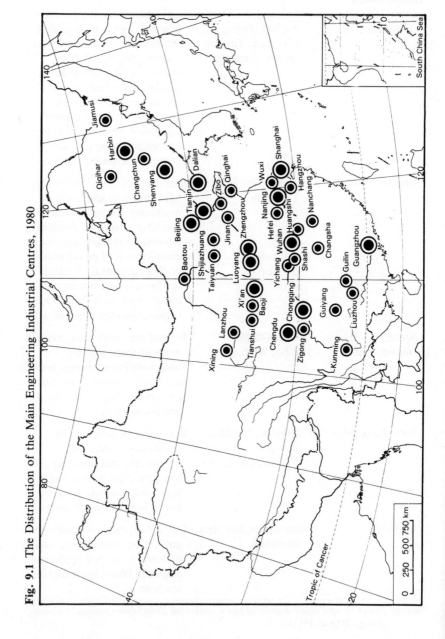

Fig. 9.1 The Distribution of the Main Engineering Industrial Centres, 1980

hand tractors, internal combustion engines, farm machinery, meters and equipment, and light industrial machinery.

Small engineering industries are also scattered in communes and brigades throughout the country. The manufacture and repair of machine tools is the main occupation of such enterprises, which serve agriculture directly and constitute a large part of the rural industrial output value. In 1978, the output of commune or brigade-run engineering industries was 522,000 pieces of farm machinery, 142,000 machine-drawn farm tools, 719.14 million fittings, and 374.15 million other farm tools. In addition, they produced 34,000 metal-cutting machine tools and automobile fittings valued at RMB800 million.[1] Some rural enterprises have recently begun to manufacture specialized equipment and spare parts for other industries as well as, in some cases, household electrical equipment.

The changes in the distribution of the engineering industry have had an important influence on regional economic development. The shift in industry to the backward and rural areas has accelerated the technical transformation of the national economy as a whole and has helped to build up the strategically important rear areas.

The biggest problem in China's engineering industry at present is its irrational structure. For example, there is a lack of large, precision, numerically controlled, highly efficient machine tools. In production, too much emphasis has also been placed on main machinery, so that auxiliary machinery and fittings remain in short supply. Since 1949, the engineering industry has serviced mainly heavy industry, providing equipment for new factories. Its development was influenced considerably by that of heavy industry, which has had the effect of limiting production as well as the upgrading of technology and specialization of the engineering industry.

The distribution of production is also irrational, without unified planning or proper division of work. Both construction and production are often repeated unnecessarily. For example, only 49 of the 600 factories producing bearings have an annual output of 100 million sets. The average output of the balance is 100,000 sets. More than 1,000 factories produce small power generators, but their average output is only 10,000 kW. The manufacture of automobiles, which requires concentrated production, is also scattered. Seventy such plants now exist in China, with an annual output of less than 100 units. Even within regions, construction is often repeated. Five factories in the Luoyang, Xi'an, Lanzhou, and Yinchuan region produce heavy equipment; there are a dozen large bearing plants; four factories manufacture material-testing machinery; and there are a large number of machine tool plants. Such duplication creates waste and limits the region's development.

The irrational distribution of the engineering industry is also apparent in the relationship between the coastal and inland areas. Since the 3rd FYP period, emphasis has been placed on construction in the rear areas, with the result that most of the funds allocated to the engineering industry were consumed by these areas. At the same time, a number of well-equipped engineering industrial enterprises were moved to the interior, while new

1. *China's Agricultural Yearbook, 1980* (Agriculture Publishing House, Beijing, 1981).

factories were built in western Henan, Hubei, Hunan, Shaanxi, Gansu, Ningxia, Qinghai, Sichuan, Guizhou, and Yunnan without overall planning. Excessive attention was paid to considerations of national defence, to the neglect of technical and economic effectiveness factors. Factories were constructed in areas remote from cities and trunk railway lines, resulting in communication and transport problems. Production costs were therefore high and economic efficiency was low. In many inland provinces and regions, the engineering industry occupied an important place in the industrial structure and these problems affected their development and that of the country as a whole.

The legacy of the irrational distribution of production in the engineering industry is a structure inadequate to serve the needs of China's modernization. The existing bases need to be consolidated and their equipment and technology upgraded. Of immediate importance is the redirection of the industry's service from new construction and heavy industry to service to the country's technical transformation, the raising of living standards, the expansion of exports, and the modernization of national defence. The product structure of the engineering industry also needs to be adjusted so that the output proportion of electrical and metal products for daily use constitutes 20 per cent of the total output; export products constitute 10 per cent; military equipment constitutes 5 per cent; and products for the technical reform of the national economy constitute 65 per cent.

The engineering industry itself needs to be upgraded, with better equipment and technology, so as to help raise the country's general technical level and the economic efficiency of other sectors of the economy. The technical transformation of the industry needs to be combined with greater specialization. Co-operation between specialized departments will rationalize the distribution of production and reduce the divisions that exist between different departments, trades, and regions, and between military and civilian production. One means of promoting specialization is to close or combine factories with inadequate or low production effectiveness. Regional advantages can also be more fully exploited so as to raise the economic effectiveness of the industry as a whole.

In addition to the reformation and reorganization of the engineering industry in the interior, co-operation between nearby factories in the coastal areas and the development of those with advanced technology into main production bases would raise their productivity levels and develop the country's export trade.

The Heavy Machine-making Industry

Heavy machinery includes metallurgical and mining equipment, heavy construction equipment, hoisting equipment, heavy machine tools, and petrochemical equipment. A large amount of metal is used in the construction of heavy machinery. In order to reduce transport costs, heavy machinery plants therefore need to be constructed near metallurgy bases. Their production leftovers can also support nearby iron and steel works, in addition to the chemical, mining, and other engineering industries (also often developed near iron and steel complexes) which are the main consumers of heavy machinery. The construction of heavy machinery plants near metallurgy bases therefore not only places them close to raw materials, but also often close to consumer areas. However, it is not always the case that raw material-producing areas are also consumer areas. In such cases, it is more economical to build forges near metallurgy bases and semi-processing and assembly plants near the main consumer areas.

Excavation machinery is also difficult to transport and needs to be suitable for different geological structures, types of wells, and means of excavation. For these reasons, this type of machinery needs to be close to consumer areas. Most of China's existing mining machinery plants are located in coal-mining areas which means that they are also close to their raw materials, such as iron ore, pig iron, and coking coal.

Heavy machinery plants produce key equipment for heavy industry and their location is an important consideration in national defence. These plants require large sites and huge equipment. They also require a solid geological structure and press-resistant soil in areas removed from residential centres.

Prior to 1949, there was no heavy machine-making industry in China, nor even a large mining metallurgy equipment factory. During the 1st FYP period, three metallurgy equipment factories of considerable size were constructed and, during the first three years of the 2nd FYP period, a number of machinery plants used their equipment to manufacture products for metallurgical production in order to support the iron and steel industry. After the 3rd FYP period, in line with the policy of strengthening construction in the interior for the purposes of national defence, a few large metallurgy equipment plants and associated factories were established in the inland areas.

Today, China's metallurgy equipment manufacturing is widely scattered, though concentrated mainly in Shanghai, Liaoning, Shanxi, Heilongjiang, Jiangsu, and Sichuan provinces. The main bases are Fulaerji (the country's largest), Shenyang, Taiyuan, and Deyang. Factories in these centres all have their own casting and forging centres which produce large and medium-sized castings. The metal material is imported from steel plants in Qiqihar, Taiyuan, Anshan, and Jiangyou.

Beijing, Dalian, and Shanghai are also important metallurgy equipment-making bases, as well as Tianjin, Xingtai, Xi'an, Fuping, Kunming, Jilin, Changzhou, Longxi, and Sanming. A group of small and medium-sized factories supplements the production of the key metallurgy machinery plants. These include metallurgy electrical machinery plants in Shenyang, Suzhou, Changzhou, Jilin, Taiyuan, and Ang'angxi; a metallurgy bearings plant and hydraulic press plant in Beijing, a metallurgy spare parts plant in Fuxin, and a metallurgy automobile and railway cars plant in Huashan.

Manufacturing bases for mining machinery are also scattered over a wide area. Almost all of the large metallurgy equipment factories also produce mining equipment. Specialized mining equipment plants are often located in coal bases or near metal material supply centres. The largest production capacity and the greatest product variety (including almost all the products of the three main kinds of mining equipment) are found in bases in the northeast, where there is a certain division of work between factories. North-central

China is the country's second largest mining equipment-producing area, centred mainly around Taiyuan. Other mining machinery plants of a considerable size are located in Shanghai, Hangzhou, Yanzhou, Jinan, Ganzhou, Quzhou, Pingxiang, Huainan, and Xuzhou in east China; Luoyang, Hengyang, Zhengzhou, Changsha, Nanning, Jiaozuo, Sanmenxia, Huangshi, and Shashi in south-central China; Chongqing, Guiyang, Luzhou, Jiangyou, Kunming, and Shifang in south China; and Shizuishan, Tianshui, Xining, Xi'an, Lanzhou, Baoji, and Yumen in north China. Many of these plants were built after 1949 as part of the development of the mining industry. Most large mines and oilfields today have their own mining machinery plants. On the whole, the distribution of China's heavy machine-making industry is related to the distribution of the country's metallurgy and mining industry (Fig. 9.2). The heavy machinery industry is restricted in its location to iron and steel bases, technological centres, and areas with convenient transportation. The main production bases of the heavy machinery industry are Shanghai, Wuhan, Deyang, Baotou, and Shenyang, as well as Tianjin, Beijing, Liaoyang, Yingkou, Qiqihar, Jiamusi, Changzhi, Huangshi, Anyang, Qingdao, Hefei, Xi'an, and Neijiang.

The manufacture of large castings for heavy machinery is scattered amongst a number of heavy machinery plants; specialization is very low. Plants that have large hydraulic presses and which produce mainly heavy castings are located at Fulaerji, Shenyang, and Dalian in the north-east; Taiyuan, Baotou, and Beijing in the north; Shanghai in the east; Luoyang, Wuhan, and Guangzhou in central-south China; Deyang, Kunming, and Chongqing in the south; and Xi'an and Lanzhou in the north.

The Precision and Complicated Machine-making Industry

The manufacture of precision and complicated machinery requires intensive technology. The products are often a combination of the most modern scientific results in a number of different fields. Precision machinery production requires sophisticated technology as well as materials of different specifications, some of which are rare. Precision machinery is light in weight and easily transported; long-distance transport costs comprise only a small part of the total production cost. The manufacture of this kind of machinery also requires, in addition to advanced technology and testing equipment, a high technical level of its operators. Industries of this type include the electronics industry, high-grade instruments and meters, high-precision machine tools, numerical control machine tools, precision tools, communications apparatus, and automatic-control equipment. Such enterprises must be located close to industrial and cultural centres that have advanced technology, scientific research institutes, and skilled workers. They are less reliant upon the distribution of their raw materials and consumer areas and are well suited to concentrated distribution.

The products of complicated machinery manufacture are also sophisticated. Their manufacture requires a great many spare parts, high-precision and good quality castings, and numerous kinds of materials. Often, several enterprises (or areas with concentrated engineering industries) co-operate in the manu-

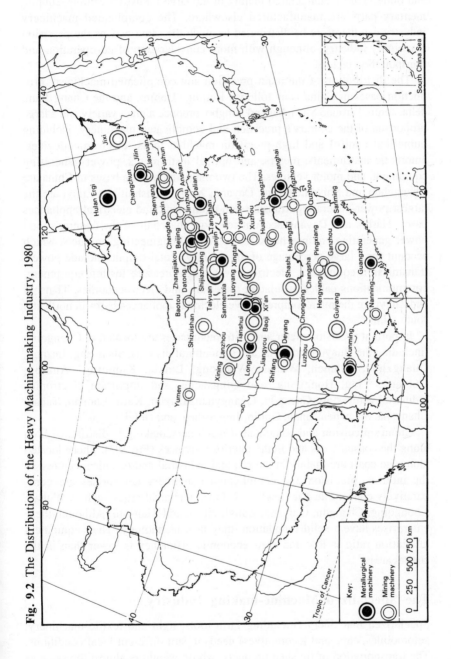

Fig. 9.2 The Distribution of the Heavy Machine-making Industry, 1980

facture of complicated machinery, which includes the products of the aviation, automobile, power generation, and power transmission industries. The main parts of complicated machinery (such as engines, steam turbine generators, and boilers) are manufactured mainly in the large industrial centres; supplementary parts are manufactured elsewhere. The complicated machinery industry can therefore be distributed in much the same way as the precision machinery industry, although with more consideration of co-operation and transportation factors.

The distribution of the main precision and complicated machinery production bases in China is as follows. Beijing, Tianjin, and the Chang Jiang delta, centred around Shanghai and Ningbo, produce a great variety and a large proportion of the country's precision and complicated machinery, including numerical control and high-precision machine tools, electronic devices, automatic instruments, meters, and optical instruments, power-generating equipment, and motor vehicles. The two main automobile bases in China are Changchun and Shiyan. Harbin, Deyang, Xi'an, Tianshui, and Zunyi are the largest power-generating, transmission equipment, and electrical appliances bases. Harbin and Deyang account for more than half of the country's total power-generating equipment. Xi'an's electrical engineering products, which account for a large percentage of the country's total output, include power-transmission equipment, electric stoves, high-pressure testing equipment, communications cables, insulating materials, and electroceramics. Tianshui and Zunyi are the main comprehensive electrical appliances bases in north and south China.

Important precision meter and instrument bases are located at Chongqing (including the Huayun industrial and agricultural district), Shenyang, Jinzhou, Guangzhou, Xiamen, Wuhan, Wuchong, Linxia, Kunming, Anning, Guiyang, Yidu, Hongjiang, and Qingsheng, and important electronics industrial centres are Chengdu, Guangyuan, Duyun, Kaili, Luonan, Tai'an, Changsha, Shenzhen, Jinan, Guilin, Jingdezhen, and Hefei.

China's precision and complicated machinery making is distributed both along the coastal areas and in the interior provinces (Fig. 9.3). Those located along the coast are mainly in the original industrial and technical centres. In the interior, precision and complicated machinery enterprises are comparatively concentrated in newly developed technical cities such as Wuhan, Chongqing, Chengdu, Guiyang, Zunyi, Xi'an, and Tianshui. Although these enterprises have a solid foundation, they lack technology. Their equipment utilization ratio is low and their economic efficiency is lower than in the coastal areas.

The Specialized Machine-making Industry

Specialized machinery (including farm tools, light and textile machinery, automobiles, cars, and locomotives) needs to suit different local conditions. The transportation of finished products, whose weight is almost the same as the raw materials required to manufacture them, is costly, necessitating the location of specialized machine-making enterprises close to consumer areas (Fig. 9.4).

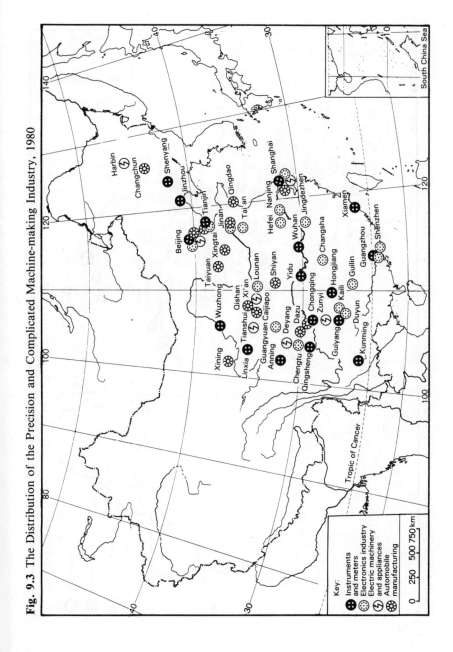

Fig. 9.3 The Distribution of the Precision and Complicated Machine-making Industry, 1980

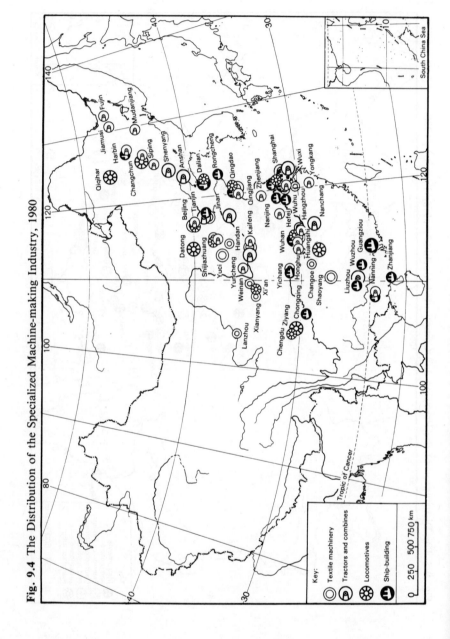

Fig. 9.4 The Distribution of the Specialized Machine-making Industry, 1980

Agricultural Machinery

The agricultural machinery industry in China is fairly well developed. Its factories, including the large specialized tractor plants, are widely scattered in the economic and technical centres of the main agricultural areas, close to convenient transport facilities and sufficient supplies of iron and steel.

Anshan, Shenyang, Changchun, and Harbin are the main agricultural machinery-producing centres in north-east China, serving both the north-east and the north-west, and accounting for a substantial proportion of the country's total output of large and medium-sized tractors. The output of tractors in Shandong and Henan provinces rank second and third respectively in the country. The main tractor-producing bases in the south-east are Nanchang, Shanghai, Changzhou, Hefei, Wuhan, and Liuzhou, and the main walking tractor bases are Wuxi, Changzhou, Yongkang, Nanchang, and Nanning, producing 60 per cent of the country's total output of walking tractors in 1980.

For the most part, the agricultural machinery industry is concentrated in the east, with large factories (particularly those manufacturing large tractors) centred in the north. Walking tractors are produced mainly in the south to cater for its natural and economic conditions. Although the industry is centred around a number of bases with a solid foundation, these bases are too widely scattered. The many factories that produce walking tractors have a particularly low economic efficiency, producing small quantities and non-standardized models. The present family responsibility system in China's rural areas requires large quantities of small agricultural machinery, of various types and standard models. The manufacture of tractors and their principal spare parts needs to be developed in line with the district division of agricultural mechanization. Nine such districts have been delineated on the basis of differing natural, economic, and technical conditions and the demand for different types of farm machinery. They are the north-east dry land district, the north China dry land district, the south-east hilly paddy land, the south-west plateau basin district, the loess plateau district, the Hetao–Hexi corridor and southern Xinjiang irrigated farm district, the Inner Mongolian and northern Xinjiang pastoral district, the Qinghai–Tibet plateau pastoral district, and the south-east hilly tropical farming district. These districts, with their different mechanization requirements, are a more rational determinant of the distribution of agricultural machinery manufacturing than the present distribution of such enterprises.

The product structure of the agricultural machinery industries, especially of small, local enterprises, needs to be adjusted to emphasize the production of small items of machinery such as walking tractors, shellers, mowing machines, driers, farm pumps, farm sideline products processing machinery, and farm transportation machinery and its spare parts. The quality of such products also needs to be raised and production costs lowered.

The level of China's industrial development is low and its technology backward. The volume of oil, electric power, iron and steel, transport facilities, and rubber available to support agriculture is limited and the rural collective economy lacks the funds to purchase modern agricultural machinery. Surplus manpower in the rural areas has also made mechanized production expensive. In addition, the specialization and socialization of agricultural production is hindered by the different farming systems which have developed as a response to varying natural conditions. For these reasons, agriculture will remain semi-mechanized for some time in China, although some areas will become more highly mechanized as a result of their more suitable local conditions. Agricultural machinery production, including the types of products and the models and scale of manufacturing, therefore needs to take local conditions into account. Mechanized and semi-mechanized machinery need to be developed simultaneously if agriculture is to be served effectively and the industry is to have a high economic efficiency.

Textile Machinery

China's textile machinery manufacturing is based on a system of specialized production. The main machinery is produced in selected factories, as are parts that are required in large quantities. Where factories producing textile machinery are concentrated, some of the work processes (such as electric plating, casting, and gear processing) are centred in a few factories which co-operate with one another to achieve higher economic efficiency. Different sectors of the industry are located in such a way as to best utilize local conditions to facilitate the development of the industry as a whole.

The Chang Jiang delta, Tianjin, and Qingdao are China's oldest textile machinery-making bases. The existing small, separate, and technologically backward plants have been reorganized and upgraded and they now constitute the country's key textile machinery manufacturing enterprises. In Shanghai, for example, four large plants have been expanded and the hundred or so smaller plants have been merged to form several large factories. The city is now an important textile machinery manufacturing base, with complete work departments and advanced technology. In 1980, Shanghai, Tianjin, Qingdao, and Jiangsu manufactured most of the country's output of textile machinery. Large textile machinery plants have also been built in north, central, and north-west China at Yuci, Beijing, Shijiazhuang, Zhengzhou, Yichang, Shaoyang, Handan, Chengde, Wuhan, Xianyang, Weinan, and Lanzhou.

The production of textile machinery spare parts has also developed. Old textile appliance plants in Shanghai, Tianjin, Jiangsu, Zhejiang, as well as other textile bases, have been renovated and expanded, while new factories manufacturing textile appliances have been established in the newly emerged textile centres of Wuhan, Zhengzhou, Shashi, Kaifeng, and Hengfeng. Textile appliances are small and are often produced in large quantities and in a number of varieties. Their production is flexible in terms of distribution, with the exception of key products requiring high technology, and textile appliance plants are therefore scattered widely over the country. The greatest number of factories and the largest production capacity is in the east; surplus products from this region supply other parts of China. In north and north-east China and in the centre, south-west, and north-west, textile appliance plants produce 70–80 per cent of local requirements.

Ships and Rolling Stock

The products of the ship and rolling stock manufacturing industries are unsuited to long-distance transportation. Production therefore needs to be close to the main consumer areas (that is, ports and railway hubs). The manufacture of the main component of transportation machinery — the engine — requires intensive technology, which further restricts efficient manufacture to industrial technological centres. When mass produced, engines, instruments, and meters can be manufactured elsewhere before being assembled in the main consumer areas.

The system of inland rivers in China favours inland navigation in the east. Ship-building is therefore concentrated in the large ports on the east coast or in the major harbours along the middle and lower reaches of the Chang Jiang. The Shanghai–Hangzhou–Ningbo area is the country's largest ship-building base as well as the site of a number of factories producing ship appliances such as diesel engines, auxiliary engines, navigation instruments, and meters. Medium-sized and small shipyards and subsidiary factories have also been built in Nanjing, Wuxi, Zhenjiang, Changzhou, and Taixing. In 1980, the area's output of steel ships for civilian use accounted for half the country's total output of ship manufacturing.

Shanghai, the country's north-south transportation centre and the mouth of the Chang Jiang system, is China's largest port and industrial base. The many rivers and waterways, the city's large population, and its developed technology and economy make Shanghai an ideal location for the development of inland passenger and freighter ship-building. The Guangzhou–Zhanjiang area in Guangdong province is also densely populated and its two large ports have an important place in the country's ocean shipping system. In 1980, Guangdong's output of civilian steel ships was second in China. The major industrial centres of Dalian, Tianjin, and Qingdao have developed iron and steel industries in addition to being the principal ports in north China. Together with Qinhuangdao, they handle a large proportion of the country's annual freight volume.

The Chang Jiang is China's most important inland navigation course. Along its middle reaches, the main ports are Wuhu, Anqing, Jiujiang, Huangshi, Wuhan, Yichang, and Chongqing. Wuhan, the largest port, is also a major iron and steel base and ship-building centre. Other ship-building centres are Chongqing and Yichang. Harbin, a navigation hub on the Songhua river in the north-east, and Nanning, Wuzhou, and Liuzhou on the Xi Jiang in the south are also important inland ship-manufacturing centres.

China's ship-building industry is now fairly well developed, with factories specializing in the manufacture of main engines, auxiliary engines, navigation instruments, and meters. The country is able to produce 16,000–50,000-tonne tankers, 13,000–25,000-tonne freighters, 16,000-tonne coal cargo ships, and 7,500-tonne passenger ships. It also builds ocean-going comprehensive survey boats, large dredging vessels, large horsepower tugboats, self-lifting drilling platforms, and other special-purpose vessels.

The country's labour and technology resources are suited to the further development of the ship-building industry, both for domestic use and export, although, in order to achieve this result, some readjustment of the product structure is required.

Rolling stock plants in China are located in the main railway hubs. The country's largest locomotive manufacturing base is at Datong, where the Beijing–Baotou and Datong–Mengyuan rail lines meet. It produces a large proportion of the country's steam locomotives of various types. Other plants are located at Dalian, Beijing, Qingdao, Ziyang, and Zhuzhou. The largest freight car manufacturing base, at Qiqihar, produces a variety of open-top cars, flatcars, boxcars, hopper cars, and other special-purpose cars. Other freight car manufacturing centres are Dalian, Chengdu, Zhuzhou, Xi'an, Wuhan, Datong, and Beijing.

10. The Chemical Industry

THE chemical industry relies on the availability of raw materials, advanced technology, and energy resources. Its importance in China relates to its contribution to the development of the national economy and the raising of living standards.

Development

China has abundant reserves of chemical resources, including those for the sodium chemical, sulphuric acid, chemical fertilizer, and organic chemical industries. Nevertheless, before 1949, the chemical industry was largely undeveloped. A few coastal cities, including Shanghai, Nanjing, Tianjin, Qingdao, Dalian, and Guangzhou, had a total of eight comparatively large chemical plants. The output value of the industry was only 3 per cent of the country's total industrial output value in 1949. Both the scale of production and the variety of products were limited. The country's main chemical industry at that time — acid and soda making — produced only 40,000 tonnes of sulphuric acid, 88,000 tonnes of soda ash, and 15,000 tonnes of caustic soda annually. The annual output of sulphuric ammonia, which was the only chemical fertilizer produced, was only 6,000 tonnes. There were few rubber products or pharmaceutical preparations. Industrial chemicals were imported and the organic chemical industry was largely non-existent.

Since 1949, China's modern chemical industry has experienced an annual growth rate of 17 per cent — higher than the national average rate of industrial development and second only to the growth rate of the oil industry. By 1980, its output value had risen to 12 per cent of the country's total industrial output value, making it the third largest industrial department after the engineering and textile industries. Of the 4,500 state-run chemical industry enterprises distributed over the country, 300 were key enterprises. Some 20,000 kinds of products were manufactured, including chemical mines, basic industrial chemicals, chemical fertilizers, pesticides, organic chemicals, pharmaceuticals, chemical articles for daily use, rubber, and plastics. Production of the main products was on a relatively large scale.

In terms of output value, the largest sector was the organic chemical industry, followed by chemical fertilizers and rubber and plastics. The production of industrial chemicals has also increased significantly since the 1970s with the completion of a number of large petrochemical complexes. The ratio between the raw material and processing industries changed from 1 : 3 at the start of the 1st FYP period to 1 : 1.05 in 1979,[1] indicating that by the 1980s China had established a solid base for the development of its chemical industry.

The development of the industry has been linked closely with its service to agriculture and light industry. Of the funds spent on its capital construction,

1. *China's Economic Yearbook, 1981 (Economic Management,* 1981).

57 per cent was used for agriculture and 20 per cent for light and textile industries. Some 77 per cent of its output value was channelled into the development of those sectors[2] and half of the main industrial chemical products were also consumed by agriculture and light and textile industries.

The emphasis since 1949 has been on the development of large and medium-sized enterprises. During the 1950s, large integrated complexes were built in Jilin, Lanzhou, and Taiyuan, and in the 1970s, a dozen large petro-chemical and fertilizer plants were built in Yanshan and Qilu, amongst other centres. In addition to these key enterprises, smaller chemical plants producing mainly fertilizer and synthetic ammonia were built in a number of localities. In 1979, the production by these small enterprises of synthetic ammonia, chemical fertilizer, dyestuffs, paint, and calcium carbide accounted for more than half the total national output of those products and the output of sulphuric acid, troilite, phosphorus ore, and tyres accounted for 40 per cent of the national total.

Distribution

In 1952, the chemical industry was concentrated in a few coastal cities and provinces. Liaoning province and Shanghai accounted for more than half the country's chemical industrial output value; Tianjin, Beijing, Jiangsu, Shandong, and Guangdong accounted for a significant part of the remainder. The interior and border regions, with the exception of Sichuan which had some chemical factories, had only very weak or no chemical industries.

After 1949, the chemical bases in the coastal areas were renovated and expanded and a number of new large and medium-sized plants were built. At the same time, plants were built in Hebei, Zhejiang, Fujian, Anhui, Sichuan, Hunan, Hubei, Jilin, Henan, Heilongjiang, Shanxi, and Gansu, and smaller enterprises were established in other provinces and regions.

Between 1952 and 1979, the output value of the chemical industry in the interior increased from 17.3 per cent of the national total to 36 per cent. The output value of the mountainous areas in the south and north increased from 3.7 to 12 per cent. During the same period, the output value of the industry in the coastal areas dropped from 82.7 to 64 per cent of the national total.[3] Every province and autonomous region (with the exception of Tibet) now has a chemical industry. However, a number of chemical bases are concentrated in Beijing, Tianjin, and Taiyuan in the north; Dalian, Jinxi, Liaoyang, Jilin, and Daqing in the north-east; Shanghai, Nanjing, Zibo, Quzhou, and Anqing in the east; Guangzhou, Wuhan, Yueyang, and Zhuzhou in central China; Chengdu, Changshou, Jintang, and Luzhou in the south; and Lanzhou in the north-west (Table 10.1).

The most highly developed bases are Shanghai, Liaoning, Jiangsu, and Beijing. Shanghai's total chemical industrial output value, and its output value of basic industrial chemicals, pharmaceuticals, daily necessity

2. Ibid.
3. Ma Hong and Sun Shanqing, *The Economic Structure of China* (People's Publishing House, Beijing, 1981), Vol. 1, Chapter 11, p. 252.

Table 10.1 The Main Chemical Industrial Bases, 1980

Enterprise	Staff and Workers (10,000 people)	Total Output (RMB100 m.)	Profit (RMB100 m.)	Main Products
Beijing Yanshan General Petrochemical Works	3.9	26.8	8.2	gasoline, kerosene, diesel oil, lubricating oil, plastic, ethylene, butadiene rubber
Jilin Chemical Industrial Company	5.5	7.9	2.0	sulphuric acid, caustic soda, synthetic ammonia, nitrogenous fertilizer, dyestuff
Lanzhou Chemical Industrial Company	3.7	7.2	0.8	concentrated nitric acid, synthetic ammonia, nitrogenous fertilizer, rubber
Zibo Qilu General Petrochemical Works	2.0	13.0	3.8	gasoline, kerosene, synthetic ammonia, urea, butadiene rubber
Nanjing Chemical Industrial Company	3.1	2.7	0.4	sulphuric acid, synthetic ammonia, nitric nitramines, phosphate fertilizer, urea
Anqing General Petrochemical Plant	0.9	4.1	0.8	gasoline, kerosene, synthetic ammonia, diesel oil, urea
Guangzhou Petrochemical Plant	0.5	3.7	0.7	gasoline, diesel oil, fuel oil, synthetic ammonia, urea
Jinxi Chemical Plant	1.1	1.3	0.2	caustic soda, BHC, benzene chloride, polyvinyl chloride
Dalian Chemical Plant	1.1	3.0	0.7	synthetic ammonia, sulphuric ammonia, soda ash, caustic acid
Yueyang Chemical Plant	1.5	2.5	0.5	short-staple polyester fibre, synthetic ammonia, sulphuric ammonia, caustic acid
Quzhou Chemical Plant	1.6	2.1	0.5	synthetic ammonia, sulphuric ammonia, caustic acid, BHC

Source: *Directory of China's Industrial and Commercial Enterprises* (Xinhua Publishing House, Beijing, 1981).

chemicals, and rubber rank first in China; its organic chemical industry and plastics rank second. Jiangsu's total chemical industrial output value ranks second, but it has the country's highest output value of chemical fertilizers, pesticides, and plastics. Its organic chemical industry and production of daily necessity chemical products rank third. Beijing's total chemical industrial output value ranks third, but its output value of organic chemicals ranks first. Liaoning has the country's fourth largest chemical industrial output value; its basic industrial chemicals rank second and its chemicals and rubber rank third. Shandong's rubber and organic chemical industries are highly developed, as are Guangdong's plastics, Tianjin's daily necessity chemicals, Sichuan and Hebei's chemical fertilizers, Zhejiang and Hunan's pesticides, Jilin's basic industrial chemicals, and Gansu's organic chemicals industries.

The distribution of chemical industrial production ranges from widely scattered with relative concentration, to centralized distribution, to highly concentrated distribution. With the exception of Tibet, all of China's provinces, autonomous regions, and municipalities produce popular industrial chemicals such as sulphuric acid, caustic soda, calcium carbide, purified petroleum benzine, synthetic ammonia, chemical fertilizers, pesticides, and daily necessity chemical products. The production of such products is not highly concentrated. For example, in 1980, Jiangsu was the largest producer of sulphuric acid, but its output was less than 15 per cent of the country's total output. Similarly, Shanghai and Liaoning had the largest caustic soda output, which constituted only 12 per cent of the national total.

By comparison, the manufacture of products such as plastic goods, concentrated nitric acid, and phosphorus is relatively concentrated because of the distribution of raw materials and consumer areas. Beijing, for example, produces one-third of the country's plastics; together with Shanghai, the figure is half the national total output. Half of the total output of concentrated nitric acid is from Jilin and Gansu provinces, and Yunnan and Hubei produce more than half of the total output of phosphorus.

Some chemical industries are even more highly concentrated in their distribution. For example, ethylene, synthetic rubber, and soda ash, as well as some other chemical products, need to be manufactured in large industrial complexes. Between them, Beijing and Shanghai produce most of the country's ethylene. Similarly, Beijing and Gansu produce most of the total output of synthetic rubber and Liaoning and Tianjin produce more than half of the total output of soda ash.

The Acid and Soda Industry

The acid and soda industry is the most basic of China's industrial chemical industries. Its main products are sulphuric acid, sodium carbonate, and caustic soda. Because the corrosiveness of sulphuric acid creates problems of transportation, its manufacture needs to be carried out close to consumer areas. Sulphuric acid is used to produce single phosphate and triamine as well as being used in oil refining, coal tar processing, dyestuff manufacture, and in the chemical fibre and some light and textile industries. The distribution of sulphuric acid production is therefore often associated with the location of these industries; raw materials are imported from elsewhere if not available locally.

Three patterns of distribution of sulphuric acid production can be distinguished. First, production is combined with other chemical industrial enterprises (as in Nanjing, Guangzhou, Kaifeng, Jintang, Beijing, Quzhou, Jilin, and Daqing). Secondly, production is distributed in consumer areas that have a concentration of chemical industries (as in Dalian, Zhuzhou, Shanghai, Taiyuan, Tianjin, Fushun, and Yumen). Thirdly, production is combined with the metallurgy industry which provides raw materials for sulphuric acid production (as in Lanzhou, Tongling, Yingkou, Shenyang, Daye, Zibo, Shaoguan, Kunming, Yuanqu, Baotou, and Benxi).

The chemical industry is one of the main consumers of sulphuric acid. Chemical fertilizer plants, particularly those producing phosphate fertilizers, are small in scale and scattered across the country. In order to meet their requirements, a large proportion of the output of sulphuric acid is produced by small or medium-sized local factories. The largest producers are Jiangsu and Liaoning, followed by Guangdong, Sichuan, Hunan, Shandong, Shanghai, and Hubei provinces.

Troilite ore, a raw material in the production of sulphuric acid, is distributed mainly in Gansu and Guangdong provinces, followed by Liaoning, Hunan, Shanxi, and Anhui. These provinces have comparatively well developed non-ferrous metal and chemical industries. With the exception of Guangdong, which has large troilite deposits, acid is produced in China using raw materials provided by the non-ferrous metal industry or near small troilite mines. The production of sulphuric acid is therefore distributed close to consumer areas as well as close to its raw material bases (Fig. 10.1).

China produces slightly more sodium carbonate than caustic soda. The manufacture of one tonne of sodium carbonate requires 1.5 tonnes of salt (100 per cent sodium chloride), its main raw material. The technique of ammonia soda or chlorine processing also consumes 1.12–1.25 tonnes of limestone per tonne of sodium carbonate. The septum and mercury methods require 2,300–2,500 kWh and 3,000–3,300 kWh of electricity respectively per tonne of sodium carbonate. The production of sodium carbonate is therefore distributed close to salt-producing areas which have reserves of limestone as well as sufficient electricity sources, or close to consumer areas with convenient transport facilities. The consumption of sodium carbonate is concentrated in areas which have chemical, metallurgy, and glass industries. For the most part, these are coastal areas, which also have rich salt resources (Fig. 10.1). The main sodium carbonate production centres in China are Dalian, Tianjin, and Qingdao. In 1980, the output of these centres accounted for most of the country's total output. The inland areas rely on rock salt for their limited output.

The distribution of production of caustic soda differs from that of sulphuric acid, although it is often manufactured in sodium carbonate plants. One tonne of caustic soda requires 1.4 tonnes of sodium carbonate and 1.7 tonnes of limestone. The electrolysis method, which combines chlorine and hydrogen to

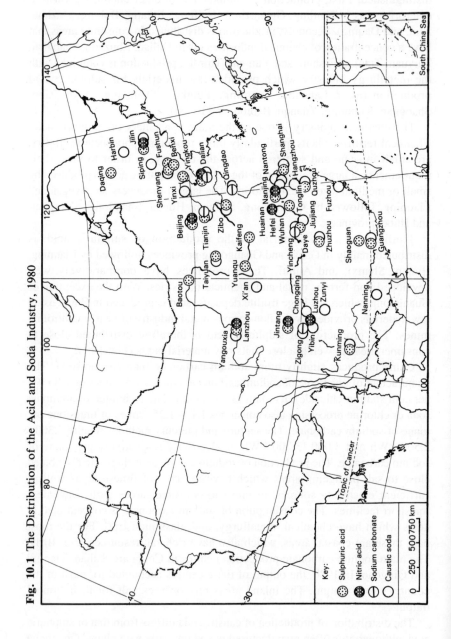

Fig. 10.1 The Distribution of the Acid and Soda Industry, 1980

produce hydrochloric acid, consumes only half the amount of crude salt but much larger quantities of electricity. Manufacturing by this method therefore necessitates proximity to power supply centres.

Caustic soda in liquid form is difficult to transport, whereas sodium carbonate in solid form and crude salt are easily transported. In addition, limestone is widely distributed and the weight of the product, when the electrolysis method is used, is almost that of the crude salt consumed. For these reasons, the production of caustic soda is distributed mainly in the large consumer areas which have convenient transport facilities. It is often associated with the chemical, light, and textile industries and its factories are usually small. The largest plant, the Liaoyuan chemical plant in Shanghai, produces less than 200,000 tonnes of caustic soda annually and other key enterprises produce only between 10,000 and 40,000 tonnes.

The four main producing areas are the Chang Jiang delta (including Shanghai, Changzhou, Hangzhou, Nanjing, Wuxi, Nantong, and Suzhou), the Beijing–Tianjin area, the southern Liaoning area (including Shenyang, Jinxi, and Dalian), and the Chongqing–Chengdu area (including Chongqing, Yibin, and Zigong) (Fig. 10.1). In 1980, the output of these areas accounted for half the country's total output of caustic soda. The balance was produced in large industrial centres that consume large quantities of chlorine and soda (including Taiyuan in the north; Jilin, Siping, and Harbin in the north-east; Fuzhou, Quzhou, Qingdao, Jiujiang, Zibo, and Hefei in the east; Zhuzhou, Wuhan, Guangzhou, and Nanning in the central-south; Zunyi and Kunming in the south; and Xi'an and Yanguoxia in the north).

The Chemical Fertilizer Industry

China's chemical fertilizer industry — producing nitrogenous, phosphate, and potash fertilizers — is fairly well developed.

Nitrogenous Fertilizer

Nitrogenous fertilizer is the main product of the chemical fertilizer industry. Its main raw material, and the main factor in the industry's distribution, is synthetic ammonia. Synthetic ammonia is produced mainly from coal, petroleum, and natural gas and the largest nitrogenous fertilizer plants are located mainly in coal bases or coal industrial areas in the north, with a few located in Shanghai, Jiangsu, and Sichuan in the south (Fig. 10.2).

In 1980, there were 1,500 synthetic ammonia factories in China, 14 of which were large and 50 medium-sized. These larger plants accounted for 45 per cent of the country's total output of synthetic ammonia; small factories produced the rest. Coal, coke, and coke oven gas constituted 62 per cent of the raw materials; natural gas, oil refinery gas, naphtha, and fuel oil constituted the balance.

Phosphate Fertilizer

There was no phosphate fertilizer industry in China prior to 1949. However, by 1958, small phosphate fertilizer plants were being built in many provinces

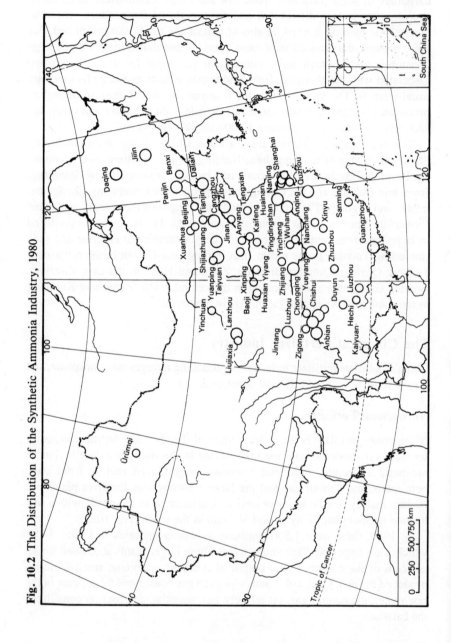

Fig. 10.2 The Distribution of the Synthetic Ammonia Industry, 1980

and regions and today there are 700 such plants. The main raw materials in the production of phosphate fertilizer are phosphate rock and troilite. Phosphate is found mainly in Yunnan, Guizhou, Sichuan, Hunan, and Hubei provinces. Approximately 70 per cent of the total output of the phosphate fertilizer industry comes from the south. Hunan, Jiangsu, and Sichuan each account for more than 10 per cent of the total; Guangdong, Hubei, Yunnan, Guangxi, and Jiangxi account for 4–6 per cent each. The largest producers in the north — Shandong, Hebei, and Liaoning — also account for 4–6 per cent each of the total output.

Less than 5 per cent of the total output of phosphate fertilizer is produced by large enterprises; 95 per cent is produced by small or medium-sized local plants. The largest production bases are Nanjing and Taiyuan, followed by Zhanjiang, Hengyang, Tongguanshan, Jinan, Handan, and Anda.

Potash Fertilizer

The potash fertilizer industry has developed slowly since its establishment in 1959 because of the inadequate supplies of its main raw material, sylvite. China's verified sylvite deposits are very small and for the most part are located in remote areas. The technology needed to separate potash chloride from sylvite ore is also lacking. Because of the limited resources, only a few small factories produce potash fertilizer. Qinghai province is the country's largest producer, its annual output accounting for 80 per cent of the total output. It is also the only province in China to use local resources in order to produce potash fertilizer. Other factories with small outputs are located in Jiangsu, Hunan, and Sichuan.

On the whole, China's chemical fertilizer industry has attained a considerable size. Its output of both nitrogenous and phosphate fertilizers ranks third in the world. However, the output of nitrogenous, phosphate, and potash fertilizer is unbalanced. Phosphate and potash fertilizer production falls far short of meeting the demand. Also, only 30 per cent of nitrogenous fertilizers have a high nitrogenous content, and efficient or super-efficient phosphate fertilizer and compound phosphate fertilizer make up less than 1 per cent of the total phosphate fertilizer output. The industry is therefore failing to meet the requirements of its consumers.

The energy consumption required to manufacture different chemical fertilizers also varies greatly. The production of one tonne of standard nitrogenous fertilizer requires 820 kilograms of standard coal; only 290 kilograms are required to produce the same amount of standard calcium magnesium phosphate. The emphasis on nitrogenous fertilizer production therefore increases the energy requirements of the country's chemical fertilizer industry. In addition, some nitrogenous fertilizer products are difficult to preserve and transport.

A further problem in the industry is that, at present, natural gas can meet the needs of only 70–90 per cent of nitrogenous fertilizer production. Naphtha is expensive and in short supply. Coke and anthracite can supply only 80 per cent of the amount needed and are usually of low quality. The supply of these raw materials to small chemical fertilizer plants, whose output constitutes a large part of the country's total output, is unstable. In many cases, they can obtain only crushed coal and coal powder, creating production difficulties and raising energy consumption. The supply of oil is also inadequate.

The supplies of phosphate and sulphur ores are also in short supply as raw material for the phosphate fertilizer industry. The cost of transporting phosphate ore reserves from the south, where they are concentrated, to the north and north-east is 2–2.5 times the cost of the ore itself. Transport capacity in the south is also limited. Even when there are adequate transport facilities, the ore is often of a low grade, which makes long-distance transportation unsuitable. And despite the great number of small phosphate mines, their output is limited and unstable. In addition, the supply of raw materials for acid manufacture is also insufficient. Half of the country's troilite mines are small in scale.

The distribution of the chemical fertilizer industry also poses problems. Although small nitrogenous and phosphate fertilizer plants are distributed over the whole country, many lack raw materials, water and power supplies, and the necessary technology and managerial expertise. Production costs are high, the quality is inferior, and plants constantly suffer deficits.

If China's chemical fertilizer industry is to develop further, the structure of its products needs to be adjusted. The production of phosphate and potash fertilizers needs to be emphasized and additional phosphate and sulphur mines need to be built. If necessary, high-grade phosphate ore, sulphur, and phosphoric acid should be imported and the production of highly concentrated compound phosphate fertilizer emphasized. Areas which have adequate phosphate and water resources could build combined ore-fertilizer bases to produce high-grade phosphate fertilizers such as phosphoric acid and yellow phosphorus. In addition, the survey and exploitation of soluble sylvite resources, such as those at Qinghai Lake, could be accelerated.

The main way in which nitrogenous fertilizer production in China can be increased is by tapping the potential of the existing plants. Small plants need to be reformed in the light of local conditions such as raw materials availability, transport facilities, and water and power supplies. In this way, small, scattered resources can be better utilized to achieve higher economic efficiency. The stable supply of oil to large plants with advanced equipment and technology would ensure that their potential is fully utilized. Medium-sized plants using coal and coke also need to be expanded, with associated anthracite bases.

Organic Chemicals

China is rich in raw materials for the organic chemical industry, particularly the petrochemical industry. Before 1965, key projects were located in Jilin, Taiyuan, and Lanzhou; a few bases were also located in Shanghai, Nanjing, and Dalian. The main product was calcium carbide, produced from coal and coke, which was then used to manufacture synthetic organic products. The rapid growth of the oil industry in China since 1965 has led to oil and gas becoming the main raw materials for the organic chemical industry. Groups of petrochemical industrial bases have been established and some existing plants using coal have been renovated and new petrochemical equipment installed. Today, organic chemical plants, and especially petrochemical plants, constitute the main part of China's chemical industry.

The basic raw material of the coal chemical industry is calcium carbide. Made from coal, its production consumes large quantities of power. Because China's coal and water resources are widely distributed, the production of calcium carbide is also scattered over the country. Twenty provinces and regions have a considerable output, although the individual enterprises are small in scale. In 1980, Jilin, Hebei, and Jiangsu each produced between 7 and 10 per cent of the country's total output; Liaoning, Beijing, Shanxi, Zhejiang, Shanghai, Fujian, Shandong, Hunan, Henan, Sichuan, Anhui, and Tianjin each produced between 3 and 5 per cent; and Guizhou, Jiangxi, Heilongjiang, Guangdong, and Gansu each produced 2 per cent. The large producers are concentrated in the north, where their development has been linked with the exploitation of coal. In the south, production is associated with the development of water and energy resources.

The basic raw material of the petrochemical industry is ethylene. To a large extent, the level of production of ethylene indicates the level of development of a country's petrochemical industry. In China, ethylene (unlike calcium carbide) is highly concentrated in its distribution and its factories are much larger than those producing calcium carbide. Beijing and Shanghai account for most of the country's total output of ethylene, followed by Gansu, Liaoning, Jiangsu, Tianjin, and Jilin.

Products of the organic chemical industry include plastics, synthetic rubber, and synthetic fibre. Their production is distributed for the most part close to large oilfields or oil refineries (Fig. 10.3).

Shanghai has a fairly complete organic chemical industrial system. From basic organic chemical raw materials, it produces plastics, synthetic rubber, and synthetic fibre. Its production of petroleum benzine and synthetic fibre rank first in China, ethylene and plastics production rank second, and synthetic rubber ranks third. The output of calcium carbide is also large.

The Yanshan General Petrochemical Works in Beijing is China's largest oil refinery, producing 300,000 tonnes of ethylene a year in addition to by-products. Beijing's output of ethylene, plastics, and synthetic rubber rank first in the country, its output of purified petroleum benzine ranks second, synthetic fibre ranks third, and calcium carbide ranks fifth.

Jilin province has rich brown coal and limestone reserves as well as abundant water and energy resources. It is a base of both the coal and oil chemical industries, producing calcium carbide, purified petroleum benzine, ethylene, plastics, and dyestuffs. Its output of calcium carbide and of some dyestuffs is the largest in the country.

Lanzhou was China's first oil refinery base established after 1949 and the country's first petrochemical industrial centre. Its synthetic rubber plant, petrochemical works, chemical fibre plant, organic chemical plant, and chemical fertilizer plant are all of a considerable size. It is now a main producer of rubber, plastics, and synthetic fibre.

Other main petrochemical bases in China are Nanjing, where a large

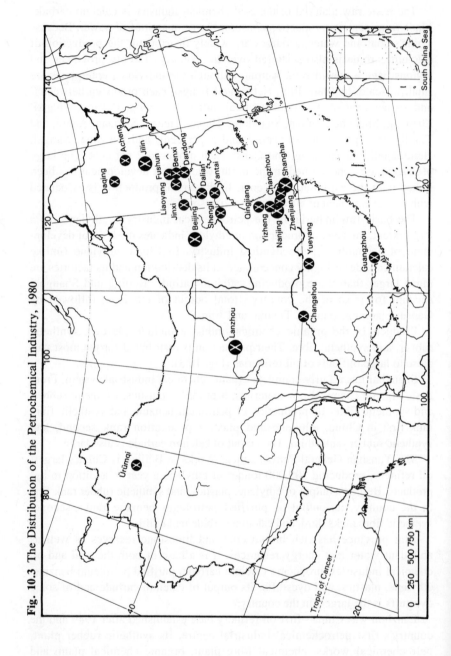

Fig. 10.3 The Distribution of the Petrochemical Industry, 1980

petrochemical base producing mainly synthetic fibre is under construction, Taiyuan, and southern Liaoning province. The production capacity of southern Liaoning's eight refineries accounts for one-third of the country's total capacity. The renovation and upgrading of its equipment and the comprehensive use of raw materials will enable southern Liaoning to increase substantially its output of chemical industrial products.

With the exception of Taiyuan, these main chemical industrial bases are of the petrochemical type. Also of importance as bases of the petrochemical industry are Tianjin, Liaoyang, Changshou, Yueyang, and Yantai, as well as Daqing, Zibo, and Yizheng which are under construction.

11. The Textile Industry

Development

The textile industry in China has a firm foundation. In 1949, its output value constituted 36.9 per cent of the gross national industrial output value. However, the low level of economic and technical development in China limited the productive power of the industry, which was at the time the largest industrial sector. Heavy industry was unable to provide adequate machinery and agriculture was unable to supply the necessary raw materials, most of which had to be imported. The cotton textile industry was the mainstay of the textile industry; wool, linen, silk, and knitted garments accounted for a very small proportion of the total output. The industry was also highly concentrated in a few coastal cities.

Since 1949, the textile industry in China has achieved a considerable increase in production capacity and output (Table 11.1). China now leads the world in annual output of cotton yarn and grey cloth as well as in the export of grey cloth and raw silk. The gross national output value of the industry

Table 11.1 Production Capacity and Output of the Textile Industry, 1949–80

Sector	Multiple of 1980 over 1949
Cotton textile industry	
Spindles	3.56
Weaving machines	4.24
Annual output of cotton yarn	9.05
Annual output of cotton cloth	7.13
Wool textile industry	
Spindles	7.62
Output of wool yarn	31.60
Output of wool products	18.20
Bast-fibre textile industry	
Spindles	6.00
Weaving machines	8.40
Output of gunny bags	44.50
Output of flax and ramie cloth	0–40 m. metres
Silk textile industry	
Filature machinery	10.00
Output of silk	22.70
Output of silk products	14.10

Source: Calculated on the basis of data from *China's Economic Yearbook, 1981* (*Economic Management*, 1981).

comprises 14 per cent of the total national industrial output value, second only to the machine-building industry.

The structure of the industry has also changed since 1949. Simultaneously with the overall development of the industry, wool, linen, and silk production have developed at a faster rate than the cotton textile industry. The proportion of the cotton textile industry in the total textile industry output value has dropped from 78 per cent in 1952 to 61 per cent in 1980. Knitted goods, wool, and silk now constitute a much higher proportion of the total output value than in 1952; only the linen textile industry has declined. This change in the structure of the industry has made possible the better utilization of raw materials and the production of a greater variety of goods.

China is now also basically self-sufficient in terms of raw materials and equipment. Textile machinery manufacture has been developed on a large scale. Its present annual production capacity of 160,000 tonnes of various kinds of textile machinery supplies 1,200 types of complete sets of equipment to 13 branches of the industry, including the weaving, dyeing, and synthetic fibre industries. Some equipment, such as spindles, is also exported.

Raw materials production, both agricultural and industrial, has increased significantly, including the production of natural fibres (especially cotton) (Table 11.2) and synthetic fibres. At present, 25 provinces, autonomous regions, and municipalities produce synthetic fibre, 13 of which have an annual output capacity of more than 10,000 tonnes. In 1980, the output of chemical fibre was 450,000 tonnes (314,000 tonnes of which was synthetic fibre), accounting for 7 per cent of the gross textile industrial output value.

Table 11.2 Natural Fibre Production, 1949–80

Category	1949	1980	Multiple of 1980 over 1949
Cotton	44.40	270.7	6.10
Sheep wool	2.66	17.6	6.62
Mulberry cocoons	—	—	—
Tussah cocoons	8.60	32.6	3.79
Jute and ramie	7.37	109.8	14.90

Source: Calculated on the basis of data from *China's Agricultural Yearbook, 1980* (Agriculture Publishing House, Beijing, 1981).

The development of textile machinery and the production of chemical fibres have played important roles in the development of China's textile industry. In addition to contributing to its modernization and improved production and technical levels, it has helped to create the conditions for an increase in the variety of textile goods and in the proportion of higher quality products. It has also made available new sources of raw materials, enabling local textile industries to develop in accordance with local conditions and to use locally available raw materials.

Since 1949, the regional distribution of the industry has become more balanced, with a relatively even spread of textile enterprises over the whole country. In 1949, the coastal cities accounted for a large proportion of the total productivity of the industry. The proportion of the industry in the hinterland and border regions was very small. Textile production was seriously divorced from the raw material-producing areas, resulting in transportation problems of both raw materials and finished products. In the cotton textile industry, for example, Shanghai and Jiangsu had to import large quantities of cotton to meet the capacity of its enterprises. On the other hand, the main cotton-producing areas in the hinterland, which lacked the necessary textile processing capacity, transported large quantities of commodity cotton to other parts of the country. The long distances and poor transport facilities made such transportation difficult, resulting in high raw material costs and expensive products which then needed to be transported to consumer areas in the hinterland.

Since 1949, the existing enterprises in the coastal centres have been updated and new textile production bases have been established in the raw material-producing areas in the hinterland. At the same time as conditions in the coastal production bases were improved and their productivity was raised, the output of raw materials in adjacent areas has been increased, chemical fibres have been developed, and conditions for the supply of raw materials have been improved. In the raw material-producing areas, such as Beijing, Shijiazhuang, Handan, Zhengzhou, Xi'an, Xianyang, and Wuhan, large cotton textile bases have been built. Wool textile enterprises have been established in the wool-producing areas of Inner Mongolia and the north-west, and silk textile bases have been established in the silk cocoon-producing areas of Jiangsu, Zhejiang, Guangdong, Sichuan, and Liaoning. Redistribution of the industry has also been effected through the establishment of small and medium-sized textile bases to take advantage of local characteristics and various raw materials.

Today, China has 4,500 textile enterprises distributed over the whole country. Co-operation and co-ordination between the raw material-producing areas, textile production areas, and consumer areas have also improved, resulting in reduced transportation of raw materials and of semi-finished and finished products.

The Cotton Textile Industry

The cotton textile industry has received the largest investment of all the textile industry sectors. As a result, it has the largest scale of all the sectors. Since 1949, the old bases and enterprises in Tianjin, Qingdao, and Shanghai have been renovated and updated. These cities have a strong textile industrial work-force and high technical and managerial levels. They are also highly co-ordinated, with integrated systems of production and efficient transport facilities. However, insufficient supplies of raw materials and backward equipment and technology in the past resulted in intensive labour and low productivity. Production was also unbalanced.

Since 1949, new processing technology has been gradually adopted and the structure of production has been adjusted so that the proportion of fine yarn, combed yarn, high-quality products, and goods for export has increased to meet the requirements of the domestic and international markets. The structure of raw materials has also been adjusted with the development of chemical fibre and polyester-cotton textile products. The effect has been not only to expand the sources of raw materials but also to increase the variety of products and their output value.

The renovation of existing enterprises requires only a small investment for a high economic return. In Shanghai, for example, increased productivity resulted in a 1.84-fold increase in the output of cotton yarn and a 1.52-fold increase in the output of cotton cloth between 1949 and 1980.

A further development in the cotton textile industry since 1949 has been the establishment of enterprises in the major cotton-producing areas, such as the North China Plain and the basin of the Wei river. High-quality cotton is produced in these areas at a high commodity rate. They are densely populated areas, providing a large market and an ample labour supply. In addition, their developed transport facilities, abundant power resources, and climate favour the development of cotton textile bases. A series of associated enterprises has also been established to support the textile industry, including textile machinery plants, thermal power stations, processing factories, and enterprises producing high-quality finished goods. The six large cotton textile bases established at Beijing, Shijiazhuang, Handan, Zhengzhou, Xi'an, and Xianyang in these areas have become the backbone of the country's cotton textile industry.

A number of smaller textile bases have been established also in populous provinces which have abundant raw materials. In most cases, one or two large or medium-sized factories form the backbone of the cotton textile industry in such bases, supported by smaller spinning, weaving, and dyeing enterprises. Other new bases are located in provinces and regions which have favourable conditions for growing cotton or which are deficient in cotton supplies. In some heavy industrial cities, particularly mining cities, cotton textile factories have also been built to improve and upgrade the industrial structure.

The development of the cotton textile industry since 1949 has resulted in the distribution of modern enterprises over the whole country (with the exception of Tibet), many of which are large enterprises (Fig. 11.1).

The Wool, Linen, and Silk Textile Industry

The production of natural fibres is widely distributed in China, although production of the various kinds of natural fibres is relatively concentrated. Cotton-producing areas are distributed mainly along the middle and lower reaches of the Chang Jiang and in the plain along the middle and lower reaches of the Huang He. Wool is produced mainly in Inner Mongolia, north-west China, Tibet, the northern part of north-east China, northern Shanxi and Hebei, and north-western Sichuan. Various kinds of natural fibre are grown for linen. Jute and ramie are grown mainly in the basin of the Chang Jiang and in the coastal areas in the south-east. Flax production is concentrated in

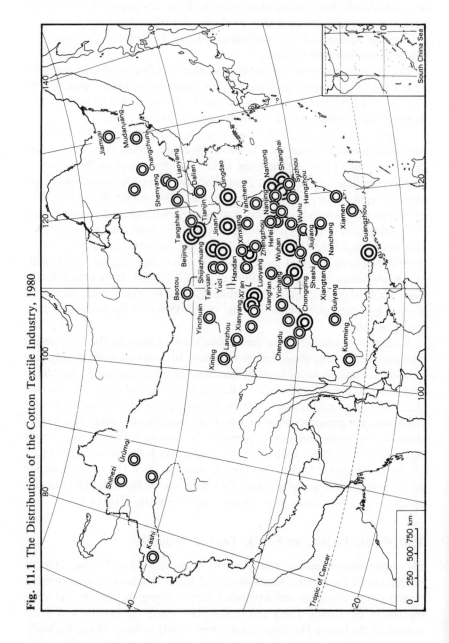

Fig. 11.1 The Distribution of the Cotton Textile Industry, 1980

Heilongjiang and Jilin. The main silk-producing areas are Sichuan, Zhejiang, Jiangsu, and Guangdong. Liaoning, Shandong, and Henan produce tussah.

Despite the favourable conditions in various provinces and regions for development of the different textile industries, in many cases their potential has been under-exploited. This was particularly the case in the past, when the textile industry was concentrated in a few coastal cities and the hinterland areas lacked the capability to process the wool, jute, flax, and ramie fibre they produced. Furthermore, poor transport facilities made shipping costly. At the same time, the coastal industries needed to import large quantities of raw materials, including wool and jute fibre. The redistribution of the wool, linen, and silk textile industries since 1949 has to a large extent remedied these irrational situations (Fig. 11.2).

Wool

The production capacity of the existing wool textile centres in Shanghai, Tianjin, Shenyang, Changzhou, Nanjing, Wuxi, Jiaxing, and Suzhou has been expanded since 1949 through renovation, expansion, and the addition of new products. A number of large and medium-sized mills have also been built in the main consumer areas such as Beijing, Baoding, Zhangjiakou, Fushun, Dandong, Qingdao, Jining, and Bengbu. Shanghai remains the largest wool textile centre. In 1980, its output of woollen fabrics exceeded 30 million metres (30 per cent of the total national output). The wool textile production capacity of Beijing and Jiangsu has increased considerably. In 1980, they ranked second and third respectively after Shanghai in terms of output.

In addition to the expansion of the existing bases, a number of new textile centres have been established in northern north-east China in Heilongjiang and Jilin provinces and in Inner Mongolia, Tibet, and five provinces in the north-west. By 1980, the number of provinces and municipalities with wool textile industries was 25, compared with 11 in 1949.

Bast-fibre

The bast-fibre textile industry was concentrated prior to 1949 in the coastal cities of Shanghai, Shenyang, Dalian, Qingdao, Wuxi, Liaoyang, and Tianjin. Since 1949, the development of the jute textile industry in the Chang Jiang basin and areas south of it — China's main jute-growing areas — has been emphasized. Jute mills have been built and equipment has been relocated from mills in Shanghai and Shenyang. China's largest comprehensive jute textile production base is now Hangzhou. The main product of the industry is gunny bags.

Before 1949, the ramie industry was concentrated in Shanghai and Guangdong province. Only small quantities of ramie cloth and yarn were produced. Since 1949, mills have been built in the ramie-growing areas south of the Chang Jiang, the largest mill being that at Yiyang. Hunan province has the largest production power, with 45 per cent of the country's spindles and 58 per cent of its weaving machines.

The flax textile industry developed in China only after 1949. Heilongjiang province is the largest flax-growing area for industrial purposes, as well as the

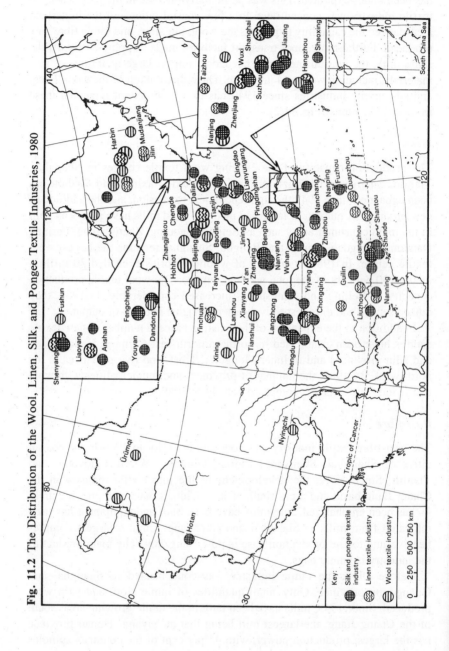

Fig. 11.2 The Distribution of the Wool, Linen, Silk, and Pongee Textile Industries, 1980

largest flax textile industrial base in the country. In 1980, it accounted for over 90 per cent of the country's total sown area and output as well as 80 per cent of the total number of flax spindles. Its main products are fine cloth, canvas, and fire hoses.

Silk and Pongee

Since 1949, three major silk fabric-producing bases in the Chang Jiang delta, Sichuan basin, and Zhu Jiang delta have been restored and developed as part of the decentralization of the filature industry and the relative concentration of silk weaving and dyeing. Printing and dyeing have now become more closely integrated with production.

China's largest silk fabric-producing areas — Shanghai, Jiangsu, and Zhejiang — account for nearly half of the national output of silk and about 40 per cent of its silk products. Zhejiang ranks first in the country in output. The Sichuan basin ranks first in the country in the output of silk cocoons, producing 20 per cent of the total raw silk output. Its silk fabric textile industry is still undeveloped, however, accounting for less than 5 per cent of the country's total output. The filature industry is widespread, covering more than 10 cocoon-producing counties and prefectures in Sichuan. Silk fabric production is centred in Chengdu, Chongqing, Mianyang, Nanchong, Suining, and Langzhong.

In the Zhu Jiang delta, Shunde and Zhongshan are the main filature centres and silk textile production is centred in Foshan and Guangzhou. A number of silk textile enterprises have also been renovated, expanded, or established in other silk cocoon-producing areas, some of which are recently developed, in Shaanxi, Xinjiang, Hubei, Jiangxi, Hunan, Guangxi, Anhui, Fujian, Hebei, and Shanxi provinces, and in Beijing.

The tussah silk textile industry is distributed mainly on the Liaodong and Shandong peninsulas and in south-west Henan. Liaoning province accounts for about 10 per cent of China's total raw silk output. It is second to the Shanghai–Zhejiang–Jiangsu area in output of silk fabric. Approximately 70 per cent of the output of tussah silk fabric is concentrated in the tussah cocoon-producing areas of Dandong, Fengcheng, Gaiping, Youyan, Zhuanghe, Anshan, Benxi, and Haicheng. Dandong and Fencheng are the country's largest integrated tussah silk fabric-producing bases. The third largest silk-producing area — the Shandong peninsula — ranks second in China in the production of tussah silk. Production is centred in Yantai, Qingdao, and Zibo. South-western Henan province is the third largest tussah silk-producing area, with bases in Zhenping, Lushan, Nanyang, and Pingdingshan. The proportion of filature machines in the hinterland areas has increased from 16 per cent in 1949 to around 33 per cent today.

China is one of the main wool and flax-producing areas in the world. Most of the wool and flax is produced in the ethnic minority areas where little or no cotton is produced. The economic growth of these regions is dependent to a large degree on the utilization of local natural resources to develop the wool and linen textile trade. Silk cocoons, flax, and ramie fibre are produced mainly in the populous parts of China where textile products are in great demand.

It is also important, therefore, to utilize the raw materials in these areas to develop the silk, flax, and ramie textile industries. Their development will contribute to the exploitation of new sources of raw materials, increased productivity of the textile industry, and a greater variety of products. The development of the various kinds of textile trades based on local conditions is an integral part of the redistribution of the textile industry and the renovation of its structure.

The Future of the Textile Industry

The rapid development of the textile industry in China since 1949 has played a large part in the growth of the national economy and in the increase in the standard of living. Compared to some other industrial sectors, the textile industry consumes less energy, employs a larger labour force, produces more profits and taxable incomes supplies greater quantities of consumer goods, and earns more foreign exchange. However, the low rate of growth of the industry compared with the development of the national economy and the daily life requirements of the population creates problems of future development and regional distribution of the textile industry.

Between 1953 and 1979, the average annual rate of growth of the textile industry was 7 per cent, compared with 11.1 per cent for the gross industrial output value, 13.4 per cent for heavy industry, and 9.1 per cent for light industry. The rate of growth of industrial and agricultural output value was 17 per cent higher than that of the textile industry, and, during the 4th FYP period, the annual rate of growth of the industry was only 4.2 per cent, a little higher than that of agriculture. The output of cotton yarn and cloth, which ranked first within the industry, developed at a slower rate than the industry as a whole. During the 4th FYP period, its output value increased by only 1 per cent.

As a result of the dramatic population increase during this period, the per-capita volume of cotton cloth between 1952 and 1979 increased from 6.7 metres to only 12.5 metres. Although the output of knitted goods, woollen yarn fabrics, and silk increased rapidly, their absolute volume and per-capita volume were very low. The average world per-capita consumption volume of cloth fibre is 6.8 kilograms compared to only 2.9 kilograms in China. The problem of shortages of cloth remains serious in China.

However, conditions in China are favourable for the further development of the textile industry. There is a large labour supply, wages are low, the potential exists to develop textile raw materials, and there is an enormous domestic market. In addition, conditions in the export trade are favourable and the industry has a developed textile machinery manufacturing foundation. Nevertheless, the proportion of investment in the industry needs to be increased. Between 1958 and 1978, the total investment in the textile industry comprised only 4.3 per cent of the gross industrial investment. This was a 30 per cent decrease in investment compared with the period of the 1st FYP. Furthermore, the investment was used mainly to produce chemical fibres; the proportion of investment in textile processing accounted for only 1.8 per cent (a 70 per cent decrease over the 1st FYP period). As a result of the decreased investment in textile processing, productivity of the industry is generally low.

In addition to increased investment in the industry, the commodity structure needs to be improved to better utilize natural resources and intensify processing. The wool, linen, and silk textile industries have always occupied a very small proportion of China's textile industrial structure. Although their supply of raw materials is more assured than in the cotton textile industry, their production capacity is low.

China produces more than 40 per cent of the world's goat wool, more than 90 per cent of its rabbit hair, and 25 per cent of its camel wool, most of which products are exported in the form of raw materials. Also, high-quality raw materials are often used as low-quality raw materials. For example, more than 90 per cent of flax and ramie is used in the production of gunny bags. The output of fine linen cloth is limited, requiring the import of certain quantities each year. However, large quantities of linen raw material are exported. The silk fabrics textile trade is a traditional industrial sector but, due to the low processing capacity of the industry following the printing and dyeing processes, large quantities of raw silk and grey silk cloth are exported. In the cotton textile industry, the production of cotton-chemical fibre cloth and broad-width cloth is low and a large proportion of exported cloth is grey and narrow-width. This irrational commodity structure wastes natural resources, reduces the variety of products, and reduces foreign exchange earnings.

Further adjustments are also required in the distribution of production within the industry and in the quality of manufactured goods. Five large national commodity cotton bases are to be built to guarantee the supply of raw materials for existing cotton textile bases in Shanghai, Beijing, Tianjin, Hebei, Shandong, Henan, Jiangsu, Zhejiang, Hubei, and Anhui. In addition, regional commodity cotton-producing bases will be built to supply the needs of local cotton textile enterprises. Elsewhere, the cultivation of cotton needs to be concentrated in suitable areas if its output is to be raised.

Although the industry is, for the most part, distributed rationally, textile enterprises in some provinces and regions are scattered, causing problems in co-ordination, production, and unified management, with consequent unsatisfactory economic results. For example, woollen mills in northern Xinjiang and cotton mills in southern Xinjiang are located 500 kilometres apart. As a result, knitting factories are also scattered and difficulties have arisen in the supply of yarn used for knitting and processing products.

The future development of the textile industry in China will be dependent upon better co-ordination of production and the supply of raw materials as well as specialization and co-operation based on local conditions.

Regional Variations in Production

Although the textile industry is distributed over the whole of China, considerable regional variations have resulted from differences in historical development, population, resources, and transport facilities. Shanghai and Jiangsu together account for over one-third of the national gross output value of the industry, producing large quantities of textile goods for the domestic and overseas markets. Tianjin and Beijing, accounting for between 3 and 10 per cent of the national output value each, also supply textile goods to other parts of China. Other main textile centres, including Shandong, Liaoning, Hubei, Hebei, Henan, Sichuan, and Shaanxi provinces, are basically self-sufficient. The remaining provinces and regions each account for less than 3 per cent of the national output value of the industry. The different levels of development of China's provinces and regions is also reflected in their textile equipment capacity and in their output of the main textile products (Table 11.3).

Table 11.3 A Comparison of the Production Capacity and Product Output of Provinces, Municipalities, and Regions, 1981

Name	Cotton Spindles (10,000)	Wool Spindles (10,000)	Printing and Dyeing (100 million metres)	Chemical Fibres (10,000 tonnes)
Shanghai	220.19	13.94	13.10	14.77
Beijing	39.43	6.11	2.20	4.00
Tianjin	69.99	4.15	4.30	3.34
Jiangsu	241.23	10.65	10.20	4.55
Liaoning	105.65	4.76	3.40	10.37
Shandong	135.17	3.65	5.50	0.80
Henan	122.16	2.39	5.30	1.42
Hebei	125.50	1.91	5.30	1.39
Hubei	155.10	2.09	7.20	0.94
Sichuan	75.52	1.06	3.10	4.90
Shaanxi	92.26	1.67	3.80	0.30
Other provinces and regions	511.36	21.30	21.15	
Total	1,893.56	73.68	84.55	63.30
% accounted for by Beijing, Tianjin, and Shanghai	17.40	32.80	23.30	34.90
% accounted for by the eight provinces	55.60	38.20	51.80	39.00
% accounted for by other provinces and regions	27.00	29.00	24.90	26.10

Source: Correspondence on Technical Economy and the Modernization of Management, 25 June 1982.

A second area of difference within the industry is the structure of production. The main sector in most provinces, regions, and municipalities is the cotton textile industry; the proportion of production of the linen textile industry is very small. However, within this basic framework, other striking differences are apparent. Shanghai, Jiangsu, Beijing, Tianjin, and Liaoning, while dominated by the cotton textile industry, have developed textile industrial systems that embrace a variety of trades and produce a wide range of products. With the exception of Beijing's output of silk products and Liaoning's output of cotton cloth, these provinces and municipalities have a per-capita output of the main textile goods far in excess of the national average and they supply large quantities of goods for the domestic market. Other parts of China where the cotton textile industry is predominant have only a low level of development of other textile industrial sectors. For example, the cotton textile industry is predominant in Yunnan, Shaanxi, Henan, Hunan, Anhui, Jiangxi, Shandong, Hebei, Shanxi, and Guizhou. However, with the exception of Shaanxi, Hubei, Shandong, Hebei, and Shanxi, the per-capita volume of cotton cloth in these areas is lower than the national average level. Similarly, with the exception of Shaanxi which produces close to the national average per-capita volume of woollen fabric, these areas are much lower in per-capita volume output of other kinds of textile goods.

By comparison, in Guangxi, Zhejiang, Inner Mongolia, Tibet, Jilin, and Heilongjiang, the cotton textile industry constitutes only a small proportion of the industry; wool, silk, or linen production predominates. The wool textile industry in Gansu, Qinghai, Ningxia, Inner Mongolia, and Tibet exceeds the cotton textile industry in terms of output by a large margin. Although the cotton textile industry in Xinjiang comprises more than half the total output of the textile industry, the proportion of the woollen textile industry is also very high. The per-capita output of woollen textile goods is also far in excess of the national average in Gansu, Qinghai, Inner Mongolia, and Tibet. Ningxia, Guangxi, Zhejiang, Fujian, Heilongjiang, and Jilin have a higher than average proportion of linen textile industry, and the silk textile industry accounts for a very large proportion of the industry in Zhejiang, Guangdong, Sichuan, and Guangxi.

The balance between processing capacity of the industry and the production of raw materials also varies within China. For example, the production of raw materials for the silk, ramie, and flax textile industries basically accords with the processing capacity of the raw material-producing areas. However, raw materials for the cotton and woollen textile industries need to be transported between provinces. Some 22 provinces, regions, and municipalities have insufficient supplies of cotton for their textile industries. Shandong, Henan, and Xinjiang have the largest quantities of surplus cotton.

The textile processing capacity of areas that have abundant resources of raw materials for the textile industry needs to be expanded in conjunction with the continued supply of materials to deficient areas. Expansion of the industry by this means will more effectively utilize local advantages and increase economic returns. In addition, the commodity structure in areas that have a strong processing capacity but insufficient raw materials should be adjusted to increase the self-sufficiency rate of raw materials. The coastal textile bases with high technical levels, but which rely on imported raw materials, need to expand their export trade. Areas which have small processing capacity and insufficient raw materials could expand their processing capacity through the production of raw materials suited to local conditions.

12. Light Industry

THE main products of light industry are consumer goods. In 1949, the output value of the industry (excluding textiles and handicrafts) accounted for more than 40 per cent of China's total industrial output value. The standard of the industry was low, however, and the few varieties of products were poor in quality.

Development

Although the proportion of light industry in the total industrial output value declined after 1949, its absolute value, output, and the variety of products expanded considerably. Notwithstanding the doubling of the population, there was a marked increase in per-capita consumption and, by 1980, the output value of light industry per capita had risen 10-fold over 1952 figures. The consumption of sewing machines, wrist-watches, clocks, and bicycles increased 16-31-fold and, by 1980, one in 12 people owned a bicycle, one in 4.3 households had a sewing machine, and one in 7.5 people owned a wrist-watch.

The structure of light industry has also improved as production has developed. New sectors, such as machines and electrical equipment for civilian use and chemical products for daily use, have become increasingly important. In addition, the distribution of the industry has improved significantly since 1949.

Light industrial goods are manufactured in many varieties to cater for a wide range of needs. As such, they are susceptible to changes in market demand. Their production is also dependent upon the availability of a range of raw materials including agricultural and sideline products, metals, minerals, and industrial chemicals. In general, light industries that use agricultural and sideline products as raw materials need to be located close to the raw material-producing areas. The transportation of mineral raw materials is comparatively easier, although, again, there are economic advantages in locating light industrial enterprises close to the raw material-producing areas.

Light industry requires a relatively low level of technology, although products such as wrist-watches, domestic electrical appliances, sensitized raw materials, and synthetic detergents and fatty acids require rather higher levels. The distribution of such industries therefore needs to be comparatively concentrated. This is also true of certain handicraft enterprises requiring specific raw materials or traditional skills.

The overall distribution of light industry is determined by the distribution of raw materials, population, markets, transport and communications facilities, and technical conditions. The concentration of light industrial enterprises in the densely populated and agriculturally prosperous areas is therefore appropriate, combined with a more widespread distribution over the whole country. However, before 1949, light industry was concentrated in a few coastal cities, while in the hinterland and border areas and in farming and stock-breeding regions, there were only a few crude processing industries centred around local handicrafts. The effect of this type of distribution was to separate production from raw materials and also from consumers. Light industry in the coastal cities was lopsided in structure, with a surplus of productive capacity in some sectors and insufficient capacity in others.

Since 1949, a number of comprehensive light industrial bases have been established in the provincial and regional capitals and in the major zones. Shanghai, Tianjin, Beijing, and Guangzhou already had a relatively solid industrial foundation based on their large populations, technical development, and established transport facilities. New products requiring greater technical skill, such as electrical appliances, machinery for daily use, detergents, and plastic products have been developed since 1949, creating a relatively complete production system. In 1980, the output value of Shanghai's light industry was RMB32.9 billion (14 per cent of the national total). It produced 55.5 per cent of the national output of cameras, 30.18 per cent of its television sets, 29.5 per cent of its sewing machines, 28.9 per cent of its bicycles, 36.8 per cent of its wrist-watches, and 17.05 per cent of its detergents. Some 20,000 different articles are produced. Between 1956 and 1960, 144 of Shanghai's light industrial enterprises were moved to other parts of the country, including Jiangsu, Anhui, Zhejiang, Yunnan, Jilin, and Gansu, as part of the economic construction of those areas and the country as a whole.

In 1980, the output value of light industry in Tianjin was RMB10.3 billion (4.4 per cent of the national total). A large proportion of its products are manufactured for the markets of north-east, north, and north-west China.

Shanghai and Tianjin are the largest light industrial bases in China today. Despite their advantages, however, the supply of raw materials, especially agricultural and sideline raw materials, is often unstable. Energy and water supplies are also inadequate. Equipment in some enterprises is outdated, their productive capacity has been reached, and there are insufficient production sites and auxiliary installations. The rate of development of production in these areas has been seriously affected as a result. In addition, the structure of the industry needs to be adjusted, with emphasis placed on processing industries that use few raw materials, consume small amounts of energy, occupy small areas of land, and require high technical skills. Co-operation with other provinces and regions would also improve the productive capacity of these main light industrial bases.

In addition to the establishment of provincial and regional light industrial bases, specialized production has been expanded since 1949 in areas with concentrated raw materials. Light industry using agricultural products as raw materials is linked closely with the distribution of their production. This has enabled higher outputs, better quality, and lower costs to be achieved. For example, the transportation of raw materials such as sugar-cane, eggs, dairy products, and glass fibre would be expensive and would reduce the quality of the end-products. Such industries need to be as close as possible to the raw material-producing areas and their scope of production should be determined accordingly.

The production of 'famous-brand' products using traditional craftsmanship and of special products in the national minority areas has also expanded since

1949. Most such products require labour-intensive production and the consumption of energy and raw materials is relatively low. These goods have a high output value and established domestic and overseas markets. Although light industrial production of this kind is distributed over the whole country, the distribution of specific products or varieties of products is relatively concentrated (Fig. 12.1).

Prior to 1949, the production of articles specifically to meet the needs of the minority nationalities was concentrated in the coastal areas; in the minority nationality areas such as Tibet, Inner Mongolia, Qinghai, and Xinjiang, there were no such production enterprises. After 1949, factories and communes were established in these areas to produce locally required articles (Fig. 12.2). More than 60 kinds of articles are now produced in Tibet, 324 in Qinghai, and 150 in Inner Mongolia.

A further change in the distribution of light industrial production in China has been its spread to rural areas. The local processing of agricultural and sideline products reduces the quantity of goods requiring transportation, thereby reducing costs and spoilage. By-products are utilized locally. This local industry reduces its over-concentration in the cities and increases the prosperity of the rural economy. In addition, it provides a source of employment, thus reducing the migration of the rural population to urban areas.

Agricultural and sideline products processing has spread extensively to the rural raw material-producing areas since 1958. Most communes and brigades now have their own grain- and oil-processing factories which supply local needs, as well as industries producing such products as soya sauce, vinegar, wine, dried fruits, and beverages. Some goods, such as preserved meats, eggs, and vermicelli, are also supplied to the urban areas and exported overseas.

The spread of light industry since 1949 in these various ways has had a significant effect on China's economic development. Although large enterprises have a considerable productive capacity, with higher technical and managerial levels, better product quality, and lower raw materials consumption than small enterprises, their distribution in the rural areas would result in low product quality because of lower technical and managerial levels. The situation might also exist that raw materials may be in short supply so that equipment cannot be fully utilized, thus negating their economic and technical advantages.

The concentration of light industries in the large cities and along the coastal areas has been reduced since 1949. In Shanghai, Jiangsu, Guangdong, Shandong, Liaoning, Tianjin, and Beijing, light industry has been transformed on a relatively large scale and productive capacity has increased accordingly. Although the absolute output value of light industry has increased in these areas, its proportion of the national total has decreased. Relatively faster progress has been achieved in Zhejiang, Hebei, Fujian, and Guangxi provinces, where the level of development in the past was lower than in the main centres. In addition, light industrial bases of considerable scope have been established as a result of the construction of key projects in Sichuan, Henan, Hubei, Hunan, Heilongjiang, and Jilin. Modern light industrial enterprises have also been established in Gansu, Qinghai, Ningxia, Xinjiang, inner Mongolia, Yunnan, and Guizhou.

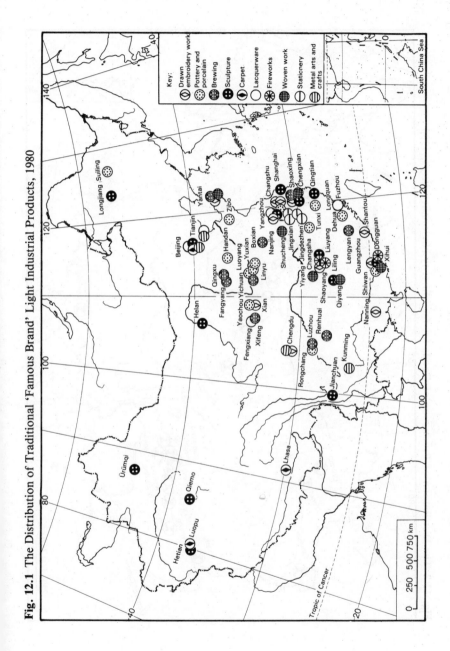

Fig. 12.1 The Distribution of Traditional 'Famous Brand' Light Industrial Products, 1980

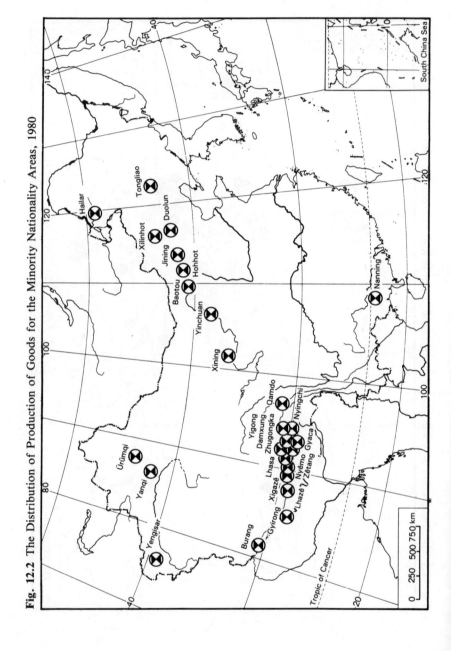

Fig. 12.2 The Distribution of Production of Goods for the Minority Nationality Areas, 1980

By 1980, the output value of light industry in Shanghai accounted for only 14 per cent of the national total, despite its being the most concentrated area of light industry in the country. Jiangsu, Guangdong, Shandong, and Liaoning provinces each accounted for between 6 and 9 per cent of the national total. With the exception of Tibet, Gansu, Ningxia, Qinghai, Xinjiang, and Guizhou, where the output value was below 1 per cent each of the total, most of the other light industrial bases scattered throughout the country accounted for between 2 and 4 per cent of the total. Such figures indicate that the differences in the level of development between the various parts of China have narrowed and that the number of light industrial bases has expanded. The widespread production of light industrial goods also indicates a greater degree of self-sufficiency as well as a degree of specialization based on local raw materials and conditions (Table 12.1).

The Food Industry

The food industry is the most important sector of China's light industry. In 1980, its output value accounted for around 25 per cent of the total output value of light industry (including textiles). The industry consists of grain and oil processing, the manufacture of cigarettes, sugar, wines, salt, canned foods, dairy products, and the processing of meat and aquatic products.

Many modern enterprises are distributed throughout the country, including the rural, mountainous, and stock-breeding areas. The highest output value is in Sichuan, Shandong, Jiangsu, and Guangdong provinces, followed by Henan, Zhejiang, Liaoning, Shanghai, Heilongjiang, Anhui, Hunan, and Hubei. Even in the more backward areas, such as Shaanxi, Inner Mongolia, Shanxi, Guizhou, and Xinjiang, the food industry is reasonably well established. The differences in the level of development of the industry in the various parts of China are therefore relatively small. Also, the industry is most prosperous and well integrated with raw materials supply and consumer markets in the densely populated areas with relatively developed agricultural production.

The structure of the industry in various parts of the country is relatively diversified. Grain and oil processing, which is closely related to daily life requirements, accounts for a large proportion (over 33 per cent) of production in most provinces and regions. Meat processing and cigarette and wine making have also developed significantly, as have sugar refining, salt making, and canned food and aquatic products processing. In most provinces and regions, there is a relatively complete system of food industries.

The joint production of more than one product (for example, sugar, paper, artificial fibres, and alcohol) has also developed in many parts of the country. This is particularly evident where raw materials supply is seasonally determined. Raw materials and equipment are more fully utilized as a result and the variety of products is increased.

Coupled with the widespread development of the food industry in the country as a whole, special products have been developed to exploit specific conditions. This has resulted in a certain degree of regional division of labour. For example, dairy production is well developed in the north-west, Hei-

Table 12.1 The Relative Importance of the Main Light Industrial Bases, 1980

Province, Municipality, or Autonomous Region	Main Products and their Rank in the Country (indicated in parentheses)
Beijing	washing machines (1), family refrigerators (1), tape recorders (2), television sets (3)
Tianjin	fatty acid for soap-making (2), bicycles (2), detergent (2), wrist-watches (3), salt (4)
Hebei	salt (1)
Inner Mongolia	sugar (2)
Liaoning	fatty acid for soap-making (1), machine-made paper (1), washing machines (2), plastic articles (3), salt (3)
Jilin	machine-made paper (2), newsprint (1)
Heilongjiang	beet sugar (1), dairy products
Shanghai	cameras (1), tape recorders (1), wrist-watches (1), television sets (1), sewing machines (1), bicycles (1), detergent (1), soap (1), bulbs (1), enamel articles for daily use (1), plastic articles (1), radios (2), dry batteries (2), fatty acid for soap-making (3), electric fans (3)
Jiangsu	radios (1), electric fans (1), leather making (1), leather shoes (1), television sets (2), wrist-watches (2), vegetable oil (3), family enamelware (3)
Zhejiang	tinned foods (1), beverages (3), leather making (3)
Anhui	cigarettes (3)
Fujian	tinned foods (2), newsprint (3)
Jiangxi	family enamelware (3)
Shandong	beverages (1), vegetable oils (1), leather making (1), leather shoes (2), cigarettes (2), salt (2)
Henan	cigarettes (1)
Hubei	family enamelware (2), detergent (3)
Hunan	family enamelware (2)
Guangdong	cane sugar (1), dry batteries (1), family enamelware (1), newsprint (2), sewing machines (2), electric fans (2), plastic articles (2)
Guangxi	cane sugar (2), tinned foods (4)
Sichuan	well salt (1), beverages (2), vegetable oil (2), tinned foods (3)
Shaanxi	dairy products (4), sewing machines (4)

longjiang, and Inner Mongolia; cane sugar production is based in Guangdong, Guangxi, Fujian, and Sichuan; and canned food production is based in Shanghai, Zhejiang, and Guangxi. Such specialized production in these areas accounts for a large proportion of the national total output of the products and a large proportion of the food industry structure on a regional level.

Sugar Refining

The raw materials required for the sugar-refining industry greatly exceed the weight of the finished product. Some 8–10 tonnes of sugar-cane or 7–10 tonnes of sugar-beet are required to produce one tonne of granulated sugar. Moreover, the raw materials easily spoil, requiring refineries to be located close to the raw material-producing areas.

The cost of raw materials in sugar refining accounts for 70–80 per cent of the total production cost. If transport costs are increased and the product quality is lowered through the need to transport raw materials some distance to refineries, production costs rise sharply. The sugar-refining industry is therefore raw materials-oriented. Sugar-cane is produced mainly in the south and sugar-beet in the northern parts of the country. The production of raw materials for the sugar-refining industry is therefore highly regional and the range of its geographical distribution limited. Even within the raw material-producing areas, sugar content varies, thus further restricting the distribution of the industry. The degree of concentration of the sugar-refining industry in certain areas is therefore much higher than in other sectors of the food industry.

Since 1949, the industry has developed simultaneously in the south and the north (Fig. 12.3). New refineries have also been established with the aim of opening up new areas of raw materials. In addition, there has been a considerable increase in the number of machine-operated refineries and their output. Between 1949 and 1980, the number of such refineries increased from 3 (producing 30,000 tonnes annually) to 400 (producing 3.2 million tonnes of sugar). The original main sugar-cane-producing areas — Guangdong, Guangxi, Fujian, and Sichuan — and the major beet-growing areas have become the country's strongest sugar production bases. In 1980, the output of sugar-cane in these main bases accounted for 84 per cent of the national total output of cane sugar or 65 per cent of the country's total sugar output. The output of beet-sugar in Heilongjiang accounted for 40 per cent of the national total beet-sugar output, or 10 per cent of the country's total sugar output. The main cane sugar production bases are Yunnan and Jiangxi, with 10 per cent of the national total output; the main beet sugar production bases are Inner Mongolia and Xinjiang, accounting for 25 per cent of the national total output.

Despite the growth of the sugar-refining industry since 1949, its output remains below the country's requirements. Around 30 per cent of the sugar consumed is imported. This deficiency in raw materials for the industry is partly a result of land-use competition in the raw material-producing areas and the under-utilization of sugar-bearing raw materials. In many refineries, the limited technical force, capital, and raw materials result in small-scale

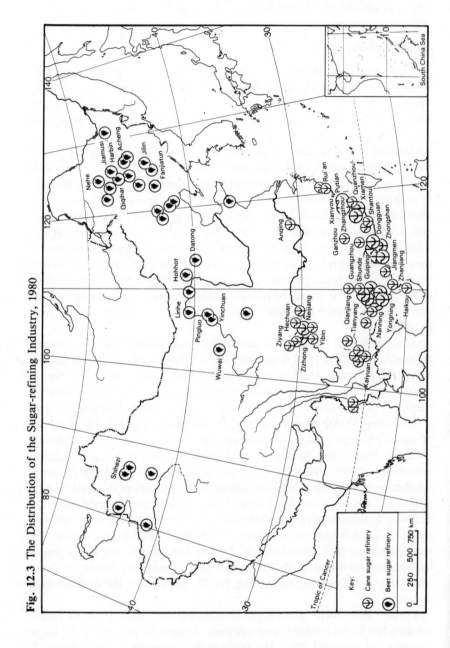

Fig. 12.3 The Distribution of the Sugar-refining Industry, 1980

production, insufficient resources, inferior product quality, high production costs, and the problem of industrial waste. Planning, rational distribution, and concentration of the industry are required if the present level of output is to increase.

Salt

The development and distribution of the salt industry is regulated by the distribution of salt resources. Conditions in China are favourable for the production of sea salt and there are a number of inland salt lakes, especially in the north and north-west. The total verified reserves of the country amount to more than 30 billion tonnes. Most provinces and regions have exploitable resources (Fig. 12.4).

The salt industry developed very slowly before 1949 and its distribution was irrational. In 1949, the output of raw salt in Liaoning, Hebei, Shandong, and Jiangsu provinces accounted for 80 per cent of the country's total output. Sea salt was marketed in the hinterland areas and salt from the north was shipped to the south because of the limited supplies in those areas. Since 1949, however, the productive capacity of the industry has been expanded and its distribution has been adjusted to accord with resources and markets.

The coastal areas are rich in sea salt and their potential for increased production is substantial due to their concentration, developed transport facilities, and proximity to the major marketing areas. However, the climate and production are unstable, resulting in fluctuations in output of up to 30 per cent annually.

Although lake salt requires only a small investment to exploit, it is distributed mainly in the vast, sparsely populated areas where communications and transport facilities are undeveloped and marketing is difficult. Like the oil industry, the production of well and mineral salts requires large amounts of engineering equipment and a long period of construction, but it is little affected by climate and production is relatively stable.

Sea Salt

The main sea salt-producing areas in northern China are Liaoning, Hebei, Shandong, and Jiangsu provinces. Their long, curved coastlines and broad beaches are suitable for production and the climate is favourable. Well-developed communications and transport facilities enable salt to be exported or shipped to the hinterland areas. Moreover, they are located near Dalian, Tanggu, Shanghai, and Qingdao, which are centres of the soda-making industry. These densely populated areas consume large quantities of salt. Salt-works in these main areas produced 65 per cent of the country's total output in 1980, a 3.7-fold increase over 1949. They form today the main part of China's salt industry.

The southern coastal areas are less suited to salt production because of high rainfall and fewer hours of sunshine. However, their long coastlines and broad beaches are suitable for building saltworks. Other advantages for the development of the industry in the south are the high temperatures and greater density of the sea water. Before 1949, there were only a few small saltworks

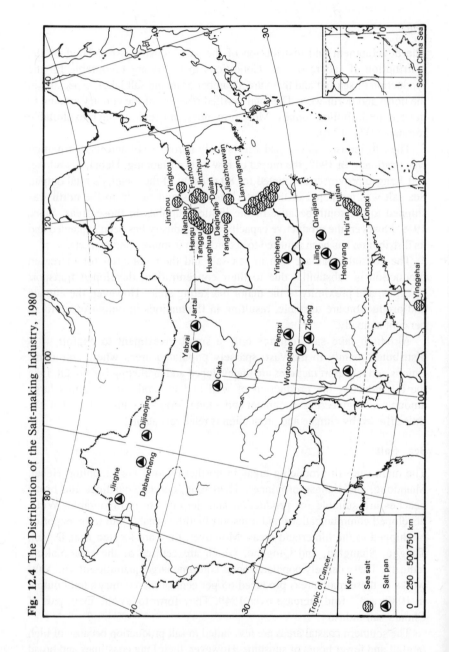

Fig. 12.4 The Distribution of the Salt-making Industry, 1980

in Zhejiang, Fujian, Guangdong, and Guangxi provinces. Since 1949, however, a number of small saltworks have been formed into collective saltworks and larger state-operated saltworks have been established in a number of suitable areas. Acreage and output have increased considerably as a result and, in 1980, the salt output of these southern provinces accounted for 13 per cent of the country's total output, a seven-fold increase over 1949.

Well, Mineral, and Lake Salts

The production of well, mineral, and lake salts has been expanded in the hinterland areas through geological prospecting. The industry was expanded in Sichuan province and a number of new salt mines were opened in Hubei, Hunan, and Jiangxi provinces where salt production was previously non-existent. In addition, the industry was expanded in Inner Mongolia, Qinghai, Xinjiang, and Yunnan. The increased productive capacity of well, mineral, and lake salts in these areas since 1949 accounts for one-third of the country's total increased productive capacity since that time. Of the country's gross output, well salt comprised 17 per cent, and lake salt 12 per cent in 1980. The development of the industry in the hinterland areas has had a significant balancing effect on the production and marketing of salt in different parts of China, thereby reducing transport requirements.

Nevertheless, the limited distribution of resources restricts the development of the salt industry in the country as a whole. The levels of output and consumption also vary over the country. Of the major producing areas, the output and consumption of salt is highest in the east and smallest in the north-west. Output is higher than consumption in both the north and the north-west. The only salt-producing area in the north-east — Liaoning province — consumes large amounts of industrial salt. In the central-south, Henan produces no salt at all and the outputs of Hubei, Hunan, and Guangxi provinces are insignificant. Output and consumption in Guangdong are high. The main deficiencies exist in the north-east and central-south. At present, the saltworks in Changlu in the north are alone capable of shipping large amounts of salt to other areas such as western Liaoning, Jilin, Heilongjiang, Shandong, the central-south, and Guizhou. A certain amount is also transported to northern Sichuan and Henan from the north-west, from Jiangsu, Shandong, and Fujian to the central-south and Guizhou, and from Inner Mongolia to the north-west and Henan.

The Paper Industry

In addition to being the raw material of a number of industries, paper is in great demand in all sectors of society. Its production is a relatively simple process, suited to small and medium-sized mills supplying local needs. On the other hand, paper for industrial technology (such as cement bags) and for newsprint requires higher levels of technology and better quality raw materials. The consumers of this kind of paper are more concentrated in distribution and are better serviced by large enterprises in the industrial and cultural centres near the raw material-producing areas.

The paper industry consumes large quantities of raw materials (around two tonnes of grass fibres are required to produce one tonne of paper) and the cost of raw materials is a considerable proportion of the total production cost. The most suitable raw material is timber, producing good quality paper at a low cost. It also has the advantage of easy storage and transportation, allowing paper mills to be set up on a large scale at some distance from the timber-producing areas.

The distribution of raw materials for paper manufacture is widespread in China. Timber and reeds are plentiful in Heilongjiang and Jilin, where there is considerable potential for further development of the industry. Liaoning and Hebei have similar potential. Other raw materials such as sugar-cane residue, bamboo, and rushes are widely distributed. Timber is in short supply, while there are abundant supplies of grass fibres of many varieties. Some 75 per cent of the total raw materials used in the paper industry are non-timber fibres and their availability affects the distribution of the industry. Most such enterprises are small and widely dispersed.

Since 1949, the backward areas with abundant resources have been developed and a number of large enterprises have been established in the relatively concentrated areas. These large paper-making bases have an assured supply of raw materials and produce high-grade products. In Heilongjiang province in the north-east, for example, a number of plants producing news-print, paper for industrial use, and commercial pulp have been established. Other main centres are Guangdong and Guangxi in the south-east, producing printing paper and industrial wrapping paper from timber, sugar-cane residue, and straw; Fujian in the east and Sichuan in the south-west, using timber and sugar-cane residue; and Hunan, Hubei, and Jiangxi on the lower reaches of the Chang Jiang, using bamboo, straw, reeds, rushes, and timber.

In areas with a large paper-making capacity but insufficient pulp, local raw materials have been used to increase the productive capacity of the industry and the variety of products. Plants in Liaoning and Jilin have been expanded or established, using timber, reeds, grasses, and waste materials to increase the pulp-producing capacity of these old paper-making bases and to increase the output of newsprint and paper for industrial use. The Chang Jiang delta area, centred around Shanghai, has a relatively large paper-making capacity but very little capacity to produce pulp. Timber from Zhejiang and Fujian is now used to produce a certain amount of pulp, as well as plants in the nearby rice-producing and reed-producing areas. As a result, the paper-making capacity of Shanghai and nearby centres has expanded.

Timber resources in the Tianjin–Beijing–Qingdao–Jinan–Xuanhua area are in short supply, although there are abundant supplies of reeds and grass fibres. The consumption of paper in these centres is high, but — with the exception of Tianjin — their productive capacity in the past was insignificant. In order to develop the paper industry, the pulp-producing capacity of the area was expanded using reeds, wheat and sorghum stalks, and waste materials. The existing plants were expanded and new, large plants, producing mainly high-grade printing paper, were established to meet increasing needs. Small and medium-sized paper-making centres have also been established in other parts of China, particularly the autonomous regions, using local resources to produce traditional hand-made paper.

Some 80 per cent of the country's total output of machine-made paper is concentrated in 14 provinces and municipalities (Fig. 12.5). These areas are rich in paper-making raw materials and provide a large consumer market.

There has been a considerable increase in the output of paper since 1949. The average output per capita has risen from 0.42 kilograms to 5 kilograms, but the ratio of the output value of the paper industry in the total industrial output value has fluctuated from 1.3 per cent in 1949, to 2.6 per cent in 1957, and 1.28 per cent in 1980. In 1980, it comprised only 4 per cent of the output value of light industry (excluding textiles). Since the 2nd FYP period, the annual rate of growth of the industry has been lower than the speed of industrial development as a whole and the contradictions between production and marketing have become increasingly apparent. At present, the output of paper meets only 65 per cent of domestic requirements. Several hundred million US dollars are spent each year on importing pulp and paper to meet the country's needs.

The main problem in the development of the paper industry is the inadequate supply of raw materials and the country's low pulp-producing capacity. Available resources need to be utilized more fully and new timber bases need to be established to increase the proportion of timber fibres in the structure of raw materials. With forethought and correct planning, suitable mountainous and waste lands could be planted to produce sufficient timber for the industry within 20 years. The residue from timber processing could also be used more efficiently to produce paper.

In addition to afforestation for paper-making and increasing the sources of timber fibres, grass fibres (particularly reeds and sugar-cane reside) could be utilized more rationally. In 1949, the annual output of reeds was four million tonnes. In 1957, reeds comprised 22 per cent of the raw materials for paper making. Changes in the system of management and the destruction of reed-growing areas by reclamation projects have since reduced the annual output of reeds to just over one million tonnes and the proportion of reed pulp to 9.5 per cent of paper-making raw materials. Improved management, the restoration of reed-growing areas, and the raising of per-unit production could improve this proportion and restore the importance of reeds as a raw material for paper making.

The distribution of the sugar-cane industry is relatively concentrated, facilitating the collection of sugar-cane residue. However, only 25 per cent of this residue is used at present for paper making, the balance being used as fuel. The substitution of coal for this residue would both increase the productivity of the sugar industry and provide a cheap raw material for the paper-making industry. The present shortage in China of raw materials for the paper-making industry and the consequent low level of productivity of the industry could thereby be remedied in a relatively short time.

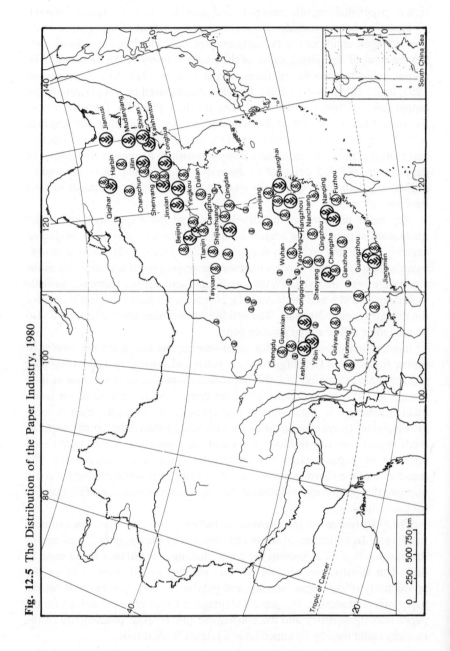

Fig. 12.5 The Distribution of the Paper Industry, 1980

13. The Main Industrial Regions of China

A NUMBER of industrial regions of a considerable size as well as many small industrial centres have been established in China since 1949. Most of the main industrial areas are concentrated east of and along the Qiqihar–Tongliao–Beijing-Guangzhou rail line. Other large industrial bases have also been established in the west, north of the Changsha–Nanning, Guiyang–Nanning, and Guiyang–Kunming lines, as well as south of the Lanzhou–Urumqi, Lanzhou–Baotou, and Beijing–Baotou lines, although they are less densely distributed than the main industrial areas and smaller in size. Approximately one-third of China's territory has no sizeable industrial bases at all, despite the abundance of raw materials and potential for development of these backward areas.

The main industrial areas are distributed for the most part along the main rail lines and the Chang Jiang and Huang He systems. In the central and southern parts of Liaoning province, however, and in eastern Hebei, the Chang Jiang and Zhu Jiang deltas, the Chengdu–Chongqing region, southern Hebei, northern Henan, and central Hunan, there are a number of blocs of industrial cities.

Most of the industrial areas in the eastern part of the country have developed as a result of the reconstruction and expansion of the pre-1949 industrial production bases; those in the west have developed as a result of state policies aimed at the development of previously unindustrialized areas. The differences in the industrial development of the east and west are apparent in the closer contact between the bases in the east and with other parts of the country than is the case between bases in the west. Such contact is particularly conducive to technical and economic collaboration.

Within the more developed industrial areas, however, the distribution of industry is inefficient and in some cases counter-productive. Pollution is also a serious problem. State planning since 1949 has been effective to a degree in solving some of the problems associated with the concentration of industry, but the situation since 1958 has been largely one of confusion.

With the exception of the mining centres, the main industrial centres have a comprehensive industrial structure dominated by the machine-building, metallurgy, and chemical industries. The lack of specialization which is characteristic of these areas is a result of the setting up of complete systems at each level of industry in the past, as well as a manifestation of the under-development of China's commodity economy.

The main industrial regions are based around the raw material, energy, or manufacturing industries, or are in areas where raw materials production and processing are well developed. Raw material and energy supplies are the main factors in the development of the industrial region in eastern Heilongjiang province, for example. It is the main coal-producing area in the north-east, as well as one of the most important timber-producing areas in China. Because the industrial structure consists mainly of coal, the output volume of the region is large, but industrial output value is low. Nevertheless, it is the principal coal-supplying base in the north-east and, as such, is of importance in the construction and development of heavy industry in that region. Light and textile industries are undeveloped.

The industrial region in western Heilongjiang province and eastern Inner Mongolia has the most abundant verified reserves of gold and oil in the country. It is also rich in timber resources, fertile grasslands, and animal husbandry. The main industries are petroleum, petrochemicals, gold mining, timber, and dairy farming. It is the country's largest energy and timber base, as well as an important metallurgy equipment-producing base. Its importance lies mainly in its supply of energy sources and in the development of the petrochemical industry in the north-east and the country as a whole.

The industrial region along the Datong–Taiyuan rail line is the largest coal-supplying base in China, occupying a crucial position in the country's energy production. The region also has abundant reserves of copper, iron ore, and bauxite. The main industries are coal, coal-chemicals, metallurgy, metallurgy equipment and textile machinery manufacturing, and thermal power production.

The Sichuan–Guizhou–Yunnan industrial region has abundant deposits of coal, iron ore, non-ferrous metals, phosphorus, and bauxite, as well as rich hydropower resources. Its coal, minerals, iron and steel, and raw materials industries are well developed, but it is backward in the manufacturing and textile industries, relying on other areas for light industrial products and textiles. The under-exploitation of hydropower resources has restricted the development of the non-ferrous metallurgy and electrochemical industries. Future development of the thermal power industry will allow for their development and the production of phosphorus fertilizer. The region's poor communications and transport facilities also affect the present exploitation of coal and phosphorus reserves. The planned Kunming–Nanning–Fangcheng railway would provide the region with access to the sea.

The industrial region in central Anhui is rich in coal, iron, copper, cotton, and tobacco. Within the region, Hefei, Bengbu, and Wuhu have comprehensive industrial structures, whereas the main focus of the other industrial centres in the region is the excavation and metallurgy industries. The region is an important coal-supplying base for the Chang Jiang delta area and pig iron supplier for the iron and steel industry in Shanghai. Convenient inland waterway communications and its location near the Chang Jiang delta industrial area enable the region's abundant natural resources to be fully utilized and the superior technology and economy of the delta area to be absorbed.

Proximity to manufacturing bases is the main factor in the development of other main industrial bases. For example, the Chang Jiang delta industrial region has intensive agriculture, a large population, convenient inland and river transport facilities, an established industrial base, and developed technology. Its textile industry is comprehensive in structure, with very high productivity. It produces a great variety of textile products of a high quality. Heavy industries such as machine building, metallurgy, chemicals, and oil refining are also well developed. The Chang Jiang delta is the largest comprehensive industrial region in China. The industrial output value of Shanghai (the country's largest industrial centre), Nanjing, Hangzhou, Wuxi, Suzhou, Changzhou, Zhenjiang, Nantong, and Ningbo accounts for one-fifth of the country's total. Large quantities of raw materials and fuel are transported to the region from the rural areas by rail, inland waterways, the highway system, and high-tension power transmission lines. Finished products, including steel products, industrial equipment, textiles, garments, cigarettes, domestic electrical appliances, and cosmetics, are distributed to other parts of the country. The region is an important base for the production of top-grade, precision, and new industrial products for the domestic and overseas markets.

The industrial region in the Zhu Jiang delta is China's largest sugar-cane-producing area, as well as an important base for the production of silk cocoons, fruit, perfume crops, and aquatic products. The region's raw materials and heavy industries are comparatively undeveloped and, with the exception of Guangzhou which has a comprehensive industrial structure, most cities in the region are relatively specialized in their structure of production. Although farm raw materials production is highly developed and concentrated in distribution, the shortage of arable land limits agricultural production. The development of heavy industry is also affected by the shortages of energy sources and mineral deposits in the region.

The region's proximity to Hong Kong and Macao provides favourable conditions for absorbing foreign capital and for importing advanced technology. Various forms of collaboration and co-operation have enabled the textiles, light, and some precision industries to be developed for the export trade. The region's two special economic zones — Shenzhen and Zhuhai — have a concentration of enterprises producing furniture, garments, wool textiles, electronic equipment, containers, and ships. In addition, there are excellent prospects for oil gas production in the South China Sea and the estuary of the Zhu Jiang. Large-scale exploitation of the hydropower resources of the Hongshui river has begun, as well as construction of the Nanning–Kunming railway and the dredging of the Xi Jiang.

The industrial region in central Heilongjiang and Jilin provinces is based on heavy industries such as the manufacture of large generating equipment, cutting and measuring tools, automobiles, railway carriages, and chemicals. Most of the region's products are distributed to other parts of the country. Most of the light and textile industries, with the exception of flax spinning, refining, beet sugar, and oil pressing, meet mainly local requirements. The region is rich in coal and hydropower resources, but is deficient in mineral deposits. The raw materials industry and excavation production are limited.

The main industrial resources in the Chengdu–Chongqing industrial region are natural gas, well salt, hydropower resources, silk cocoons, sugar-cane, rape seeds, cotton, and limited quantities of iron and coal reserves. Light industries such as sugar, paper, salt, salt-chemicals, silk weaving, and oil pressing are well developed; heavy industry consists mainly of machine building, iron and steel, nitrogen fertilizer, and natural gas. It is a large hydropower base for the local cotton textile industry. The region's industrial centres are densely distributed and comprehensive in industrial structure, making it the most developed industrial region in south-west China. Transport and communications facilities are well developed.

The main industrial resources of the industrial region in western Hubei province are hydropower, ores, phosphorus, cotton, and some oil. The automobile and hydropower industries occupy an important position and there is great potential for further development of the hydropower industry, the exploitation of ores and phosphorus, and the development of energy-consuming industries.

The Guanzhong industrial region, based around Xi'an, Xianyang, Baoji, Tongchuan, and Huxian, produces mainly cotton and woollen textiles, transformer and electrical equipment, and machinery for the petroleum industry.

The third main type of industrial region has both well-developed raw materials and processing industries. For example, central and south Liaoning province has abundant deposits of coal, limestone, magnesite, dolomite, and manganese for the metallurgy industry, and large amounts of non-ferrous metal resources. In addition, there are large reed-growing areas and abundant quantities of tussah cocoons. It is the largest and most important industrial base in the north-east, with well-developed heavy, light, and textile sectors. Since 1949, the region has become an important heavy industrial base centre around the iron and steel, non-ferrous metallurgy, and oil refining industries. Machine building, petrochemicals, salt-alkali chemicals, and nitrogen fertilizer production are also well developed. Although the proportion of light and textile industries is small, the production of tussah silk, paper, pressed oils, and synthetic textiles is significant. The region's cotton textile industry is the largest in north-east China. It is also the only salt-producing area in the north-east. Communications and transport facilities are well established and the region has a large urban population.

The main problem in the industrial development of the region is the shortage of energy resources. Large-scale exploitation of coal deposits has depleted resources so that despite the still large output, supplies are unable to meet the requirements of the iron and steel industry in terms of quantity or variety. Oil deposits and hydropower resources are also limited. As a result, the direct use of energy sources limits the development of the secondary energy and heavy industries. The solution to the problem of energy shortages lies in the exploitation of the coalfields in eastern Heilongjiang province and Inner Mongolia. A further problem is the self-servicing nature of heavy industry in the region and the inadequate development of light industry and agriculture.

There are abundant resources of iron ore, salt, coal, and oil in the Beijing–Tianjin–Tanggu industrial region, but limited resources of agricultural raw materials. Tianjin, with cotton textiles as the main industry in addition to well-developed light and heavy industries, is a comprehensive industrial centre. Tangshan is a coal-mining centre. Beijing, the political and cultural centre of China, has the largest number of new projects completed since 1949. The industrial structure of the region consists of well-developed branches of heavy industry (such as machine building, iron and steel, petrochemicals, salt-alkali chemicals, and coal) and advanced light industry (including cotton and woollen textiles, salt, and electrical machinery). It is second only to the Chang Jiang delta in the production of light industrial and textile products. However, the region relies on other parts of the country for agricultural raw materials such as cotton, wool, and tobacco. Transport and communications facilities are well developed; the region is the railway and aviation hub of China.

Although Beijing and Tianjin are the main energy-deficient areas in China, they are located near the coal-producing areas of Hebei and Shanxi. Future emphasis in the region will be on the production of high-grade, precision, and advanced industrial products, as well as the development of the light and textile industries.

The industrial region along the Jinan–Qingdao rail line has abundant gas, coal, bauxite, sea salt, tussah cocoons, and considerable reserves of coal and iron ore. It is close to the country's most important cotton, tobacco, and peanut-producing areas and the large coal and ore mines in Shandong. As a result, the region's heavy and light industries are of a considerable scale. It is also an energy-surplus region supplying oil and petroleum products to other parts of the country.

The Lanzhou–Tianshui–Yinchuan–Xining industrial region has abundant hydropower resources and non-ferrous metal reserves. Large-scale exploitation of hydropower resources has enabled the rapid development of the copper, lead, zinc, nickel, chlorine, and rare earth and metals industries and aluminium smelting. It also has well-developed materials-testing machinery, machine tools, petroleum, and petrochemicals machinery industries. With the exception of the woollen textile industry, the region's light and textile industries are backward. As the largest railway hub in the north-west, Lanzhou is linked not only with the main industrial centres of the region, but also with the north-west, making it a convenient base for the future large-scale exploitation of north-west China.

A number of other industrial regions are of this third type, including the Wuhan–Daye region (iron and steel, machine building, and cotton textiles), central Hunan province (machine building, metallurgy, and jute textiles), southern Hebei and northern Henan (coal, iron and steel, and cotton textiles), western Henan (coal, aluminium smelting, machine building, and cotton textiles), and Hohhot and Baotou (iron and steel, rare earth metals, machine building, and woollen textiles) (Fig. 13.1).

Fig. 13.1 The Distribution of the Main Industrial Regions, 1980

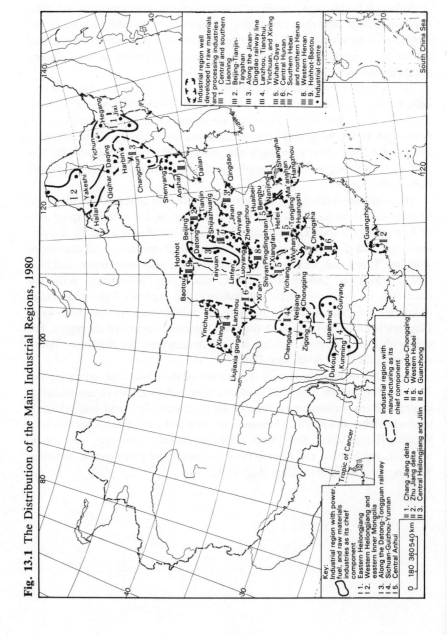

Part III: Agricultural Geography

14. The Development of Agriculture before 1949

AGRICULTURAL production was the mainstay of China's national economy for several thousand years. The country's agricultural resources are amongst the richest in the world and agriculture remains today of major importance in the national economy.

The Development of the Main Agricultural Zones

The cultivation of agricultural crops and the breeding of stock first developed some 9,000 years ago during the Shang dynasty on the plains of the middle and lower reaches of the Huang He and in the valleys and basins of what are now Henan, Shaanxi, and Shandong provinces. Animal husbandry was the main agricultural sector, although millet and wheat cultivation occupied an important place in production.

During the Western Zhou dynasty (11th century-770 BC), the variety of farm crops increased to include rice, millet, wheat, beans, and hemp. Agricultural development led to the growth of the handicraft industry, commerce, and ultimately to the rise of cities.

Between 770 BC and AD 581, agricultural production spread south, west, and north from the Huang He as production techniques developed and the country progressed from a slave society to a feudal one, based on individual households and private land ownership. Water conservation projects improved the irrigation of farm land, as well as transport and communications facilities. The improvements in irrigation increased the amount of land available to agricultural production and changed the composition of farm crops. The area given over to the cultivation of corn gradually expanded and, during the later Warring States period, the cultivation of winter wheat paved the way for increased production through multiple cropping and crop rotation. Winter wheat, millet, and corn became the main crops.

The expansion of the agricultural zones and the change in the structure of agriculture was apparent in the development of regional economic differences. In the north and north-west, stock breeding was the main economic activity. Forestry predominated in areas south of the Chang Jiang, Huai He, and Tongbai, and around the Qin Ling in the west. Intensive crop cultivation, which constituted the main economic activity, centred around the densely populated Chang Jiang, Huai He, and Tongbai river valleys. Agricultural production also developed to some degree in the north in the border regions.

During the Western Han dynasty (206 BC–AD 24), crop cultivation expanded in the vast area bordered by the eastern coastline, the Gansu corridor in the west, and the Yan Shan in the north. However, a period of great upheaval followed, which devastated the once flourishing rural economy. Large-scale migration to areas south of the Chang Jiang increased the population in the south-east dramatically and the economic development of the region was boosted as the relatively advanced production techniques of the north filtered south.

Following the unification of the country during the 3rd century, the population and economy stabilized. This period of stability was short-lived, however, and a second large migration south during the years of upheaval at the close of the Jin dynasty further shifted the country's economic focus to the south. The consolidation of the areas south of the Chang Jiang continued as the population of the north was further depleted by warfare and migration. This shift in population had a decisive effect on the agricultural development of both north and south China.

Agricultural production in the south was by this time relatively advanced, with large-scale irrigation and dredging works creating favourable conditions for development. The production of the main crop — paddy rice — increased dramatically and, by the later Tang dynasty, the lower reaches of the Chang Jiang contributed the greatest part of the taxes paid to the ruling dynasty and supplied surplus grain to the grain-deficient north.

Industrial crops, such as mulberry and hemp, developed in the south during the Northern and Southern Song dynasties in the 12th and 13th centuries and tea was produced in sufficient quantities to be exported. At this time, the Chang Jiang basin was the largest agricultural region in the country.

The devastation of the country during the Yuan dynasty was followed in the 15th and 16th centuries by measures to revive production. Agriculture not only recovered and developed along the Huang He and the Chang Jiang, but made considerable progress in Yunnan, Guizhou, Guangdong, and Guangxi provinces in the south. The period of the Ming and Qing dynasties also saw the commercialization of farming and a rise in the commodity rate of farm produce. The production of sugar-cane and fruit in Fujian and Guangdong provinces and cotton, silk, and tea south of the Chang Jiang was concentrated, with a relatively high level of commercialization. Nevertheless, agricultural production remained feudal in character rather than capitalistic.

During the Qing dynasty, crop cultivation expanded in the north-east and border regions, and waste lands were gradually reclaimed for agriculture. Cultivation also developed in the semi-agricultural and semi-stock breeding highlands of Qinghai and Tibet as the population in those areas increased through migration from the interior.

The development and distribution of agriculture in China up to the 19th century was therefore influenced to a large degree by demographic and political as well as natural conditions. As productive forces developed and the amount of land available for agricultural production expanded, the rate and nature of agricultural development became uneven throughout the country.

The Development of Agricultural Production, 1840–1949

At the time of the Opium War of 1839–42, China was in the final phase of feudalism. The national economy was backward, despite the development of a commodity economy based on farm produce. Following the Opium War, China became a semi-feudal, semi-colonial society. Although the influence of the foreign powers in the coastal areas in the south-east led to a certain degree of agricultural specialization and commercialization of the rural economy, in general, small-scale production continued to dominate in the national economy, and the distribution of the main agricultural zones remained unchanged.

The commercialization of agricultural production after the Opium War was apparent in the specialized production of cotton, tobacco, soya beans, silk, tea, peanuts, sugar-cane, sesame seeds, fruits, and vegetables in certain areas. Rice also began to be cultivated as a commodity crop. Although this process of commercialization continued for one hundred years after the Opium War, the economy remained basically a small peasant economy. The appropriation of land for agricultural production continued under the system of feudal land ownership, and farming implements remained backward. Self-sufficiency in farm produce and the exchange of commodity surpluses were the basis of production. In all areas, grain crops predominated, supplemented by other crops as dictated by natural and economic conditions. The cultivation of the limited amount of land permitted to each household was intensive in order to produce sufficient quantities of farm produce over and above the needs of self-sufficiency for commodity exchange. The limited amount of land and the feudal system of production prevented further development of production. Natural conditions also contributed to the low level of production, particularly in the western regions and north China, where the continental climate, low rainfall, mountainous terrain, and vast expanses of grassland and desert were not conducive to crop cultivation on a large scale.

Despite the profound influence of natural conditions on agricultural production, the determining factor was the socio-economic conditions resulting from the semi-feudal, semi-colonial system in force. Poverty in the rural areas was rife as the peasants struggled to pay high land rents and loan interest rates to landlords during a period when the country was ravaged by war and natural disasters. The peasants had few resources: farming implements were outmoded and draught animals were in short supply. As a result, production methods were inefficient, with little potential for improvement.

The area of land under cultivation also decreased throughout the country, resulting in a steadily decreasing total output of agricultural products. Grain production during the Sino-Japanese War was 20 per cent lower than in 1936 and the output of industrial crops such as cotton, tobacco, peanuts, hemp, sugar-cane, tea, and silkworms declined steadily. In effect, by 1949, the rural economy was in a state of bankruptcy.

15. The Development of Agriculture since 1949

THE socialist system of land reform and collective and public ownership has both improved the conditions in China for agricultural production and developed the country's productive forces. Despite these measures, however, the level of production remains low owing to the rapid increase in population since 1949 and the effects of long-term shortages of the main agricultural products. Agriculture in China today is unable to meet the requirements of the national economy. Nevertheless, notable changes have occurred in both the production and distribution of agriculture in terms of the conditions of production, the level of output, and the structure and distribution of production.

The Conditions of Production

Technical, economic, and natural conditions have had a significant impact on the development of agriculture in China. Improvements in the technical and economic conditions since 1949 have been instrumental in improving the conditions of production. In addition, natural conditions have been improved in many areas through better land utilization measures, the application of organic and chemical fertilizers, land reclamation, and soil erosion control and water conservation projects. Agricultural machinery has also been updated (Table 15.1), with the result that agriculture in China has become modernized in terms of its conditions of production (Table 15.2).

The Level of Output

Improvements in the conditions of production have been reflected in a rapid increase in the level of output of agricultural products. Calculated at 1970 prices, the gross agricultural output value in 1980 was RMB162.7 billion, a 3.8-fold increase over 1949 (Table 15.3).

The increase in the level of output can be broken down into five main stages, as indicated in Table 15.3. Between 1949 and 1957, agricultural production developed rapidly. The total output value increased 88.3 per cent, an average annual increase of 8 per cent. Between 1958 and 1962, the period of the 2nd FYP, agriculture suffered serious set-backs. The total output value decreased by 19.9 per cent, an average annual decrease of 4.3 per cent. Production recovered in the period 1963–5, with a 37.2 per cent increase in total output value, an average annual increase of 11.1 per cent. During the 3rd and 4th FYP periods (1966–76), the disruption and destruction caused by the Cultural Revolution slowed the development of agriculture. By 1976, the total output value had increased by 51 per cent, an average annual increase of 3.8 per cent. By 1980, the total output value of agriculture had increased by 23.5 per cent.

Table 15.1 China's Main Agricultural Machines, 1952–80

Year	Total Power of Agricultural Machinery (10,000 hp)	Large and Medium-sized Tractors	Small and Walking Tractors	Combine Harvesters	Irrigation and Drainage Machinery (10,000)	Irrigation and Drainage Machinery (10,000 hp)	Trucks for Farm Purposes	Motorized Fishing Vessels (10,000 hp)	Motorized Fishing Vessels
1952	25	1,307		284	4.0	12.8	4,084	1,485	10.3
1957	165	14,674		1,789	55.8	56.4	11,063	7,789	64.0
1965	1,494	72,599	3,956	6,704	389.1	907.4	39,585	33,701	213.6
1975	10,168	344,518	598,533	12,551	538.4	4,866.6	97,105	55,225	312.9
1979	18,191	666,823	1,671,000	23,026	563.0	7,122.1	135,000	61,022	351.4
1980	20,000	745,000	1,874,000	27,045		7,464.5			

Source: China's Economic Yearbook, 1981 (Economic Management, 1981).

Table 15.2 The Level of Agricultural Modernization, 1952–80

Year	Area Plowed by Tractors (10,000 mu)	Percentage of Area Plowed by Tractors of the Total Cultivated Area	Area Electrically Irrigated (10,000 mu)	Chemical Fertilizer Applied (10,000 tonnes)	Chemical Fertilizer Used per mu (jin)	Electricity Used in Rural Areas (100 million kWh)
1952	204	0.1	476	29.5	0.4	0.5
1957	3,954	2.4	1,803	179.4	2.1	1.4
1965	23,369	15.0	12,140	881.2	11.3	37.1
1975	49,805	33.3	34,333	2,657.9	35.5	183.1
1979	63,329	42.4	37,981	5,247.6	70.3	232.7
1980	61,487	41.3	37,973	6,214.6	78.7	321.0

Source: China's Agricultural Yearbook, 1980 (Agriculture Publishing House, Beijing, 1981).

Table 15.3 The Increase in Total Output Value of Agriculture, 1949–80

Period	Amount of Increase (RMB100 million)	Average Increase per annum (RMB100 million)	Ratio of Increase (%)	Ratio of Average Annual Increase (%)
Reconstruction period (1950–2)	207.7	69.23	48.5	14.1
1st FYP (1953–7)	157.5	31.50	24.8	4.5
2nd FYP (1958–62)	–158.0	–31.60	–19.9	–4.3
1963–5	136.4	78.80	37.2	11.1
3rd FYP (1966–70)	185.8	37.16	24.4	3.9
4th FYP (1971–5)	227.5	45.50	21.5	4.0
5th FYP (1976–80)	342.0	68.40	26.6	4.8
1949–80	1,199.0	38.67	280.1	4.4

Source: China's Agricultural Yearbook, 1980 (Agriculture Publishing House, Beijing, 1981).

The rapid development of agriculture after 1949 resulted in a 2.8-fold increase in grain production by 1980. In addition, cotton production increased 5.09-fold, oil-bearing crops production doubled, sugar-bearing crops increased 9.2-fold, draught animals increased in number by 58.7 per cent, the number of pigs increased 4.29-fold, sheep increased 3.42-fold, aquatic products increased 9.03-fold, and forestry and sideline production (including brigade-run industries) also increased significantly (Table 15.4).

Notwithstanding the developments in production since 1949, production is not yet able to meet the country's requirements because of China's large population and poor economic base. The per-unit yield, labour productivity, and the average produce per capita are lower than the world average. Natural conditions continue to have a significant impact on production levels and many main crops are cultivated only in sufficient quantities to meet domestic requirements. The development of agriculture also varies throughout the country, resulting in wide variations in production and income levels. The future development of agricultural production will require the continued expansion and modernization of the means of production if the level of output is to increase.

The Structure of Production

The emphasis in the past on grain production restricted the development of other agricultural sectors such as forestry, animal husbandry, and the production of sideline, aquatic, and cash crops. Local conditions also tended to be ignored in the emphasis on grain crops. Furthermore, a lack of co-operation between the various agricultural departments limited the development of grain production. In 1980, grain still constituted a large percentage of the total output value of agriculture (64.3 per cent compared with 82.5 per cent in 1949). Between 1949 and 1980, forestry increased by only 2.5 per cent, animal husbandry by 1.8 per cent, and aquatic production by 1.1 per cent. A significant increase in the output value of sideline products (12.8 per cent) resulted from the development of commune- and brigade-run enterprises (Fig. 15.1).

The structure of agricultural production today is still dominated by grain production; cash and other crops constitute only 20–30 per cent of the total output value. The area of land under cultivation is also used mainly for grain production (80 per cent in 1980) (Fig. 15.2).

Within the animal husbandry sector, the raising of pigs constituted 55 per cent of the total output value in 1980 and pork accounted for 94 per cent of the total meat output. The other main products are cattle, sheep, rabbits, and poultry. Within the forestry sector, timber forests predominate; economic forests and shelter belts account for only a small percentage of the total afforested area. Marine products constitute the bulk of aquatic products. Despite the country's abundant rivers and lakes, freshwater products account for only 25 per cent of the total output value.

The structure of production is characterized by a narrow focus and the under-exploitation of natural resources. The imbalance between agriculture, forestry, animal husbandry, sideline production, and aquaculture has led to

Table 15.4 The Output of Main Agricultural Products, 1949–80

Item	Unit	1949	1952	1957	1965	1975	1979	1980
Grain	100 million *jin*	2,263.6	3,278.3	3,900.9	3,890.5	5,690.3	6,642.3	6,364.4
Cotton	10,000 *dan*	888.8	2,607.4	3,280.0	4,195.5	4,761.6	4,414.7	5,414.0
Total of oil crops	10,000 *dan*	5,127.0	8,386.3	8,391.9	7,250.7	9,041.5	12,870.7	15,382.0
Bluish dogbane and jute	10,000 *dan*	73.7	611.0	601.9	558.4	1,398.7	2,178.9	2,196.0
Sugar-cane	10,000 *dan*	5,284.3	14,231.6	20,784.8	26,782.9	33,333.7	43,015.0	45,614.0
Sugar-beet	10,000 *dan*	381.1	957.1	3,002.1	3,968.7	4,952.7	6,211.6	12,610.0
Draught animals[1]	10,000 head	6,002.0	7,646.0	8,775.0	8,421.0	9,686.0	9,459.0	9,524.6
Pigs[2]	10,000 head	5,775.0	8,977.0	14,590.0	16,693.0	28,117.0	31,971.0	30,543.0
Sheep[2]	10,000 head	4,235.0	6,178.0	9,858.0	13,903.0	16,337.0	18,314.0	18,731.1
Aquatic products	10,000 tonnes	44.8	166.2	311.6	298.4	441.2	430.5	449.7
Timber	10,000 cu m^2	567.0	1,120.0	2,787.0	3,978.0	4,626.0	5,439.0	5,359.0
Total output value of agriculture[3]	RMB100 million	428.1	635.8	793.3	871.7	1,285.0	1,584.3	1,627.0

Notes: 1. Includes cows, horses, donkeys, mules, and camels.
2. Heads at the end of the year.
3. Calculations made according to fixed prices of 1970.
Source: China's Agricultural Yearbook, 1980 (Agriculture Publishing House, Beijing, 1981).

Fig. 15.1 A Comparison of the Outputs of the Main Agricultural Sectors

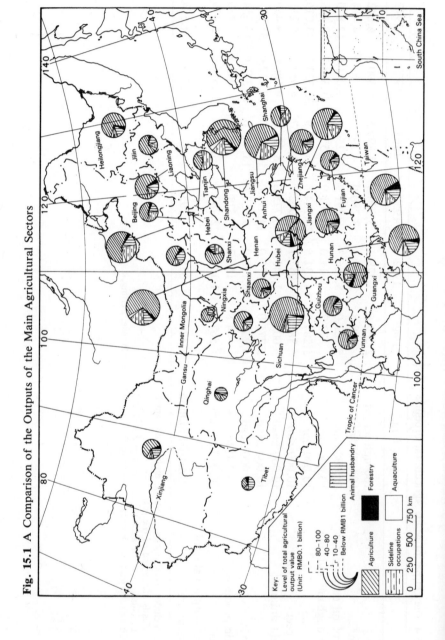

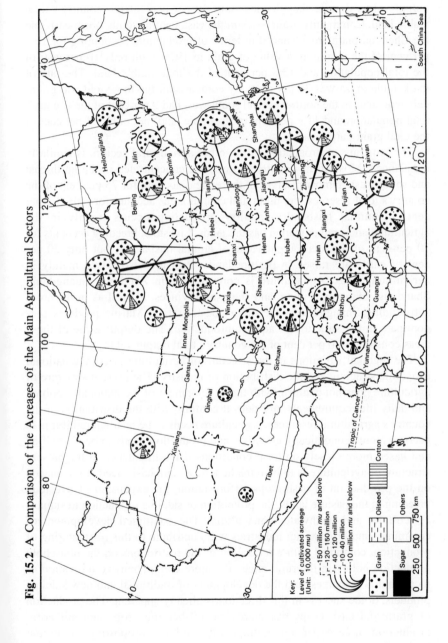

Fig. 15.2 A Comparison of the Acreages of the Main Agricultural Sectors

economic stagnation in the rural areas and a low rural income. This imbalance is particularly apparent in the economies of the advanced and backward regions. Of the country's 29 provinces, municipalities, and autonomous regions, 14 in south China are comparatively developed. The agricultural output value of these areas constitutes 60 per cent of the country's total output value, despite their having only 40 per cent of the country's total arable land. Community grain bases in the east, central-south, north-east, and the Chengdu plain are advanced in terms of production, accounting for 15.3 per cent of the total output value of grain in 1979, with only 10 per cent of the total population and 13.8 per cent of the total arable land. The rate of marketable grain was 30 per cent. By comparison, the low-yield and grain-deficient areas in the north-west and south-west had 9 per cent of the country's total population and 11.9 per cent of its arable land, but only 8.4 per cent of the total grain output value.

The structure of production in the other agricultural sectors is similarly unbalanced. Most of the country's forests are concentrated in the north-east and south-west. Timber reserves in these areas account for 75 per cent of the country's total reserves; the north and central areas account for only 3.2 per cent. In animal husbandry, poultry production occurs mainly in the agricultural areas rather than in pasture lands. Livestock breeding accounts for 70 per cent of the total output value of animal husbandry, but only 20 per cent of cattle are raised in pasture lands. Pigs are also raised mainly in agricultural areas. Aquaculture is concentrated in Zhejiang, Guangdong, Shandong, Liaoning, Fujian, and Jiangsu provinces, as well as in the areas surrounding Shanghai and the other coastal cities. Marine products predominate in the structure of aquatic production. The output value of these areas constitutes 80 per cent of the country's total output value.

The regional variations in the structure of agriculture affect the national economic structure and the distribution of industry. The present structure of agriculture does not conform with the development of the national economy and daily life requirements, nor does it conform with the distribution of the country's agricultural resources. Agriculture needs to be restructured if it is to become more economically effective, and production needs to be diversified and based more closely on local conditions if the imbalance in the present structure of agriculture is to be remedied. More emphasis needs to be placed on the pro-duction of cash crops, afforestation, the expansion of livestock breeding in the pasture lands, the promotion of sideline production to support agriculture, and freshwater aquaculture. The continued development of commune- and brigade-run industries will contribute to this restructuring of production, combined with a relaxation of the restrictions on the household production policy in the rural areas, the more comprehensive utilization of local natural resources, and the development of traditional and new sideline products. Some success in this direction is already apparent. The production of grain and cash crops has increased, oil-bearing crops and silkworm production have expanded dramatically, and the proportion of animal husbandry in the total agricultural output value has risen. Continued restructuring along these lines is necessary to achieve a more rational balance of the main agricultural sectors.

The Distribution of Production

The distribution of agricultural production has become steadily more rational since 1949 as the distribution of industry, communications, transport facilities, and urban construction has changed. An important development has been the recovery and strengthening of the original agricultural and pastoral areas. The concentration of agriculture in the middle and lower plain of the Chang Jiang, the middle and lower plain of the Huang He, the Zhu Jiang delta, the Chao Shan plain, the Liao He plain, and the Songhua Jiang plain has a long history. These areas have abundant natural resources, a comparatively high technical level, a large population, and plentiful labour. The population accounts for 70 per cent and the arable land for 60 per cent of the country's total. Furthermore, they are close to large cities and mining areas, with their convenient communications and transport facilities and large markets for agricultural products. Grain and cash crop production, pig and cattle raising, and aquaculture are the main sectors. Since 1949, priority has been given in these areas to water conservation projects and investment in the modernization of agricultural technology. The further development of these areas is important because of the need for agricultural commodity bases to meet the needs of factories and mines and for export to accelerate national economic development.

Capital investment and the modernization of technology have also been instrumental in raising the agricultural output of low-yield and backward areas such as the Huang He, Huai He, and Hai He plains and the north-west pastoral areas, the loess plateau, and some mountainous areas, thereby redressing to some degree the imbalance in the distribution of agricultural production throughout the country.

Another important development since 1949 has been the establishment of new agricultural bases, taking into consideration the needs of factories, mining areas, cities, and the development of communications facilities. State farms have also been established in many of these areas to provide large quantities of marketable grain and industrial raw materials for the new industrial bases.

A number of agricultural raw materials and city subsidiary food bases have also been established since 1949 to service the main industrial cities and to develop industry in the agricultural regions. Cotton textile and flour processing mills have been set up in the important cotton- and wheat-producing areas in the interior and various new industries have been established in the agricultural regions to serve agriculture and to use agricultural raw materials. Such industries include factories producing tractors, pesticides, chemical fertilizers, farm tools, sugar, oil, tea, and livestock products. The distribution of agricultural raw materials bases was planned so as to supply regional requirements to industrial bases with a high processing capability but a shortage of agricultural raw materials without affecting the supply of raw materials on a national level. In return for grain, other foodstuffs, and agricultural raw materials, the cities provide electricity, agricultural machinery, chemical fertilizers, and technical know-how to the surrounding rural areas.

Improvements in farming techniques, science, the conditions for production, the development of new crop varieties, as well as the development of industry, communications, and transport facilities have affected the traditional distribution of farm crops. For example, the double cropping of rice has spread from south of the Nanling river to the Huai He area, to the north as far as latitude 34 degrees, and to mountainous areas such as the Yuan Jiang area in Yunnan province. Single cropping has also spread north as far as Heilongjiang province and to some mountainous areas. Winter wheat is now grown as far north as latitude 47 degrees and in Tibet. The cultivation of corn has spread throughout the country, and cash crops, cotton, sugar-cane, sugar-beet and tobacco have also changed in their distribution. In some cases, however, the redistribution of farm crops has been irrational in terms of the conditions and cultivation methods necessary for production.

16. China's Land Resources

CHINA'S total land area of 9.6 million square kilometres comprises one-fifteenth of the world's total land area. It is the third largest country in the world after the USSR and Canada.

The Main Land Resources

Land resources are influenced by such factors as geography, geomorphology, climate, water resources, soil types, vegetation, economic conditions, and land reclamation measures. China's land surface has a complex topography. Approximately one-third of the total area is mountainous terrain; plateaux account for 26 per cent of the total; basins account for 19 per cent; plains account for 12 per cent; and rolling hilly terrain accounts for 10 per cent. Of the mountainous areas, one-third is higher than 3,000 metres in elevation and conditions for cultivation are poor. However, conditions in the mountainous areas, particularly in the tropical and subtropical areas of south China, are in many cases suitable for afforestation and the cultivation of special local products. The mountainous north-west region is an important grazing area as well as the source of rivers which irrigate the agricultural regions in the plains.

The main forms of land use in China are as follows: crop land, 10.4 per cent; fruit, tea, mulberry, and rubber plantations, 12.7 per cent; pasture and grazing land, 33 per cent; inland river and alluvial basins, 3.1 per cent; public facilities in urban areas, 6.9 per cent; and deserts, marshes, swamps, glaciers, and land under snow cover, 19.4 per cent (Fig. 16.1). The large proportion of grazing land and the small proportion of crop land indicate the importance of livestock raising in the future development of China's agriculture.

China is one of the world's richest countries in terms of natural resources. Its area of crop land ranks fourth in the world, forests rank eighth, and grazing land in the north and west alone rank third in the world. The country's large population, however, and the average population density of over 100 per square kilometre (four times the world average) mean that the land resources per capita figure is very low (between one-fifth and one-third the world average). Since 1949, strict policies of land use and population control have been in force to eliminate wasteful land-use practices, such as construction in the densely populated and land-deficient areas in the eastern part of the country, and to reduce the population pressure on the available land.

The distribution of land resources and their productivity, as well as water resources, climate, and soil fertility, vary throughout the country. The three main regions are the eastern monsoon region, the north-western hinterland region, and the western Qinghai–Tibet plateau. The eastern monsoon region accounts for 90 per cent of the country's crop land, forests, and water resources. Animal husbandry is also centred in this region, which suffers from droughts, flooding, and an uneven rainfall. The distribution of forests is also uneven, the main forested areas being the north-east and south-west. Climatic

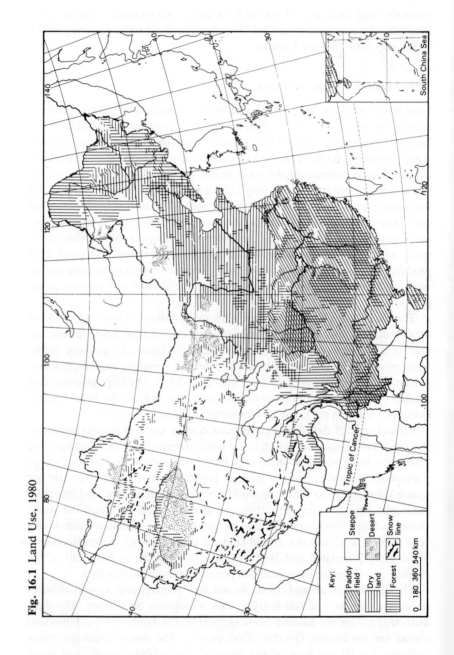

Fig. 16.1 Land Use, 1980

conditions vary from a temperate climate in the north-east (where there are large plains, areas of forest, and fertile soil, but also much waste land, and where the short growing season allows only one crop a year), to a warm temperate climate in the north of the region, and a tropical and subtropical climate in the south. In the northern part of the region, vast amounts of crop land suffer from a shortage of water resources, as well as droughts, flooding, and alkaline soil. There is little forest area. The loess plateau has deep gullies, steep slopes of loess soil, and a fairly long growing season. However, the precipitation is low, vegetation is sparse, and erosion is a serious problem. The southern parts of the region are rich in water and other resources and have a long growing season, but the area lacks flat land and the soil is strongly acidic. Two or three crops are produced each year.

The north-western hinterland region has large areas of desert and a saline-alkaline soil. The eastern half of the region is under pasture, but there is no irrigation or farming in the arid wilderness in the west because of the low soil fertility. The high elevation, steep slopes, short growing season, and the low productivity of the Qinghai–Tibet plateau also prohibit intensive land use.

The uneven distribution of land resources, the varying topography, and the differences in land productivity throughout China have had a significant impact on the distribution of agriculture and must be taken into account in any plans for the future development of agriculture in the three main regions.

Land reclamation has been a common means to increase the area of land under cultivation. Since 1949, 490 million *mu* have been made available in this way to agriculture. However, only 1.88 billion *mu* of land suitable for the development of agriculture, forestry, and animal husbandry remains for reclamation. Of this amount, only about 500 million *mu* are suitable for cultivation and pastures.[1] The amount of land suitable for farming is therefore scarce, although the potential for forestry is large. The vast area of land in China which is unsuitable for cultivation limits the exploitation and utilization of the country's abundant land resources.

The Utilization of Land Resources

The physical geography of China has been adapted for agriculture by the transformation of the physical features of the land, by the use of intensive cultivation, and by the raising of the productive capacity of the land. Since 1949, significant achievements have been made in the development of farm lands, pastures, and forests, and in the construction of water conservation projects.

In 1980, China had 1.49 billion *mu* of farm land, of which 25.5 per cent was paddy rice fields and 74.5 per cent was dry agriculture and irrigated fields. One-third of the total area of farm land is of a poor quality. Since 1949, the total area of land under cultivation has been expanded by land reclamation, but the absolute increase has been small because most of the newly reclaimed land has been used for rural construction, forestry, and grazing, and because of the devastation caused by natural disasters. The total increase in cultivable land

1. *China's Agriculture Yearbook, 1980* (Agriculture Publishing House, Beijing, 1981).

since 1949 is only 24 million *mu*. The increase in the population (at an annual rate of 2 per cent) over the same period has also reduced the total area of farm land and the amount of farm land per capita (Table 16.1).

Table 16.1 The Relationship between Population and Crop Area, 1949–80

Item	1949	1952	1957	1965	1975	1980
Total population (100 million)	5.42	5.75	6.46	7.25	9.19	9.80
Rate of population growth (%)	16.00	20.00	23.20	28.50	15.80	12.00
Total area of crop land (100 million *mu*)	14.68	16.19	16.77	15.53	14.95	14.90
Per-capita area of crop land (*mu*)	2.71	2.82	2.59	2.14	1.62	1.52

Source: *China's Economic Yearbook, 1981* (*Economic Management*, 1981).

Since 1949, 420 million *mu* of newly afforested land has also been added to the total area of forest, which totalled 1.83 billion *mu* in 1980. More than half of the forested area is concentrated in north-east and south-west China, with little or no forest in the agricultural and pastoral regions in the north and north-west. The unit number of timber stock is also comparatively low and little attention has been paid in the past to the replanting and cutting of forests to improve growth. As a result, the average annual per-*mu* output of timber is only 0.12 cubic metres. Scientific management of afforestation is necessary if the output of timber is to increase. The Ministry of Forestry has estimated that 1.17 billion *mu* of waste land and mountainous terrain are suitable for afforestation. Measures have been taken in the form of the establishment of 80 nature reserves in 20 provinces and regions to protect the existing forest resources.

More than 60 per cent of the 4.29 billion *mu* of grassland in China is located in low-yield deserts, wildernesses, and cold highland areas. Some 1.17 billion *mu* of grassland is unused because of the lack of water resources and wells. Climatic conditions in the grasslands are also harsh, with long winters which restrict the growth of grass. In southern and central China, only 20 per cent of the grazing area is utilized and some 200 million *mu* of pastures and prairies in north and west China are suitable for cultivation. The potential therefore exists to raise the productivity level of the available land and to increase the output of cultivated grass. The country's inland waterways and coastal areas are also under-utilized for the development of aquaculture.

The Problems of Land Use

The total area of crop land in China is relatively small and the existing crop land is under-utilized. Farming, forestry, and grazing compete for the use of the available land, especially in the mountainous areas in the south, the semi-agricultural and semi-pastoral areas in the north, and the semi-forest and semi-agricultural areas in the loess plateau and on the fringes of forests. In the agricultural regions, the land use is often not suited to the specific require-ments of agriculture, forestry, and stock breeding, or to the production of grain and cash crops. As a result, the productive capacity of the land is not fully utilized.

A second problem in land use is the over-reclamation of waste land and the unplanned expansion of crop land. The intensive cultivation which has been practised in many farming areas has exhausted the fertility of the soil and fertilization is inadequate. In addition, the over-felling of trees in timber areas, without regard for replanting, and the neglect of young forests have resulted in a low survival rate of timber stock. Furthermore, grazing in the pasture lands tends to be concentrated in the areas of natural pasture, with the effect of depleting the natural resources in these areas. The over-exploitation of ponds and lakes has also depleted these natural resources. The excessive utiliza-tion of resources in some areas has led to problems of soil erosion, soil infertility, despoiled grazing land, exhausted resources, and a disruption of the ecosystem.

Thirdly, China has a low land reclamation index, an uneven distribution of reclamation, and a low yield per unit area. The national index of reclamation is 10.4 per cent, but this figure varies significantly between different parts of the country. In areas with a long history of farming and in the densely populated plains, such as those around Shanghai, Tianjin, and Shandong, and those in Jiangsu, Henan, Hebei, and Anhui provinces, the index varies from 34 to 63 per cent. In the more mountainous and hilly areas with a similar history and population density, such as Beijing and Shaanxi, Hubei, Liaoning, and Shanxi provinces, the index varies between 20 and 27 per cent. Even lower index figures are recorded in the more mountainous provinces and regions and in the border areas in the north-west, north, and south-west, where the topography and harsh natural conditions hinder agricultural production. In the provinces and regions which have a high index of reclamation there is little potential for further reclamation of waste land, whereas those areas where there is sufficient waste land are generally unsuitable for agricultural production.

The yield per unit area in China is also relatively low. In 1980, the national average grain output per *mu* was only 360 *jin*, and the country's average grass output per 100 *mu* was only one-tenth that of Australia. The average output of timber per hectare in areas growing trees of young and middle age was only 1.8 cubic metres.

In spite of the considerable land-use problems that are apparent in agriculture in China today, the potential exists for further development and a rise in productivity if these problems are dealt with appropriately.

The Rationalization of Land Use

The rational use of land resources is determined by natural conditions combined with soil conservation, fertilization, and improvement measures. At present, China's land resources are not being utilized effectively to increase the level of productivity. One way in which the available resources could be used more effectively is by exploiting favourable conditions more fully through multi-purpose utilization. The country's developed transport and marketing networks have made possible regional specialization in crop and sideline production in addition to grain production. In the southern mountainous regions, for example, the land is suitable for crop cultivation, animal husbandry, and, particularly, forestry. The potential of these areas for plantations and sideline production remains undeveloped, as does their potential for forage crop production and beef cattle raising.

In the dry steppe lands of the north, crop yields are low and extensive cultivation has caused the soil to become eroded and sandy, making grazing impractical. The pattern of mixed farming and grazing in these areas is unsuited to the natural conditions. In the pastoral areas, animal husbandry is more suited to the local conditions than agriculture and the rotation of forage with grain cultivation would raise productivity beyond its present low level. In the mixed farming and forestry areas, the same degree of specialization would reduce the present encroachment of crop land upon forested land, which is the most suitable type of production in hilly and mountainous areas.

The expansion of the capital construction of crop lands and improvements in the conditions of production are also means by which the use of land resources may be rationalized and the per-unit output raised. The capital construction of farm land includes measures to reduce the effects of drought and flooding in order to increase the acreage of stable and high-yield land, soil improvement measures, and modernization of the conditions of production. Low-yield land, which comprises one-third of China's total crop land, is in danger of further deterioration unless measures are implemented to improve the soil fertility and the conditions of production by rational land use.

The fertilization of existing crop lands and reclaimed waste land is an important means of transforming low-yield land into high-yield land. Green manure crops and legumes, which add nutrients to the soil, are suitable for cultivation in association with non-nutrient supplying crops such as corn, sorghum, wheat, and rice, or those which are self-sufficient in nitrogen production, such as beans and peanuts. A balance of these types of crops fertilizes the soil while it is in use.

Despite the steady increase in the land utilization ratio since 1949, the available land resources can be further utilized through the expansion of the system of multi-cropping, the combined use of organic and inorganic fertilizers to increase soil fertility, and the scientific improvement of crop strains.

In addition to capital construction and improvement of the conditions of production, cultivable waste land has the potential for further exploitation. China has 500 million *mu* of cultivable waste land, 150 million *mu* of which is average or above in quality. There is also 16 million *mu* of silted coastal land suitable for reclamation. Of the total area of waste land suitable for cultivation, approximately 44 per cent is natural steppe, suitable for the growing of forage, and 16–20 per cent in the hilly areas of the southern provinces is suitable for plantations of oil-bearing crops, tea, and tangerines. There is considerable potential, therefore, for the development of waste land into pasture land and, to some extent, crop land, especially in eastern and northern Heilongjiang province and in Inner Mongolia. In these areas, some 80 million *mu* of the 110 million *mu* of waste land is relatively fertile. The largest area of reclamation, the San Jiang plain, accounts for approximately 40 per cent of the total grain output of Heilongjiang province. It is also an important producer of commodity grain and soya beans.

Many of the areas of cultivable waste land in Heilongjiang province and Inner Mongolia are open and level and are therefore suitable for large-scale mechanized farming. The cultivation of waste lands in other parts of China, such as in Xinjiang autonomous region and the semi-arid and arid steppes of the north-west, is dependent upon the availability of water resources and other conditions of production. In most cases, the land is suitable for the growing of fodder and forage crops for livestock and the establishment of pastures rather than for the growing of grain, cotton, and oil-bearing crops. The silted coastal areas are suitable for the cultivation of cotton, rice, and wheat in the temperate north, rice in the south, and sugar-cane in Fujian and Guangdong provinces.

The hilly and mountainous areas in the south are also under-utilized at present. Covering the provinces of Yunnan, Guizhou, Sichuan, Hunan, Hubei, Guangdong, Guangxi, Fujian, Zhejiang, Jiangxi, Jiangsu, and Anhui, these mountainous areas are rich in flora and fauna, mineral resources, and potential energy resources. Since 1949, significant restructuring of the land has improved the natural conditions and increased the suitability of these areas for forestry, grazing, and, in the valleys and basins, the cultivation of rice, dry crops, and cash crops. With the exception of those areas most suited to forestry and animal husbandry, most of the hilly and mountainous areas in the south are suitable for a mixed economy of farming, forestry, and (to some extent) grazing.

The level of productivity in these areas could be raised further through the capital construction of farm land, an increase in grain production and in the proportion of the total output of forestry and animal husbandry, the development of fir, pine, and bamboo timber forests, and the expansion of fuel wood stock and shelter belts. In addition, the local conditions are appropriate for tea, oil-bearing crops, and subtropical fruit plantations and for the setting up of industries to process local products. The mountain slopes are also suitable for livestock such as cows, sheep, and rabbits. The rational use of land resources in these areas requires specialization in one or two main areas of production, with some secondary areas.

In the cultivable waste land in the south (approximately 80 million *mu*), most of which is located in Yunnan province and Hainan Island, the hot, humid, and wet subtropical and tropical climate is suitable for the cultivation of oil-bearing crops, grains, rubber, and other tropical crops. The soil fertility is poor, however, and erosion has seriously damaged the vegetation. If the land resources in these areas are to be exploited more fully and the level of productivity is to be raised, improvement measures which take into consideration the local conditions will need to be implemented.

17. Grain Crops

GRAIN is the principal food crop for China's one billion people, accounting for 70–80 per cent of the total output value of agricultural products and 80–8 per cent of the total sown area of all crops. These high proportions have remained basically unchanged since 1949.

The Structure of Grain Production

The main grain crops in China are rice, wheat, sweet potatoes, corn, sorghum, millet, and soya beans. Rice has long ranked first in the total grain output, followed by wheat, corn, and the other main crops (Table 17.1).

Since 1949, the proportions of rice and wheat in the total grain output have increased steadily (rice by 2 per cent and wheat by 6 per cent between 1952 and 1980). The proportions of sorghum, millet, and soya beans have decreased accordingly (by 4.6, 5.3, and 3.3 per cent respectively). Rice, wheat, potatoes, and corn accounted for 88.9 per cent of the total grain output in 1980. The significant increase in the output of wheat and corn can be attributed to their adaptability to various conditions, the less sophisticated farming techniques required compared with rice, and the large area of non-irrigated farm land suitable for their cultivation.

The outputs of sorghum, soya beans, and, especially, millet have decreased since 1949, partly because of the traditional view that they are low-yield crops. In fact, millet is particularly suited to the conditions in the North China Plain and sorghum produces high yields in low-lying, damp areas. These crops therefore have the potential for higher outputs in the future.

A further change in the structure of grain production since 1949 has been the rapid expansion in the area devoted to the cultivation of sweet potatoes. In general, the main changes since 1949 have been in the relative importance of rice and wheat and the coarse food grains, in the proportion of high-yield and low-yield crops in the total output, and in the proportion of summer, early season, and autumn grain crops (Table 17.2). The increase in the summer grain output since 1957 is due largely to the increased wheat yield per unit area. By 1980, the total wheat output had more than doubled. The use of double- and triple-harvest rice in south China during the same period increased the sown area of early season rice, its yield per unit area, and its proportion in the total rice output. The total sown area of early season rice rose from 118 million *mu* in 1957 to 180–90 million *mu* in 1971, while the per-*mu* yield increased from 328 *jin* in 1957 to 590 *jin* in 1980. Its total output increased 250 per cent between 1957 and 1980 and its proportion in the total rice output increased from 22.3 to 35.3 per cent during the same period.

Multiple cropping since 1949 has reduced the area of farm land devoted to grain crops and the multiple crop index has risen accordingly (Table 17.3). Fluctuations in the amount of farm land used for grain crops and in the total sown area were the main factors affecting the output of grain between 1949 and 1980.

Table 17.1 China's Grain Output, 1952–80 (100 million *jin*)

Year	Rice	Wheat	Sweet Potatoes*	Corn	Sorghum	Millet	Soya Beans	Other
1952	1,369.0	363.0	327.0	337.0	222.0	231.0	190.0	241.0
1957	1,736.0	473.0	438.0	429.0	153.0	171.0	201.0	301.0
1962	1,260.0	333.0	489.0	325.0	122.0	106.0	135.0	382.0
1965	1,754.0	504.0	397.0	473.0	142.0	124.0	123.0	372.0
1970	2,200.0	584.0	510.0	613.0	164.0	176.0	184.0	362.0
1975	2,511.0	906.0	571.0	944.0	215.0	143.0	145.0	272.0
1979	2,875.0	1,255.0	569.0	1,201.0	153.0	123.0	149.0	289.0
1980	2,785.2	1,083.2	556.9	1,234.5	135.5	108.9	157.6	302.6

Note: Five *jin* of sweet potatoes is equivalent to one *jin* of food grain.
Source: China's Agricultural Yearbook, 1980 (Agriculture Publishing House, Beijing, 1981).

Table 17.2 Seasonal Food Grain Output, 1957–80 (100 million *jin*)

Year	Summer Grain	% of Total Grain Output	Early Rice	% of Total Grain Output	Autumn Grain	% of Total Grain Output
1957	606.3	15.5	386.8	9.9	2,907.9	74.5
1963	473.9	13.9	334.2	9.8	2,591.9	76.2
1965	600.9	15.4	511.7	13.2	2,778.4	71.4
1970	681.6	14.2	748.2	15.6	3,369.2	70.2
1975	998.4	17.6	974.0	17.1	3,717.6	65.3
1977	881.2	15.6	924.1	16.3	3,849.7	68.1
1978	1,187.5	19.5	1,016.2	16.7	3,891.3	63.8
1979	1,357.3	20.4	1,039.5	15.7	4,245.2	63.9
1980	1,157.5	18.2	982.8	15.4	4,224.1	66.4

Source: China's Agricultural Yearbook, 1980 (Agriculture Publishing House, Beijing, 1981).

Table 17.3 The Total Grain Output and Cultivated Area, 1949–80

Year	Total Output (100 million *jin*)	Sown Area	Farm Land for Grain Crops	% of Multiple Cropping Farm Land
1949	2,264.0	164,938.0	—	—
1952	3,278.0	185,968.0	—	—
1957	3,901.0	200,450.0	140,335	142.8
1965	3,891.0	179,441.0	135,303	132.6
1976	5,726.0	181,115.0	116,212	155.8
1979	6,642.0	178,894.0	116,572	153.5
1980	6,364.4	174,708.8		

Sources: China's Agricultural Yearbook, 1980 (Agriculture Publishing House, Beijing, 1981) and *China's Economic Yearbook, 1981* (*Economic Management*, 1981).

Significant changes have also occurred since 1949 in the distribution of the grain-deficient and grain-surplus regions. Many provinces, particularly the eight coastal provinces, were grain-deficient before 1949 and few inland provinces were grain-sufficient. Following the Opium War, even the traditionally grain-surplus provinces of Hunan, Jiangxi, and Anhui experienced reductions in their surplus grain output. After 1949, the coastal grain-deficient provinces of Guangdong, Fujian, Jiangsu, Hebei, and Shandong became self-sufficient and Jiangsu was able to supply some surplus grain to other regions. Surplus grain was also produced in Zhejiang, Sichuan, Hunan, and Hubei provinces. Heilongjiang province became the largest granary in the country.

Grain bases established in the developed areas along the middle and lower reaches of the Chang Jiang assisted in the economic recovery of those areas, increased their level of productivity, and made available to the state surplus grain for distribution to the grain-deficient areas. New grain bases were also established in Heilongjiang and Jilin provinces, which improved the supply of grain to the grain-deficient regions in north-east China. The steady increase in the output of grain since 1949, the restructuring of production, and improved marketing have laid a solid foundation for the continued development of China's grain production.

The Characteristics of Grain Production

Insufficient grain was produced in China before 1949 to meet the country's requirements. By 1980, however, the total national output of grain had increased to 636.44 billion *jin* from 226.4 billion *jin* in 1949 (an annual growth rate of 3.4 per cent). This growth rate exceeded that of the other main grain-growing countries (Table 17.4), despite variations in the rate over the period 1949–80 (Table 17.5).

The rapid growth in the output of grain during the periods of rehabilitation (1950–2) and national economic readjustment (1963–5), the decline in growth during other periods, and the dramatic decline during the 2nd FYP period were due to natural as well as political factors. The country was affected by frequent natural calamities during these periods when prevention

Table 17.4 The World Total Grain Output and Growth Rate, 1949–78

Country	Total Output (100 million jin)			1949–78		1970–8	
	1949	1970	1978	Growth Rate (%)	Annual Average Growth Rate (%)	Growth Rate (%)	Annual Average Growth Rate (%)
China	2,264	4,799	6,095	169.2	3.5	27.0	3.1
United States	3,148	4,433	6,561	108.4	2.6	48.0	5.1
Japan	356	384	361	1.4	0.1	–6.0	–0.7
France	322	674	944	93.2	2.3	40.1	4.3
Federal Republic of Germany	290	413	522	80.0	2.1	26.4	3.0
Great Britain	205	300	374	82.4	2.1	24.7	2.8
Romania	112[1]	227	403	259.8[3]	4.5	77.5	7.4
Yugoslavia	158	249	293	85.4	2.2	17.7	2.0
India	1,257[2]	2,542	3,091	145.9	3.2	21.6	2.5
Brazil	224	551	736	228.6	4.2	33.6	3.7
Canada	400	696	856	114.0	2.8	43.6	4.6
Argentina	154	412	610	296.1	4.9	48.1	5.1
World total	15,149	27,850	35,952	137.3	3.0	29.1	3.3

Notes: 1. 1950 figure.
2. Sweet potato output not included.
3. Between 1950 and 1970.

Source: China's Agricultural Yearbook, 1980 (Agriculture Publishing House, Beijing, 1981).

Table 17.5 Changes in the Growth Rate of Grain Output, 1949–80

Period	Increased/ Decreased Amount (100 million jin)	Annual Average Increased/ Decreased Amount (100 million jin)	Growth Rate (%)	Annual Average Growth Rate (%)
Reconstruction period (1950–2)	1,014.0	338.2	44.80	13.1
1st FYP (1953–7)	623.0	124.5	19.00	3.5
2nd FYP (1958–62)	−701.0	−140.2	−18.00	−3.9
1963–5	691.0	230.2	21.60	6.7
3rd FYP (1966–70)	967.0	193.6	24.90	4.5
4th FYP (1971–5)	832.0	166.4	17.10	3.2
5th FYP (1976–80)	674.4	134.9	11.85	2.2
1949–80	4,100.4	132.3	181.10	3.4

Source: *China's Agricultural Yearbook, 1980* (Agriculture Publishing House, Beijing, 1981).

and control measures were undeveloped. Droughts, flooding, frosts, typhoons, low temperatures, and plant diseases and pests reduced grain yields and reflected the country's inability to withstand natural influences on production.

The political instability of the years 1958–62 and 1966–76 also affected agricultural production through the misuse of funds and material resources. The restructuring of production following the Cultural Revolution also led to a drastic reduction in the sown area of grain, resulting in a 2.7 billion *jin* decrease in the total grain output in 1980 over the previous year.

A second characteristic of grain production is its relatively low level and its low marketing rate despite China's being one of the largest grain-growing countries in the world (second only to the United States). The low level of production is due largely to the low yield per unit area. In 1949, the national average yield per *mu* of sown area of grain was 137 *jin*. By 1980, the yield had increased to 364 *jin*, an average annual increase of only 3.2 per cent. The growth rate of the grain yield per *mu* also varied during different periods (Table 17.6). Whilst the average grain yield was higher than the world average, it fell below that of the developed countries (Table 17.7).

China also lags behind most other countries in terms of labour productivity. For example, in 1979, each Chinese worker cultivated an average of 4.88 *mu* of land and produced 2,141 *jin* of grain, compared with 8.9 *mu* and 4,932 *jin* in Japan, 143.3 *mu* and 21,428 *jin* in the Soviet Union, and 1,198.1 *mu* and 281,965 *jin* in the United States in 1978. In 1979, each Chinese worker supported 3.5 persons, including himself, in terms of the level of productivity, compared with 80 persons in the United States.

The rate of marketable grain is also low in China. For many years after 1949, the state purchased only slightly more than 20 per cent of the total

Table 17.6 The Average Growth of Grain Yield per *mu*, 1949-80

Period	Increase/Decrease of Yield per *mu* (*jin*)	Growth Rate of Yield per *mu* (%)
Reconstruction period (1950-2)	13.0	8.7
1st FYP (1953-7)	6.3	2.1
2nd FYP (1958-62)	-4.0	-2.1
1963-5	14.0	7.4
3rd FYP (1966-70)	11.0	4.6
4th FYP (1971-5)	8.2	2.8
5th FYP (1976-80)	10.2	3.1
1949-80	7.3	3.2

Source: China's Agricultural Yearbook, 1980 (Agriculture Publishing House, Beijing, 1981).

grain output, half of which was supplied to the grain-deficient areas. By 1979, only 11 provinces and regions had a surplus of grain and Hunan province, the largest supplier, was able to supply only 3 per cent of its total grain output. Less than 1 per cent of the total national grain output in that year was surplus grain.

The traditionally grain-deficient areas include the Beijing, Tianjin, and Shanghai municipalities, and the provinces and regions of Liaoning, Shanxi, Shaanxi, Gansu, Ningxia, Inner Mongolia, Qinghai, Xinjiang, and Guizhou. The deficiencies in these areas are met by the grain-surplus provinces of Heilongjiang, Jilin, Jiangsu, Anhui, Zhejiang, Hunan, Hubei, Jiangxi, Guangdong, and Sichuan. The rest of China is self-sufficient in grain production. In recent years, however, the supply of surplus grain has diminished and the requirements of the grain-deficient areas have increased. The resulting imbalance in the supply and demand for state commodity grain requires a rapid increase in the level and stability of grain production if the present situation is to improve.

A further characteristic of China's grain production is its uneven development since 1949 in different parts of the country. Only four provinces have experienced an average annual increase of more than 4 per cent; five provinces have averaged less than 3 per cent. The remaining 20 provinces and regions have experienced an average annual growth rate of between 3 and 4 per cent. Low-yield areas (producing less than 800 *jin* per *mu*) account for 77.5 per cent of the national total. These areas are distributed mainly in the north-west loess plateau, in low-lying land and areas prone to waterlogging on the Huang He, Huai He, and Hai He plains, in the semi-drought stricken areas in the western part of north-east China, the eastern part of Inner Mongolia, and the Yunnan-Guizhou plateau.

The uneven development of production in different parts of the country is due in part to the natural conditions in those areas. Another important factor is the degree of technical transformation of agriculture in different areas. In Jiangsu province, for example, the average annual rate of increase in grain output since 1949 is 4.7 per cent. This steady growth in output is attributable

Table 17.7 The World Grain Yield per *mu* and Growth Rate, 1949–78

Country	Per-*mu* Yield (*jin*)			1949–78		1952–78	
	1949	1952	1978	Annual Average Increase (*jin*)	Growth Rate (%)	Annual Average Increase (*jin*)	Growth Rate (%)
China	137	176	337	6.9	3.2	6.2	2.5
United States	218	231	465	8.5	2.6	9.0	2.7
Japan	399	431	743	11.9	2.2	12.0	2.1
France	217	235	618	13.8	3.7	14.7	3.8
Federal Republic of Germany	356	372	610	8.8	1.9	9.2	1.9
Great Britain	350	357	605	8.8	1.9	9.5	2.0
Romania	101*	131	355	8.8	4.6	8.6	3.9
Yugoslavia	172	90	383	7.3	2.8	11.3	5.7
India	96	93	160	2.2	1.8	2.6	2.1
Brazil	156	149	149	-0.2	-0.2	0.0	0.0
Canada	135	235	302	5.8	2.8	2.6	1.0
Argentina	141	183	310	5.8	2.8	4.9	2.0
World average	154	163	261	3.7	1.8	3.8	1.8

Note: Figure for 1950.
Source: China's Agricultural Yearbook, 1980 (Agriculture Publishing House, Beijing, 1981).

to the province's favourable natural conditions as well as to the emphasis placed on the capital construction of farm land and the technical transformation of agriculture. In 1979, irrigated land accounted for 72.4 per cent of Jiangsu's total cultivated land; electricity used for farming averaged 1 horsepower per 5.1 *mu*; and 139.6 *jin* of fertilizer was used per *mu*. In addition, the cropping system was reformed and advanced scientific farming methods were adopted. By comparison, some low-yield areas have unfavourable natural conditions and serious soil erosion problems. In addition, extensive cultivation, unplanned land reclamation, and the neglect of soil and water conservation measures have further upset the ecosystem, resulting in poor soil and low yields.

The uneven development of grain production is also reflected in the distribution of commodity grain bases. The 170 state commodity grain bases are situated in east, central-south, and north-east China, and in the Chengdu plain, whereas the low-yield and grain-deficient counties are located in the north-west and south-west. This imbalance between supply and demand exacerbates the problem of uneven development in different regions.

The Distribution and Production of Staple Food Crops

The main staple food crops in China are rice, wheat, soya beans, and sweet potatoes. Their sown area is large, producing high yields.

Paddy Rice

Rice is the most important of the grain crops and the staple food of two-thirds of the country's population. Its total output and sown area rank first in China. In 1980, the output of rice accounted for 43.8 per cent of the total grain output and 29 per cent of the total sown area of grain crops.

The warm temperatures and frequent monsoons of the tropical, subtropical, and warm temperate zones, the large areas of plains and hilly land, and the abundant inland water resources provide favourable conditions for the cultivation of rice, particularly in the south, in the middle and lower reaches of the Chang Jiang, and on the Yunnan–Guizhou plateau. Cultivation in the north is dependent upon the improvement of hydrological conditions. The popularization of improved strains has also increased rice yields.

China's total annual output of rice comprises one-third of the world's total. Between 1949 and 1978, the output of rice rose by 181.5 per cent (an average annual increase of 3.6 per cent — higher than the world average increase). In addition to the increase in output, the yield per unit area and the sown area have also expanded steadily (Table 17.8). Between 1949 and 1980, some 120.7 million *mu* of sown area was added to the total area of rice cultivation (an increase of 31.3 per cent). During the same period, the per-*mu* yield of rice increased by 118.3 per cent, while the total output rose by 186.3 per cent.

Rice production in China is notable not only for its high output, but also for its wide distribution. Rice is cultivated over a vast area stretching from Hainan Island in the tropical south to Heilongjiang province in the cold

Table 17.8 Rice Production, 1949–80

Item	1949	1952	1957	1965	1980
Sown area (10,000 *mu*)	38,563.0	42,573.0	48,362.0	44,737.0	50,633.0
Average per-*mu* yield (*jin*)	252.0	322.0	359.0	392.0	550.0
Total output (100 million *jin*)	972.9	1,368.5	1,735.5	1,754.4	2,785.2

Source: *China's Agricultural Yearbook, 1980* (Agriculture Publishing House, Beijing, 1981).

temperate north, and from Taiwan in the east to Xinjiang in the west. Moreover, it is cultivated in low-lying areas, marsh lands, and tidal fields along the coast as well as in hilly areas 2,500 metres or more above sea level, such as northern Yunnan province, where the temperature is warm and there are sufficient water resources.

The distribution of the rice-growing regions is related closely to natural conditions. The main rice-growing regions are located in the eastern part of the country where monsoons are frequent, in the provinces on the Yunnan–Guizhou plateau, and along the Chang Jiang valley south of the Qin Ling and the Huai He. Rice is produced mainly on the plains by rivers and lakes, in low-lying areas, hilly land, and low mountainous areas. Some 94 per cent of the country's total output of rice is grown in the provinces, municipalities, and regions of Sichuan, Yunnan, Guizhou, Hubei, Hunan, Guangxi, Guangdong, Fujian, Jiangxi, Zhejiang, Anhui, Jiangsu, and Shanghai. These areas have abundant water resources, a high rainfall, and warm temperatures. In the north, where natural conditions are less favourable, paddy fields are scattered in a few areas, and wheat is the predominant grain crop.

In the south, long-grained rice is double-cropped; in the areas along the Chang Jiang valley, it is both single- and double-cropped. Further north, short-grained rice is single-cropped. The main rice-producing regions can be classified according to their natural conditions, cropping systems, and rice varieties. In the south, for example, two crops of rice are grown each year in Guangdong and Fujian provinces and in the Guangxi Zhuang autonomous region south and east of the Nan Ling. The cultivation of early and late season crops is possible because of the high temperature and rainfall and the long growing season. This part of the country ranks first in the production of long-grained rice.

The most concentrated rice-producing areas in this region are the Zhu Jiang delta and the Chao Shan plain in Guangdong province, the coastal plain in Fujian province, and the area along the Xi Jiang in Guangxi. Next in importance are the valleys and basins in the hilly and mountainous areas.

A second type of rice-producing area lies in central China, where one or two crops are grown each year. This region, situated in the middle and lower reaches of the Chang Jiang, north of the Nan Ling, and south of the Qin Ling and the Huai He, includes Sichuan, Hunan, Hubei, Anhui, Jiangxi, Jiangsu, and Zhejiang provinces, as well as the Shanghai area. The total rice output and the sown area of the region constitute over half of the national total. Improvements in water conservation and cultivation techniques and the introduction of new varieties of rice have changed the area from a single-cropping to a double-cropping area, producing mainly long-grained rice.

The third main area is the rice-producing region on the Yunnan–Guizhou plateau. Of the rice-producing areas in the south-west, this region ranks second after central and south China in total output and sown area. The climate and topography of the plateau vary to the extent that long-grained rice is grown on the lower flat land and hilly areas, while short-grained rice is grown in the higher mountain areas. In the centre of the plateau, both short- and long-grained rice are grown, as well as dry, deep water, glutinous, and soft rice. Double-cropping is practised in the river valley.

The other main rice-producing area is in the north, where single-grained rice is single-cropped. The north ranks first in the region in terms of sown area of rice, followed by the north-east. The north-west has scattered paddy fields only, with the exception of large rice-growing areas in Inner Mongolia and the Ningxia Hui autonomous region. In Qinghai and Tibet, the low temperatures and unfavourable topography restrict rice growing to the low lying areas of the river valleys.

This present distribution of rice cultivation in China (Fig. 17.1) is in the process of being transformed as water conservation measures are improved, cropping systems are reformed, and new varieties of rice become popular, resulting in an expansion of the sown area. For example, the middle and lower reaches of the Chang Jiang have changed from single to double cropping.

Wheat

Wheat is the main cereal crop in China, second only to rice in total output and sown area. In 1980, the wheat-producing area accounted for 24.8 per cent of the total grain-producing area, and wheat accounted for 17 per cent of the total grain output.

A number of varieties of wheat can be cultivated in a temperate climate. It is the main non-irrigated summer crop, able to withstand the spring droughts which occur over much of the country. Winter wheat is also important in China due to its suitability to the natural conditions and the consequent increase in the total wheat output.

China ranks second in the world in wheat output and sown area (15 and 12 per cent respectively). Between 1949 and 1978, the total output of wheat increased by 290.2 per cent (an average annual increase of 4.8 per cent — higher than the world average). Before 1949, wheat and flour had to be imported in order to meet the country's requirements. However, improvements in irrigation and in the conditions of production since 1949 have led to a rapid increase in the output and the sown area (Table 17.9).

The increase in the total sown area (from 320 million *mu* in 1949 to 430 million *mu* in 1980) was the result of the opening up of land and the increased use of multiple cropping methods and improved seed varieties. Land

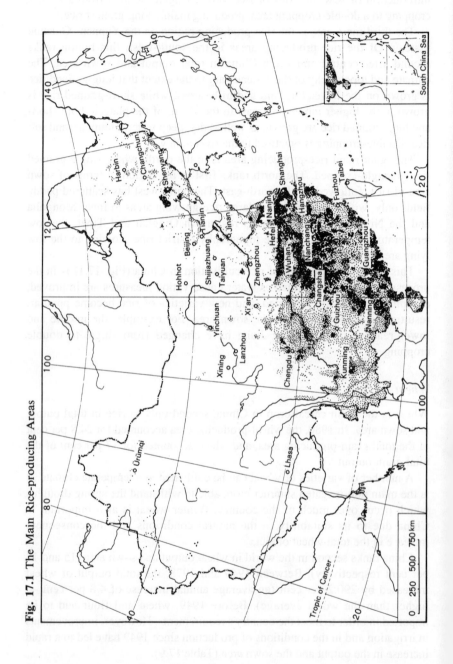

Fig. 17.1 The Main Rice-producing Areas

Table 17.9 Wheat Production, 1949–80

Item	1949	1952	1957	1965	1980
Sown area (10,000 *mu*)	32,273	37,170	41,313	37,064	43,266.7
Average per-*mu* output (*jin*)	86	98	114	136	250
Total output (100 million *jin*)	276.2	362.5	472.8	504.4	1,083.2

Source: China's Agricultural Yearbook, 1980 (Agriculture Publishing House, Beijing, 1981).

was opened up, for example, in the provinces and regions of Heilongjiang, Inner Mongolia, Xinjiang, Gansu, Qinghai, and Anhui, which had rich waste land resources. In the southern provinces and regions, the multiple cropping area was increased, in many cases by rotating wheat with rice. Improved seed varieties were an important factor in the increase in the sown area in the provinces and regions along the Huang He.

The per-unit yield of wheat has increased during the period since 1949 through improvements in the management of wheat cultivation. The degree of improvement has varied, however, due to the natural conditions in different parts of the country. Heilongjiang, Jilin, Inner Mongolia, and Xinjiang had the highest and fastest increase in the per-unit yield, compared with Guangxi, Jiangxi, Hunan, Liaoning, Guangdong, and Fujian, where the increase was low and unsteady.

Although the average yield per hectare in China is higher than the world average, it is lower than some agriculturally advanced countries. Furthermore, the level of development of production varies throughout the country. In 1980, for example, the per-*mu* yield in Jiangsu province was 437 *jin*, compared with only 80 *jin* in Guangxi. This difference in yield can be attributed to the differences in climate, soil, and water resources; the differences in the economic conditions of the labour force, production experience, and the availability of farm animals, fertilizers, seeds, and so on; and the differences in the level of management and the importance of wheat in grain production. Future increases in the per-unit yield of wheat will depend on improvements in the irrigation network, the spread of improved varieties, the increased use of fertilizers, crop rotation, and the rational utilization of natural resources.

The three main wheat-producing regions in China are the spring wheat region, the north China winter wheat region, and the south China winter wheat region (Fig. 17.2). The spring wheat region includes the provinces of Heilongjiang, Jilin, and Liaoning in the north-east; Inner Mongolia, Qinghai, Xinjiang, and Tibet; and most of Gansu, western Sichuan, Shaanxi, Shanxi, and north-western Hebei provinces. The main wheat-producing areas are Heilongjiang, Inner Mongolia, Gansu, and Xinjiang. The Songliao and San Jiang plains in the north-east are also potentially major producing areas, with

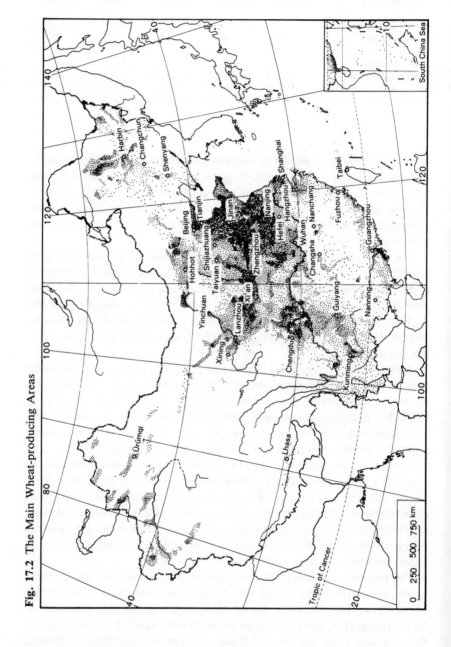

Fig. 17.2 The Main Wheat-producing Areas

fertile soil and flat terrain suitable for large-scale mechanized farming. In 1980, the sown area of Heilongjiang province was 31.578 million *mu* and the total wheat output was 7.9 billion *jin* (both accounting for 40 per cent of the total spring wheat sown area and output). Inner Mongolia accounted for 20 per cent of the sown area and 14 per cent of the total wheat output.

The spring wheat region is characterized by a dry, cold climate, with very cold winters and a short frost-free period. Cultivation is annual. The large area of waste land in the region is suitable for wheat production and mechanized ploughing. The potential exists, therefore, for enlarging the sown area of this wheat-producing region. The north China winter wheat region — the main wheat-producing region in the country — includes Henan, Hebei, Shanxi, most of Shaanxi, southern Gansu, northern Jiangsu and Anhui provinces, and all of Shandong province. The region accounts for approximately two-thirds of the total wheat sown area and output, and Shandong, Henan, Hebei, and Shaanxi are the most important wheat-producing provinces in the country. The climate and soil are favourable for wheat production, allowing three crops every two years. Improvements in the conditions of production since 1949 have increased considerably the sown area of winter wheat. The main problem of the region — spring droughts — can be rectified by improved irrigation systems.

The south China winter wheat region includes Zhejiang, Fujian, Jiangxi, Guangxi, Hunan, Hubei, Yunnan, eastern Sichuan, southern Anhui, southern Jiangsu, and southern Henan provinces. The most important wheat-producing areas are Anhui, Jiangsu, Sichuan, and Hubei provinces, where the commodity rate of wheat is higher than in other parts of the country because of the importance of rice as a food crop. The natural conditions in these provinces, the main commodity wheat-producing region in China, are suitable for wheat and the growing period is long. Wheat is rotated with rice or cotton, using a two-crops-a-year cultivation system, or with rice and other grains or with two crops of rice, using a three-crops-a-year system. Heavy rains during the spring and summer cause occasional floods and wheat diseases; drainage and disease prevention measures therefore need to be improved in this region.

Soya Beans

Before the start of this century, China was the only country in the world producing soya beans. In 1930, soya beans were exported for the first time from the north-east provinces to England and the United States and they have since become an important commodity in world agricultural trade. Before 1937, the average annual output of soya beans was approximately 20 billion *jin*. The north-east provinces accounted for 35 per cent of the total output and 50 per cent of the total exports. During the Second World War, the production of soya beans was seriously affected and by 1949, the total output was only 10.17 billion *jin* (half that of the pre-war period).

The development of soya bean production remained slow after 1949, increasing by only 48 per cent between 1949 and 1978 (an average annual increase of 1.4 per cent). The total output in 1980 was only 65 per cent of the total output in 1938. The main reasons for the low output in the post-war years have been poor management, backward irrigation systems, a shortage of fertilizers, droughts, and floods.

Soya bean cultivation in China is widespread (Fig. 17.3). With the exception of Tibet and Qinghai, where temperatures are too low, soya beans are grown in every province. There are five main soya bean-producing regions. The north spring soya bean region consists mainly of the north-eastern provinces of Heilongjiang, Jilin, and Liaoning. One crop is produced each year and soya beans are usually rotated annually with wheat, millet, sorghum, and corn. The region is the most important soya bean-producing region in China, accounting for 37 per cent of the total sown area and 42 per cent of the country's total output in 1980. Heilongjiang province alone accounted for 20 per cent of the country's total sown area and 25 per cent of the total output. It is the largest commodity soya bean production base in China.

Summer soya beans are grown using a three-crops-in-two-years system along the middle and lower reaches of the Huang He and the Huai He valley. This region includes Shandong, Henan, Hebei, Shaanxi, Shanxi, northern Jiangsu, and northern Anhui provinces. It is the second largest soya bean-producing region in the country. Soya beans are usually rotated with wheat and the commodity rate is low. Summer soya beans are also grown in the Chang Jiang valley region using a two-crops-a-year system. Most of the output is used in the production of non-staple foodstuffs; very little is used for export and oil extraction.

Autumn soya beans are grown using a three-crops-a-year system in the region south of the Chang Jiang, including southern Zhejiang, Jiangxi, and Hunan, northern Guangdong and Guangxi, and most of Fujian province. The soya beans are grown in the rice fields to increase the fertility of the soil and the output of other crops.

In the subtropical region that includes southern Guangdong, Guangxi, and Yunan, two crops of soya beans are grown each year. Despite the favourable climate, however, the sown area is small and the output low.

Other Food Grains

Apart from rice and wheat, the main food grains in China are corn, sorghum, millet and potato varieties, barley, oats, broom-corn millet, buckwheat, and bean varieties. Their cultivation is widespread because of their suitability for all soils and natural conditions, their short growing season, and their suitability for rotation with other crops. Such food grains help to increase the utilization rate of the existing cultivated land and to increase the total grain output. In the north, north-east, and north-west, where they comprise about two-thirds of the total grain output of the region, they are essential grain crops.

Corn

Corn is the third most important grain crop after rice and wheat. Its sown area and output accounted for 17.2 per cent and 19.4 per cent respectively of the total grain production of the country in 1980. Corn also ranked second only

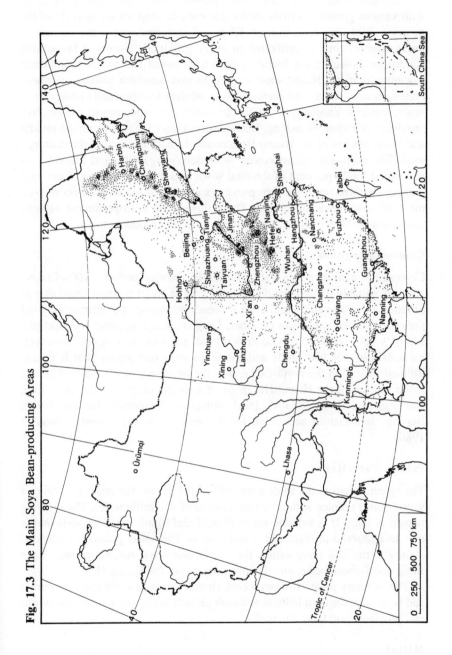

Fig. 17.3 The Main Soya Bean-producing Areas

to the United States in world production, accounting for 16 per cent of the world total. The per-*mu* yield in 1980 of 410 *jin* was second only to that of rice.

Corn grows well in a warm, damp climate. The many varieties of corn, with various growing periods, make it a suitable crop for many parts of the country. With the exception of Tibet and Qinghai, where the climate is unfavourable, corn is cultivated in every province. The most favourable conditions, however, are found in the hilly areas of Heilongjiang, southern Liaoning, northern Hebei, south-eastern Shanxi, southern Shaanxi, northern Hubei, western Henan, the Sichuan basin, western Guizhou and Guangxi, and south-western Yunnan. In 1980, the sown area and output of the five provinces of Hebei, Shandong, Henan, Shanxi, and Shaanxi along the middle and lower reaches of the Huang He accounted for 40 per cent of the country's total. The north-eastern provinces — Heilongjiang, Jilin, and Liaoning — accounted for 24 per cent of the total sown area and 27 per cent of the total output; the three south-western provinces accounted for 16 per cent of both the total sown area and output. These three main corn-producing regions accounted for 80 per cent of the country's total corn production.

Chinese Sorghum

Chinese sorghum favours a warm climate. Its growing period is 100–40 days and it is suitable for semi-arid areas. It is also a water-tolerant crop, able to produce a considerable yield even if inundated during the autumn growing period. With the exception of Tibet, Qinghai, Zhejiang, and the Shanghai area, Chinese sorghum can be grown in all parts of the country. However, its suitability for low lands and saline-alkaline soil means that it is distributed mainly in the north-east and in the provinces along the middle and lower reaches of the Huang He. Its sown area and output in Liaoning, Jilin, Heilongjiang, Hebei, Shanxi, Inner Mongolia, Shandong, Henan, Anhui, Beijing, and Tianjin accounted for 90 per cent of the country's total in 1980.

Potato Varieties

The sweet potato is the most important of the potato varieties. It favours a warm, sunny climate with an annual rainfall of 450 millimetres. The growing season is long. It is suitable for both acid and lightly alkaline soils and is able to withstand droughts, hail, and insects. The sweet potato is cultivated mainly in the Zhu Jiang valley, the middle and lower reaches of the Chang Jiang, the Sichuan basin, and the lower reaches of the Huang He.

The ordinary potato favours a cool climate. It has a short growing period and is suitable for high latitude and high altitude areas, particularly the north-east provinces and Inner Mongolia.

Millet

Millet is a traditional crop, with a short growing period and the ability to resist drought. It favours sunny conditions and requires half as much water as wheat. Millet is particularly suited to the conditions in the north, north-east, and north-west, where there is a dry climate, a short growing season, and variable rainfall. The main millet-producing areas are Heilongjiang, Inner Mongolia, Shanxi, Hebei, Jilin, Henan, Shaanxi, Shandong, and Liaoning provinces. Their combined sown area and output account for 95 per cent of the country's total.

The Distribution of Commodity Grain Bases

China's vast area and population mean that the establishment of commodity grain bases, the raising of the commercial rate of grain, and an increase in the country's food reserves are necessary if the quality of life is to improve, the economy is to advance, and social stability is to be achieved.

The main grain production bases in China are concentrated along the middle and lower reaches of the Chang Jiang. Since the time of the Eastern Jin dynasty in the 4th century up to the end of the Qing dynasty (1911), these bases supplied surplus grain to north China. However, as foreign involvement in China increased in the early 20th century, more and more rice and flour were brought into the country from outside. In addition, the building of factories and railways stimulated the development of industrial crop production. These changes had a serious effect on grain production in the traditional 'bread baskets'. At the same time, however, the formation of industrial and com-mercial cities and the expansion of the industrial crop planting areas led to the development of commodity grain production in such areas as the plains of the Donting, Poyang, and Chaohu lakes in Hunan, Jiangxi, and Anhui provinces respectively, and in some counties on the Lake Taihu plain in Jiangsu province. Located at the centre of these grain-planting areas, and with developed transport facilities, Changsha, Jiujiang, Wuhu, and Wuxi became the main commodity rice bases in the country. During the Second World War, however, these areas were damaged considerably and grain production dropped to a very low level.

Since 1949, the country's economy has developed rapidly and many industrial bases have been established or expanded. Increases in the standard of living and the growth of the urban population have been accompanied by steady increases in the need for commodity grain. The restoration of the old commodity bases and the establishment of new ones became a major concern, along with the development of grain production throughout the country. Thirteen commodity grain bases are in the process of being established or are planned, including bases in Jiangsu, Zhejiang, Guangdong, Hunan, Hubei, Jiangxi, Jilin, Liaoning, Anhui, Gansu, Ningxia, Inner Mongolia, and Heilongjiang. The per-capita area under cultivation, the per-capita grain output for the agricultural population, the yield per unit area, and the rate of commodity grain in these areas are higher than the country's average.

The commodity grain bases in China fall into four categories (Fig. 17.4). The bases in the Chang Jiang and Zhu Jiang deltas, the Jianghan plain, and the areas around the Dongting and Poyang lakes are the traditional 'bread baskets', which have long supplied the country with commodity grain. These areas have 70 million *mu* of cultivated land and an agricultural population of 53 million (1.4 *mu* per person). In 1980, the rate of commodity grain in the

Fig. 17.4 The Main Commodity Grain Bases

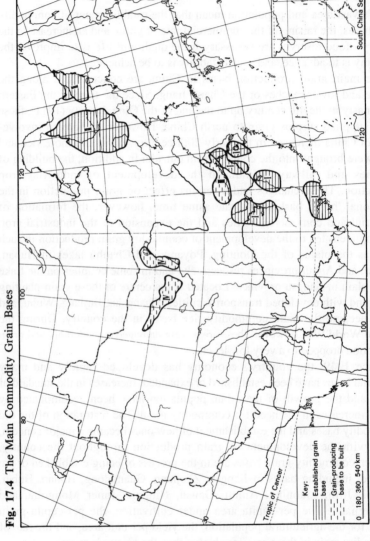

Notes: I The Changjiang delta, Zhujiang delta, Jianghan plain and areas around Dongting and Poyang Lakes. II The 31 counties and cities in Heilongjiang province and the central areas of Jilin and Liaoning provinces. III The northern areas of Jiangsu and Anhui provinces. IV The Hexi corridor in Gansu province and the Hetao areas at the great bend of the Huang He in Ningxia and Inner Mongolia.

delta areas of the Chang Jiang and Zhu Jiang was 30 per cent; in the other areas it exceeded 20 per cent.

These areas have a subtropical climate, a favourable natural environment, fertile soil, a high year-round temperature, and a long frost-free period. With an average annual rainfall of 800–1,200 millimetres, the region has the richest water resources in the country. Because of the favourable natural conditions, crops grow quickly and there are several high yields each year. Advanced irrigation systems and a high technical level of agriculture have also contributed to the region's position as the largest grain producer in the country. In the Zhu Jiang delta and the plains around the Taihu and Dongting lakes, the superior irrigation systems and the immunity of 55–69 per cent of the land to both drought and excessive rainfall have expanded grain production to 1,000 *jin* per *mu* of cultivated land. In the areas around Suzhou in Jiangsu province and Jiaxing in Zhejiang province, the output per *mu* is 1,500 *jin*. Though densely populated, these areas have a per-capita grain output of 800–900 *jin*. The abundance of other foodstuffs, such as aquatic products, poultry, vegetables, and fruit, means that they also consume less grain than other parts of the country and so are able to supply other areas with large quantities of surplus grain. Jiaxing county in Zhejiang province, for example, provides the country with 450 million *jin* of grain each year, second only to Yushu county in Jilin province, which has an annual surplus of 700–800 million *jin*. Located around the large cities of Shanghai, Guangzhou, Nanjing, and Wuhan, in the most prosperous industrial and commercial region of the country, these areas also enjoy easy transportation on both water and land. The main problem in these low-lying areas is their susceptibility to waterlogging and the need to improve soil and drainage conditions as well as to raise the level of intensive and scientific farming.

The second category of commodity grain bases includes 31 counties and cities in Heilongjiang province and the middle areas of Jilin and Liaoning provinces in the north-east. The area has a total of 100 million *mu* of cultivated land and an agricultural population of 22 million (4.4 *mu* per person). Situated in the frigid-temperate and temperate zones, these areas have a frost-free period of only 120–50 days and one harvest a year. Since they are sparsely inhabited, the per-capita area of cultivated land is twice the country's average and there are large areas of undeveloped land. The flat terrain and vast areas of fertile land have facilitated mechanized farming, thereby raising the level of agricultural productivity and the land utilization rate. In 1980, the rate of commodity grain in these areas was 35 per cent. The main problems are susceptibility to drought and waterlogging caused by the inadequate irrigation and drainage facilities, and frosts because of the high altitude.

The third category consists of the commodity grain bases in northern Jiangsu and Anhui provinces. The area has 57 million *mu* of cultivated land and an agricultural population of 32 million. In 1980, the average grain yield per *mu* was 500 *jin* and the commodity rate exceeded 20 per cent. The production background and natural conditions in the area are favourable for agriculture, with a longer growing period and higher temperatures and rainfall than areas north of the Huang He. With a frost-free period of 200–25 days and an annual rainfall of 600–800 millimetres, three yields are possible every two years or two yields a year. The area also has rich underground water resources suitable for the development of irrigation networks.

The northern Jiangsu and Anhui bases are located near large industrial bases and cities and are bordered by Shandong and Hebei provinces where the natural conditions are unfavourable for grain production. The Grand Canal and the Tianjin–Pukou and Lanzhou–Lianyungang railways play an important role in supplying commodity grain to the cities and industrial bases and supporting the establishment of cotton and vegetable oil bases in Hebei, Shandong, and Henan provinces. The grain yields in this area can be increased through improvements in the water conservation facilities and measures to resist natural disasters.

Finally, the commodity grain bases in the Hexi corridor in Gansu and the Hetao areas on the Huang He in Ningxia and Inner Mongolia autonomous regions have a total of 16 million *mu* of cultivated land and an agricultural population of 5 million (3.2 *mu* per person). In 1980, the per-*mu* output of grain was 370 *jin* (a per-capita output of 950 *jin*). One-fifth of the grain produced is sold to the state. These areas have been grain-producing bases since the Qin dynasty (221 BC). The climate is dry and the annual rainfall is low (50–200 millimetres). With a frost-free period of 140–60 days, short periods of sunlight, and large daily temperature variations, only one yield is produced a year. However, there are rich water resources. In 1980, 78 per cent of the land was artificially irrigated. Situated in the vicinity of Baotou, Hohhot, Wuhai, Shizuishan, Yinchuan, Lanzhou, Jinchang, Yumen, and Jiayuguan, these bases are strategically important in the development of these pastoral areas, industrial bases, and cities. Because of the low productivity and poor management of water conservation facilities in these areas, however, water resources are wasted, the soil is becoming impoverished and salinized, and the grain yield per unit area is still relatively low.

18. Industrial Crops

INDUSTRIAL crops, the second most important agricultural crop in China, include all crops with the exception of cereals, forage, and green manure. The main crops grown for industrial purposes are fibre crops, oil- and sugar-bearing crops, vegetables, tea, pharmaceutical crops, and tobacco.

Industrial crops have a very high economic value. At the present level of production, the net output value of sugar-cane is RMB113 per *mu*, compared with RMB88.7 per *mu* for rice. In northern China, the net output value of sugar-beet is 50 per cent higher than that of corn. The planting of industrial crops stimulates the development of light and textile industries, increases revenue, and enlivens the market. Most of the raw materials for these industries are agricultural raw materials (70 per cent in the 1970s). The greater the supply of agricultural raw materials, the faster the growth of light and textile industries, and the more prosperous the market.

The sale of industrial crops is also very profitable for farmers, most sales being to the state. Industrial crops also earn foreign exchange through exports and reduce the quantity of imported goods. The main export items are farm and sideline products and processed goods.

The Production of Industrial Crops

Some of China's industrial crops are world famous and of importance in the international market. The production of such crops was affected, however, by the political and economic turmoil of the years preceding the formation of the People's Republic. By 1949, the total output of industrial crops was half that of the period before the Second World War. The output of tea and silk decreased during the period by over 80 per cent and established production centres were destroyed. Since 1949, however, the production of the main industrial crops has revived. By 1980, the total area under cultivation had doubled and was 10 per cent higher than the total sown area of cereal crops. The development of different industrial crops during the period was uneven, however. For example, the proportion of cotton in the total cultivated area of industrial crops decreased from 44.7 per cent in 1952 to 30 per cent in 1980; that of peanuts decreased from 14.9 per cent to 14 per cent; and that of sesame seeds decreased from 8.5 per cent to 4.8 per cent. The cultivated area of bluish dogbane and jute increased from 1.3 to 2 per cent of the total; sugar-cane increased from 1.5 to 3 per cent; sugar-beets increased from 0.3 to 2.8 per cent; and flue-cured tobacco increased from 1.5 to 2.5 per cent of the total. One reason for the change in the proportion of these crops was the rapid development of the sugar, linen fabrics, and tobacco industries and the consequent growth in demand and higher purchase prices for raw materials. The decline in the proportion of cotton and oil-bearing crops was due in part to the increase in the sown area of cereal crops and the low purchase price. In recent years, the emphasis on the overall development of agriculture, and on cotton and sugar production particularly, has moderated this decline to some extent.

The production of industrial crops is relatively concentrated, although this pattern is beginning to change. Such crops require specific growing conditions, developed cultivation techniques, and more funds, labour, and materials compared with cereal crops. Because of the importance of natural conditions, the distribution of production is usually highly concentrated. Sugar-cane, sugar-beet, and bluish dogbane, for example, are suitable only for specific kinds of conditions and 60 per cent of the country's total sugar-cane growing area is in Guangdong province and Guangxi. Other crops, such as cotton and tobacco, are more adaptable and are consequently more widely dispersed throughout the country. Oil-bearing crops, such as rape and peanuts, are even more widely distributed.

In the 1950s, the production of industrial crops was concentrated over a large area, the level of production was high, and industrial crops accounted for a large proportion of the total output value of agriculture. Such distribution was economical and convenient in terms of management, the popularization of techniques, the introduction of new products, and the sale and shipment of products. Between 40 and 80 per cent of the total growing area and output of cotton, jute, ramie, flue-cured tobacco, sugar-cane, sugar-beet, and peanuts was concentrated in a few areas.

Between 1958 and the 1970s, the production of all industrial crops became more dispersed. For example, in 1977, the 70 million *mu* of cotton-growing area in the country was distributed over 70 per cent of all the counties in China. Only 21.6 per cent of these had a growing area in excess of 100,000 *mu*. The distribution of sugar-cane, sugar-beet, flue-cured tobacco, and other industrial crops was similarly scattered over a large part of the country. The per-unit area yield and quality of crops declined as a result of this scattered distribution.

The production of industrial crops is often in conflict with that of cereal crops. The output value of industrial crops for the same area is up to 10 times that of cereal crops and their commodity rate is as high as 70–90 per cent of that of grains. Industrial crops also consume much more water, fertilizer, labour, animal power, and investment, and use more complicated techniques than do cereal crops. The income and standard of living in areas which produce industrial crops are consequently higher than in areas which produce cereals. The development of industrial crops is therefore an important means of increasing agricultural incomes. Because grains are the basic food crop, however, and because conditions suited to the cultivation of cereal crops are also suitable for industrial crops, there is often a problem of conflicting land use. The over-planting of industrial crops reduces the land available for cereal crops. The production of industrial crops must therefore be developed according to the degree of self-sufficiency of an area in grain, as well as according to natural conditions, the available labour force, animal power, technical equipment, expertise, water and fertilizer resources, and the potential for expanded production.

A close relationship exists between the production of industrial crops and the development of the light and textile industries. Industrial crops are the main source of agricultural raw materials for these industries and their value is largely determined by those industries. Ideally, the light and textile industrial bases should be located near concentrated industrial crop-producing areas so as to facilitate the transportation of raw materials, and the concentrated areas of industrial crops should be located close to transport facilities. Since 1949, transportation has improved in the main industrial crop areas (including the sugar-cane, cotton, peanut, tobacco, tea, and fruit-growing areas), thereby facilitating transportation to the processing industries. This has stimulated the production of industrial crops and the associated industries. In general, the distribution of industrial crops in China is rational.

Fibre Crops

The main fibre crops, which provide raw materials for the textile industry, are cotton, linen, and silk.

Cotton

China is one of the world's main cotton producers. In 1949, as a result of the preceding years of instability and disruption, the cotton yield was only 52 per cent of its previous highest output in 1936. Since 1949, the production of cotton has been revived: in 1952, the yield was 26.074 million *dan* (compared with 8.888 million *dan* in 1949); in 1957, it was 32.8 million *dan*; and in 1980, the yield had risen to 54.134 million *dan* (Table 18.1). Although China's total cotton output was high during the period 1949–78, its average annual rate of increase is only average when compared to other countries (Table 18.2).

The yield per unit area has also grown significantly. In 1980, the average output of ginned cotton per *mu* was 73 *jin*, compared with 22 *jin* in 1949 (an increase of 231.8 per cent). The average annual increase was 3.9 per cent. China's average annual cotton yield per *mu* is a little higher than the world average (Table 18.3).

Tables 18.2 and 18.3 indicate the importance of China's cotton production in the world output and the yield per unit area. In 1980, China accounted for 16 per cent of the total world output (ranking third after the United States and the Soviet Union).

The production of cotton requires a warm climate, sunlight, and adequate and reliable rainfall. Most of the country's cotton-producing areas have favourable natural conditions. The five main cotton areas are the Chang Jiang valley, the Huang He valley, and north, north-west, and south China (Fig. 18.1). The Chang Jiang valley is the most important of these cotton-producing areas. It has the highest yield per unit area and produces the largest quantity of marketable cotton. The main cotton areas within the region include Zhejiang province, the Shanghai area, Jiangxi, Hunan, and Hubei provinces, the areas south of the Huai He in Jiangsu and Anhui provinces, the Sichuan basin, and Nanyang and Xinyang in Henan province. Other scattered growing areas are the southern part of Shaanxi province and northern Guizhou, Yunnan, and Fujian provinces.

Table 18.1 The Total Annual Output of Cotton, 1949–80

Period	Increase in Output (million dan)	Average Annual Increase (dan)	Ratio of Average Increase (%)	Ratio of Average Annual Increase (%)
Reconstruction period (1950–2)	17.186	5.729 million	193.3	43.2
1st FYP (1953–7)	6.726	1.345 million	25.8	4.7
2nd FYP (1958–62)	–17.805	–3.56 million	–54.3	–14.5
1963–5	26.955	8.985 million	179.7	40.9
3rd FYP (1966–70)	3.585	717,000	8.5	1.7
4th FYP (1971–5)	2.076	415,000	4.6	0.9
5th FYP (1976–80)	6.518	1.306 million	13.7	2.6
1949–80	45.246	1.459 million	509.0	6.0

Source: *China's Agricultural Yearbook, 1980* (Agriculture Publishing House, Beijing, 1981).

Table 18.2 The Total Output and Rate of Increase of the Main Cotton-producing Countries, 1949–78

Country	Total Output (million *dan*)			Ratio between 1949 and 1978		Ratio between 1952 and 1978	
	1949	1952	1978	Increase (%)	Average Annual Increase (%)	Increase (%)	Average Annual Increase (%)
China	8.888	26.074	43.34	387.6	5.6	66.2	2.0
United States	70.160	66.640	47.20	-32.7	-1.4	-28.1	-1.3
Soviet Union	16.880	25.200	52.80	212.8	4.0	109.5	2.9
India	10.360	10.840	25.00	141.3	3.1	130.6	3.3
Turkey	2.080	3.300	10.30	395.2	5.7	212.1	4.4
Brazil	7.930	10.320	9.20	10.2	0.5	-10.9	-0.4
Pakistan	4.420	6.380	10.96	148.0	3.2	71.8	2.1
Egypt	7.740	8.920	8.70	12.4	0.4	-2.5	-0.1
Mexico	4.160	5.300	6.64	59.6	0.5	25.3	0.9
The Sudan	1.340	1.660	3.34	149.3	3.2	101.2	2.7
Iran	0.420	0.720	3.00	614.3	7.0	316.7	5.6
World total	1,440.8	1,420.0	2,590.2	79.8	2.0	82.4	2.3

Source: China's Agricultural Yearbook, 1980 (Agriculture Publishing House, Beijing, 1981).

Fig. 18.1 The Main Cotton-producing Areas

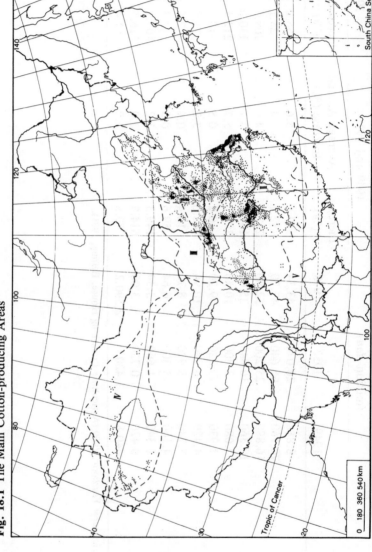

Notes: I Cotton-growing area in the Huang He valley.   II Cotton-growing area in the Chang Jiang valley.   III Early cotton-growing area in the north.   IV Inland cotton-growing area in the north-west.   V Cotton-growing area in south China.

Table 18.3 The Yield per *mu* and Rate of Increase of the Main Cotton-producing Countries, 1949–78

Country	Per-unit Yield (*jin/mu*)			Increase 1949–78 (*jin*)	Increase 1952–78 (*jin*)
	1949	1952	1978		
China	22	31	59	37	28
United States	42	42	63	21	21
Soviet Union	64	59	116	52	57
India	14	11	21	7	10
Turkey	43	33	105	62	72
Brazil	21	23	30	9	7
Pakistan	25	30	38	13	8
Egypt	73	72	114	41	42
Mexico	50	45	126	78	83
The Sudan	51	44	52	1	8
Iran	28	27	71	43	44
World total	33	29	52	19	23

Source: China's Agricultural Yearbook, 1980 (Agriculture Publishing House, Beijing, 1981).

In recent years, the cotton-producing areas in this region have reached 32 million *mu* (approximately 40 per cent of the total in the country). The total output of the region accounts for 53–64 per cent of the country's total output and its per-*mu* yield is as high as 80 *jin* in some areas. The region has the advantage of a warm climate, adequate rainfall, and sunny summers, which make it suitable for summer and autumn cotton. However, the spring rains, dry summers, and frequently wet autumns are less suitable conditions for production. In most areas, cotton is planted with other crops and is harvested twice a year.

The Huang He valley region is the largest of the cotton-producing areas in China. It consists of Hebei province south of the Great Wall, Shandong, Henan (with the exception of Nanyang and Xinyang), southern Shanxi, the central Shaanxi plain, southern Gansu, areas north of the Huai He in Jiangsu and Anhui provinces, and the areas around Beijing and Tianjin. Between the 1950s and 1970s, the cotton-producing area in this region decreased by one-third. In recent years, the area of production has reached 36 million *mu* and the per-*mu* yield is 40–50 *jin*. The total output accounts for 32–43 per cent of the country's total output of cotton. The moderate climate and plentiful sunlight in summer provide favourable conditions, with the exception of the rainy season. One harvest a year is the normal practice. In some areas, cotton is planted with other crops (including oil-bearing crops).

In the north of China, the cotton-producing areas are comparatively small, with only a short history of cotton production. The main growing area consists of Liaoning and mid-Shanxi provinces, as well as scattered areas such as northern Hebei and Shaanxi provinces and eastern Gansu province. Because of the low temperatures, the region is suitable only for early upland cotton.

However, there is adequate sunlight during the summer and because the temperature varies greatly during the day, summer cotton is a suitable crop. The cotton is harvested once a year. The cotton-producing areas in the north are declining because of the harsh conditions and the increase in the area of cereal crops. At present, the cotton-growing area is 1.8 million *mu* (2 per cent of the country's total) and the average output per *mu* has decreased to approximately 30 *jin* (the lowest per-*mu* output of all the industrial crops). The total output of cotton is slightly more than 1 per cent of the country's total output.

The north-west inland region has a long cotton-producing history and considerable potential for future development. It consists of Xinjiang, the Hexi corridor in Gansu province, and an irrigated area along the Huang He. Sufficient sunlight, dry weather, and great daily temperature variations promote steady growth. However, the soil is poor and its salinity hinders growth. Cotton is harvested once a year. The growing area is 2 million *mu* (3 per cent of that of the country) and the average output per *mu* is approximately 30 *jin*. The output of the region accounts for 20 per cent of the country's total output.

South China is the oldest cotton-producing area but it is now the smallest and most scattered of the regions producing cotton. It includes most of Yunnan province, the Sichang area in Sichuan, Guangxi, Guangdong, and southern Guizhou and Fujian provinces. The area is exceptionally rich in heat energy and it has adequate rainfall but poor sunshine. In the frost-free areas, cotton grows throughout the winter. In most cases, the fields are double-harvested. Because of the hot weather and abundant rainfall, pests and plant diseases are serious problems. The growing area in this region is now only several thousand *mu*.

Bast-fibre Crops

China produces a wide variety of bast-fibre crops (Fig. 18.2). In 1979, bluish dogbane, flax, hemp, jute, and ramie accounted for 96.7 per cent of the total output of bast-fibre crops and 8.2 per cent of the total acreage (Table 18.4).

Jute, an annual plant, thrives in tropical and subtropical zones. It is produced mainly in Zhejiang, Guangdong, Hunan, Jiangxi, and Jiangsu provinces in the Chang Jiang and Zhu Jiang basins. Bluish dogbane, which is adaptable to poor quality, low-lying land, saline-alkaline soil, and extremes of weather is distributed over 20 provinces and autonomous regions from Liaoning in the north-east to Guangdong in the south, and from Xinjiang Uygur autonomous region in the north-west to Zhejiang in the east. Bluish dogbane and jute, which rank first among China's bast-fibre crops, account for half of the total bast-fibre crop acreage and 80 per cent of the country's total output. Their per-unit area yield is 50 per cent higher than that of the average output of all the bast-fibre crops. The main producers, Anhui and Zhejiang provinces, harvest 150,000 tonnes each year, followed by Shandong, Guangdong, Henan, and Sichuan provinces, which each produce 100,000 tonnes a year.

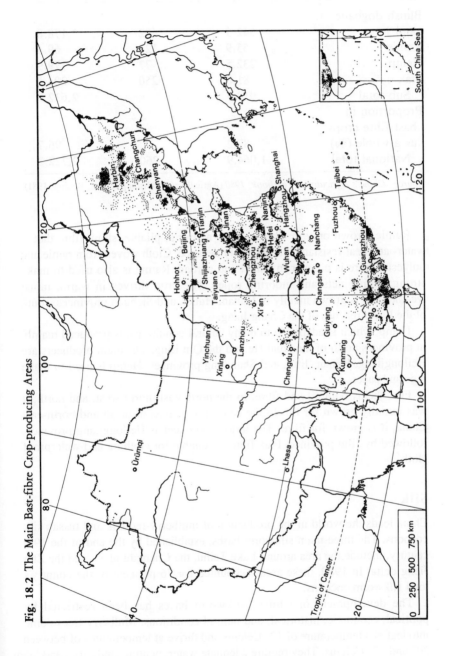

Fig. 18.2 The Main Bast-fibre Crop-producing Areas

Table 18.4 The Area and Output of Bast-fibre Crops, 1979

Crop	Cultivated Area (10,000 *mu*)	Yield per *mu* (*jin*)	Total Output (10,000 *dan*)
Bluish dogbane and jute	542.5	402	2,178.8
Ramie	55.9	124	69.4
Hemp	232.5	77	179.9
Flax	81.8	250	204.1
Sub-total	912.7		2,632.2
Proportion in bast-fibre crops as a whole (%)	87.2		96.7
National total	1,064.9	260	2,722.3

Source: China's Agricultural Yearbook, 1980 (Agriculture Publishing House, Beijing, 1981).

Ramie, grown only in China, yields a strong, pliable, shiny fibre that is water- and heat-resistant and not easily decayed. Cloth woven from ramie and polyester fibre is popular in China and abroad. Ramie is also used to make strong fishing nets and mooring ropes. The crop thrives in warm, moist weather and is grown mainly in Hunan, Hubei, and Sichuan provinces, south of the lower reaches of the Chang Jiang.

Hemp, which is adaptable to many natural conditions, is produced mainly in provinces north of the Huai He and the Qin Ling. The main producers are Heilongjiang, Henan, Jilin, and Shandong provinces. Hemp is used to make rope and paper.

Flax yields both oil and fibre. In the north-east, north-west, and north, it was initially grown for oil. In the cold, moist areas of north and north-east China, it is grown for fibre. The largest producer is Heilongjiang province, followed by Jilin province. Flax fibre is suitable for clothing and waterproof cloth.

Silk

China leads the world in the production of mulberry-fed silk and tussah silk cocoons. The three main silkworm bases, established by the end of the 19th century, include the area around Lake Taihu, the Chengdu plain, and the Zhu Jiang delta. In 1980, these areas accounted for 76 per cent of the country's total silkworm cocoons.

The development of China's silkworm bases has been restricted by political, economic, historical, and natural conditions. Mulberry trees come into leaf at a temperature of 12° Celcius and thrive at temperatures of between 20° and 27° Celcius. They require adequate water, neutral sandy soil, and loam with a rich organic content. Sericulture is a complicated form of agriculture, requiring great care, intensive labour, and adequate expertise and investment.

The main sericulture areas are located in the Chang Jiang and Zhu Jiang basins where conditions are warm and moist and where there is a comparatively long frost-free period. Seven or eight generations of silkworms can be raised annually in the Zhu Jiang basin and three or four in the Chang Jiang basin; two are usual in the Huang He basin. The four main sericulture areas in China today — the Suzhou area around Lake Taihu in Jiangsu province, the Jiaxing area in Zhejiang province, the Nanchang area around the Jialin Jiang in Sichuan province, and the Foshan area in the Zhu Jiang delta in Guangdong province (Fig. 18.3) — account for more than half of the country's total output of silk. In 1980, the four provinces produced 215,000 tonnes (86 per cent of the total output).

Sericulture has developed rapidly since 1949. By 1980, the total output had increased by 219,000 tonnes over the 1949 total (an average annual increase of 6.9 per cent). China's output of silk accounts for 35 per cent of the world total; it is one of the country's major exports. Additional sericulture centres are planned to be established between latitudes 30° and 40° north.

The tussah silk industry also has the potential for further development. China produces 90 per cent of the world's total of tussah cocoons, mainly in Liaoning, Shandong, and Henan provinces. Liaoning produces 75 per cent of the total.

Oil-bearing Crops

Oil-bearing crops, one of China's main industrial crops, have developed rapidly since 1949. The total area in 1956 was 102.4 million *mu* (compared with 63.418 million *mu* in 1949) and the total output was 5.085 million tonnes (compared with 2.563 million tonnes in 1949). The output of the three principal oil-bearing crops — peanuts, rape seed, and sesame seeds — increased by 95.7 per cent over the 1949 figure, making possible the export of several hundred million tonnes of edible oil by 1957.

In the 1960s and 1970s, however, because of the over-emphasis on grain production, the acreage and output of oil-bearing crops declined and edible oils had to be imported to make up the deficit. Since the 1970s, the situation has improved and the output has increased steadily (Fig. 18.4). The gross output of oil-bearing crops in 1980 was 7.69 million tonnes, 6.24 million tonnes of which consisted of the three main crops (Tables 18.5 and 18.6).

Compared with China's other industrial crops, oil-bearing crops have had the slowest growth in output, with the exception of the periods 1963–5 and 1976–80.

Peanuts

Peanuts are an annual crop which grows best in a warm climate and non-alkaline-saline soil. Peanuts are grown in most parts of China, with the exception of Tibet, Ningxia, Gansu, Qinghai, Inner Mongolia, and the northern part of the north-east.

Of all the oil-bearing crops, peanuts rank first in total growing area and output. In 1956, they accounted for 65.5 per cent of the total output of oil-bearing crops and 37.8 per cent of the total growing area. The average output

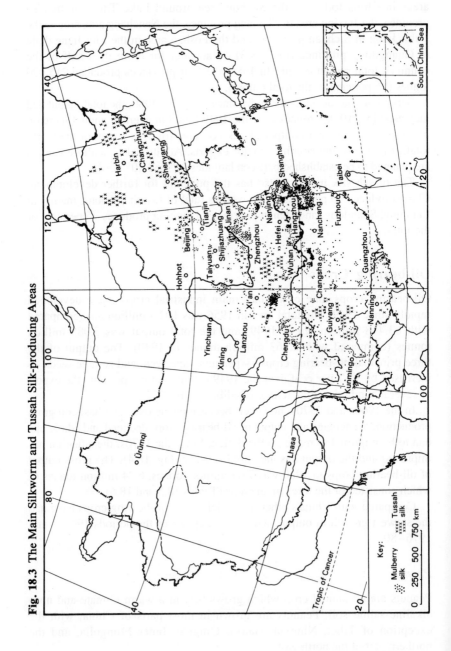

Fig. 18.3 The Main Silkworm and Tussah Silk-producing Areas

Fig. 18.4 The Main Oil-bearing Crop-producing Areas

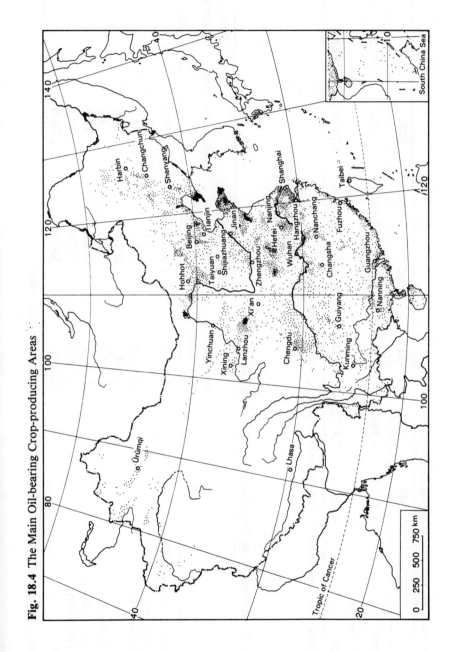

Table 18.5 The Total Output of Oil-bearing Crops, 1949–80

Item	1949	1952	1957	1962	1965	1970	1975	1980
Total output	5,127.0	8,386.3	8,391.9	4,006.6	7,520.7	7,543.6	9,041.5	15,381.1
Output of the three main types	4,655.0	7,457.0	7,542.0	3,684.0	6,544.0	6,754.0	8,082.0	12,485.0

Source: China's Agricultural Yearbook, 1980 (Agriculture Publishing House, Beijing, 1981).

Table 18.6 The Increase in the Total Output of Oil-bearing Crops, 1949–80

Period	Increase (10,000 dan)	Average Annual Increase (10,000 dan)	Ratio of Increase (%)	Ratio of Average Annual Increase (%)
Reconstruction period (1950–2)	3,259.3	1,086.4	63.6	1.70
1st FYP (1953–7)	5.6	1.1	0.1	0.01
2nd FYP (1958–62)	–4,385.3	–877.1	–42.3	–13.70
1963–5	3,244.1	1,081.4	81.0	21.90
3rd FYP (1966–70)	293.0	58.6	4.0	0.80
4th FYP (1971–5)	1,497.8	299.6	19.9	3.60
5th FYP (1976–80)	6,339.6	1,267.9	70.1	11.20
1949–80	10,254.1	330.8	200.0	3.60

Source: China's Agricultural Yearbook, 1980 (Agriculture Publishing House, Beijing, 1981).

per *mu* was 86 kilograms, 36.5 kilograms more than that of the other oil-bearing crops. After 20 years of neglect of the industry, the output in 1980 rose to 3.6 million tonnes and the growing area to 35.088 million *mu*, placing China second in the world in the production of peanuts. The main producing areas are Shandong, Hebei, Guangdong, Henan, Anhui, Sichuan, Liaoning, Fujian, and Jiangsu provinces, and the Guangxi Zhuang autonomous region. The output and growing area of these regions account for 90 per cent of the country's total.

In the north, the main peanut-producing areas are in the Shandong peninsula, the lower reaches of the Luan He in east Hebei province, the area formerly flooded by the Huang He in east Henan, the area north of the Huai He, and the Liaoning peninsula. In south China, peanuts are grown in the sandy soil along rivers, the sea coast, and on the mountain slopes, and are often rotated with rice. The main producing areas in the south are along the rivers of middle and south Hebei province, north and east Henan, north-western Shandong, north Jiangsu, the middle part of Anhui, south Jiangxi, east Hubei, south Hunan, the middle part of Sichuan, south Yunnan, and north-eastern Guizhou.

Further increases in the output of peanuts will depend on an increase in the growing area. In the north, land that is unsuited to grain production could be planted with peanuts. The rotation of peanuts with grains would increase the output in areas that are suited to both crops as well as fertilize the soil. In the south, peanuts could be grown in the unused autumn and winter fields. In addition to the capital construction of farm land and the improvement of soil cultivation and field management, the selection and popularization of fine peanut varieties, the prevention and control of plant diseases, and the elimination of pests are necessary for an increase in the per-unit area yield of peanuts.

The establishment of peanut production bases in suitable areas in Shandong, eastern Henan, Hebei, Guangdong, and the Guangxi Zhuang autonomous region — where the output per unit area, the total output, and the commodity rate are already high — would guarantee a supply of peanuts for export.

Rape Seed

Rape belongs to the mustard family. In many areas south of the Yan Shan, rape is grown as a winter crop and is not in competition with grain and cotton. In recent years, its production has developed considerably. In 1980, China produced 2.383 million tonnes of rape seed (second in the world) and the total growing area was 42.662 million *mu* (third in the world).

The main rape seed-producing areas in China are concentrated in Anhui, Hubei, Hunan, Jiangsu, Jiangxi, Sichuan, and Zhejiang provinces, and the Shanghai area in the Chang Jiang basin. Approximately 10 per cent of the paddy fields in these areas are sown with rape seed and in 1980 they yielded 77 per cent of the country's total output. Their output per *mu* was 30 per cent higher than the national average. The largest producer in terms of output per unit area is Shanghai (120 kilograms per *mu*), followed by Jiangxi, Hubei, and Hunan (each producing 50 kilograms per *mu*). However, Shanghai's output per unit area fluctuates considerably. In 1979, it was 155.5 kilograms per *mu*, dropping 22 per cent by 1980 to 122.5 kilograms.

Unless the total growing area is increased, any future increases in the total output of rape seed will be dependent upon an increase in the output of the low-yield areas and maintenance of the output of the high-yield areas. For example, some of the winter paddy fields in the Chang Jiang area could be utilized to a greater extent if irrigation of the area was improved. In addition, the Huang He, Huai He, and Hai He plains in the north have considerable potential for expanding the growing area of rape seed by using winter fields not otherwise in use. The selection of new cold- and drought-resistant, early maturing, and high-yield varieties would also increase the total output.

Cabbage-type rape is suited to many conditions and has a short growing period. It is suitable for the cold, dry north-west where there are long hours of sunshine and the daily temperature variation is extreme. In Liaoning province, it is suitable for rotation with maize, sorghum, and rice.

Sesame Seeds

Sesame is an annual crop which requires a warm climate and well-drained soil. The oil-bearing rate of sesame seeds is 53 per cent, the highest of all the oil-bearing crops. Sesame seeds have a short growing season, are drought-resistant, and can be inter-planted with other crops as well as planted alone in small plots.

Before the Second World War, China ranked first in the world in sesame production. In 1933, its total output was 970,000 tonnes (60 per cent of the world total). During the following two decades, however, the annual output declined and by the early 1950s the highest national average yield per *mu* was only 30 kilograms. By 1978, the yield had increased slightly, to an average output per *mu* of 33.5 kilograms. In recent years, the output has declined once more. In 1980, the total growing area was 11.642 million *mu* and the total output was 258,550 tonnes (accounting for 12 and 20 per cent of the world total respectively, and ranking third and second respectively).

Of the three varieties of sesame — spring, summer, and autumn — spring sesame is grown north of the Huang He, summer sesame is grown in areas between the Huang He and the Chang Jiang, and autumn sesame is grown south of the Chang Jiang. Sesame is grown in 24 of the provinces and regions, the main producing areas being Anhui, Hebei, Henan, Hubei, Jiangxi, and Shandong, which produce 80 per cent of the country's total output. In order to increase the per-unit area yield, farming techniques and field management need to be improved, particularly in Anhui, Henan, Hubei, and Jiangxi, where the growing area is large but the output is low (half that of Hebei and Shandong provinces).

Flax and Sunflower Seeds

Flax and sunflower seeds are also important oil-bearing crops in China. Distributed in the cool and semi-arid Inner Mongolian plateau, the loess plateau, the Gansu corridor, and two basins south and north of the Tian Shan, flax is grown on small plots, is cultivated roughly, and is not in competition with grain crops. The total cultivated area — 9 million *mu* — is relatively stable.

Sunflower seeds are an increasingly important and adaptable crop. In 1980, the total growing area was 12 million *mu* and the total output was 900,000 tonnes. Most of the provinces in the north-east grow sunflowers, including Heilongjiang, Jilin, Liaoning, and the Hetao area in Inner Mongolia. Resistant to the cold, heat, droughts, and water, sunflowers are suitable for barren and saline-alkaline soil. There is considerable potential for the development of sunflower seeds production bases in the future.

Sugar-bearing Crops

Sugar-bearing crops, such as sugar-cane and sugar-beet, are important industrial crops in China. Sugar-cane was exported as far as England in the mid-19th century and sugar-beet was first grown experimentally in the north-east in 1906. Before 1949, however, the production of sugar-bearing crops was in decline and, in 1949, the total output was only 2.832 million tonnes. Since that time, although the output per *mu* has fluctuated (Table 18.7), the development of the established areas and the opening up of new bases has increased production at a rate faster than other industrial crops (Tables 18.8 and 18.9).

Table 18.7 The Output per *mu* of Sugar-cane and Sugar-beet, 1949–80

Year	Output per *mu* of Sugar-cane (kg)	Output per *mu* of Sugar-beet (kg)
1949	1,625.5	797.0
1952	2,600.0	909.5
1957	2,599.0	628.0
1965	2,548.0	774.0
1975	2,122.0	546.0
1980	3,170.0	949.5

Source: China's Agricultural Yearbook, 1980 (Agriculture Publishing House, Beijing, 1981).

The increase in the output per *mu* of sugar-cane between 1949 and 1980 was 94.8 per cent (a 2.2 per cent average annual increase). The average annual increase per *mu* in the output of sugar-beet was 0.6 per cent. China's per-unit area yield of both sugar-cane and sugar-beet is lower than that of the main sugar-producing countries in the world.

The main reasons for the low yield of sugar-bearing crops are their irrational distribution and dispersed growing areas. The country's 7.6 million *mu* of sugar-cane fields are scattered over 700 counties and municipalities in 15 provinces and regions, and sugar-beet fields are scattered over 24 provinces and regions. The over-emphasis in the past on self-sufficiency in grain

Table 18.8 The Total Output of Sugar-bearing Crops, 1949–80

Item	1949	1952	1957	1962	1965	1970	1975	1979	1980
Sugar-cane	5,284.3	14,231.6	20,784.9	6,886.7	26,782.9	26,914.0	33,333.7	43,015.0	45,614.8
Sugar-beet	381.0	957.1	3,002.1	677.5	3,968.7	4,128.9	4,952.7	6,211.6	12,610.7
Total output	5,655.3	15,188.7	23,787.0	7,564.2	30,751.6	31,042.9	38,286.4	49,266.6	58,225.5

Source: *China's Agricultural Yearbook, 1980* (Agriculture Publishing House, Beijing, 1981).

Table 18.9 The Increase in the Total Output of Sugar-bearing Crops, 1949–80

Period	Increase (10,000 dan)	Average Annual Increased (10,000 dan)	Ratio of Increase (%)	Ratio of Average Annual Increase (%)
Reconstruction period (1950–2)	9,523.4	3,174.5	168.1	38.9
1st FYP (1953–7)	8,598.3	2,866.1	56.6	9.4
2nd FYP (1958–62)	−16,222.8	−3,244.6	−68.3	−7.4
1963–5	23,187.4	7,729.1	306.5	59.6
3rd FYP (1966–70)	291.3	58.3	0.9	0.2
4th FYP (1971–5)	7,243.5	1,448.7	23.3	4.3
5th FYP (1976–80)	19,399.1	3,879.8	52.1	8.7
1949–80	52,560.2	1,695.0	927.7	7.8

Source: *China's Agricultural Yearbook, 1980* (Agriculture Publishing House, Beijing, 1981).

production reduced the level of production of some of the main sugar-cane producers. Poor conditions for production, low state purchasing prices, a shortage of expertise, and low planting and management levels also lowered the total output as well as the sugar content of the crops. The same problems beset the sugar-beet industry. Dispersed growing also caused transportation difficulties and increased costs. The development of China's sugar-bearing crops industry is therefore dependent upon the suitability of local conditions and the rational distribution of production.

Sugar-cane

Sugar-cane, a member of the grass family, grows in tropical and subtropical climates. Temperatures of around 30° Celcius best suit its long growing period. It requires deep fertile soil and 1,500–2,000 millimetres of annual rainfall. The conditions required for its growth restrict sugar-cane production to areas south of the Qin Ling and the Huai He. The most suitable areas are the coastal areas in south-east Fujian province and the area from Xinfeng and Yingde in Guangdong province to parts of Guangxi Zhuang autonomous region. Conditions in these areas are such that even in the coldest months, sugar-cane is still able to grow. Yields are high if spring and autumn droughts are overcome, typhoon damage is reduced, and irrigation is provided.

The conditions in the Tuo Jiang basin in Sichuan and the Hegu basin in southern Yunnan province are also suitable for the establishment of sugar-cane bases. In the areas between the Chang Jiang and the Nan Ling, conditions are suitable for production, although temperatures are often low and there is competition with grain for land use. North of the Chang Jiang, sugar-cane is produced only in the Sichuan basin where conditions are poor.

Sugar-cane is grown in 14 provinces (Fig. 18.5), the main producing areas being Fujian, Guangdong, Guanxi, Sichuan, and Yunnan. These areas accounted for 89.3 per cent and 88.7 per cent respectively of the country's total growing area and output in 1979 (Table 18.10).

Sugar-beet

A biennial root tuber plant, sugar-beet is resistant to the cold, droughts, and alkaline soil. It is adaptable to both warm and cool climates, with a growing period of 140–60 days. The longer the hours of sunshine, the higher the sugar content; crops grown in the higher latitudes also tend to have a higher sugar content. Sugar-beet is best suited to loam that is deep, porous, fertile, and rich in organic matter with a low water level. It is grown in 23 provinces, regions, and municipalities (Fig. 18.5), the main producing areas being those north of the Chang Jiang (such as Heilongjiang, Jilin, Inner Mongolia, and Xinjiang) (Table 18.11). Heilongjiang is the largest producer, accounting for 44.9 per cent of the total growing area and 40 per cent of the country's total output.

The future development of sugar-beet production will depend upon the further development of areas such as the north Songnen plain in Heilongjiang province, western and middle Jilin province, the Hetao area in Inner Mongolia and Ningxia, and the Manas area in Xinjiang where the natural conditions are

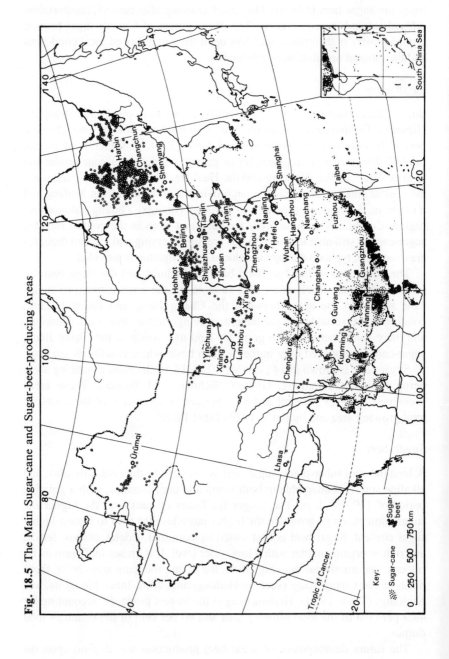

Fig. 18.5 The Main Sugar-cane and Sugar-beet-producing Areas

Table 18.10 The Cultivated Area and Output of the Main Sugar-cane-producing Areas, 1979

Province	Cultivated Area (10,000 mu)	Yield per mu (jin)	Total Output (10,000 dan)
Guangdong	272.7	6,027	16,436.4
Guangxi	191.6	3,977	7,620.0
Fujian	67.9	9,167	6,222.8
Sichuan	82.6	5,139	4,244.6
Yunnan	70.9	5,118	3,628.9
Total	685.7	5,885.6	38,152.7
Total output of China	767.7	5,604	43,015.0
Proportion of the total output of China as a whole (%)	89.3		88.7

Source: *China's Agricultural Yearbook, 1980* (Agriculture Publishing House, Beijing, 1981).

Table 18.11 The Cultivated Area and Output of the Main Sugar-beet-producing Areas, 1979

Province	Cultivated Area (10,000 mu)	Yield per mu (jin)	Total Output (10,000 dan)
Heilongjiang	218.9	1,134.0	2,480.9
Jilin	77.2	1,474.0	1,138.7
Inner Mongolia	67.7	1,447.0	979.4
Xinjiang	33.0	1,799.0	593.2
Total	396.8	1,463.5	5,192.2
Total output of China	487.5	1,274.0	6,211.6
Proportion of the total output of China as a whole (%)	81.4		83.6

Source: *China's Agricultural Yearbook, 1980* (Agriculture Publishing House, Beijing, 1981).

appropriate and local conditions are suitable for the building of sugar refineries.

Tobacco

Tobacco has a high economic value as an industrial crop. The proper development of tobacco production depends upon due consideration being given to the necessary natural, economic, and technological conditions. Tobacco has specific climate and soil requirements and during the long growing period, an average daily temperature above 20° Celcius and adequate water are necessary. The soil must be deep, porous, well drained, and rich in organic matter. Labour and fuel requirements are also important for the curing of tobacco.

Tobacco is either sun- or flue-cured. Before 1949, the production of tobacco was controlled by the foreign powers in China. Since then, state planning has enabled the level of production to increase considerably. In 1949, the total output of tobacco was 42,900 tonnes; by 1952, it was 221,600 tonnes; and in 1979, it had increased to 806,150 tonnes. The highest output, 1.052 million tonnes, was recorded in 1978. Between 1949 and 1979, the average annual increase in production was 9.5 per cent (Table 18.12). The average annual increase for the years 1949–78 was 11.5 per cent — the highest rate of all the tobacco-producing countries.

Flue-cured tobacco is produced in Anhui, Guizhou, Henan, Jilin, Liaoning, Shandong, and Yunnan provinces (Fig. 18.6). The highest output and best-quality tobacco are produced in the Xuchang area in Henan province, the Yuxi and Qujing areas in Yunnan, Zunyi in Guizhou province, and the Changwei area in Shandong province. These areas are suitable for expanded production and the establishment of flue-cured tobacco bases in the future.

Although sun-cured tobacco accounts for only 20 per cent of the country's total output of tobacco, its production is distributed over the whole of the country, particularly in south China. It is grown mainly for local consumption.

Tea

Tea bushes were first grown in China and tea was exported for the first time during the Ming and Qing dynasties (1368–1911). Between 1880 and 1888, approximately 100,000 tonnes were exported each year. Between 1888 and 1949, however, the output declined and by 1949, the total output was only 41,050 tonnes, 18 per cent of which was exported. After 1949, the level of production began to increase and by 1952, the total output was 82,400 tonnes; in 1957, it was 111,600 tonnes; and by 1980, the output had reached 303,750 tonnes (Table 18.13). One of the main tea producers in the world, China's rate of increase in the level of production during this period was higher than that of any other country.

Since they are perennial and evergreen, tea bushes thrive in tropical and subtropical zones where the annual temperature averages 15–25° Celcius, the annual precipitation is 1,000 millimetres, and the relative humidity is 85 per cent. The most suitable areas for tea cultivation are mountain slopes with

Table 18.12 The Increase in the Total Output of Flue-cured Tobacco, 1949–80

Period	Increase (10,000 dan)	Average Annual Increase (10,000 dan)	Ratio of Increase (%)	Ratio of Average Annual Increase (%)
Reconstruction period (1950–2)	357.4	119.1	416.6	72.9
1st FYP (1953–7)	68.9	13.8	15.5	2.9
2nd FYP (1958–62)	–254.6	–50.9	–49.7	–12.8
1963–5	486.7	162.2	189.0	42.4
3rd FYP (1966–70)	53.1	10.6	7.1	1.4
4th FYP (1971–5)	604.2	120.8	75.8	11.9
5th FYP (1976–80)	31.8	6.4	2.3	0.5
1949–80	1,347.5	43.5	1,570.5	9.5

Source: *China's Agricultural Yearbook, 1980* (Agriculture Publishing House, Beijing, 1981).

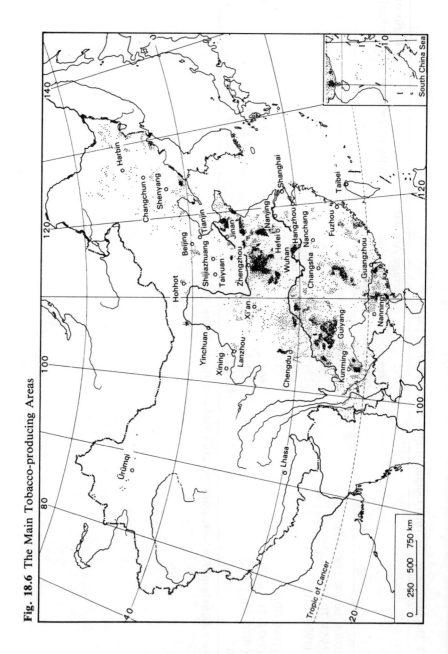

Fig. 18.6 The Main Tobacco-producing Areas

Table 18.13 The Increase in the Total Output of Tea, 1949–80

Period	Increase (10,000 dan)	Average Annual Increased (10,000 dan)	Ratio of Increase (%)	Ratio of Average Annual Increase (%)
Reconstruction period (1950–2)	82.7	27.6	100.7	26.1
1st FYP (1953–7)	58.4	11.7	35.4	6.2
2nd FYP (1958–62)	–75.5	–15.1	–33.8	–7.9
1963–5	53.4	17.8	36.2	10.7
3rd FYP (1966–70)	70.9	26.3	35.2	6.2
4th FYP (1971–5)	149.0	29.8	54.8	9.1
5th FYP (1976–80)	186.5	37.3	44.3	7.6
1949–80	525.4	16.9	640.0	6.6

Source: *China's Agricultural Yearbook, 1980* (Agriculture Publishing House, Beijing, 1981).

deep fertile soil which is well drained and has a pH value of 4.5–6.5. The main tea-producing areas are the mountainous and hilly areas in Anhui, Hunan, Sichuan, and Zhejiang provinces (Fig. 18.7). In 1979, these areas produced 65.4 per cent of the country's total output of tea. The output of Fujian, Hubei, and Yunnan provinces constituted 19.7 per cent of the total. A number of varieties of tea are produced, including black, green, Wulong, Bian, perfumed, and other special kinds. Approximately 80 per cent of the total output of black tea is exported.

The production of tea is affected by poor management, extensive cultivation, and a low per-unit area yield. The growing areas are scattered, the scale of production is small, equipment is backward, and the quality of the tea produced is unstable. The distribution of production is irrational, particularly in the north and west of the country. The distribution of different varieties will need to be readjusted, production bases will need to be established, and the quality of the tea produced will need to be improved if production is to develop efficiently so that it is able to meet domestic and international demands.

Industrial Crop Production Bases

Agricultural commodities include commodity grain and industrial crops. The establishment of industrial crop bases is necessary if the level of production of these crops is to expand. However, their establishment and development are often restricted by regional, natural, social, and economic conditions.

Cotton Bases

Since the early 1960s, the distribution of cotton production has become more dispersed. By 1978, 1,200 counties grew cotton, although 78 per cent of these had a growing area of less than 100,000 *mu*. In most of the cotton-growing counties, production was not concentrated. In Luancheng county, in south Hebei province, for example, the 130,000 *mu* of cotton-growing area was spread amongst 1,000 production brigades. Few fields were larger than 100 *mu*. Similarly, in Henan province, only 60 per cent of the cotton-growing counties have more than 100,000 *mu* of fields; in Hebei province, the figure is 50 per cent, and in Shandong province, it is 39 per cent. The per-unit area yield of the three main cotton-producing provinces is 24.5, 13.5, and 16.5 kilograms and the commodity rate is 87.8, 88, and 88.9 per cent respectively.

The concentration of cotton-producing areas makes possible high per-unit area yields and commodity rates. In Jiangsu and Hubei provinces, for example, over 90 per cent of the cotton-producing counties have over 100,000 *mu* of cotton fields. Their per-unit area yields are 40 and 53.5 kilograms and their commodity rates are 98 and 99 per cent respectively.

The natural, social, and economic conditions are most suitable on the Jianghan, Huanghuai, and Binhai–Yan Jiang plains in the lower reaches of the Chang Jiang, in south and mid-Hebei province, in north-west Shandong province, on the north Henan plains, and in the Nan Jiang area for the establishment of large cotton production bases. The climate in these areas is

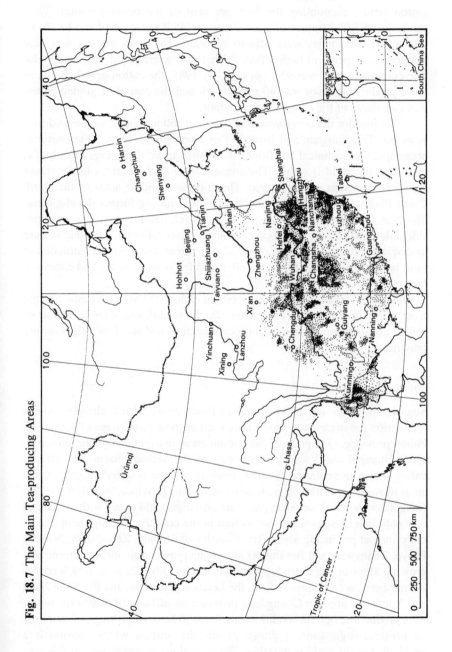

Fig. 18.7 The Main Tea-producing Areas

suitable for production on a large scale: the frost-free period is approximately 250 days, there is adequate rainfall, and where rainfall is insufficient, there are abundant underground and other water resources.

In 1978, the 138 counties in these five areas had 28.79 million *mu* of cotton fields, accounting for 39.4 per cent of the country's total. They produced 995,000 tonnes of ginned cotton (45.9 per cent of the total), of which 937,000 tonnes were sold to the state. The yield per *mu* was 32.9 kilograms, 11 per cent higher than the national average per-unit area yield. The commodity rate was 95.1 per cent. By 1985, the cotton-growing area of these production bases was 40 million *mu* and the output of ginned cotton was two-thirds of the country's total output.

Conditions for the development of the main cotton production bases differ, however. The Jianghan and Binhai–Yan Jiang plains have better natural, economic, and technical conditions than other areas; their level of output is high; and the yield is stable. The consolidation of these areas in the future would further increase their yield. The north and middle areas of the North China Plain are established production areas requiring further development. The Nan Jiang and Huanghuai plains have rich natural resources and considerable potential for development, but the foundations for production are inadequate and require expansion. In all these areas, the capital construction of farm land is essential to offset the effects of frequent droughts and excessive rain.

Other areas appropriate for development include the Sichuan basin, and the river plains in Anhui province, where the local authorities are in favour of capital construction so as to meet local demands and those of neighbouring provinces.

Sugar-cane bases

Sugar-cane bases are most suited to those areas which already have a foundation for sugar-cane production, such as the coastal areas of south-east Fujian province, Qionglei and the coastal areas in mid-Guangdong province, south Guangxi and Yunnan provinces, and the Sichuan basin. The coastal valley plains in south-east Fujian province are the country's highest yield areas of sugar-cane. The delta areas in Guangdong province, including the Zhu Jiang delta and the Chao Shan plain, are also high-yield areas, with the largest concentration of sugar-cane production in the country, making them one of the principal producing areas. The counties of Shunde, Zhongshan, Nanhai, Panyu, Doangwan, and Jieyang in Guangdong province are either concentrated growing areas or sugar production centres. The Qionglei area, which covers the northern part of Hainan Island, the Leizhou peninsula, and the Yang Jiang and Yangchun areas in Guangdong province, is sufficiently warm for sugar-cane production, but the conditions are liable to be dry in spring and summer. At present, sugar-cane is grown on the dry slopes, where erosion is a problem, and the yield is unstable. The conditions of production in this area will need to be improved if production is to expand.

In the south of the Guangxi Zhuang autonomous region, sugar-cane is grown in the valley plains along the You Jiang, Yong Jiang, and Yu Jiang, and in the hilly areas. The main growing areas and production centres are Hengxian, Guixian, Yongning, and Hepu counties. Intensive cultivation over the years in the Tuo Jiang basin in Sichuan province has lowered the per-unit area yield. The production of sugar-cane in the valley basins in southern Yunnan province is dispersed and cultivation techniques are backward. An increase in the level of output of the area will require concentration of production and an increase in the per-unit area yield.

Sugar-bearing crops, particularly sugar-cane, are more suitable than cotton for concentration in production bases, but the establishment of sugar production bases is dependent upon the natural and socio-economic conditions and the conflict in land use of grain and sugar-bearing crops. In Fujian province, for example, the conditions for sugar-cane production are superior to those in Hunan and Zhejiang provinces and both the per-unit area yield and the sugar content are higher than in those provinces. In 1980, the output per *mu* was 4,985 kilograms (compared with 3,637.5 kilograms in Zhejiang and 3,367.5 kilograms in Hunan). Although the land use for sugar-cane production in Fujian is also suitable for rice and is able to produce comparatively high per-unit area yields, the production of rice is less important than in Hunan and Zhejiang where, in 1980, the per-*mu* yield was 260 and 281 kilograms respectively (compared with 245.5 kilograms in Fujian). Hunan and Zhejiang provinces are more suitable, therefore, for rice production and Fujian is more suitable for sugar-cane production.

Communications and transport facilities in the three provinces are advanced. Specialization in production is therefore possible, with the result that the costs of producing sugar-cane in Fujian and rice in Hunan and Zhejiang would be lowered.

At present, China imports large quantities of sugar. If the production of sugar-cane were to be expanded in those areas less suitable for rice, the deficit in rice could be made up by the state and sugar imports could be reduced. In Fujian province, 200,000 *mu* of land suitable for sugar-cane production has not yet been utilized. The consolidation and expansion of sugar production bases and the rationalization of their distribution is therefore dependent to a large degree upon improving the arrangements between administrative areas.

19. Forestry

THE forestry industry is an important part of China's agricultural economy. In addition to providing timber and timber products, forests regulate weather conditions, preserve soil and water, act as a barrier to wind and shifting sands, protect fauna, promote farm and animal husbandry production, and play an important ecological role.

China's vast land area is suitable for various kinds of tree growth, and large areas of land remain to be opened up. At present, there are some 2,800 varieties of arboreal trees, including species unique to China such as dawn redwood, water pine, Taiwan cedar, Fujian cypress, and Chinese cedar. The most economically valuable trees are tung-oil, tea-oil, Chinese tallow, varnish, rubber, and eucommia trees. The main broadleaf timber trees include the Manchurian, black walnut, camphor, and manmu trees.

Three thousand years ago, the country was covered by forests. However, natural disasters (such as forest fires) and human factors (such as the great increase in population, indiscriminate felling, and the damage caused by war and domestic upheaval) have seriously depleted the forest resources. By 1949, China had only 1.15 billion *mu* of forests, covering 8.6 per cent of the total land area. Some 1.5 million *mu* of new trees were planted annually and the annual output of timber was 5 million cubic metres. Virtually no particle board was produced at the time. Since 1949, the total area of newly planted forests has reached 420 million *mu*, and naturally regenerated forests cover 490 million *mu*. Forests now cover 12.7 per cent of the country, and 70 million *mu* of new forest is created each year. The annual output of timber is 50 million cubic metres and that of particle board is 600,000 cubic metres. Some 86 per cent of the country's state-run forest farms are mechanized (compared with 17 per cent in 1949) and new technology is being introduced and promoted. In addition to large-scale afforestation campaigns, farmers are also being encouraged to plant trees on unused cropland.

China's Forest Resources

The main characteristics of China's forest resources are their insufficiency, their uneven distribution over the country, and the inadequate protection they provide to agriculture, animal husbandry, and the environment. China has large areas of mountainous land, but only a small area of forests (1.8 billion *mu*). Of the total storage area of 9.5 billion cubic metres, 3.5 billion are ready to be cut. The percentage of forest cover is lower than the world average of 22 per cent, and the per-capita areas of forest and wood storage volume are also low (1.9 *mu* and 10 cubic metres respectively).

The main forested areas are in the north-east, the south-west, and in Zhejiang and Fujian provinces. The forests in north-east and south-west China account for almost half the total forested area, and their storage volume accounts for around 75 per cent of the total. Heilongjiang and Jilin provinces in the north-east alone account for 26.9 per cent of the country's total forested area and 31.6 per cent of the total storage volume. Sichuan and Yunnan provinces in the south-west account for a further 14 per cent of the total forested area and 24.6 per cent of the total storage volume. The densely populated northern and central parts of the country, where agriculture and industry are comparatively advanced, account for only 10.4 per cent of the total forested area and 3.7 per cent of the storage volume. Gansu, Ningxia, Qinghai, Xinjiang, and the western parts of Inner Mongolia, which constitute 37 per cent of the total land area, have only 3.2 per cent of the country's forest area and an even smaller storage volume.

The paucity of forested land and its uneven distribution throughout the country provide little protection for agriculture, animal husbandry, and the natural environment. Between Heilongjiang in the north-east and Xinjiang in the north-west, 1.9 billion *mu* of deserts and gobi threaten 200 million *mu* of farm land and pastures. Since 1949, some 90 million *mu* of farm land have become sandy desert and, in Inner Mongolia, the sandstorm line is moving steadily south, threatening northern Shaanxi and western Shanxi provinces and even Beijing. Soil erosion in the Chang Jiang valley has also become progressively more serious. Hainan Island, in the south, now has 7.2 per cent forest coverage, compared with 25 per cent in 1955. In the early 1960s, naturally irrigated crop land accounted for half of the island's total farm land; it has now been reduced to 20 per cent. Guizhou province is affected by droughts two years out of three since its forest cover has been depleted. In addition, the destruction of forests in Yunnan province has deprived rare animals such as elephants of their natural habitat. Forests have a vital role in maintaining the ecological balance; their destruction both upsets this natural balance and affects the level of agricultural production of a region.

A second characteristic of forestry is the large percentage of timber forests and the small proportion of economic, fuel, and shelter forests in the total forested area (Table 19.1). Although timber forests account for a large percentage of the total, they are poor in quality. Most are natural forests, which have been depleted by excessive felling and insufficient replanting. The care of new and established forests has also been inadequate, and denudation and forest fires have taken their toll. The main forest areas are decreasing as a result. In Sichuan, Yunnan, Guizhou, Fujian, Jiangxi, Zhejiang, Anhui, Hunan, Guangdong, and Shaanxi provinces, for example, approximately 110 million cubic metres of forest resources have been consumed annually since 1977, 40 million cubic metres more than the annual forest growth volume. The destruction of forested land has contributed to the problems of drought,

Table 19.1 The Composition of China's Forest Area, 1980 (%)

Total Forest Area (*mu*)	Composition					
	Timber Forests	Shelter Forests	Economic Forests	Fuel Forests	Special-use Forests	Bamboo Groves
1.8 billion	80.3	6.5	7.1	2.7	0.5	2.7

Source: China's Agricultural Yearbook, 1980 (Agriculture Publishing House, Beijing, 1981).

flooding, and sandstorms, as well as to the reduction in the supplies of wood and forest products.

Since 1949, 100 million *mu* of shelter forests have been established, lessening to some extent the effects of the depletion of the natural forests and protecting agricultural production in the process. They are limited in area, however, and sandstorms and soil erosion remain major problems. In the north-west, the northern parts of Shanxi and Hebei, and in the western part of the north-east — areas which are close to the Gobi desert — tree coverage is sparse and the climate dry. The existing shelter forests are inadequate to protect the land against sandstorms. In the eastern coastal provinces, too, the forested area is small and unable to provide adequate protection. The need for a significant expansion in the area of shelter forests, including shrub and grass coverage, is paramount.

Economic forests comprise only 0.88 per cent of the country's total forested area, and many areas specialize in single-product production. Oil- and fruit-bearing trees, as well as other forest types, are necessary to provide specific products and to guarantee the development of timber forests. Their percentage of the total forested area needs to be increased accordingly.

Forests in China also have an important water conservation function in that they adjust the run-off volume of the rivers and their tributaries and slow the accumulation of sand in river beds. Most of the large forested areas are located on the upper reaches of the large rivers, such as the Chang Jiang, Zhu Jiang, Min Jiang, and Songhua, where they assist in keeping the rivers' middle and lower reaches open to navigation. They are therefore important in the economic construction of those areas.

Finally, China's forestry industry is characterized by slow reafforestation and a low survival rate. Of the 1.5 billion *mu* of forests planted in China since 1949, less than one-third have survived. On average, only 15 million *mu* have been established each year, and existing forests are frequently depleted by fires, plant diseases, and insect pests. Between 1950 and 1979, some 330 million *mu* of forests were damaged by forest fires — equivalent to 73 per cent of the existing forests built up over the same period and almost equal to the planned felling volume. Plant diseases and insect pests have also become a more serious problem in recent years, affecting 25 per cent of the country's forests each year.

The Main Forested Areas

China's forested areas are concentrated in the north-east and the south-west. These areas are the main natural forest production bases and a natural defence for the north-east plain, eastern Inner Mongolian grassland, and the upper reaches of the Chang Jiang. The two areas, where production is well developed, have been the country's largest timber suppliers since 1949. The forested area of south China is another important production base (Fig. 19.1).

The north-east forest area, including Heilongjiang, Jilin, and Liaoning provinces, the Hinggan mountains in eastern Inner Mongolia, and the Changbai Shan forest area, has the country's largest forest resources. Broadleaf trees — mainly poplar, birch, and oak — constitute 40 per cent of the forests.

Fig. 19.1 The Distribution of the Main Forest Areas

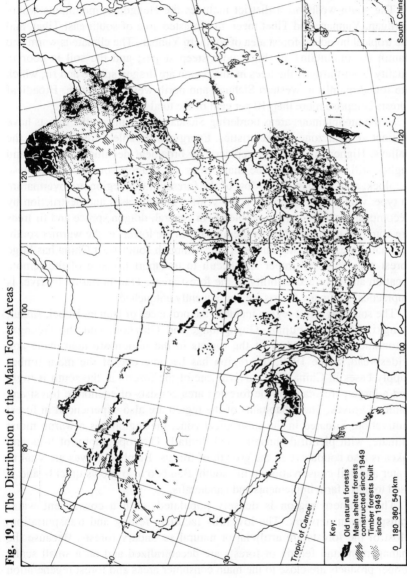

Key:
Old natural forests
Main shelter forests constructed since 1949
Timber forests built since 1949

0 180 360 540 km

Tropic of Cancer

South China Sea

The forested areas are in broad valleys or on gentle slopes which are suitable for mechanized felling. They are also close to rail transport facilities and water courses. Since 1949, the north-east region has become the country's largest state forest, with the highest level of mechanization, the longest forest railway, and the longest forest roads. It is the biggest timber-producing area in China, with trees of a high economic value, and the most favourable conditions of all the forested areas of China.

The south-west forest district includes the Hengduan mountains where Sichuan, Yunnan, and Tibet meet, the forested area of south-east Tibet, and the tropical broadleaf forest area of southern Yunnan. The climate is warm and damp; the mountains are high, with steep slopes; and the soil is poor in quality. Two-thirds of the trees in this region are dragon spruce and fir, which are found mainly in western Sichuan and north-western Yunnan. Broadleaf forests comprise more than 10 per cent of the total area.

In the mountainous areas bordering Sichuan and Yunnan, the forests have distinct vertical zone characteristics. Evergreen broadleaf trees grow in the valleys. Higher up, these are replaced by broadleaf deciduous species, and higher still, by conifers. The main trees are dragon spruce, fir, Chinese hemlock, and Yunnan pine. Most of the forests in this region are overmature in type, with an average age of 160 years. Plant diseases and destruction by decomposition are common problems. In general, dragon spruce and fir trees are common in the north where temperatures are lower; in the warmer south, the main forest trees are Yunnan pine. Although south-west China has large forest resources, its timber is difficult to transport because of the remote location and poor accessibility of the forest areas. Transportation by river is impractical and many forests are consequently untouched.

The southern forest region includes the provinces of Hunan, Hubei, Anhui, Jiangxi, Zhejiang, Fujian, Guangdong, and Guizhou, and the Guangxi autonomous region. Most of the forests in the region are man-made and widespread. Since 1949, the region has become one of the main timber supply bases in China. The survival rate of the forests in the south is high, and a large percentage of the forested area consists of economic forest and bamboo groves. The inhabitants of the region are also experienced in forest cultivation. Situated in the subtropical zone, the region has a warm, moist climate, with plentiful sunshine and rainfall. The topography of hills and lakes is also conducive to the growth of forests. Bamboo groves are vital to water and soil conservation in the south. Bamboo also grows quickly and is used to make farm implements and handicrafts.

The southern region is densely populated, with a convenient water transportation network. The low hills facilitate felling and transportation. Most of the forests are artificial or natural secondary forests. Because the management and felling of forests are decentralized and on a small scale, timber products are close to the main consumer areas and forest regeneration is carried out properly. Most trees are felled by hand because the widespread nature of production hinders mechanization. Forest workers typically move around the region and labour productivity is low. Nevertheless, the region produces 20 per cent of the country's total output of timber each year, second only to the north-east region.

The Future Development of the Forestry Industry

The forestry industry in China is still very backward. Forests cover only a small area and they are far from meeting the needs of national economic development. Measures planned to expand the industry and to place it on a sounder economic base include the construction of large shelter forests, afforestation in the plains areas, and the construction of coastal shelter forests, orchards, and economic forests, especially tropical economic forests such as rubber.

The Construction of Large Shelter Forests

Large shelter forests are to be planted in 11 provinces and regions, including Xinjiang, Qinghai, Ningxia, Gansu, Shaanxi, Inner Mongolia, Shanxi, Hebei, Liaoning, Jilin, and Heilongjiang. At present, the rural population in these areas totals 44 million. There are 290 million *mu* of cultivated land, 500 million *mu* of grasslands and pastures, and the forest coverage is 2.1 per cent. Between Xinjiang and Heilongjiang are 1,900 million *mu* of desert land. The sandstorms in this region are a serious threat to agricultural production, destroying farm land and pastures and removing surface soil. Water and soil erosion in the counties along the middle reaches of the Huang He are serious problems, with more than 10,000 tonnes of soil per square kilometre being removed each year. Nitrogenous, phosphate, and potash fertilizers are also seriously depleted each year. The region accounts for 70–80 per cent of the sand found in the Huang He.

The frequent natural disasters in this area — which comprises 25 per cent of the total area of China — have affected agricultural production, particularly the production of grain. A grain-deficient area, its requirements are met by the grain-surplus provinces and regions. Although there are vast pastures suitable for animal husbandry, livestock production is also very low and the output of sheep and of large farm animals has remained unchanged since 1965. In addition, there are shortages of fuel, fodder, fertilizer, and timber.

Since 1949, forests have been planted in the region. In eastern Inner Mongolia and in the western part of Heilongjiang, Jilin, and Liaoning provinces, for example, 4.05 million *mu* of shelter forest had been planted by 1978 to act as a barrier for 45 million *mu* of farm land (half the area's cultivated land). In the north-west, 10 million *mu* of forest, 15 million *mu* of pasture land, and 30 million *mu* of oases have also been developed. A 170-kilometre shelter forest has been constructed in Inner Mongolia along the north-eastern edge of the desert, and a forest belt of trees, shrubs, and grass has been formed on the northern edge of the Hexizhouliang region in Gansu. Man-made and natural forests now cover 81 million *mu* in this area.

The western part of the shelter forest belt is desert or semi-desert, with an average annual rainfall of less than 200 millimetres and strong winds. Approximately 85 per cent of the country's deserts are in this region, 75 per cent of which consist of migratory dunes which threaten farm land and create serious wind erosion. Expansion of the deserts can be checked by the rational use of the region's water resources, which consist mainly of mountain ice and snow and underground water. These resources can be used to support the growth of shrubs, which in turn can be used to develop animal husbandry, agriculture, and forestry.

The eastern part of the region consists of steppe or steppe deserts, with an annual rainfall of 200–400 millimetres. These deserts account for approximately 14 per cent of the country's total desert area. The main threat to cultivation is wind erosion, though the conditions are less severe than in the western part of the region and there is a natural layer of vegetation which protects the soil. Careful use of the land resources will allow for the development of animal husbandry and agriculture.

The planting of forests in this region should have as its main aim the control of erosion. Of the 80 million *mu* of forest planned to be developed, 10.3 million *mu* are to be shelter forests to protect farm land; 2.54 million *mu* will be shelter forests to protect pasture land; 10.31 million *mu* will act as sand breaks; 8.27 million *mu* will be to hold sand; 31.5 million *mu* will be fuel forests; 12.75 million *mu* will be timber forests; and 4.22 million *mu* will be economic forests. At the completion of the first stage of the afforestation project, the percentage of forest cover in the agricultural or semi-agricultural and semi-pastoral areas will have increased from 4 to 10 per cent. In the areas worst affected by water and soil erosion — along the middle reaches of the Huang He — the forest cover will have increased from 4 to 18 per cent. Approximately 100 million *mu* of farm land and 50 million *mu* of pasture land will be protected as a result of the project, and the forests will also supply fuel, fodder, and fertilizer for the local inhabitants.

Afforestation in the Plains Areas

North and central China, and that part of east China around the middle and lower reaches of the Chang Jiang, are China's most important areas for the production of food, cotton, edible oil, and pigs. However, these areas have a sparse tree coverage, and large quantities of timber are imported each year from the north-east and the south. The tree coverage of the plains could be increased by planting trees along river courses, beside lakes, channels, and canals, in dried-up river beds, and on waste, saline, and alkaline land. Such forests would also shelter farm land. The soil, water, and climatic conditions of the plains areas are suitable for forestry and there is sufficient labour for afforestation. Within 15 years, these areas could supply 40 million cubic metres of timber annually, in addition to fuel, fodder, and fertilizer. The conditions are also suitable for mechanized production. The most common fast-growing tree species in the region is the paulownia. It is easily regenerated and its deep roots do not interfere with crops, thus making it an ideal species for intercropping.

Since 1949, some 3 million *mu* of sandy and alkaline land in Henan province has been converted to forests and orchards, and trees have been planted between fields on 40 million *mu* of farm land. As a result of these measures, the threat of flooding, drought, sandstorms, alkalinization of the soil, and other problems have been reduced and agricultural production has increased.

The Construction of Coastal Shelter Forests

China has 18,000 kilometres of coastline, along which are 10 million *mu* of sandy desert, saline and alkaline beaches, and badly eroded hilly land. Sandstorms and typhoons occur frequently and shifting sand often inundates farm land. Soil erosion and drought are serious problems. Occasionally, sea dykes and adjacent crops are destroyed. Consequently, agricultural production in these areas is unsteady and there are shortages of fuel.

Since 1949, the government has conducted campaigns to control the sand and wind damage along the coast. One means of reducing the damage has been the construction of shelter forests, which in 1980 totalled a million *mu*. In the north, coastal shelter forests have been established in Jiangsu, Shandong, Hebei, and Liaoning provinces. Where wind erosion is a serious problem, trees, shrubs, and grass have been planted together with fast-growing trees. In the saline-alkaline marshes along the northern coastline, afforestation has been combined with basic capital construction and water conservation measures. Coastal shelter forests have also been established in Zhejiang, Fujian, and Guangdong provinces in the south. Two-thirds of the southern coastline is sand and mud, and drifting sands and wind storms are common. Since 1949, 1,000 kilometres of coastal forest shelter belt have been planted in Guangdong province. Afforestation is also well established in Fujian province, where dykes are used to control shifting sand.

The Construction of Orchards and Economic Forests

Orchards and economic forests of various types are widely distributed in China and some of their products occupy an important position in the international market. They have a higher and faster return than timber forests, and fruit trees are suitable for cultivation in large orchards or in scattered areas, in fertile or poor quality soil, and on plains as well as in hilly areas.

China produces 10,000 varieties of fruit, making it one of the main fruit-growing countries, and its cultivation technology is well developed. The main fruits are apples and pears. In 1980, the total output of apples was 47.261 million *dan* (1 dan is equivalent to 50 kilograms), a 19-fold increase over the 1952 output. Production bases have been expanded in the Liaodong and Shandong peninsulas, and new bases have been established along the old Huang He course north of the Qin Ling. Pears are grown mainly in Hebei, Shandong, and Liaoning provinces, and production in Hebei and Shandong has in recent years expanded considerably. In 1980, the total output of pears was 29.326 million *dan*, a 2.7-fold increase over the 1952 output. The largest grape production base is Turpan in Xinjiang autonomous region. The main producers of oranges — the principal subtropical fruit — are Sichuan, Guangdong, and Zhejiang. In 1980, the total output of oranges was 14.252 million *dan*, a 2.4-fold increase over 1952. Guangdong province is the main producer of bananas and pineapples, the principal tropical fruits. Other products of the economic forests in China include wood-grain alcohol and wood-related oil, crude drugs, and industrial materials, all of which have a high economic value.

There are more than 200 varieties of wood-oil trees in China, the most common being tea-oil, tung-oil, raw lacquer, Chinese tallow, walnut, and mountain apricot trees. The tea-oil tree — grown mainly in Hunan, Jiangxi, and the hilly parts of Sichuan, Guizhou, Hubei, Anhui, and Zhejiang — supplies a large proportion of the edible oil in the south. Some 200 million *mu* of tea-oil trees are grown in China, more than two-thirds of them in Hunan and Jiangxi. The largest output of tung oil is from the three-year variety, which grows mainly in the mountainous areas along the middle and lower reaches of the Chang Jiang. The biggest producers are Sichuan, Hubei, Hunan, Guizhou, Guangxi, southern Shaanxi, and south-western Henan, with Sichuan producing one-third of the country's total output of tung oil. The oil produced in Xiushan in the Wu Jiang valley is exported to many countries.

Red lacquer — also an important export commodity — has a similar distribution to that of tung oil. Chinese tallow grows mainly in the provinces south of the Qin Ling and the Huai He. The walnut tree grows over the whole of the country; the mountain apricot is grown mainly in the semi-moist and semi-dry regions in the north; and coconut and palm oil are produced in the south. Other important economic trees include chestnut, jujube, pepper, anise, Chinese cassia, camphor, and Chinese fan palm.

The hilly areas of the south are particularly suited to the cultivation of tea-oil, tung-oil, Chinese tallow, and olive trees, whereas conditions in the north are more suitable for walnut, mountain apricot, and pepper trees. The expansion of economic forests is necessary for the supply of edible oils, crude drugs, and raw materials for industrial development and export.

The Construction of Tropical Economic Forests

Located south of the Tropic of Cancer, Guangdong, Yunnan, Guangxi, and Fujian have a tropical-subtropical monsoon climate. The high temperatures and plentiful rainfall provide ideal conditions for the cultivation of rubber, coconut, pepper, sisal hemp, olives, cocoa, coffee, and fruit trees.

The most suitable areas for the cultivation of rubber are Hainan Island and Xishuangbanna in Yunnan. Since 1949, they have become important natural rubber production bases, with a total of 3.41 million *mu* of rubber plantations. Small plantations have also been established in Guangxi and Fujian. In 1981, there were 5.3 million *mu* of state-operated rubber plantations and a number of state-run rubber processing factories. Of the country's 6.4 million *mu* of plantations, 2.8 million *mu* are in production, yielding an average annual output of 128,000 tonnes of latex rubber. The area of natural rubber plantation and its output rank fourth and sixth respectively in the world. China is also the first country successfully to grow rubber in large tracts in areas between 18 and 24° north.

There is still considerable potential for growth of the rubber industry through expansion of the area under cultivation in suitable areas and by the replacement of the relatively low-yielding varieties with new varieties. New high-yielding varieties could be expected to increase the average per-*mu* dried rubber output to 80–100 kilograms, thus ensuring self-sufficiency in rubber output.

20. Animal Husbandry

ANIMAL husbandry is the raising of domestic animals and poultry — using natural or cultivated grass or fodder — to produce meat, eggs, dairy products, leather, and fur products. It is also important in the production of raw materials for light industry and export. The present low level of production of the animal husbandry industry — livestock products account for only one-seventh of the country's total export value — is an impediment to national economic development.

The Conditions of Production

Conditions in China are favourable for the development of the animal husbandry industry. In 1978, for example, there were 4.29 billion *mu* of grassland in the northern and western parts of the country, 3.35 billion *mu* of which were suitable pasture land. Xinjiang autonomous region alone had 1.2 billion *mu* of land suitable for grazing. The other vast grasslands are in Inner Mongolia, Gansu, western Sichuan, Heilongjiang, Ningxia, Jilin, and Liaoning. Grassy mountain slopes in south and central China also totalled 670 million *mu*.

The output of grass in the north-east and in eastern Inner Mongolia is stable. These areas are ideal for raising cows, beef cattle, and fine-wool sheep. Central Inner Mongolia and northern Hebei province have poorer meadows, suitable for fine-wool sheep and sheep raised to produce leather. In central and south China, conditions favour beef cattle production. In the desert areas of Qinghai and Tibet, and in the high-altitude colder regions of western Sichuan province, conditions are very poor for animal husbandry.

China has the largest variety of livestock and poultry in the world today and there is a long tradition of raising domestic animals and poultry in conjunction with grain cultivation and agricultural sideline production. In addition to providing a source of income, farm animals provide fertilizer for crops.

Since 1949, animal husbandry has developed rapidly in China in terms of its output and its proportion of the total value of agricultural production. However, this development has been unstable (Table 20.1). Between 1949 and 1980, the output value of the industry increased 3.2-fold and the average annual increase was approximately 3.9 per cent. During the same period, the proportion of animal husbandry in the total value of agricultural production increased 1.8-fold.

The number of animals and of animal by-products has also increased significantly since 1949. In 1980, there were approximately 588 million domestic animals, a 2.67-fold increase over the 1949 figure of 160.12 million. The number of pigs increased 4.29-fold during the period, and the number of sheep increased 3.42-fold; however, the number of large animals increased only 0.58-fold. In 1980, there were also 5.888 million bee hives (a nine-fold increase over the figure in the early 1950s), 200 million rabbits,

Table 20.1 The Output Value of Animal Husbandry and its Percentage of the Total Agricultural Output Value, 1949–80

Year	Livestock Husbandry Output Value (RMB100 million)	Percentage of Agricultural Output Value
1949	33.7	12.4
1952	47.9	11.5
1957	69.0	12.9
1962	44.5	10.3
1965	82.7	14.0
1970	92.6	12.9
1975	179.4	14.0
1978	193.0	13.2
1979	221.2	14.0
1980	230.9	14.2

Note: The figures before 1970 are based on 1957 fixed prices; those between 1971 and 1980 are based on 1970 fixed prices.

Sources: China's Agricultural Yearbook, 1980 (Agriculture Publishing House, Beijing, 1981) and *China's Economic Yearbook, 1981* (*Economic Management*, 1981).

24.11 billion *jin* of pork, beef and mutton products, and a high output of poultry, eggs, milk, leather, and fur.

The development of the industry has provided the country with increased quantities of animal products. In 1979, the state purchased 130.041 million pigs (a 2.52-fold increase over 1957), 1.643 million head of cattle (a 32 per cent increase over 1965), 11.289 million sheep (a 1.2-fold increase over 1957), and 125.48 million poultry (a 57 per cent increase over 1957). In the early 1950s, raw materials for the wool textile industry were imported entirely from abroad. By 1978, however, the country was able to supply 80 per cent of its raw material requirements. In that year, the output of fine wool and reprocessed wool totalled 80,000 tonnes.

The structure of the industry has also changed since 1949, although all varieties of livestock have increased in number (Table 20.2). Between 1949 and 1980, the number of pigs increased by 5.5 per cent annually, but production was unstable. The number of sheep increased more steadily at 5 per cent per annum. However, the number of large farm animals increased at an average annual rate of only 1.5 per cent. The varying rates of increase have also affected the structure of the industry (Table 20.3). The percentage of pigs in the total number of domestic animals increased by 15.8 per cent between 1949 and 1980, making them the main domestic animal. The percentage of sheep increased by 5.5 per cent during the period, and the percentage of large farm animals decreased by 21.3 per cent as draught animals were gradually replaced by farm machinery.

In 1979, pork accounted for 94.3 per cent of the country's total meat output, mutton accounted for 3.6 per cent, and beef accounted for only 2.1 per cent (Table 20.4). Pork has long been the staple meat in China, though its percentage of the total has varied at different times. In 1979, pork was propor-

Table 20.2 The Increase in the Number of Livestock, 1949–80 (10,000 head)

Year	Pigs	Sheep	Farm Animals
1949	5,775.2	4,234.7	6,002.2
1952	8,977.0	6,177.8	7,645.9
1957	14,589.5	9,858.2	8,382.2
1962	9,997.2	13,464.6	7,020.1
1965	16,692.5	13,903.0	8,421.0
1970	20,610.1	14,704.2	9,436.2
1975	28,117.3	16,336.7	9,686.0
1978	30,128.5	16,993.7	9,389.2
1979	31,971.0	18,314.2	9,459.1
1980	30,543.1	18,731.1	9,524.6

Source: China's Agricultural Yearbook, 1980 (Agriculture Publishing House, Beijing, 1981).

Table 20.3 Changes in the Structure of the Animal Husbandry Industry, 1949–80 (%)

Year	Pigs	Sheep	Farm Animals
1949	36.1	26.4	37.5
1952	39.4	27.1	33.5
1957	44.5	30.0	25.5
1962	32.8	44.2	23.0
1965	42.8	35.7	21.5
1970	46.1	32.8	21.1
1975	51.9	30.2	17.9
1978	53.3	30.1	16.6
1979	53.5	30.7	15.8
1980	51.9	31.9	16.2

Source: China's Agricultural Yearbook, 1980 (Agriculture Publishing House, Beijing, 1981).

tionally more important than mutton and beef in the south compared with the north. Although pork is still the principal meat in the north, the percentage of mutton and beef is much larger than in the south. The agricultural areas produced much more pork than mutton and beef; the agricultural-pastoral areas produced slightly more beef and mutton than did the farming areas; and in the pastoral areas, mutton had the largest percentage, followed by pork and beef.

Animal husbandry is the weakest of all the agricultural sectors, due to backward production techniques, the poor supply of fodder, low-quality breeding stock, animal diseases, and the lack of a consistent state policy with respect to animal husbandry production.

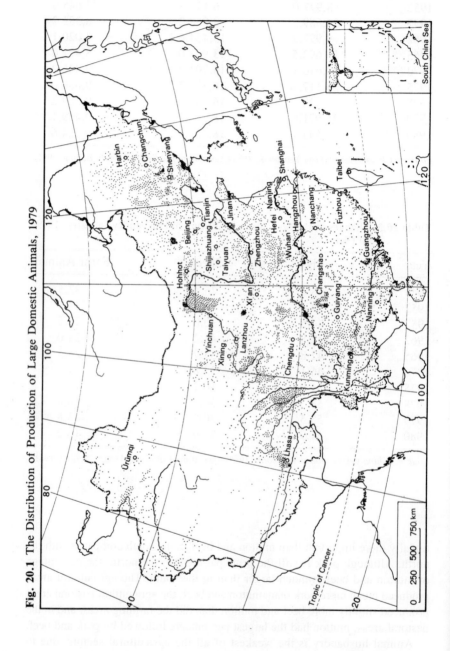

Fig. 20.1 The Distribution of Production of Large Domestic Animals, 1979

Table 20.4 The Proportion of Pork, Mutton, and Beef in the Total Output of Different Regions, 1979 (%)

Region	Pork	Mutton	Beef
Entire country	94.3	3.6	2.1
Divided by northern and southern districts			
Northern district	89.8	6.9	3.3
Southern district	96.5	1.9	1.6
Divided by farming and pastoral areas			
farming area	97.0	1.9	1.1
pastoral area	38.5	40.9	20.6
mixed pastoral-farming area	95.8	2.1	2.1

Source: *China's Agricultural Yearbook, 1980* (Agriculture Publishing House, Beijing, 1981).

The Distribution of Production

The distribution of animal husbandry production is determined by natural and socio-economic conditions. The main large domestic animals — the ox, water buffalo, horse, donkey, mule, and camel — are raised mainly as draught animals, although a few are raised as a source of meat and dairy products. The relative importance of these large animals is shown in Table 20.5 and their distribution is shown in Fig. 20.1.

Table 20.5 The Relative Importance of Large Domestic Animals, 1979

Type of Domestic Animal	Number of Domestic Animals (10,000 head)	Percentage (%)
Oxen	5,241.3	55.4
Water buffalo	1,837.7	19.4
Fine strain or improved strain of cow	55.7	0.6
Horse	1,114.5	11.8
Donkey	747.3	7.9
Mule	402.3	4.3
Camel	60.4	0.6
Total number of domestic animals	9,459.1	100.0

Source: *China's Agricultural Yearbook, 1980* (Agriculture Publishing House, Beijing, 1981).

Oxen are the main draught animals in China except in Heilongjiang province and Tianjin. Their value as a source of meat, skin, and milk is also high. They are raised mainly in the farming and pastoral areas. The Mongolian ox is found in the northern pastoral areas, where its meat and milk have a high economic value and where it is an important draught animal. The north China ox is found in the North China Plain and in the dry crop-cultivating areas such as western and southern Henan province, the mountainous area in southern Shandong province, southern and western Shanxi, the Qin Ling area of Shanxi, and the mixed farming-pastoral areas in the north where conditions are favourable. The south China ox is used as the main form of draught power in the dry crop-growing areas in the Chang Jiang and Zhu Jiang valleys.

The water buffalo is the main draught animal in the fertile plains south of the Huai He, along the middle and lower reaches of the Chang Jiang, and in the paddy fields in south and south-west China. On the Qinghai−Tibet' plateau, where conditions are harsh, the main large animals are the yak and the pienniu (the hybrid of a bull and a yak). They provide meat, milk, and fur and act as a means of transport.

Horses are also an important animal in many parts of the country. The Mongolian horse is the most common breed of horse in China, particularly in the north-east, north, and north-west. Other main breeds include the Sanhe, Yili, and Hequ, and the breeds found in the mountainous south-west region where horses are a principal means of transport.

Donkeys and mules are more common in China than in any other country. Donkeys are an important draught animal and means of transport in the north, the north-west, and the southern part of the north-east. Mules are found mainly in Hebei, Henan, Shanxi, Gansu, Shaanxi, and Shandong provinces. Camels are the only means of transport in the desert areas of western Inner Mongolia and Gansu province.

The most common small domestic animals in China are pigs and sheep. Pig production exceeds that of any other country. Although they are found in all parts of the country, they are most common in the Chang Jiang and Zhu Jiang valleys in north and north-east China. They are less important in north-west China and Inner Mongolia (Fig. 20.2). The varieties of pigs and production techniques vary throughout the country according to natural and socio-economic conditions. The abundance of fodder in the subtropical areas of Guangdong, Guangxi, southern Yunnan, and Fujian, where crops ripen three times a year, provides ideal conditions for pig production. The main commercial pig-producing areas in China are Sichuan, Jiangsu, Hunan, Shandong, and Guangdong provinces.

The Chang Jiang valley has a warm, subtropical climate, fertile soil, and abundant fodder from farm production. This area accounts for some of China's most developed agriculture and the highest proportion of pigs. Another main pig-producing area is the middle and lower reaches of the Huang He, which supplies Beijing and Tianjin as well as other large cities in the region. Pig production is relatively undeveloped in Inner Mongolia, Xinjiang, and the Qinghai−Tibet plateau.

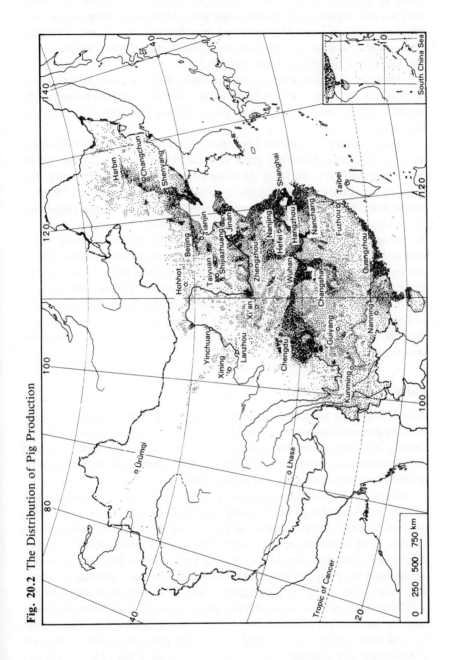

Fig. 20.2 The Distribution of Pig Production

Sheep are raised in most of the country's farming and pastoral areas. In the pastoral districts, it is the principal small domestic animal, being the main food supply. Approximately 60 per cent of the total number of sheep are found in Xinjiang, Inner Mongolia, Qinghai, and Gansu; Henan and Shandong are also important sheep-producing areas. Mongolian sheep are the most common breed in Inner Mongolia and in north-west, north, and north-east China, where they are an important food supply. Other main breeds are the Tibetan, Kazak, and Altay breeds (Fig. 20.3).

Although goats have a low economic value, they are an important source of meat, fur, and milk in mountainous areas. They are found over much of the country, particularly in Inner Mongolia, Gansu, Xinjiang, Shaanxi, and Shandong.

Poultry raising is another important sector in the animal husbandry industry. Chickens, ducks, and geese have the highest economic value. China was one of the first countries to introduce artificial incubation of poultry. The industry is mainly a sideline occupation, with a high output. Chicken production is the main aspect of poultry raising, having the largest output and the widest distribution. The main producing areas — Hebei, Jiangsu, Shandong, Anhui, Guangdong, Hunan, Hubei, and Henan — produce 80 per cent of the country's total output of egg-laying and broiler chickens. Ducks and geese are found mainly in the paddy areas of the Chang Jiang and Zhu Jiang valleys. Guangdong, Guangxi, Jiangsu, Anhui, Hunan, and Sichuan provinces produce 80–90 per cent of the country's total output of duck meat and eggs. Geese are raised mainly in the lower reaches of the Chang Jiang and the Zhu Jiang, the main producers being Jiangsu, Anhui, and Guangdong provinces.

Patterns of Land Use

Animal husbandry production is distributed over four main areas in accordance with the predominant pattern of land use. These areas are the natural pastoral-herding areas, the agricultural areas, the mixed agricultural-pastoral areas, and the suburban areas where livestock production is carried out on the outskirts of cities and around industrial and mining areas.

The natural pastoral-herding areas include the plateaux, mountains, and valleys in Inner Mongolia, Xinjiang, Qinghai, Gansu, Tibet, and north-western Sichuan. They comprise 40 per cent of the total land area and are China's most important animal husbandry bases. Predominantly minority nationality areas, they depend on livestock production as the main economic activity and the principal means of subsistence. The main animals are sheep and goats, followed by cattle and horses, and, in the desert regions, camels.

The pastures in these areas are vast, and nomadic herding has traditionally been the main means of production. In recent years, however, production has become more settled. Natural conditions are the most important determinant of the output and distribution of production because of the lack of grain and fodder in these areas. For example, in the Inner Mongolia pastoral area, the amount of natural pasture land decreases from the east to the west. The eastern part of the region is more suited to livestock production for meat and milk,

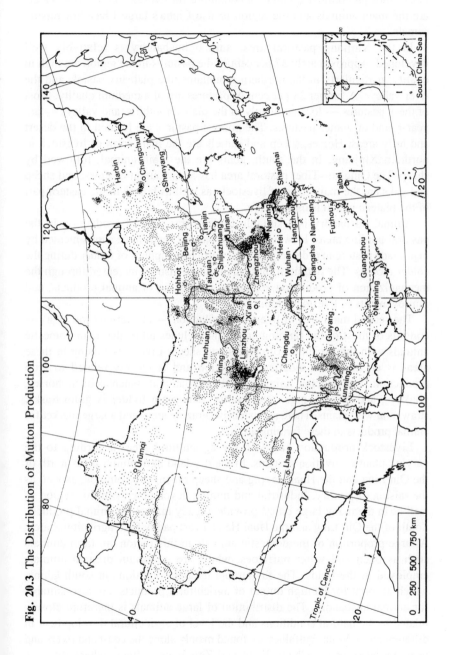

Fig. 20.3 The Distribution of Mutton Production

and the western parts are more suited to the raising of animals for fur. From east to west, the principal form of livestock production varies therefore from cattle to horses, sheep, goats, and camels. In the west, semi-desert and desert grass-lands predominate, with poor conditions for livestock production. Goats are the main animals and the region is also China's largest base for raising camels.

In the Xinjiang pastoral area, animal husbandry is relatively well developed. Approximately 37 per cent of the pastures in the region are high in quality, particularly in the northern mountains, the plateaux basins, and the river valleys. A further 28 per cent of pastures are of a medium quality. Most of these pastures — located mainly in the plains, foothills, and valleys — are year-round or winter pastures. The poorest pastures are located in the desert and hilly areas. Horses, sheep and camels are the main form of livestock in northern Xinjiang. In the south, goats are the main animal, followed by sheep. The Qinghai–Tibet pastoral area has a low output of grass, and sheep and yaks are the main form of livestock, as well as horses in the eastern part of the plateau which is more fertile.

Animal husbandry is a suitable form of agricultural production in the pastoral-herding areas. However, natural pasture needs to be supplemented by man-made pasture in order to guarantee sufficient supplies of fodder during the colder months. The output of these areas could also be increased through the mechanization of production, expanded processing of animal products, and improvements in livestock strains.

The second main area of livestock production — the agricultural areas — consists of most of the farming areas and includes all of the main domestic animals with the exception of camels and sheep. Livestock raising in these areas is an important sideline occupation and is closely related to crop production. The principal animals are draught animals (such as oxen, horses, donkeys, and mules), pigs, and poultry. The main fodder is grain husks, straw, and wild plants. There are extensive grazing areas and a large market for animal products in these farming areas.

Livestock production varies in the agricultural areas according to the varying plant cultivation systems. In the dry land agricultural areas north of the Qin Ling and the Huai He, pig and sheep raising are common, as well as the raising of poultry. Industrial and mining developments in this region as well as in the many large cities, provide a ready market for animal products. South of the Qin Ling and the Huai He is a vast paddy field agricultural area. A large proportion of the domestic animals in this region are farm animals such as oxen and water buffaloes, which are important draught animals employed in the fields. The favourable natural conditions in south China, which account for its high output of agricultural products, are also suitable for animal husbandry. The distribution of large animals is therefore closely related to the natural conditions and the level of agricultural development in different areas. Water buffaloes are found mainly along the coast and rivers and near the lakes in the Chang Jiang and Zhu Jiang valleys, where they are important draught animals. Oxen are found mainly in the hilly and mountainous areas. Pig and poultry production is widespread, the main commodity pig production bases being Sichuan, Guangdong, Jiangsu, and Hunan provinces. The main geese and duck production areas are Jiangsu, Anhui, Guangdong, and Guangxi.

The mixed agricultural-pastoral areas are a third main area of livestock production. Situated between the agricultural and pastoral areas, the land use is mixed, although pastures are tending to replace farm land. There is considerable potential in these areas for expanded livestock production and the development of a national stock-raising base.

Animal husbandry is also practised in the suburban areas, where it provides milk, eggs, poultry, and meat to consumers without incurring high transportation costs.

The Establishment of Livestock Production Bases

Livestock production bases require favourable natural, socio-economic, and technical conditions in order to supply large quantities of high-quality livestock products to the cities. In general, however, the production of livestock products in China is unstable, and products are of a low quality. Production is unable to meet the needs of the development of the national economy. Modern, stable, high-quality production bases need to be established and developed in areas with favourable natural and production conditions. One such area includes western Heilongjiang and Jilin provinces and eastern Inner Mongolia where the large tracts of pasture land and high-quality grass provide ideal conditions for breeding cattle, fine-wool sheep, lambs, and other livestock. At present, the shortages of grass and fodder hinder the further development of the area. These problems could be overcome by the expansion of the pasture areas, the expanded cultivation of grass and other fodder crops, and the mechanization of production.

A second area suitable for further development as a livestock production base includes the Altay, Tacheng, and Yili districts of northern Xinjiang where the main forms of livestock are fine-wool sheep, beef cattle, meat sheep, and horses. There are natural and seasonal pastures and fertile soil in the mountain plateaux and valleys suitable for growing fodder crops. The main problems in this area are the waste of summer pastures and the insufficient area of winter pastures. Further development of livestock production will require sufficient quantities of high-quality grass and fodder and the rational management of the existing pastures.

The south-eastern Qinghai–Tibet plateau has varied topography with relatively poor conditions for livestock production. However, there are rich water resources, forests, pastures, and varied vegetation. The main animals are sheep, goats, yaks, oxen, pienniu, and horses. The main problems in the area with respect to its development as an important livestock production base is the lack of proper management and processing technology.

The north and north-west agricultural-pastoral area has favourable climatic, water, and soil conditions for grass and crop production to support a beef cattle, sheep, and wool production base. There are high-quality natural pastures and sufficient quantities of fodder, making it particularly suitable for fine-wool sheep and beef cattle production. Pigs are also important in some of the predominantly agricultural areas. The emphasis on agriculture in this area has reduced the importance of animal husbandry, despite the area's suitability for livestock production. The development of forestry and agriculture needs to be co-ordinated with livestock production, with the development of a meat and wool production base being emphasized.

The valleys and basins of the Chang Jiang, the Zhu Jiang delta, and Shandong and Henan provinces are pig, poultry, and egg production bases, as well as important producers of oxen, buffaloes, and dairy cows. The area's developed agriculture provides abundant sources of fodder in addition to the natural pastures and water plants. The area is also highly developed in terms of technology and mechanization. Future expansion of animal husbandry in this area should emphasize pig and poultry production, as well as the production of herbivorous animals as a source of meat.

21. Aquaculture

AQUACULTURE — the production of aquatic animals and plants — includes fishing, breeding, preservation, and the processing and transportation of aquatic products. China has favourable natural conditions and rich resources for the development of aquaculture. Of the 3,000 varieties of aquatic products produced in China, approximately 800 are produced in the inland waterways. There are 250 million *mu* of freshwater waterways in China (in addition to 170 million *mu* of swamp land and 380 million *mu* of rice fields), 18,000 kilometres of coastline, 200 million *mu* of offshore shoals, and 1.6 million square kilometres of continental shelf waters of a depth less than 200 metres. In addition to the rich natural resources, aquaculture has a long history in China, dating back to the 11th century BC. Prior to 1949, however, the level of production was seriously affected by feudalism, imperialism, and warfare. In 1936, the output of the industry was 1.5 million tonnes; by 1949, this had been reduced to 448,000 tonnes. Conditions were generally very poor and techniques backward, producing a low output of aquatic products.

Development since 1949

Aquaculture has undergone considerable development since 1949. In 1979, 1.74 million *mu* of the total marine arable area of 7.38 million *mu* (23.5 per cent) and 48 million *mu* of the total freshwater arable area of 75.44 million *mu* (64 per cent) was cultivated. In 1980, the total output of aquatic products was 4.497 million tonnes (ranking third in the world). This output was a 10-fold increase over the 1949 figure, producing an average annual growth rate of 7.8 per cent. The 1980 output value was RMB2.1 billion (1.3 per cent of the total agricultural output value).

The increase in the output of the industry is due mainly to the establishment of state-run fishing communes and brigades, the popularization of updated methods and equipment (such as chemical-fibre nets), and the increase in the number of motorized fishing vessels and cold-storage facilities. Freshwater fishing also developed in the suburban districts after 1949 and a number of commodity bases were established. In 1980, the cultivated water surface area was 50 million *mu*, producing an output of 800,000 tonnes (an average output per *mu* of 20 kilograms). Freshwater breeding techniques and management have improved significantly since the 1950s and the output of freshwater aquatic products now ranks first in the world. When combined with sericulture or animal husbandry, aquaculture is an appropriate form of agriculture for conserving energy, exploiting local resources, and maintaining the ecological balance.

Since 1970, the output of kelp has increased considerably in the marine fishing grounds which cover 1.8 million *mu*. The annual output of 0.4 million tonnes is an average per-*mu* output of 235 kilograms. Marine fishing has been extended to waters between 80 and 200 metres in depth.

The development of aquaculture has been unstable, despite the increased output since 1949. In addition, natural resources have been depleted, technical standards have remained relatively low, and the economic results of the industry have been generally poor. The offshore aquatic resources have been over-exploited, resulting in a reduction in the output and quality of commercial fish. In 1978, the eight main commercial fish comprised only 28 per cent of the total harvest, compared with 46 per cent in 1970; the percentage of small fish of various kinds has increased accordingly. Freshwater resources have also been damaged, particularly by the construction of sluices and dams on rivers, by the reclamation of land from lakes, and by industrial pollution. A further problem in the industry is the inadequate facilities and their irrational distribution. There are insufficient fishing ports and docks, and the preservation and processing facilities are inadequate. Fish breeding is also under-utilized in the industry as a means to increase output, and marine cultivation is emphasized over freshwater cultivation (Tables 21.1 and 21.2).

Although freshwater resources greatly exceed marine resources in terms of total usable area, the output of marine products is greater than that of freshwater products. Between 1952 and 1980, the output of marine products increased by 8.8 per cent (an average annual increase of 0.3 per cent). Table 21.3 indicates that caught fish greatly outnumber those that are bred. While the marine output is increasing, that of freshwater products is decreasing. In terms of cultivated products, however, freshwater aquaculture is of major importance. The proportion of cultivated products in the country's total output of aquatic products has increased by 16.8 per cent between 1952 and 1979. However, the output of cultivated aquatic products remains short of the demand. China's aquatic products are derived mainly from inshore fishing (accounting for approximately 83 per cent of the total output), whereas artificial cultivation is the main form of aquaculture in more advanced countries. Deep-sea fishing is also very backward in China and the proportion of the major commercial species of fish in the total output has decreased (Tables 21.4 and 21.5).

The decrease in the proportion of the main commercial fish (especially yellow croaker and hairtail) in the total output of marine products may be attributed to intensive fishing. The volume of aquatic resources in the coastal areas has been estimated to have dropped from over 10 million tonnes to 4.8 million tonnes in 1980. Annual catches of around 3 million tonnes have therefore seriously impaired propagation and the renewal of marine fish resources. Furthermore, in 1977, young fish were estimated to comprise 60 per cent of the total marine catch, thereby threatening the extinction of some species.

Both marine and freshwater aquaculture need to be developed simultaneously through fish farming. Freshwater aquaculture is more suited to small-scale management, such as at the collective or individual level. Marine aquaculture, on the other hand, should be expanded (though with an eye to the protection of marine resources) through large-scale ventures in the outer waters of the Yellow and East China Seas, in the southern South China Sea, and in the Pacific Ocean east of Taiwan.

Marine and freshwater resources need to be cultivated in order to reduce the reliance upon caught aquatic products. The world marine output — approxi-

Table 21.1 The Composition of Marine and Freshwater Resources

Marine Resources (%)		Freshwater Resources (%)	
Total area (3.54 million km²)		Total area (250 million *mu*)	
Bohai Sea	2.3	Rivers	45.6
Yellow Sea	12.4	Lakes	33.6
East China Sea	24.3	Reservoirs	12.8
South China Sea	61.0	Ponds	0.8

Source: China's Agricultural Yearbook, 1980 (Agriculture Publishing House, Beijing, 1981).

Table 21.2 The Output of Aquatic Products, 1949–80

Year	Total Output (million tonnes)	Marine Products (%)	Freshwater Products (%)
1949	0.448	—	—
1952	1.666	63.6	36.4
1957	3.116	62.2	37.8
1962	2.283	65.6	34.4
1965	2.984	67.5	32.5
1970	3.185	71.6	28.4
1975	4.412	75.9	24.1
1977	4.695	77.1	22.9
1978	4.656	77.3	22.7
1979	4.305	74.1	25.9
1980	4.497	72.4	27.6

Source: China's Agricultural Yearbook, 1980 (Agriculture Publishing House, Beijing, 1981).

Table 21.3 The Proportion of Marine and Freshwater Products in the Total Outputs of Aquatic Products and Cultivated Products, 1952–79

Year	Percentage of Aquatic Products (%)			Percentage of Cultivated Products (%)		
	Total	Marine	Freshwater	Total	Marine	Freshwater
1952	88.2	60.0	28.2	11.8	3.6	8.2
1957	78.0	58.3	19.7	22.0	3.9	18.1
1962	82.3	61.7	20.6	17.7	3.9	13.8
1965	79.3	64.0	15.3	20.7	3.5	17.2
1970	75.9	65.8	10.1	24.1	5.8	18.3
1975	76.6	69.6	7.0	23.4	6.3	17.1
1977	74.6	68.1	6.5	25.4	9.0	16.4
1978	73.9	67.6	6.3	26.1	9.7	16.4
1979	71.4	64.4	7.0	28.6	9.7	18.9

Source: China's Agricultural Yearbook, 1980 (Agriculture Publishing House, Beijing, 1981).

Table 21.4 The Proportion of the Main Marine Products in the Total Aquatic Output, 1957–78 (%)

Year	Big Yellow Croaker	Small Yellow Croaker	Hairtail	Giant Prawn	Kelp	Others
1957	9.2	8.4	10.3	0.9	—	—
1962	9.3	4.8	17.5	0.7	2.6	65.1
1965	5.1	2.2	18.8	1.1	1.3	71.5
1970	7.0	1.3	17.2	0.6	3.9	70.0
1975	4.2	1.6	14.4	0.9	4.8	74.1
1976	3.6	1.5	12.7	0.3	4.4	77.5
1977	2.5	1.2	10.9	0.7	6.1	78.6
1978	2.6	0.7	10.8	1.1	7.0	77.8

Source: China's Agricultural Yearbook, 1980 (Agriculture Publishing House, Beijing, 1981).

Table 21.5 The Proportion of the Main Marine Products in the Total Marine Output between 1950–2 and 1978 (%)

Year	1950–2	1953–7	1958–62	1963–5	1966–70	1971–5	1976–7	1978
Proportion	74.27	78.60	66.00	68.00	63.00	51.00	38.00	31.88

Source: China's Agricultural Yearbook, 1980 (Agriculture Publishing House, Beijing, 1981).

mately 60 million tonnes a year — appears to be declining. It is imperative, therefore, that breeding be developed in suitable areas of the continental shelf and in the inshore areas. China has favourable conditions for the development of breeding and propagation, which have high economic results. Aquaculture is also suitable for development on a collective basis. Collective fish farming would also contribute to rural employment and the comprehensive utilization of natural resources.

Marine Aquaculture

China has a vast area of marine fishing grounds, with favourable currents and a rich food supply which ensures the steady propagation of many varieties of fish. Major commercial fish, such as yellow croaker and hairtail, are scattered amongst the inshore fishing grounds, and the South China Sea abounds in tropical fish. The natural resources of marine aquaculture are affected mainly by the water depth, which in turn affects the water temperature, salt content, and biological profile of an area. The main zones — which require different fishing vessels, equipment, and methods — are the coastal, inshore, and deep-sea fishing zones.

The Coastal Fishing Zone

The coastal zone consists of those areas which are less than 40 metres in depth. In China, they comprise 500 million *mu*. Such areas receive the runoff of continental rivers and are consequently rich in bait, with water of a low salt content. They provide ideal propagating grounds for shrimp, prawns, crabs, jellyfish, herring, as well as for schools of commercial fish. Because of their importance in this respect, coastal waters are protected.

One such zone is the Bohai Sea, in the north, which has an average water depth of 18 metres. Surrounded on three sides by land, it covers an area of 100.2 million *mu*. Its bed of refined sand and soft clay makes it an ideal spawning ground for small yellow croaker, hairtail, prawns, pike, perch, and crabs. The annual output of plankton of the area is estimated to be more than 5 million tonnes, and the potential annual catch is about 300,000 tonnes. Many of the traditional aquatic products have been depleted, however, so that prawns, crabs, and herring comprise the bulk of the catch. Nevertheless, the favourable location and conditions of the Bohai Sea make it suitable for breeding on a large-scale.

The Yellow Sea coastal fishing zone covers an area of 200 million *mu*. Fish which spawn along the 4,000-kilometre coastline include hairtail, cod, giant prawns, inkfish, yellow croaker, silvery pomfret, goatfish, herring, and crabs. The annual output of commercial fish and shrimp reaches as high as 400,000 tonnes. The land fronting the Yellow Sea is amongst the most densely populated in China, with the most advanced industry, agriculture, and transport facilities in the country. There is consequently a great demand in the region for aquatic products. The marine resources have been severely depleted, however, and half the catch consists of young fish. The resources of the Yellow Sea need to be protected in order to ensure their recovery, and fish breeding needs to be actively developed as an alternative to reliance upon the present dwindling resources.

The coastal fishing zones of the East China Sea cover an area of 50 million *mu*. The zone has a low salt content and plentiful bait as a result of the rivers which empty into it (including the Chang Jiang). It provides an ideal spawning ground for commercial fish, shrimp, and yellow croaker, amongst others. Because the resources in the upper and middle depths of the East China Sea are relatively plentiful, the exploitation of fish in the bottom depths has been reduced. Nevertheless, regulations need to be enforced as to authorized fishing areas and times.

The fishing zone along the South China Sea coastline covers an area of 100.3 million *mu*. It is a favourable area for grouper, prawns, and inkfish. Here again, regulations are necessary in order to most effectively utilize the available resources and to prevent damage by trawling vessels. The climatic conditions in the zone are particularly suitable for breeding.

The Inshore Fishing Zone

The inshore fishing zone consists of those areas between 40 and 100 metres in depth. They cover a total area of approximately 800 million *mu*. The meeting of coastal and outer sea waters provides plentiful supplies of bait and suitable feeding grounds for commercial fish and shrimps during the winter months. China's inshore zone passes through 20° of latitude, creating variable conditions between north and south. In the Yellow Sea area north of 34° latitude, for example, year-round fishing grounds are suitable for cod, herring, plaice, and flounder. The movement of currents determines the distribution of other species of fish at certain times of the year. The inshore fishing grounds between 34° latitude and the Taiwan Straits are favourable for mild-water species such as yellow croaker, hairtail, conger pike, silvery pomfret, and long-finned herring. The annual catch of commercial aquatic products in this area is greater than one million tonnes. The inshore fishing zone of the South China Sea is situated south of the Taiwan Straits.

The resources in the inshore fishing zone are becoming more widely utilized as trawling becomes a more widespread practice. Its use should be restricted, however, so that it does not prevail over other fishing methods.

The Deep-sea Fishing Zone

This zone consists generally of areas which are 80–100 metres or more in depth. The deep-sea zone of the East China Sea is the feeding and wintering area for a number of varieties of fish, including chub, mackerel, Spanish mackerel, and scad. These fish form large schools during the autumn and winter months. The main fishing grounds in this area are the Wudao, Duima, Haijiao, and Jizhoudao grounds, although the Wudao and Duima grounds are at present under-exploited.

The deep-sea fishing zone of the South China Sea has considerable potential for further development of its chub, mackerel, scad, and deep-water redcoat resources. Similarly, the resources of tuna, bonito, and shark in the deep-sea areas of the Pacific Ocean east of the Nansha Islands and Taiwan are under-exploited at present.

The main areas for the future development of deep-sea fishing are located in the south-eastern part of the Yellow Sea, that part of the East China Sea east of 124° longitude, that part of the southern East China Sea that is 80 metres or more in depth, areas in the South China Sea that are 60 metres or more in depth, as well as areas around the islands in the South China Sea and in the Pacific Ocean.

Freshwater Aquaculture

Freshwater acquaculture in China is influenced by the geographical distribution of rivers, by climatic conditions, and by topography. Most of the rivers in eastern China which empty into the sea are rich in organic matter as well as aquatic animals and plants. Areas north of the Huang He are favourable for cold-water fish such as salmon. The rivers in north China and the middle and lower reaches of the Chang Jiang are suitable for lukewarm-water fish such as carp, while the rivers in south China are suitable for warm-water fish. The densely populated and well-developed areas south of the Chang Jiang have a solid foundation for aquaculture and a high level of output.

Freshwater aquaculture has also developed rapidly in the outskirts of the large cities in north China, where its products are an important food source for the population. It is still relatively undeveloped, however, in the vast rural areas. Western China, particularly in the north-west, is deficient in the water resources required for freshwater aquaculture; most of the lakes are of salt water and there are few inland rivers. Cold-water species are bred in the plateau areas, but in general the north-west is undeveloped in its aquaculture production.

Freshwater aquaculture varies throughout the country according to natural conditions, the distribution of water resources, other aquaculture resources, and the conditions of production. One distinct type of freshwater aquaculture is pond fish farming in south China, including the tropical and subtropical zones of Guangdong, Guangxi, and southern Fujian. The high temperatures and abundant rainfall in these areas provide ideal conditions for year-round production of lukewarm-water fish. Warm-water species which are reared in ponds are also suitable for production in the southern parts of the region. The water resources consist mainly of scattered ponds and reservoirs because of the topography which is too hilly for lakes. The Zhu Jiang delta — the only flat area in the region — is criss-crossed by rivers which offer favourable conditions for aquaculture. Half of the region's fish-ponds are located in the delta area. The region has approximately 11.29 million *mu* of water surface (5 per cent of the national total). However, only 5 million *mu* (10 per cent of the national total) have been utilized for aquaculture.

In the Zhu Jiang delta, aquaculture has long been combined with other forms of agriculture, making it a high-yield area. In Shunde county, for example, fish-ponds cover an area of 250,000 *mu* and the average annual catch is 400 *jin* per *mu*. Some 20 townships in the counties of Shunde, Nanhai,

Zhangshan, Xinhui, and Gaohe in Guangdong province have become leading commodity fish production bases, with 430,000 *mu* of fish-ponds. The output of these counties is transported for sale mainly in Guangzhou, Hong Kong, and Macau. Live fish exported from the region account for 80 per cent of the national total of exported freshwater fish and approximately one-third of the national total of exported marine and freshwater fish.

The plains along the middle and lower reaches of the Chang Jiang — north of the Nan Ling and south of the Qin Ling and the Huai He — are a second important freshwater aquaculture region. The area consists of plains, basins, and hilly land. Situated in the subtropical zone, the climate is warm and humid, with plentiful rainfall. Water resources are abundant (including a network of rivers, lakes, ponds, and reservoirs), providing favourable conditions for the propagation of freshwater fish. The total water surface area is approximately 120 million *mu* (54 per cent of the national total). The slow-flowing rivers and relatively shallow lakes are rich in fish and plant life, providing not only ideal conditions for freshwater aquaculture, but also conditions suitable for the spawning of some marine species. Both agriculture and animal husbandry are well developed and the proximity of large cities and towns further enhances the region's suitability for commercial aquaculture.

There are over 260 varieties of fish, 10 of which are important commercial varieties, in addition to shellfish varieties and water plants such as lotus roots and water chestnuts. The region ranks first in the country in its output of freshwater fish as a result of its long history of aquaculture production and cultivation of aquatic plants and the sophisticated fish farming techniques employed in production. The annual output of between 600,000 and 700,000 tonnes comprises 60 per cent of the national total output. Of this total, approximately 500,000 tonnes comprises the output of ponds and reservoirs, while the balance is produced in the region's rivers. It is the largest freshwater aquaculture area in China.

A third main area is the extensive pond and reservoir areas of the North China Plain and the loess plateau. The region — situated south of the Great Wall and north of the Qin Ling and the Huai He — has a moderate climate but cold winters. The average annual rainfall varies between 500 millimetres in the east and 200 millimetres in the west. The total water surface area is relatively small (17.9 million *mu*, accounting for 7 per cent of the national total), and the discharges from the Huang He and the Hai He are unstable. During the wet season, the rivers are heavily silted and some dry up during the summer months. The lakes and low-lying areas in the lower reaches of the region's rivers are relatively shallow, with a small surface area. In addition, the lakes, ponds, and reservoirs are scattered over the region. The principal freshwater aquaculture areas are the Baiyang, south Beidagang, Dongping, and Nansi lakes.

There are approximately 140 varieties of fish, including around seven important commercial species. The main fish-producing areas are Shandong and Henan provinces; the western part of the region has a poor foundation for production. Shandong has favourable conditions for production in its lakes, whereas Henan is more suited to reservoir production. The production bases in Baiyang lake in Hebei province and in the outlying areas of Beijing and

Tianjin are relatively well developed. The annual output of 90,000 tonnes comprises 9 per cent of the total national freshwater fish output.

The region has considerable potential for further development since at present only 5.6 million of the 10 million *mu* of lakes, ponds, and reservoirs are utilized for aquaculture. Nansi lake in Shandong province is planned to be developed as a national commodity fish base and other bases are to be developed at Dongping lake in Shandong, Baiyang and Wen'an lakes in Hebei province, south Beidagang lake in the Tianjin area, Guanting and Miyun reservoirs in the Beijing area, Liujiaxia reservoir in Gansu province, Danjiangkou reservoir in Henan province, and Qingtongxia reservoir in Ningxia Hui autonomous region.

A fourth main aquaculture region is located on the Yunnan–Guizhou plateau. It includes Yunnan and Guizhou provinces and the Greater and Lesser Liang Shan areas of western Sichuan province. The moderate climate, plentiful rainfall, and abundant water resources (including numerous basins, reservoirs, ponds, and lakes) are favourable for year-round production. The main lakes include the Dianchi, Erhai, Xingyun, Qionghai, and Caohai lakes, which are relatively shallow, with abundant organic matter. The region has a total water surface area of 4.71 million *mu* (2 per cent of the national total), 1.7 million *mu* of which have been developed as aquaculture production bases. The main form of production is river production, although fish farming has begun to be developed in the ponds and reservoirs. The region's annual output of approximately 15,000 tonnes (2 per cent of the total national output) is low because of the fast-flowing nature of the rivers.

Aquaculture is also practised in the rivers, lakes, and reservoirs of Liaoning, Jilin, and Heilongjiang provinces in north-east China. In this region, the water temperature is low and there is a long winter season. Rainfall decreases from east to west. However, the region has many rivers with a considerable volume of water. The total water surface area is 60 million *mu* (24.1 per cent of the national total). Aquaculture has a long history in Heilongjiang province, but only since 1949 has production developed significantly. During the late 1960s, resources were depleted by over-fishing. The present annual output is approximately 60,000 tonnes (5 per cent of the national total).

In the grasslands of Inner Mongolia, Xinjiang, Ningxia Hui autonomous region, and part of Gansu province, pond fish farming is the main form of aquaculture. The region has a continental climate, with low temperatures. Rainfall decreases from 400–500 millimetres in the east to 100 millimetres in the west, and the region is subject to frequent droughts. Water resources are limited, most of the rivers being short and rapid flowing. The volume of water is also affected by the annual rainfall. The main rivers suitable for aquaculture are the Ertix, Ili, and Tarim rivers in Xinjiang. Most of the lakes are salt-water lakes, with no production value. The most important lakes for aquaculture include the Daihai, Huangqihai, Buir Nur, Dari Nur, Ulansuhai Nur, Bosten, and Fuhai lakes. The few reservoirs in the region are also suitable for production. The total freshwater surface area in the region is 11 million *mu* (6 per cent of the national total).

The Qinghai–Tibet plateau, consisting of Qinghai, Tibet, and the western part of Sichuan province, is planned to be developed gradually as a lake fish farming region. The region is characterized by mountainous terrain (4,000 metres or more above sea level), an arid, cold climate, and low rainfall. Lakes comprise the main water resources, although these are mainly of salt water. Both rivers and lakes are affected by the seasonal rainfall fluctuations and by the long winter months when they tend to freeze over. The water temperature is low even during the summer months. The conditions in the region are therefore unfavourable for aquaculture production.

Aquatic Products Breeding

Aquatic products breeding comprises marine and freshwater fish farming. China has abundant resources for and a long history of fish farming. The designated areas for marine fish farming are the inter-tidal zone and that zone within 15 metres of the lowest tide level. The estimated total of such areas is 200 million *mu*, 7.4 million *mu* of which are suitable for fish farming. At present, however, only 1.68 million *mu* are used for this purpose. There is therefore considerable potential for further development of marine fish farming in China. The main products include mud carp, grey mullet, eel, milkfish, red snapper, globe-fish, prawns, lobsters, crabs, oysters, abalone, mussels, clams, scallops, sea cucumbers, sea chestnuts, and algae. Giant kelp was first introduced from Mexico in 1978 and has since become one of the principal cultivated species in China. The total annual output of marine fish farming products (including kelp and shellfish) is 400,000 tonnes. The most favourable areas for this form of aquaculture are Zhejiang, Fujian, and Guangdong provinces, and Guangxi Zhuang autonomous region (Fig. 21.1). Land reclamation projects during the 1960s reduced the output of marine products in these areas, particularly the output of mud clams in Zhejiang province.

The main problem in marine fish farming is the lack of processing technology which would enable the supply of processed products using kelp and mussels, for example, to meet the market demand. The cultivation of prawns, abalone, and sea cucumbers is also restricted by the lack of modern fish farming techniques, despite the abundant natural resources.

The Yellow Sea coastline of Liaoning province has become an important kelp-producing area, and mussels are an important product of the shallow coastal waters of Shandong province. The kelp-producing area accounts for half the national total, while its output accounts for 80 per cent of the national total output. Prawn and scallop production have also developed rapidly in these provinces, in some places reaching a per-*mu* output of 1,000 *jin*. The southern Yellow Sea coastline is traditionally a producer of hard clams, and the East China Sea area has long used sophisticated techniques in the cultivation of shellfish and seaweeds.

Since 1949, Fujian and Zhejiang provinces have become important marine fish farming bases, with particular emphasis on the cultivation of red laver. The output of marine products accounts for 27 per cent of the national total. The South China Sea coastline has favourable conditions for the cultivation of oysters, mud clams, razor clams, mussels, and pearl oysters, in addition to milkfish and prawns which are presently under trial cultivation.

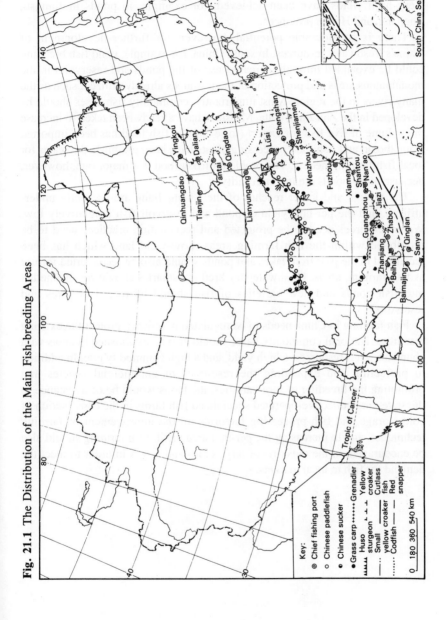

Fig. 21.1 The Distribution of the Main Fish-breeding Areas

Key:
- ⊚ Chief fishing port
- ○ Chinese paddlefish
- ◉ Chinese sucker
- ● Grass carp
- ⊔ Huso sturgeon
- ‧‧‧‧‧ Grenadier
- Yellow croaker
- Small yellow croaker
- Cutlass fish
- Codfish
- Red snapper

0 180 360 540 km

Yingkou
Dalian
Qinhuangdao
Tianjin
Yantai
Qingdao
Lianyungang
Lüsi
Shengshan
Shenjiamen
Wenzhou
Fuzhou
Xiamen
Shantou
Nan'ao
Guangzhou
Jiazi
Zhabo
Zhanjiang
Beihai
Qinglan
Baimajing
Sanya

Tropic of Cancer

South China Sea

China was the first country in the world to engage in freshwater fish farming. Since 1949, breeding techniques have improved, including the introduction of artificial incubation of carp. In the Zhu Jiang delta, fish farming has been combined with agriculture to produce good economic results. The output per *mu* of pond surface exceeds 1,000 *jin* in some areas where fish farming is combined with sericulture or sugar-cane production. Very high yields have been achieved, for example, in ponds in Jiangsu, Zhejiang, and Hunan provinces.

There is considerable potential, however, for further development of China's freshwater resources. In south China, for example, pond fish breeding could be expanded through increased use of the ponds and reservoirs in the mountainous areas and protection of the resources already utilized, such as the many rivers in the region. Most importantly, commodity fish bases should be developed in the Zhu Jiang delta. Measures have already been taken to increase the volume of live fish for export (for example, fish food has been imported from abroad and fish food processing plants have been established to cater for local fish farming needs). The problem of fish food is a major one, however, because many ponds are low in fertility.

The middle and lower reaches of the Chang Jiang are presently under-utilized, and the per-unit yield of pond and reservoir fish is relatively low. Water resources need to be protected and reclamation practices need to be prohibited within the fish farming areas. Low-yield land which has been reclaimed in the past from lakes and ponds should also be reconverted for use as fish farming areas. Freshwater fry bred in estuaries should be channelled into fish ponds and new varieties of fish should be reared in lakes and reservoirs.

Fish farming in China needs to be regulated in order to protect the existing resources. National commodity bases should also be established in areas with abundant water resources, a high yield, and a high commodity rate. In addition to protecting and expanding the resources of commercial species and promoting the breeding of rare varieties, the bases would be of assistance to the state- and collective-operated specialized fish farms in the construction of cold-storage and fish-processing factories, in the improvement of farming techniques, and in increasing the per-unit area yield. Fish farming should also be encouraged on the outskirts of large cities and towns in order to meet the demand for fish in local markets.

22. The Main Agricultural Regions of China

THE conditions for agricultural production in China are determined by natural conditions, traditional land use practices, and economic and technical conditions. As a result, distinct agricultural regions have developed. On one level, differences exist between east and west and between north and south China. The eastern part of the country has favourable climatic conditions and water and soil resources. Agriculture is well developed in this densely populated region, with relatively advanced and concentrated farming, forestry, aquaculture, and sideline production. The production of pigs and poultry ranks first in the country. The conditions and resources in western China are less favourable for agricultural production and the area under cultivation is small and scattered. Most of the land is used for animal husbandry, the traditional form of agriculture of the minority nationalities who are the main inhabitants of this sparsely populated part of the country. The region is China's main livestock region.

Distinct agricultural regions are also apparent in north and south China. North-east China, above the Qin Ling and the Huai He, is the country's main dry land crop-growing region. In the south-east, the basic method of production is wet paddy field production. It is China's main rice-growing area and an important producer of various subtropical and tropical plants and crops. In the west, the Gansu–Xinjiang area north of the Qilian mountains is a vast dry-weather region where agricultural production is totally dependent upon irrigation. Animal husbandry is the main form of production in the deserts and mountainous areas. South of the Qilian mountains, on the Qinghai–Tibet plateau, animal husbandry, agriculture, and forestry are the main agricultural practices.

These four main regions — the north-east, south-east, north-west, and south-west — may be further classified according to their natural resources and socio-economic conditions into the eastern monsoon region, the north-western continental region, and the Qinghai–Tibet plateau region (Fig. 22.1).

The Eastern Monsoon Region

China's most important agricultural region, the eastern monsoon region spans the tropical, subtropical, warm temperate, temperate, and frigid zones. High summer temperatures and rainfall and the fertile plains and hilly areas are favourable for the cultivation of farm crops. The region includes most of the country's cultivated farm land and agricultural population as well as the two most important cotton-growing areas — the plains on the middle and lower reaches of the Huang He and the Chang Jiang. Other important economic products include pigs, chickens, ducks, rabbits, bees, and freshwater and marine aquatic products. The region consists of five main agricultural areas: the north-east, the middle and lower reaches of the Huang He, the Sichuan basin, the middle and lower reaches of the Chang Jiang, and the south.

Fig. 22.1 The Main Agricultural Regions

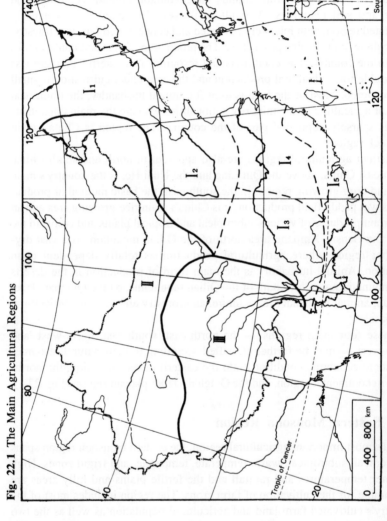

Notes: I Eastern monsoon agricultural region.   I1 North-east.   I2 Middle and lower reaches of the Huang He.   I3 South-west.   I4 Middle and lower reaches of the Chang Jiang.   II North-east continental agricultural region.   III Tibet-Qinghai plateau.

The North-east Region

The north-east region consists of Heilongjiang, Jilin, and Liaoning provinces, most of which lie in the temperate zone. Although it has low temperatures, there are rich land, water, and forest resources. The long, cold winters (frost-free days vary from 80–120 in the north to 140–80 in the south of the region) restrict the growing period. With the exception of southern Liaoning province where the climate is mild, only one crop is grown each year. The annual rainfall is 500–700 millimetres. The fertile Songliao plain, covering 300,000 square kilometres in the central part of the region, is suitable for agricultural mechanization and there are large tracts of arable virgin land, much of which has been reclaimed. Since 1949, a number of mechanized state farms have been established in the Songhuajiang–Ruijiang and Sanjiang plains. The region's farm and forestry products occupy an important place in the country's total output of those products. For example, sorghum, soya beans, and millet production account for 45–50 per cent of the total output, and the output of sugar beets constitutes 60 per cent of the country's total output. The area is also China's largest timber base. Forests cover 30 per cent of the total area and the output of timber products accounts for one-third of the country's total output. Tussah cocoon production accounts for 60 per cent of the national total. In terms of per-capita volume, the area also ranks first in the output of grain. Large quantities of grain and soya beans are supplied to the state.

The main problems in agricultural production in this area are extensive cultivation, the unstable and low per-unit output, natural disasters, and the irrational utilization of soil and forest resources. In order to increase the per-unit yield, mechanization should be expanded and the existing resources utilized rationally. In addition, animal husbandry should be developed and food production bases established near the cities.

The Middle and Lower Reaches of the Huang He

Located north of the Qin Ling and the Huai He, the area around the middle and lower reaches of the Huang He is situated mainly in the warm temperate zone. Agricultural cultivation consists of three dry land crops every two years. The land in this area is the most intensively cultivated in China, with the longest history of agriculture. It is the largest tract of cultivated land in the country as well as the largest sown area of wheat, cotton, peanuts, sesame seeds, and tobacco. The output of apples, pears, and persimmons is also the highest in the country. Forestry and animal husbandry are relatively backward and the forest cover is a low 7–8 per cent. In addition to the annual rainfall of 500–800 millimetres, there are abundant surface and underground water resources. However, agricultural production in the area is seriously affected by the problems of drought, waterlogging, and saline soil.

The North China Plain, situated within this agricultural area, is the highest stable-yield area in north China. Its favourable water and soil resources make it also the most advanced dry land farming area. Irrigation is well developed and the problems of drought and waterlogging have largely been overcome. Agricultural production is further facilitated by a ready supply of labour, convenient transport facilities, and the existence of a large market and scientific and technical support in the cities. The superior socio-economic conditions and the sound foundation in grain and cotton production of the North China Plain have contributed to its being the highest-yield grain- and cotton-growing area in the north. There is considerable potential, however, for further increases in the level of output.

The loess plateau, along the middle and lower reaches of the Huang He, produces dry-land and other grain types. However, the plateau area is seriously eroded and the crop yield is low and unstable. The annual rainfall is 400–600 millimetres. The weather conditions are variable and drought is a common problem during the spring months. In addition, the vegetation is sparse and the soil is loose and soft. Ridges and gullies criss-cross the land.

The flat Wei river plain and the Qinchuan plain have fertile soil and abundant surface and underground water resources. It is one of the major wheat- and cotton-producing areas, with a long history of cultivation and a large population. The main problems for agriculture in this area of the middle and lower reaches of the Huang He are the low and unstable yield of grain, cotton, edible oils, and tobacco; drought, waterlogging, and saline soil; the lack of fertilizer; and the emphasis upon grain production to the exclusion of animal husbandry and forestry.

The Sichuan Basin

The Sichuan basin area of the eastern monsoon region is situated south of the Qin Ling and west of the western Sichuan plateau. Subtropical in climate, it is an important agricultural and forestry base. Consisting mainly of mountainous areas and hilly land, there are abundant water resources. The winters are mild and there is a long growing period. With the exception of the highest areas, two crops of wheat and rice are grown annually. The annual rainfall is high (800–2,000 millimetres). The Sichuan basin is an important producer of grain, edible oils (rape seed and peanut), sugar-cane, tobacco, tea, oranges, and silk, as well as one of the major timber and animal products bases in the country. In the Chang Jiang valley and the lower reaches of the Min, Tuo, and Jialing rivers in the southern part of the basin, the climatic conditions are even more favourable for agricultural production, especially oranges, sugar-cane, and double-cropped rice. Some tropical fruit trees (such as longan and litchi) are grown even during the winter months in parts of Luzhou and Hejiang, where conditions are superior to other areas at the same latitude.

The main problems for agricultural production in the Sichuan basin area are the low multiple-crop index, the low per-unit yield of grain, and the lack of self-sufficiency in grain. In addition, the output of forestry comprises only a small proportion of the area's total agricultural output and animal husbandry is under-developed. These agricultural sectors need to be developed in order to diversify the economy of the area, and self-sufficiency in grain needs to be achieved through increases in the grain yield. The area also has potential for further cultivation of economic crops such as fruit trees.

The Middle and Lower Reaches of the Chang Jiang

Situated south of the Qin Ling and the Huai He, the middle and lower reaches of the Chang Jiang are densely populated areas with limited farm land, abundant water resources, and well developed agriculture, forestry, and aquaculture. The subtropical climate is warm and humid and the frost-free period is 210–300 days. Wheat is grown during the winter months and double- and triple-cropping are carried out in most parts of the region. The most important crops are double-cropped rice, tea, oranges, tung oil, tea oil, fir trees, and bamboo. The annual rainfall is 800–2,000 millimetres and the rainy season is long. South of the Chang Jiang, the rainfall is concentrated during the spring months. Summer droughts often threaten the summer crop of rice.

The topography of the area is varied, consisting of plains, hills, low-lying land, and basins. The fertile plains are criss-crossed by rivers and dotted with lakes. It is the most intensively cultivated area in China, with advanced irrigation, an abundant supply of labour, a high level of agricultural technology, and an intensive farming system. It is an important base for the production of grain, cotton, edible oils, tea, silk, and freshwater aquatic and forestry products. The raising of pigs is the main animal husbandry occupation. One of China's main farm produce bases, the Chang Jiang delta, river valleys, and areas surrounding the lakes are the most densely populated and agriculturally developed areas in China. Most of the region consists of fertile alluvial plains. The abundant water resources provide favourable conditions for aquatic plants and animals and there is considerable potential for further development of freshwater aquaculture. The proximity of many large cities and towns further facilitates agricultural production in the region through the availability of large markets, communications and transport facilities, and agricultural technology. Cultivation, irrigation and drainage, crop protection measures, and grain and fodder processing are mechanized and the high level of scientific cultivation ensures high and stable yields. The main problems in the Chang Jiang area are flooding, drought, large temperature fluctuations, typhoons, hail, and dry heat waves. The intensive cultivation methods also affect crop yields to some extent.

The Jianghan, Dongting lake, and Poyang lake plains along the middle reaches of the Chang Jiang — consisting of alluvial and silted land — are the main farming areas in Hubei, Hunan, and Jiangxi provinces. The plains are low-lying and the cultivated land is concentrated in large tracts with thick soil of a high organic content. The many rivers and lakes on these plains make up the largest continental water surface area in China and there are abundant resources for the development of freshwater aquatic products such as fish, shellfish, shrimps, and lotus plants and seeds. The subtropical climate provides ample sunshine and a frost-free period of 250–80 days — conditions favourable for double-cropped rice, cotton, and peanuts production. The annual rainfall is 900–1,400 millimetres. The main grain crop in the plains area is rice, large quantities of which are supplied to the state each year. The commodity rate of ginned cotton exceeds 90 per cent and the output of the other main agricultural product — freshwater aquatic products — comprises 25 per cent of the country's total output. Also of importance are pigs, eggs, poultry, edible oils, other foodstuffs, and light industrial materials such as ramie, flax, and reeds. In order to stabilize and increase yields, the water resources of the plains need to be protected and used rationally. Measures need to be implemented to prevent flooding and waterlogging, and reclamation of the lakes areas needs to be controlled.

The hilly and mountainous areas south of the middle reaches of the Chang Jiang and north of the Nan Ling are located in the intermediate subtropical, humid zone. Large in area and densely populated, the region has favourable conditions for the development of subtropical economic forests, producing timber and special forestry products. It is one of the most advanced agricultural regions at such an altitude in the world. Much of the annual rainfall of 1,200–2,000 millimetres occurs during the spring, and the relative humidity is usually higher than 80 per cent. Some 70 per cent of the land consists of mountains, 20 per cent is farm land, and 10 per cent is water surface area. The region has rich natural resources, a high level of productivity, and considerable potential for further development of agricultural production. It is one of the main areas in the country for the production of tea, orange, tung-oil, and tea-oil trees, as well as for pine, cypress, and bamboo, making it one of the most important forestry bases in south China. The main factors which limit production are the high temperatures during summer and autumn, the heavy rainfall during spring and summer, and soil erosion and infertility.

The level of output of different areas within the region encompassing the middle and lower reaches of the Chang Jiang varies according to the degree to which the problems of drought, flooding, and waterlogging have been overcome. Water conservation measures are necessary if such problems are to be minimized. In addition, the system of cultivation and the distribution of agriculture need to be combined with soil improvement measures and more rational land use if forestry, animal husbandry, sideline production, and aquaculture are to be developed further.

The South China Region

The south China region is located in the southern subtropical and tropical zones south of the Nan Ling. The region includes Guangdong, Fujian, and the southern parts of Guangxi and Yunnan. It is the only area in China where tropical plants and crops are cultivated. There are abundant water resources and both the annual rainfall and average temperatures are high. The frost-free period is often year-round, providing favourable conditions for winter crops and short growing periods. Although the annual rainfall is between 1,500 and 2,000 millimetres, its seasonal distribution is uneven, resulting in serious soil erosion in the mountainous areas, heavy flooding in the plains and valleys, and droughts during the dry season. Droughts are a particular problem during winter and spring in the western parts of Hainan Island, in western Guangxi, and in southern Yunnan. In summer and autumn, the coastal areas are often subjected to typhoons, resulting in damage to crops and reduced output levels. The region consists mainly of mountains, with a little farm land; plains and basins suitable for agriculture are limited. The large population of the region means that the per-capita amount of farm land is therefore very low. However, in the hilly and mountainous areas, there are rich commercial forest and animal resources and the area is an important base for forestry and aquaculture. It is also the largest sugar-cane production base in the country, as well as one of the main producers of tropical and subtropical fruits such as bananas, pineapples, litchis, longans, and oranges. Moreover, it is the main producer in the country of tropical economic crops such as rubber trees. The Zhu Jiang delta is also an important grain, sugar-cane, silk, and freshwater aquatic products base. Hainan Island and Xishuangbanna are important producers of such tropical plants as rubber, coconuts, palm oil, cashews, pepper, coffee beans, mangoes, and betel nuts.

The main problems in the south China region are the regional differences in the level of agricultural production and the lack of self-sufficiency in grain. The potential of the region remains to be fully developed, particularly in the production of sugar-cane and rubber. Fertilization and irrigation improvements are required in order to raise the cropping index and the per-unit output of grain. Forestry, fruit trees, and sideline production also remain to be fully developed.

The North-western Continental Region

The second main agricultural region in China in terms of its natural resources and socio-economic conditions is the north-western continental region. The region consists of that area west of the Greater Hinggan mountains, the loess plateau, and the area north of the Qilian and Kunlun mountains. It is a vast agricultural region which is sparsely inhabited by ethnic minority groups whose main agricultural pursuits are animal husbandry on the grasslands and crop production in fertile areas supported by irrigation. The climate is temperate continental, with wide daily temperature fluctuations. Annual evaporation exceeds the annual rainfall. The widely distributed grasslands provide excellent natural pasture land and the region is one of China's most important pastoral areas, producing sheep, goats, horses, and cattle. Due to the dry climate, crop cultivation depends entirely upon irrigation, and farm sizes are determined by the available water resources.

The area east of Baotou in Inner Mongolia is a transitional zone between the eastern plain and the highlands of Inner Mongolia and between the semi-humid and semi-dry and dry areas. Although the region has inadequate water and heat resources, there are vast areas of grassland which render it more suitable for animal husbandry than for crop cultivation. With a frost-free period of 80–150 days, one crop is produced each year. The annual rainfall is small and unevenly distributed. In the north-western part of the region, the annual rainfall is 200–300 millimetres; in the south-east, it is 400–500 millimetres. Conditions during the spring months are windy and dry, and drought is a serious problem. The area between the south-eastern foot of the Greater Hinggan mountains and the Daqing mountains is the most important pasture land in China. The highlands of Hulun Buir Meng in the eastern part of the region and the eastern part of Xilin Gol Meng are grassy marsh lands, with a cover rate of 65–80 per cent. It is the best grassland area in China, gradually changing in the west to dry grassland and waste land. In the grassland west of the Hinggan mountains in Hulun Buir Meng in northern Inner Mongolia, in the central northern part of Xilin Gol Meng, and in the northern part of Ulanqab Meng, animal husbandry is the main agricultural system, including cattle, sheep, and horse breeding. In southern Hulun Buir Meng in central southern Inner Mongolia, in northern Jirem Meng and Ju Ud Meng, in southern Xilin Gol Meng and the foothills of the Yin Shan in Ulanqab Meng, and in north-eastern Ih Ju Meng, crop cultivation is combined with animal husbandry in this mixed agricultural zone between the pasture land in the north and the farming areas in the south.

Although in the past this region was an important pastoral area, large-scale reclamation, the conversion of pasture land into farm land, extensive cultivation, and the crop rotation system by which farm land is left to lie fallow have reduced the area of pasture land. The remaining grassland has been over-grazed, resulting in the spread of waste land in the region to a serious extent. Crop cultivation and animal husbandry have become unstable and farm yields are presently very low. The over-emphasis on crop cultivation is contrary to the natural conditions of the region and needs to be de-emphasized in favour of animal husbandry if the conditions of production and the level of output are to improve.

The transitional area of Chifeng in Ju Ud Meng and the area south of Wuchuan–Jining in Ulanqab Meng in southern Inner Mongolia, as well as Hohhot, Baotou, and the transitional zone between the pastoral area of the highlands of Inner Mongolia and the farming area in north China are mixed farming, animal husbandry, and forestry areas, with farming as the main agricultural system. A variety of crops are grown using extensive cultivation. The area is prone to natural disasters, however, and the per-unit yield is low.

Most of the land in Ganxin, west of Baotou in Inner Mongolia, is dry desert with unfavourable natural conditions. The large daily temperature fluctuations during the growing season combined with adequate sunshine, provide favourable conditions for the cultivation of melons and sugar-beets. Most of this region consists of vast tracts of land and highland areas. The plains near the mountain foothills and those parts of the Gobi desert which have soil cover are potentially fertile farm land if supported by irrigation. However, the annual rainfall is less than 250 millimetres, falling in some areas to less than 100 millimetres. The higher annual rainfall in the mountains and basins which criss-cross the region, combined with snow and glaciers, provides the main source of water for irrigation in the mountain valleys during the summer months. Wind and sand erosion are also major problems, as is salinization of the soil. The plant cover rate in most parts of the region is sparse and the soil is poor in organic matter. The grasslands in this region are therefore unsuitable for grazing.

The north-western continental region has a long history of agricultural production and, since 1949, a number of state-owned farming and animal husbandry bases have been established. The farm land in the crop cultivation areas is scattered throughout the plains near the foothills where water is available for irrigation and on the plains along the Huang He in Ningxia and Inner Mongolia. The size of farms is determined by the available water resources because irrigation is essential for agriculture in this region. The main grain-producing bases are the plains along the Huang He in Inner Mongolia, the Yinchuan and Weining plains in Ningxia, the Gansu corridor, and the Ili area in Xinjiang (where cotton is the main crop). The plains along the Huang He in Inner Mongolia and the Shihezi area in Xinjiang are also important sugar-beet production bases. However, because over 95 per cent of the region consists of deserts, semi-deserts, and mountains, the main form of agriculture is livestock grazing. In the desert areas, seasonal nomadic grazing is combined with grazing on pastures on the plains and in the basins and on mountain pasture farms. The pasture lands of the Altay, Tian Shan, Qilian, and Kunlun mountains are used as seasonal pasture for large numbers of sheep, goats, horses, and cattle. In some areas, there are few mountain pasture farms. In the desert pasture areas, the main animals are sheep, goats, and camels.

The main problems in the north-western continental region are the scarce water resources and the poor conditions for water conservation, extensive cultivation, and the low per-unit yield. There is inadequate grassland for the development of animal husbandry which is the most suitable form of agriculture for the region. The planting of forests and the expansion of the present area of grassland would also reduce the problems of soil and wind erosion.

The Qinghai-Tibet Plateau Region

The third main agricultural region in China, the Qinghai–Tibet plateau includes the greater part of Tibet and Qinghai, western Sichuan, north-western Yunnan, and part of Gansu. It is the largest plateau in the country, with many mountains between 4,000 and 6,000 metres above sea level, terraces at an altitude of 3,000–5,000 metres, and lake basins and valleys. Because of the high altitude of the plateau, the conditions are unsuitable for crop cultivation, and animal husbandry is the main form of agriculture. However, in the eastern and southern parts of the region, below 4,000 metres in altitude, conditions are suitable for cold-resistant crops and, in the river valleys in the far south of the plateau, the mild climate is suitable for some corn and rice cultivation. The region has long hours of sunshine and wide daily temperature fluctuations.

Pasture land and grassland cover 2 million *mu* of the region. In the east and the semi-humid south-east, grassy marsh lands provide excellent natural pasture, whereas the semi-dry and dry areas in the north-west are unsuitable for grazing. The south-eastern and eastern parts of the region comprise the second largest area of forest in China.

Crop cultivation, animal husbandry, and forestry in the Qinghai–Tibet plateau region are influenced by the low temperatures of the highlands. Livestock, crops, and forest types are suitable for the cold climate. The main animals are yaks, Tibetan sheep, and goats, and farm crops are mainly such cold-resistant crops as highland barley, wheat, peas, potatoes, and rape seeds.

Most of the forests consist of dragon spruce and fir trees. In the river valleys at lower altitudes and in the warmer south-eastern part of the region, cattle and pigs are raised, corn and rice are cultivated, and there is a higher proportion of broadleaf trees in the forests. In recent years, winter wheat has been cultivated in the valleys along the Yarlungzangbo river in southern Tibet where the winters are less severe and where the low temperatures in spring and summer prolong the growth period. The per-unit yield of winter wheat is high where the conditions are suitable for cultivation.

In general in this region, however, crop cultivation is backward, and animal husbandry and forestry are the main forms of agriculture. The economic development of the region is restricted by its altitude and topography, the climate, sparse population, and the lack of manpower and transport facilities. Fodder bases need to be constructed in order to upgrade the quality of livestock. In addition, grain production bases need to be established so that the region can become self-sufficient in grain. Forestry resources also need to be protected and used rationally.

Part IV: Transport and Communications

23. The Development and Distribution of Transport and Communications

TRANSPORT and communications play an important role in industrial and agricultural production in that they enable commodities to be exchanged, thereby promoting production as well as expanding its range. The level of development of such facilities is a direct reflection of the level of economic development of a province or region and of the country as a whole.

Transport and Communications Facilities before 1949

China has a long history of land development. For centuries, it was one of the most economically and culturally developed countries in the world, with established transport and communications facilities. The country's inland waterways have been used for transportation for as long as 7,000 years. During the Spring and Autumn Warring States period (475–221BC), canals were dug to supplement the over-burdened natural waterways which were used for both freight and passenger traffic as well as for irrigation. Following the unification of China during the Qin dynasty (221–207BC), both water and land transport networks became an important means of strengthening economic and cultural exchanges between various parts of the country. The two main river systems — the Chang Jiang and the Zhu Jiang — were connected by canals and natural waterways. Many roads were also built during this period, forming the beginnings of a national land transport system.

Both water and land transport were developed further during the Han, Sui, and Tang dynasties. The famous 'Silk Road' was opened during the Han dynasty (206BC–AD220). In addition to providing access to and from countries in the West, it made trade possible between the central plain of China and the western border regions. The Da Shou Ling mountain road, built during the Tang dynasty (618–907), brought the central plain into contact with the regions south of the Qin Ling. During the Tang dynasty, there is estimated to have been some 25,000 kilometres of trunk roads, and water transport facilities were also expanded at this time. The canals built during the Han dynasty include the Wei, Yang, and Bian canals and, during the Sui and Tang dynasties, the Yongji, Tongji, Shangyang, and Meng canals were joined to form the Grand Canal. Some 1,500–2,000 kilometres in length, the Grand Canal links north and south China. Some 30 smaller canals were also dug in various parts of the country during the Tang dynasty.

At the time of the Northern and Southern Song dynasties (960–1279), China's political and economic centre moved southward and transport and communications systems in the south developed accordingly. The favourable conditions in the south for water transport enabled grain to be shipped over long distances and the system of rivers and canals soon became the main arteries along which goods flowed between the north and the south. The Bian, Huang He, Huiming, and Guangji rivers alone carried 50,000–60,000 tonnes of grain each year.

During the Yuan dynasty, the capital of China was moved to Da Du (Beijing), although the economic centre of the country remained in the regions along the lower reaches of the Chang Jiang and the south-east coast. The transportation north of grain during the early years of the dynasty relied mainly upon the already established canals and, to some extent, upon the land transport network. However, the opening of the Grand Canal, which reached as far north as Beijing, eliminated the need for changes in the mode of transport en route from the south. The use of the canal was restricted to some extent, however, because of its narrow size and its unsuitability for heavy loads. In order to overcome the problem, coastal routes were opened towards the end of the Yuan dynasty for the transportation of grain to the capital. Sea transport subsequently developed and Guangzhou, Quanzhou, and Mingzhou became the largest sea ports in the country.

China's maritime links with other countries also have a long history. As early as the Qin dynasty, ships sailed to the Korean peninsula and, during the Han dynasty, sea routes to Japan were opened up and ships sailed as far as India and Italy. By the time of the Tang dynasty, sea links extended as far as the Persian Gulf and there were close and frequent exchanges with the Arab countries. By the time of the Ming dynasty, maritime transport had developed to the extent that fleets of Chinese ships had reached the coast of East Africa.

The development of land and water transport and communications enhanced the economic and cultural development of the country, thereby consolidating it as a unified nation. Despite these developments, however, transport and communications remained relatively backward as a result of the feudal system then in force. The modernization of transport and communications, which only really commenced after the Opium War of 1840, occurred in a number of stages. The first stage of modernization occurred between 1840 and the Sino-Japanese War of 1894–5 when China was opened to the West following the signing of the Treaty of Nanjing in 1842 which opened the ports of Guangzhou, Fuzhou, Xiamen, Ningbo, and Shanghai to foreign trade. The Qing government later signed other similar treaties with the United States and France which gave those countries the right to navigate in Chinese waters and deprived China of its customs rights. Rights were also obtained by force to navigate the inland waterways, and Tianjin, Niuzhuang (Yingkou), Chaozhou, Qingzhou, Hankou, and Jiujiang became inland trading ports. Following the opening of these ports to foreign trade, the foreign powers opened shipping services and constructed ports, harbours, wharves, and warehouses. Shipping corporations were set up in Shanghai, Tianjin, Hankou, and Dalian by the foreign powers to run China's coastal shipping services and the Chang Jiang service. The sole Chinese-owned and operated service was established in 1872 as a comprador shipping company. A number of small, non-governmental shipping enterprises with very limited funds were also later established. Most of the non-governmental companies were restricted to the small or remote routes in which the foreign companies were uninterested. China's first modern shipping industry was therefore under foreign control.

The second stage of modernization of transport and communications occurred between the Sino-Japanese War of 1894–5 and the founding of the Republic of China in 1911. As capitalism evolved into imperialism, the foreign powers began to construct railways in order to establish spheres of influence and hence to divide the country between them. The main railway lines built during this period include the Kunming–Hekou line in Yunnan (built by France in 1895), the north-east line (built by Russia in 1896), and the Jinan–Qingdao line in Shandong (built by Germany in 1898). The Qing government also built, using foreign loans, all or part of the Guangzhou–Hankou line (1896), the Beijing–Hankou line (1897), and the Shijiazhuang–Taiyuan, Beijing–Fengtian (Shenyang), Daokou–Qinghua, and Nanjing–Shanghai lines in 1898. Between 1895 and 1911, 9,200 kilometres of railway lines were built. Because most of the railways served the interests of the foreign powers, they were mainly in the coastal regions of eastern China and were linked with the coastal and inland ports in order to facilitate the movement out of the country of industrial raw materials and agricultural products in exchange for foreign-produced industrial goods (Fig. 23.1). The railways were also important for the development of production in the foreign-owned factories and mines (Fig. 23.2).

Between 1911 and the Sino-Japanese War of 1937, a third stage of modernization occurred with a second wave of railway construction and the commencement of large-scale highway construction and civil air transport services. A feature of railway construction during this period was the scale on which the foreign powers constructed railways in the interior regions. In 1905, Japan took control of the previously Russian-owned Changchun–Dalian railway before it occupied by force the north-east provinces of Heilongjiang, Jilin, and Liaoning. It then proceeded to build a large number of trunk and branch lines in the north-east. During this second period of railway construction, 11,000 kilometres of track were laid, bringing the total length of China's railway network to 22,000 kilometres (Fig. 23.3).

The construction of highways lagged behind that of the water and rail transport systems and only began to develop after 1913 when the country's first highway was built between Changsha and Xiangtan in Hunan province. Roads were later built in Hebei, Shanxi, Shandong, Anhui, Zhejiang, Hunan, Hubei, Guangdong, Guangxi, Yunnan, and Sichuan provinces, totalling 30,000 kilometres by 1926. Most of these roads followed the traditional postal roads and cart ways and were of an uneven standard, consisting mainly of earth surfaces. Very few roads had sand or stone surfaces or permanent bridges, and their use was often restricted to certain times of the year. Between 1927 and 1936, many roads were built by the Guomindang government in an attempt to buttress its rule. In 1928, the Ministry of Communications and Transportation drew up a national highway construction programme, with Lanzhou at its centre, consisting of national, provincial, and county highways. Roads were constructed in Jiangsu, Zhejiang, and Anhui — the three provinces surrounding Nanjing which was the seat of the nationalist government. By 1936, some 4,000 kilometres of highways were open to traffic in these provinces. Next in priority were the provinces of Jiangxi, Fujian, Guangdong, Guangxi, Hunan, Hubei, Henan, Sichuan, Shaanxi, and

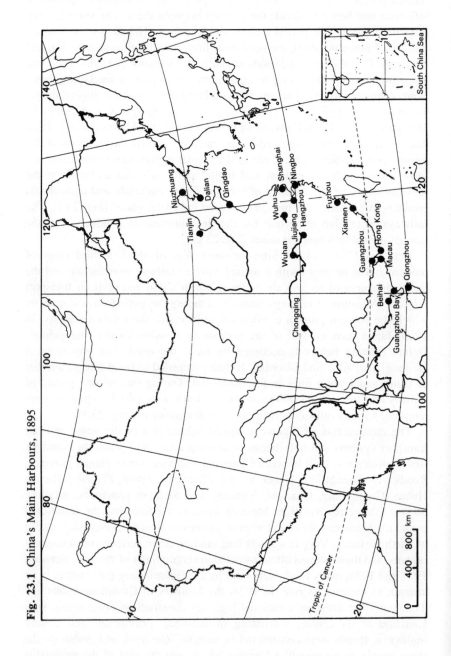

Fig. 23.1 China's Main Harbours, 1895

Fig. 23.2 China's Main Harbours and Railways, 1912

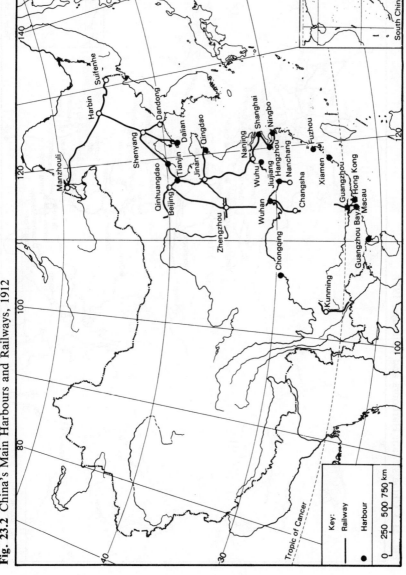

Fig. 23.3 China's Main Harbours and Railways, 1937

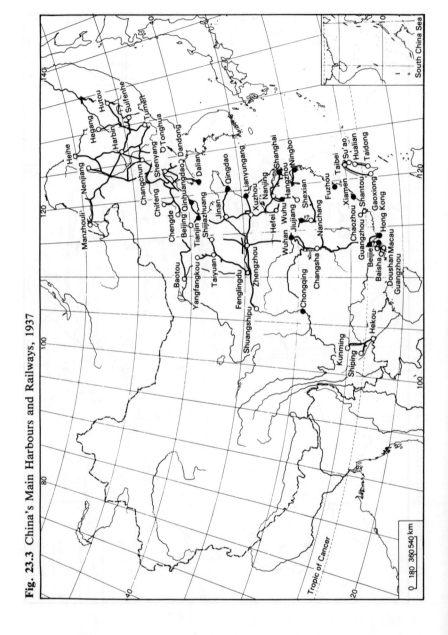

Gansu, where 20,000 kilometres of highway were constructed by 1936. At the same time, Japan built military highways, police patrol roads, and other major roads in the north-east in order to strengthen its position in the region. By 1936, highways open to traffic in the north-east totalled over 10,000 kilometres. In all, some 95,000 kilometres of road were in use throughout the country, forming a nation-wide network of highways.

Air transport developed only from 1929 when the state-run, United States'-funded China National Aviation Corporation was established. This was followed in 1931 by the German-financed Euro-Asia Aviation Corporation. Air routes centred on Shanghai and Nanjing were opened and, by 1936, air routes in the country covered 22,000 kilometres.

The years between 1937 and 1949 were a period of warfare and economic decline which had a severe impact on the development of transport and communications. By 1943, the total ship tonnage was only 37,000 tonnes (5 per cent of the total in 1936). Many main rail trunk lines were heavily damaged during this period and there was very little construction carried out with the exception of the Hunan–Guangxi and Guizhou–Guangxi lines in the south-west. Between 1938 and 1948, the total length of track in the country increased by only 4,000 kilometres. Highway construction continued, however, particularly in the north-east and the north where the Japanese continued to build roads to facilitate its military invasion of China. The government also built a number of trunk highways in areas under its control. Air routes were opened in the south-west, centred on Chongqing. In general, however, the construction and modernization of the country's transport and communications systems came to a standstill during the period leading up to 1949.

Following the defeat of Japan in 1945, further damage was inflicted on the existing transport and communications systems by the civil war between the nationalist and Communist forces. By the end of 1948, the total length of usable track was only 11,000 kilometres and many aircraft, ships, and much rolling stock had been destroyed.

The main characteristics of the transport and communications systems in China prior to 1949 were their small size, poor quality, uneven distribution, and their semi-feudal, semi-colonial nature. Between 1876, when the first railway line was built, and 1949, only 22,000 kilometres of track were laid. This total represented only 0.23 kilometres for every 100 square kilometres of land area — one of the smallest rail systems in the world. In spite of its vast territorial seas, long coastline, and many rivers, the country's water transport system was also backward. By 1949, the total ship tonnage was only 1.16 million tonnes, with practically no ocean shipping. The inland river transport routes, which totalled 73,600 kilometres, covered only 17 per cent of the total river length. Highways open to traffic totalled only 80,700 kilometres and half of the country's counties were inaccessible by road transport. Civil aviation was even more backward: aircraft were few in number and outdated in design, and civil air routes with regular services totalled only 10,000 kilometres.

The quality of the railways in China was affected by their foreign operation and management and by the fact that the materials and technology varied according to the country of origin of funding. Management was chaotic, technology and equipment were incomplete, and the overall efficiency of the operations was extremely low. Railway gauges differed throughout the country, one-third of the railway stations had no signal facilities, and half the sleepers were ineffective. Such conditions greatly reduced the efficiency and safety of rail transport. The most advanced railway at the time — the Beijing–Wuhan line — provided for a locomotive speed of only 15–30 kilometres per hour and a tonnage limit for freight trains of only 800 tonnes. Ships were mainly small, old, and outdated in technology and equipment. Half the fleet was 20 or more years old and 60 per cent consisted of ships with a tonnage of between 100 and 1,000 tonnes. Port facilities were rudimentary and the level of mechanization was low. The inland river channels were mainly natural channels which lacked navigation facilities. More than half of the country's highways were unpaved, and freight motor vehicles accounted for less than half of all vehicles. The equipment for civil air transport was even more backward, resulting in frequent accidents and very low efficiency.

In addition to the problems of size and quality, China's transport and communications systems prior to 1949 were unevenly distributed throughout the country. Following the Opium War, the important ports along the east coast were controlled by the foreign powers who used them to extend their spheres of interest over the coastal and interior regions. The development of transport and communications was concentrated as a result in the north-east and in the eastern coastal regions. The eastern part of the country comprises only 40 per cent of the total land area, yet in 1949 it accounted for 94 per cent of the total length of railway track (Fig. 23.4). The three north-eastern provinces (which make up less than 9 per cent of the total area) alone accounted for 50 per cent of the total track in the country. The vast area to the south-west and north-west, beyond the Beijing–Wuhan–Guangzhou rail line, was serviced by only 6 per cent of the total length of track (and most of those lines were short), despite the fact that it covers 60 per cent of the total land area. Water transportation was concentrated mainly along the east coast where, each year, Shanghai alone handled half the goods which passed through China's ports. Shanghai also accounted for over half the total number of motor vehicles in the country.

The semi-feudal, semi-colonial nature of China's transport and communications systems prior to 1949 can be attributed to the fact that from their beginnings, the modern systems were controlled by foreign capital and, hence, foreign powers. In 1931, 84.3 per cent of the total length of track was controlled in this way and, by 1937, this proportion had increased to 90.7 per cent. Transport routes were used by the foreign powers to export raw materials in exchange for foreign-produced goods and by the nationalist government to move grain, fodder, and troops around the country. In this sense, the railway system in China prior to 1949 can be said to have served semi-feudal, semi-colonial ends.

Fig. 23.4 China's Main Harbours and Railways, 1949

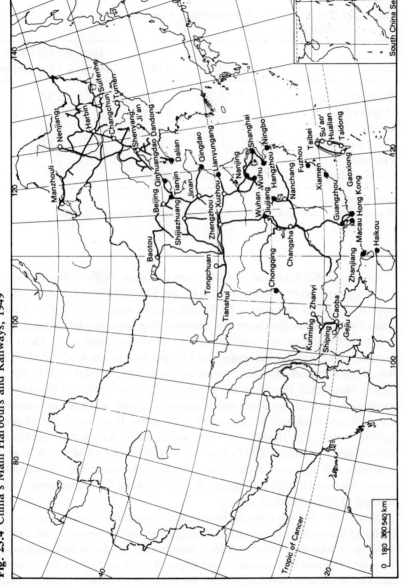

Development since 1949

Since 1949, transport and communications services in China have developed significantly (Table 23.1). The total length of the national transport network increased 6.6-fold (to 1.239 million kilometres) between 1949 and 1980.

Table 23.1 The Increase in Transport and Communications Services, 1949–80 (10,000 km)

Item	1949	1980	Increase between 1949 and 1980 (times)
Railways	2.20	5.19	2.36
Highways	8.07	87.58	10.85
Inland rivers	7.36	10.78	1.46
Civil aviation	1.14*	19.16	16.82
Pipelines	—	0.86	—
Local railways	—	0.34	—

Note: 1950 figure.
Source: China's Economic Yearbook, 1981 (Economic Management, 1981).

Of the 51,900 kilometres of rail lines in use in 1980, 8,000 kilometres (15.4 per cent) were multiple tracks. Of the 875,800 kilometres of highway open to traffic in that year, 110,000 kilometres were major national trunk lines, 130,000 kilometres were inter-provincial or intra-provincial trunk lines, and 630,000 kilometres were county or commune highways. First- and second-class highways accounted for 17.2 per cent of the total. In 1961, the inland river channels open for navigation totalled 172,000 kilometres, but the failure since then to utilize the rivers comprehensively, the blockage of navigation channels by dams and irrigation systems, and poor maintenance have reduced the length of the navigable channels. However, ocean shipping had developed significantly by 1980, and pipeline transport — previously non-existent — totalled 8,000 kilometres, 5,438 kilometres of which were oil pipelines. Air transport routes showed a rapid increase: the 159 domestic routes totalled 110,400 kilometres in 1980, and the 23 international routes totalled 81,200 kilometres.

Since 1949, the railways, highways, and coastal and inland river shipping routes in the north-east and coastal regions have been improved, and railway trunk lines with large freight volumes have been upgraded in their technology in order to exploit the economic advantages of those regions for the benefit of national economic construction. At the same time, railways and highways have been constructed in the south-west and north-west, and existing facilities have been improved, changing in the process the national distribution of the railway and highway networks. As a result, the proportion of railway mileage open to traffic in these regions has increased from 5.5 per cent of the national total in 1949 to 24.8 per cent in 1980, and the proportion of highway mileage has increased from 24.2 per cent of the national total in 1950 to 31.9 per cent in 1980. At present, Tibet is the only region in the country which has no rail system, and Mêdog county in Tibet is the only county in China which has no highway. Approximately 90 per cent of the communes in the country are accessible by vehicle.

The dredging since 1949 of that part of the Chang Jiang which passes through Sichuan province has also played a significant role in promoting the economic development of the interior regions. The development of civil aviation has opened up the remote regions and those with poor land or inland river transport facilities. For example, an air route was opened in the early 1950s between Tianjin and Chongqing and, in the early 1960s, a route was opened between Beijing and Lhasa. Civil air routes now connect more than 80 large and medium-sized cities, including cities in the border areas of Yunnan, Xinjiang, and Tibet. The expansion west of the transport network has been significant in improving the national distribution of transport facilities, in promoting the development of the interior provinces and border areas, and in strengthening China's national defence capabilities.

Along with the development of the country's transport network, the standard of vehicles and equipment has also improved since 1949. By 1980, the number of locomotives had increased 2.67-fold over the total in 1949, and the number of railway carriages had increased 5.69-fold. Locomotives of over 2,200 horsepower accounted for 60 per cent of the total, and railways with heavy rails of over 50 kilograms accounted for over 40 per cent of all rail lines. Railways with automatic and semi-automatic blocks accounted for over 90 per cent of the total; 20 per cent of locomotives were diesel or electric; and over 40 per cent of loading and unloading facilities were mechanized. Between 1950 and 1980, the horsepower of inland river tugs increased 8.7-fold, and the carrying capacity of ships and barges increased 41.4-fold. The proportion of freight volume handled by mechanized ships increased from 68 per cent to 88 per cent during the same period. The number of coastal ships increased 18.5-fold, and, by 1980, the loading and unloading facilities in large and medium-sized harbours had been basically mechanized. The number of privately owned motor vehicles increased 46-fold, and the proportion of all-weather highways open to traffic increased from 42 per cent of the total highway mileage in 1949 to 68 per cent in 1980.

These developments in the transport and communications network and the improvements in facilities have led to a significant, though uneven, increase in passenger and freight volumes and volume turnover since 1949 (Table 23.2). The most noticeable increase has been in the volume of passenger traffic on the highways: in 1980, it accounted for two-thirds of the total passenger traffic. Passenger traffic on the railways and waterways accounted for one-third of the total. The volume of freight traffic carried by the railways has increased steadily: in 1980, it accounted for 46 per cent of the national total of freight traffic and 50 per cent of the total national turnover. Inland river freight has decreased accordingly. However, the increase in the volume of ocean shipping has led to a sharp increase in the overall volume of freight turnover by water transport (43.9 per cent of the total in 1980). The handling capacity of the coastal harbours and the Chang Jiang also increased 21.2-fold

Table 23.2 The Increase in Passenger and Freight Volume and in the Volume of their Turnover, 1949–80

Item	1949	1980	Increase, 1949–80	Growth Rate (% p.a.)
Passenger traffic				
Total volume (100 m. persons)	1.37	34.18	24.94	10.9
Railways	1.03	9.22	8.95	7.3
Highways	0.18	22.28	123.78	16.8
Water transport	0.16	2.64	16.50	9.5
Civil aviation	—	0.03	—	—
Total volume turnover (100 m. persons/km)	155	2,280.60	14.71	9.1
Railways	130	1,383.00	10.64	7.9
Highways	8	729.00	91.13	15.6
Water transport	15	129.00	8.60	7.2
Civil aviation	2	39.60	19.80	—
Freight traffic				
Total freight volume (10,000 tonnes)	16,097	240,506.00	14.94	9.1
Railways	5,589	111,279.00	19.91	10.1
Highways	7,963	76,017.00	9.55	7.5
Water transport	2,543	42,676.00	16.78	9.5
Pipelines	—	10,525.00	—	—
Civil aviation	2	8.89	4.45	4.9
Total volume turnover (100 m. tonnes/km)	255.47	11,517.44	45.08	13.1
Railways	184.00	5,717.21	31.07	11.7
Highways	8.14	255.06	31.33	11.8
Water transport	63.12	5,052.76	80.05	15.2
Pipelines	—	491.00	—	—
Civil aviation	0.21	1.41	6.71	6.3

Source: China's Economic Yearbook, 1981 (Economic Management, 1981).

between 1949 and 1980. Coal, oil, and mineral products accounted for approximately one-third of this increase. Foreign trade goods also account for one-third of the total goods handled by the coastal harbours.

The railways are today the main component of China's transport and communications system. Notwithstanding the importance of the highways, the water transport system, civil aviation, and pipelines in the overall transport network, the railways play an important role in heavy, long-distance freight transport and their development has been a priority since 1949 (Table 23.3). Heavy freight constitutes a large proportion of the total freight volume. Iron, steel, metallurgy products, and raw materials account for approximately 60 per cent of the total rail freight and 75 per cent of the total water freight. Over 70 per cent of the total rail freight is carried in north, north-east, and east China. These regions also account for an even higher proportion of the total volume of water, highway, and pipeline freight transport.

Table 23.3 The Proportion of Different Forms of Transport in the Total Transport and Communications System, 1980 (%)

Form of Transport	Passengers		Freight*	
	Passenger Volume	Volume of Passenger Turnover	Freight Volume	Volume of Freight Turnover
Railways	27.0	60.6	46.3	49.6
Highways	65.2	32.0	31.6	2.2
Water transport	7.7	5.7	17.7	43.9
Civil aviation	0.1	1.7	4.4	4.3

Note: Pipeline transport not included.
Source: China's Economic Yearbook, 1981 (Economic Management, 1981).

Future Development

Despite the developments which have occurred since 1949, China's transport and communications services have not kept pace with industrial growth. The discrepancy between carrying capacity and freight volume is a serious impediment to the growth of the national economy. Transport and communications facilities need to be developed further and their carrying capacity needs to be expanded if the problem is to be resolved. The transportation of passengers and freight requires close collaboration between a number of forms of transport and the setting up of a comprehensive transport network on both the provincial or regional and national levels according to the requirements of production.

At present, the development of the various forms of transport is unco-ordinated, and insufficient use is made of the country's inland and coastal waterways. Whilst the railways and coastal shipping will remain the most important forms of transport, their development needs to be co-ordinated with that of the highways, civil aviation, inland rivers, and pipelines. There is also considerable potential for expansion of the ocean-going fleet and of the shipping facilities along the Chang Jiang, particularly if the handling capacity of the existing ports is expanded and the construction of new harbours is accelerated. Additional small and medium-sized harbours in the coastal provinces would facilitate the dispersal and distribution of goods. The inland waterways are at present under-utilized. Some of the main waterways would require little investment to significantly expand their capacity. Inland river transport is planned to be developed in the coastal provinces and municipalities and along the Chang Jiang where conditions are suitable for handling ships of 3,000 or more tonnes.

The existing forms of transport will in the future be more co-ordinated when the railways, the Chang Jiang, and the coastal navigation facilities are utilized more fully for the transportation of heavy freight over long distances and when the local inland rivers and highways are developed further for freight transport over shorter distances. Additional pipelines will be constructed for the transportation of oil and gas. The development of aviation will be determined mainly by the requirements of international exchange and tourism.

The development of transport and communications on a regional level will be determined by local conditions. For example, the railways are the most important transport system in the north-east because of the region's heavy industry and the established rail network needed to carry a large volume of freight. In east China, in the areas along the Chang Jiang and along the eastern seaboard, industry and agriculture are highly developed and the area is densely populated. The conditions for water transport are favourable and the freight and passenger volumes are large. The most suitable forms of transport are therefore waterways and railways. In the vast south-western and north-western regions, the conditions for water transport are poor. Railways are presently the most important form of transport, although their construction to date has been slow. In future, priority should be given to the construction of highways for both freight and passenger transportation.

In addition to the development of appropriate forms of transport in different parts of the country, transport facilities need to be developed in a co-ordinated manner if their efficiency is to be raised. Large-scale industrial and agricultural production requires that supply, transport, and marketing be integrated. In the past, however, China's transport and communications were dislocated and segmented, giving rise to both shortages and waste. The co-ordination of water, land, and air transport would require little investment, while producing fast results in terms of the efficient transportation of goods. Such a through-transport system requires certain basic conditions of technology and equipment for the efficient collection, loading, unloading, and distribution of goods, as well as co-operation in the form of transport agreements and contracts. In this way, a national through-transport network may be established. Already, the through-transport of large quantities of goods on water and land has been developed. There are presently more than 4,000 railway stations and 98 harbours providing water-land through-transport services and the number of service centres is increasing. Through-transport for passenger traffic has also developed noticeably and, as a result, vehicles, mileage, and carrying capacity have been more fully utilized. As more and more departments co-operate and participate in the through-transport system, transport and communications will play a more important role in production and distribution.

24. The Rail Network

RAILWAYS are the mainstay of China's modern transport system. Equipped with modern technology, they are important in the transportation of primary products such as coal, ores, timber, iron and steel, building materials, and grain, which play a decisive role in the development of the national economy. In addition to transporting goods from the producing areas to the consuming areas, rail transport is itself a productive sector, contributing to the production of other sectors of the economy.

The Development of China's Rail Network

The rail network in China prior to 1949 was small in size, outdated in quality, and uneven in its distribution throughout the country. Since 1949, the existing railways have been upgraded, new railways have been built, their transport capacity has been increased, and the distribution of rail facilities has been improved in order to meet the demands of industry and agriculture.

In 1949, the railways were in a state of disorder. Some 14,000 kilometres of track and more than 3,000 railway bridges were out of operation and locomotives were in a state of disrepair. Only 1,200 kilometres of track — mainly in the north-east and in the coastal areas — were in operation. The repair and upgrading of the existing railways was therefore a first priority. The rail transport service of the main trunk lines was also expanded, thus increasing the transport capacity of the existing railways. Many new railways were built during this period of reconstruction and, by the end of 1952, 24,518 kilo-metres of railways were in operation.

During the 1st FYP period, beginning in 1953, many new industrial construction projects were carried out along the old rail lines north of the Chang Jiang and east of Baotou and Lanzhou. Since the construction of these new industrial bases required the support of the existing coastal industrial bases, rail transport volume increased considerably. The first railways to be upgraded included the Harbin–Dalian, Beijing–Shenyang, Beijing–Hankou, and Beijing–Baotou lines amongst others. At the same time, double tracks were constructed, the number of locomotives and rolling stock was increased, communications equipment was installed, and the transport capacity was expanded. In addition, the construction of railways to the interior and to the north-west and south-west regions commenced. Eight main trunk lines (totalling 4,000 kilometres) and two branch lines of 600 kilometres were constructed during this period, including the Lanzhou–Xinjiang, Baoji–Chengdu (which connected the north-west and the south-west), Fengtai–Shahekou (in association with the Baotou steel base), Baotou–Lanzhou (which connected north China, Inner Mongolia, and the north-west), and Yingtan–Xiamen lines. The reconstruction during the 1st FYP period of the existing railways and the construction of new railways changed the distribution of the country's rail network and increased the volume of rail freight turnover.

During the 2nd FYP period, a greater rail transport capacity was required to meet the needs of increased industrial and agricultural production, the expansion of capital construction, and the exploitation of the interior and border regions. Many of the existing railways were extended and 22 new lines were built, including the Lanzhou–Xinjiang, Lanzhou–Qinghai, Baotou–Lanzhou, and Gansu–Wuhan lines in the north-west; the Guizhou–Guangxi, Guiyang–Kunming, Chengdu–Kunming, Neijiang–Yibin, Sichuan–Guizhou, and Yingtan–Xiamen lines in the coastal regions; and the Hangzhou–Changchun line. During this period, 8,000 kilometres of track were added to the existing railways, and 3,000 kilometres of new lines and 1,500 kilometres of branch lines were built, bringing the total length of track in operation to 34,600 kilometres, of which 5,000 kilometres were double-tracked.

Between 1961 and 1965, when capital construction was curtailed and industrial production targets were lowered, only one new railway was built; the extension of existing lines was the main priority. During the period 1963–5, over 2,000 kilometres of railways were extended, 2,000 kilometres of new lines were built, and 700 kilometres of branch lines were laid.

The decade of the Cultural Revolution (1966–75) was one of widespread chaos in China. Economic construction and expansion of the railways in the interior regions was emphasized. After 1971, construction of a number of main railways (including the Houma–Xi'an, Beijing–Taiyuan, Hunan–Guizhou, and Jiaozuo–Zhicheng lines) brought the total length of new lines constructed between 1966 and 1975 to 7,600 kilometres, including 1,500 kilometres of double-tracked lines and 400 kilometres of electrified lines. By the end of 1975, the total rail mileage in operation in China was 46,000 kilometres, of which 7,000 kilometres were double-tracked.

At the end of the 1970s, a second period of readjustment of the national economy occurred and, in railway construction, emphasis was placed on the extension of existing lines, though a few new lines were laid. By 1980, the rail mileage open to traffic totalled 51,900 kilometres, of which approximately 8,000 kilometres were double-tracked. The average annual increase in mileage since 1949 was 800 kilometres. In addition, more than 4,000 tunnels (with a total length of 1,800 kilometres) and 14,000 railway bridges (totalling 1,000 kilometres) were built during the same period.

Although the development of China's rail network since 1949 has been considerable, it has failed to keep pace with national economic development. For example, the length of track is still relatively small and the technology and equipment are backward. In 1980, there were only 0.54 kilometres of rail lines per million square kilometres (one-twelfth of the United States' figure and one-quarter that of India), and 0.5 kilometres of railways per 10,000 people (one-sixth of the United States' figure and half that of India). The distribution of rail lines is also inadequate, with the result that a complete national rail network does not exist. Despite the efforts to technically upgrade the rail system, China's railway technology and equipment are also still outdated. Steam locomotives account for the main part of the country's total engine stock; diesel and electric engines handle only 13 per cent of the total transport volume. In many other respects, China is behind the developed countries in terms of modernization of its rail system.

A second problem which is apparent despite the developments since 1949 in railway construction is the rapid growth in transport volume and the insufficient transport capacity. Although the rail mileage open to traffic has increased 2.5-fold since 1949, the development of the national economy and the expansion of capital construction during the same period have increased the rail transport volume 11-fold and the volume of freight turnover 31-fold, thereby far exceeding the increase in rail transport capacity. This discrepancy between transport volume and transport capacity is particularly apparent in the industrial and agricultural production bases of east China where the economy has developed rapidly, resulting in a rapid increase in rail freight transport volume. The existing rail facilities are unable to meet the demands of economic development in this region. The railways which have been built in the vast areas west of the Beijing–Guangzhou line account for 75 per cent of the country's total new railways. They have promoted the economic development of the west and strengthened the economic contacts between east and west, while at the same time they have increased the transport volume of the eastern railways, thus exacerbating the problem in the east of insufficient transport capacity.

The Distribution of the Main Railways

Most of China's railway lines are located close to the industrial and agricultural production areas. Beijing is the centre of the national rail network, which radiates out to all parts of the country (Fig. 24.1). In the north-east, the 70 rail lines total 15,000 kilometres (30 per cent of the national total). The railway density in this region averages 1.2 kilometres per square kilometre (double the national rail density).

China's rail network consists of 10 main trunk lines:

(a) the Harbin-Dalian, Harbin–Manzhouli, and Harbin–Suifenhe trunk lines;

(b) the Beijing–Shenyang, Beijing–Chengde, and Beijing–Tongliao trunk lines;

(c) the Tianjin–Shanghai, Anhui–Jiangxi, and Yingtan–Xiamen trunk lines;

(d) the Beijing–Guangzhou line;

(e) The Jining–Erlian, Datong–Puzhou, Taiyuan–Jiaozuo, Jiaozuo–Zhicheng, and Zhicheng–Liuzhou trunk lines;

(f) the Baoji–Chengdu, Chengdu–Kunming, and Yunnan–Vietnam trunk lines;

(g) the Beijing–Baotou and Baotou–Lanzhou lines;

(h) the Longhai, Lanzhou–Xinjiang, and Lanzhou–Qinghai lines;

(i) the Chengdu–Chongqing, Xiangfan–Chongqing, and Xiangfan–Hankou lines; and

(j) the Shanghai–Hangzhou, Zhejiang–Jiangxi, Hunan–Guizhou, and Guiyang–Kunming lines.

(a) The north-east rail network, with Harbin and Shenyang as its main centres, consists of the Harbin – Manzhouli, Harbin – Suifenhe, and Harbin–Dalian lines. The 50-odd lines which make up the network link the cities

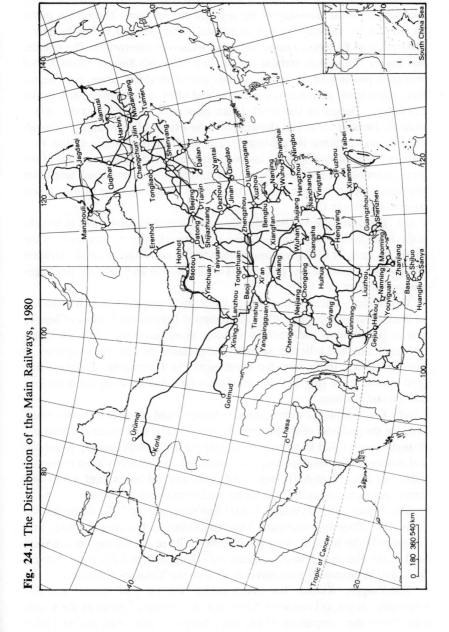

Fig. 24.1 The Distribution of the Main Railways, 1980

with the industrial and mineral bases. The double-tracked Harbin–Dalian line runs for 944 kilometres between south and north; the Harbin–Manzhouli line (935 kilometres in length) and the 548–kilometre Harbin – Suifenhe line run between east and west, connecting with rail lines of the Soviet Union at both ends. All three lines service the capitals of the three north-western provinces (Harbin, Changchun, and Shenyang) and the harbour city of Dalian. They therefore form the mainstay of the region's rail network. The region in the vicinity of the railways is rich in natural resources and is highly indus- trialized, with factories, mines, and other industrial enterprises. The Greater and Lesser Hinggan mountains are the largest timber base in China. Other important products of the region include animal products, grain, soya beans, flax, sugar-beet, petroleum, coal, iron and steel, automobiles, and heavy machinery. Dalian in the south is an important industrial centre and a strategic harbour for ocean shipping and the export of petroleum. Although the rail freight volume is very heavy, particularly on the Harbin–Dalian line, there is an imbalance between in-going and out-going freight because of the great quantities of coal, petroleum, grain, timber, iron and steel, and other products which are transported to the south. The area has one of the highest freight densities in China.

(b)   The double-tracked Beijing–Shenyang line (841 kilometres in length) is the main line linking the north-east rail network with the networks to the south. As such, it is of great importance in the exchange of goods between the north-east and the rest of China. The line is also an important passenger transport service.

The Beijing–Chengde line, which has a small transport capacity, crosses an area of varied topography and steep slopes. It joins the Jinzhou–Chengde line at its northern end, thereby serving as an auxiliary to the Beijing– Shenyang line and relieving some of the pressure on that line's capacity to transport goods south from the north-east. The Changping–Tongliao line (870 kilometres in length) is the third main land link between the north-east and the rest of China.

(c)   The Tianjin–Shanghai, Anhui–Jiangxi, and Yingtan–Xiamen trunk lines are the mainstay of the eastern rail network. The double-tracked Tianjin– Shanghai line (1,325 kilometres in length) passes through densely populated and economically developed regions (including the country's most important industrial city, Shanghai), large coal, iron, and oil bases, and grain- and cotton-producing areas. It is one of the busiest railways in China.

The Anhui–Jiangxi (Wuhu–Guixi) line stretches for 550 kilometres and joins the Zhejiang–Jiangxi, Yingtan–Xiamen, Huiyin–Nanjing, and Nanjing–Wuhu lines. It plays an important role in alleviating the transport load of the Nanjing–Shanghai, Shanghai–Hangzhou, and Zhejiang–Jiangxi lines, and in promoting transport contact with the Yingtan–Xiamen line.

The Yingtan–Xiamen line (built during the 1st FYP period and 697 kilometres in length) connects Yingtan with the coastal areas of the south- east. Since the completion of the line, the previously inaccessible Fujian province has been linked with other parts of the country. The railway has promoted the exploitation of the forest resources of the Jiulong Jiang valleys and the production of agricultural sideline products, local products, and mineral resources in southern and northern Fujian province. It has also stimulated the development of new industrial bases such as Nanping, Sanming, and Zhangzhou. The line is important for national defence in its consolidation of the coastal defences in the south-east in addition to its economic importance.

(d) The Beijing–Guangzhou line (2,324 kilometres in length) is the north-south railway hub of China. It runs from Beijing through five provinces (Hebei, Henan, Hubei, Hunan, and Guangdong) to the Zhu Jiang delta. It links the rail networks of the north-east, the north, and the south, and both freight and passenger transport are heavy. As such, it is one of the main north-south transport arteries in the country. At its southern end, it joins the 1,085-kilometre Hunan–Guangxi line which ends on the Sino-Vietnamese border at the Youyiguan Pass. This line is the main trunk line linking the central-south with the south-west.

(e) The Jining–Erlian, Datong–Puzhou, Taiyuan–Jiaozuo, Jiaozuo–Zhicheng, and Zhicheng–Liuzhou trunk lines form a second important north-south transport artery. The Jining–Erlian line leads to Mongolia and the Soviet Union; it spans the vast grasslands and desert of Inner Mongolia before reaching Erlian on the Sino-Mongolian border. The Datong–Puzhou (Datong–Mengyuan) line is 883 kilometres in length. It handles a great volume of passengers and freight and is the main trunk line running through Shanxi province. The Taiyuan–Jiaozuo line (400 kilometres in length) links the Datong–Puzhou, Beijing–Baotou, Shijiazhuang–Taiyuan, Beijing–Guangzhou, and Longhai lines. It plays an important role in China's rail network, contributing to the transportation of Shanxi coal, the development of local economies, and the promotion of national construction. Since its completion, the Jiaozhi–Zhiliu line links the Datong–Puzhou, Beijing–Baotou, Shijiazhuang–Taiyuan, Longhai, Hunan–Guangxi, and Litang–Zhanjiang lines with the main waterway of the Chang Jiang, forming in the process a rail trunk line running parallel to the Beijing–Guangzhou line in central China.

(f) The Baoji–Chengdu, Chengdu–Kunming, and Yunnan–Vietnam trunk lines are important trunk lines in the south-west. The 669-kilometre Baoji–Chengdu line (constructed during the 1st FYP period) runs mostly through mountainous terrain. Tunnels account for 12.6 per cent of the total length, and rail bridges account for 4 per cent of the total. Running through Shaanxi, Gansu, and Sichuan provinces, the line joins the Longhai line in the north and the Chengdu–Chongqing and Chengdu–Kunming lines in the south. It is an important transport artery between the south-west areas and those in the north-west, north, and north-east.

The Chengdu–Kunming line passes through western Sichuan and northern Yunnan. These areas are rich in natural resources; the Panzhihua iron and steel plant is located here. The railway has contributed significantly to the exploitation of coulsonite and ilmenite in western Panzhihua and of the water resources of the Yalong Jiang. It has also contributed to the economic prosperity and culture of the minority nationality areas as well as playing an important role in national defence.

The Yunnan–Vietnam line, running between Kunming and Hanoi (where it joins the Vietnamese rail network) is narrow, poor in quality, and low in transport capacity. It is planned to be upgraded, widened, and modernized.

(g) The Beijing–Baotou line extends for 833 kilometres between Beijing and the Baotou iron and steel industrial base in Inner Mongolia. The varied terrain, including steep slopes and sharp curves on the Nankou–Kangzhuang section of the line, restricts the amount of traffic the line can carry. The Fengtai–Shacheng line (104 kilometres in length) was constructed to increase the transport capacity and meet the demands of economic construction in north-western Inner Mongolia. It is regarded as a double track of the Beijing–Baotou line. Double tracks were also laid along the Shacheng–Datong section of the line, thereby increasing the transport capacity of the Beijing–Baotou line and stimulating the transportation of coal from Shanxi and construction in Baotou and Hohhot.

The Baotou–Lanzhou line extends for 990 kilometres, following the Huang He along part of its route. It is one of the main trunk lines built during the 1st FYP period and is linked with the Lanzhou–Xinjiang line by the Gantang–Wuwei line. The Beijing–Baotou and Baotou–Lanzhou lines link north and north-west China, forming the second main east-west transport artery. These lines have reduced the transport distance between the north-east and Lanzhou and between Beijing and Lanzhou; they have relieved the northern section of the Beijing–Guangzhou line and the western section of the Longhai line of some of their transport volume; and they have accelerated economic construction in the north-west whilst consolidating national defence in the north-western border regions.

(h) The Longhai, Lanzhou–Xinjiang, and Lanzhou–Qinghai lines together comprise the longest rail trunk line in China. The Longhai railway, which extends for 1,736 kilometres between Lianyungang in the east and Lanzhou, the most important city in the north-west, is one of the main east-west transport arteries. Some parts of the line are poor in quality, however, and pass through difficult and dangerous terrain, thus reducing the speed of transportation. Since 1949, the capacity of the line has been increased through the upgrading of equipment and technology and the completion of electrified and double-tracked lines east of Baoji. The line connects with the Tianjin–Shanghai, Beijing–Guangzhou, Baoji–Chengdu, Lanzhou–Qinghai, and Baotou–Lanzhou lines. The Longhai railway transports materials in and out of the north-western and south-western provinces and, as such, it is of great importance in the linking of the east and west and in stimulating the economic development of the western areas.

The Lanzhou–Xinjiang railway is the only line that extends to the north-western border areas of Xinjiang. It extends for 1,904 kilometres between Lanzhou and Ürümqi, passing through the difficult and sparsely populated Gobi desert area. The line has now been extended between Turpan and Korla in Xinjiang, which has helped to promote the economic development of Xinjiang as well as to improve national defence.

The Lanzhou–Qinghai line is the main plateau line in China. Some 1,020 kilometres in length, it is the first phase of the projected Qinghai–Tibet railway. The line links important minority nationality areas and the Qaidam basin (rich in petroleum, natural gas, non-ferrous metals, salt, and industrial chemicals) with Gansu province and, hence, central north China. As such, it has contributed to the prosperity of the minority nationality areas and strengthened national unity in the border regions.

(i) The Chengdu–Chongqing, Xiangfan–Chongqing, and Xiangfan–Hankou lines are the most convenient form of land transport in and out of Sichuan province. The Chengdu–Chongqing line runs through the economically developed Sichuan basin, linking it with the Chang Jiang. The line also connects with the country's rail networks through the Baoji–Chengdu and Xiangfan–Chongqing lines and Chongqing's Chang Jiang bridge, thus forming close links between north-west, south-west, and east China. The railway is important in promoting the exchange of goods between Chongqing and other parts of Sichuan province.

The Xiangfan–Chongqing line links with the Chengdu–Chongqing and Sichuan–Guizhou lines. It is 916 kilometres in length; its 405 tunnels and 716 railway bridges account for 41 per cent of its total length. The line is an important trunk line between the south-west and central-south. The Xiangfan–Hankou railway, 328 kilometres in length, has reduced the passenger and freight volume of the Chang Jiang in and out of Sichuan.

(j) The east-west trunk line comprising the Shanghai–Hangzhou, Zhejiang–Jiangxi, Hunan–Guizhou, and Guiyang–Kunming lines links Shanghai with six provinces and forms the main rail trunk line connecting east China with the central-south and south-west. The western end of the Zhejiang–Jiangxi line also connects with the Beijing–Guangzhou and Hunan–Guizhou lines as well as intersects lines leading to the important harbours of Ningbo, Xiamen, Fuzhou, and Jiujiang. As far as Jiangxi, the line passes through densely populated areas with advanced industry and agriculture. The western section of the line passes through areas with rich coal and iron resources. This main trunk line for the south-eastern provinces is an important passenger and freight transport line.

The Hunan–Guizhou line (902 kilometres in length) provides an important link between Beijing and the south-west and between east and central China. The Guizhou–Kunming line (467 kilometres in length) passes through the coal bases of Lupanshui and the coal-mining areas of Yangchang, Tianba, Enhong, and Zhaotong. The railway is an important means of transporting coal and iron ore to the Shuicheng iron and steel plant and phosphate from Yunnan province. It is also an important artery linking Yunnan with other parts of the country.

Future Development

In spite of its vast size, China has at present only 50,000 kilometres of railways and, with the exception of the north-eastern provinces, the rail network has not been fully developed in most parts of the country. The railways east of the Beijing–Guangzhou line are for the most part relics of pre-1949 development. Although a few lines have been built in the areas west, south-west, and north-west of the Beijing–Guangzhou line, none exist south of the Lanzhou–Xinjiang and Lanzhou–Qinghai lines or west of the Baoji–Chengdu and Chengdu–Kunming lines in areas which comprise one-third of China's total territory and which are rich in energy resources, metals, and phosphate and sylvite reserves. The upgrading of the existing rail network and its expansion into the vast areas presently without a rail system are therefore a priority in the future development of China's rail transport.

Of first importance is the construction of parallel, trunk, and feeder lines in the coastal areas east of the Beijing–Guangzhou line in order to reduce the transport volume of the main lines and increase the density of the rail network. Lines are required leading to the south-west, the north-west, and the coal bases in the areas west of the Beijing–Guangzhou line.

The Beijing–Shanghai and Beijing–Guangzhou lines, the main north-south lines in the east, have insufficient transport capacity to cope with the present transport volume. At Pingshikou, in the southern section of the Beijing–Guangzhou line, for example, transport capacity is only 60 per cent of the transport volume. Double tracks are therefore required for this section of the line and another major trunk line between Beijing and Jiujiang is necessary in order to relieve the pressure on the Beijing–Shanghai and Beijing–Guangzhou lines. A second route from Beijing to Guangzhou (between Xiangtang, Ganzhou, and Longyan and between Tanzhou and Guangzhou or between Ganzhou and Shaoguan) would also ease the transport problems in the eastern part of the country as well as develop the economies of Jiangxi, Fujian, and Guangdong provinces.

Of the east-west rail trunk lines, the Zhejiang–Jiangxi and Longhai lines both have a low transport capacity. A line is to be built between Nanjing and Xiangfan to increase the capacity of the east-west network and reduce the transport distance between Shanghai and Sichuan province. The upgrading of existing lines and the construction of new lines would also help to meet the increasing demand for coal transportation between the west and the east.

The few railways in the south-west and the north-west (including the Hunan–Guizhou, Guizhou–Guangxi, and Longhai lines) have a low capacity in some sections for the transportation to eastern China of coal from Ningxia and Shaanxi, sulphur and iron ore from Gansu, coal from Sichuan and Guizhou, and phosphate from Yunnan. In a bid to increase the carrying capacity of these lines, electrification is to be carried out between Baoji and Lanzhou on the Longhai line, as well as on the Guiyang–Kunming, Hunan–Guizhou, and Baoji–Chengdu lines. New lines are also to be built to develop further the western areas, develop the border regions, consolidate national defence, and promote the economies of the minority nationality areas.

The upgrading of existing lines will be emphasized in the coastal areas, where such lines as the Harbin–Manzhouli, Harbin–Suifenhe, Harbin–Dalian, Beijing–Shenyang, Beijing–Baotou, Tianjin–Shanghai, Beijing–Guangzhou, Shanghai–Hangzhou, Longhai, Dezhou–Shijiazhuang, and Jiaoxian–Jinan lines handle 70 per cent of the country's total volume of freight turnover. The east-west railways, which are important for the long-distance transportation of primary materials as a result of the present imbalances in the distribution of production and the growth of foreign trade, are also to be upgraded.

Since 1949, considerable progress has been made in the upgrading of the north-south trunk line, especially those lines which are situated west of the

Chang Jiang. Double tracks have been laid upon the northern section of the Beijing–Guangzhou line and along the Tianjin–Shanghai and Harbin–Dalian lines. A number of new north-south trunk lines have also been constructed, including the Jiaozuo–Zhicheng and Zhicheng–Liuzhou lines. As a result, with the exception of the southern section of the Beijing–Guangzhou line, the north-south railways are less over-burdened than those between the east and the west. The single-track east-west lines are particularly low in transport capacity. Accordingly, their upgrading is of primary importance (particularly in the case of the Dezhou–Shijiazhuang, Jiaozhou–Jinan, Shanghai–Hangzhou, and Zhejiang–Jiangxi lines and the section of the Longhai line between Zhengzhou and Lianyungang.

In addition to the upgrading and expansion of the present rail network, a priority in the further development of China's rail transport is the modernization of its rail technology. At present, steam, diesel, and electric engines are used. Steam locomotion is low in efficiency and economy, requiring twice the amount of fuel and producing half the power of electrically powered engines which have a larger transport capacity at higher speeds. Diesel locomotives are heavy and slow, but they are suitable for towing over-loaded freight and passenger trains.

Before 1949, the only locomotives in China were outdated steam engines. In 1958, the first diesel and electric locomotives were trial-manufactured and, in 1969, construction began of the first electrified line (the Baoji–Fengzhou line, 91 kilometres in length) and Chinese-manufactured electric engines came into use. By 1980, over 1,000 kilometres of electrified line were open to traffic and more than 7,000 kilometres of track for diesel-engined trains. In addition, diesel-engined trains are used along 10,000 kilometres of the Beijing–Guangzhou, Beijing–Shanghai, Shanghai–Hangzhou, and Shenyang–Danyang lines.

The freight turnover of electric and diesel trains accounted in 1980 for 18.2 per cent of the total rail freight turnover and 50 per cent of the total passenger turnover. Considerable potential therefore exists for further develop-ment of the rail system in terms of modernization of rail technology, as indicated by a 30 per cent reduction in travel time and a 350 per cent increase in transport capacity following the adoption of electric engines on the Baoji–Fengzhou and Baoji–Chengdu lines in 1969.

At present, steam locomotives account for 80 per cent of locomotives in China; diesel engines account for 18 per cent and electric engines account for 2 per cent of the total. As such, the present rail technology is unable to meet the demands of national economic development. The transport capacity of many trunk lines is 30–50 per cent below present volume requirements and it is unlikely to be increased using steam engines alone. Diesel and electric engines are necessary if the transport capacity of the present rail network is to be increased. Electric engines are particularly suitable for mountainous areas. For this reason, priority should be given to the electrification of those lines west of the Beijing–Guangzhou line and those leading to the south-west and north-west where there are many tunnels and steep slopes. The main railways for the transportation of coal between the west and the east (the Hunan–Guizhou, Guiyang–Kunming, Chengdu–Chongqing, Baoji–Lanzhou, Shijiazhuang–Taiyuan, Fengtai–Shacheng, Taiyuan–Jiaozuo, and Xiangfan–Chongqing lines) are also of priority, as are the main coastal railways (such as the Beijing–Guangzhou and Harbin–Dalian lines).

In addition to the electrification of appropriate lines, diesel locomotives need to be introduced along more lines in order to ease the heavy steam railway traffic and conserve fuel resources. At present, the high production costs of diesel locomotives prohibit such expansion, and the electrification of rail lines involves engineering difficulties. Electric and diesel engines will therefore replace steam locomotives only very gradually. In the immediate future, the most pressing need is to raise the efficiency of steam engines so that their full potential may be utilized.

25. The Navigation Network

RIVER and marine transport are much more limited by natural conditions than are other forms of transport. They are also slower and more discontinuous than rail or highway transport. However, water transport is low in cost, energy consumption, and investment; marine transport, in particular, is the most convenient and cheapest form of transport in China. As such, marine and river transport are particularly suited to the long-distance transportation of bulky goods such as petroleum, coal, timber, and mineral ores when speedy delivery is not a prime consideration.

The Distribution of Resources

One of the largest countries in the world, China has a long coastline and many lakes and rivers which are suitable for navigation. The rivers, totalling 430,000 kilometres in length, include 15 which are over 1,000 kilometres in length and which empty into the sea. More than 100,000 kilometres of navigable river courses have been opened to date, some 40,000 kilometres of which are suitable for barges (almost double the combined length of the navigable inland courses of Britain, France, and the Federal Republic of Germany). Of the 24,880 lakes, 28 are 500 square kilometres or more in size.

The main navigable river systems are distributed mainly in the densely populated, economically advanced areas such as the Chang Jiang delta (based around Shanghai), the Hunan, Hubei, and Jiangxi basin of central China (based around Wuhan), the Sichuan basin (based around Chengdu and Chongqing), and the Zhu Jiang delta (based around Guangzhou) (Fig. 25.1). Most of these large river systems run from west to east, and their tributaries run from the south and the north. As a result, they cover a vast area for the transportation of goods and passengers, while connecting the inland regions with marine transport and promoting the economic development of the river basins.

Bordering the Pacific Ocean in the south-east, China has vast ocean areas suitable for the development of marine transport. The inshore area consists of the Bohai, Yellow, East China, and South China seas. The continental coastline, extending from the mouth of the Yalu river in the north to the mouth of the Beilun river in the south, is over 18,000 kilometres in length — one of the longest coastlines of any country in the world.

The inshore area spans the temperate, subtropical, and tropical zones where the natural conditions are suitable for the development of marine transport, including the construction of harbours in the natural bays and river mouths along the coast. Close to the mainland are also more than 5,000 islands, most of which are rocky islands near mountainous coastal areas. A number of alluvial islands are located in the estuaries of the large rivers, the largest being Chongming Island in the estuary of the Chang Jiang. Many of the islands are suitable as harbours, navigation marks, or shelters in strong winds; as such, they play an important role in coastal navigation and fishing.

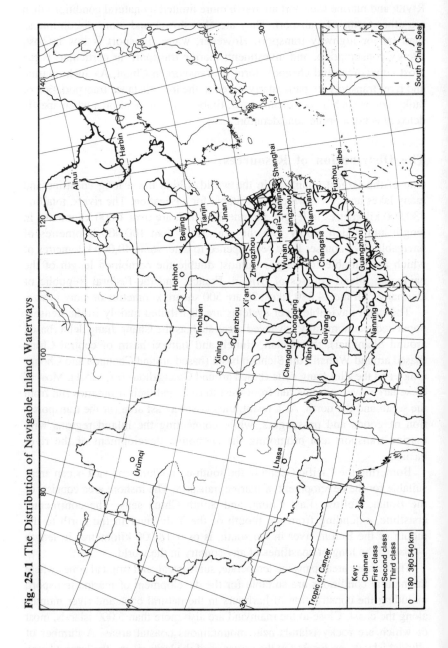

Fig. 25.1 The Distribution of Navigable Inland Waterways

The Development of China's Navigation Network

Notwithstanding the favourable natural conditions in China for navigation and its long history, inland navigation was very backward prior to 1949. Most vessels were wooden junks; there were only a few barges and most of those were in poor condition. As a result, the inland river courses were under-utilized; by 1949, there were only 73,600 kilometres of inland river navigation lines, 24,200 kilometres of which were navigable by motorized boats and ships. The navigation lines along the coast and most of the steamships used for coastal and inland river navigation were in the hands of foreign owners and capitalists. In 1936, the tonnage of merchant ships in Chinese hands constituted only 30.56 per cent of the total tonnage of such ships used for navigation along the coast and rivers. This was less than half the tonnage in the hands of Britain and Japan. In ocean transport, the tonnage of merchant ships owned by China constituted only 0.14 per cent.

Since 1949, however, considerable progress has been made in the development of water transport. During the 1st FYP period, the development of inland navigation was emphasized, particularly navigation along the Chang Jiang; marine transport was also developed to some extent. During this period, Yuxikou harbour in Anhui province was constructed, and the harbours of Shanghai and Wuhan were expanded. Communications equipment was installed along the entire course of the Chang Jiang and the river course was improved. The Zhu Jiang and Grand Canal were also improved for navigation. Many other rivers were dredged, using local manpower, materials, and funds, in order to open them for navigation and to meet local needs. During this period, the mileage of the inland navigation network increased to 144,000 kilometres (a 95.7 per cent increase over 1949), 39,000 kilometres of which were navigable by motorized craft (an increase of 25 per cent). During the 1960s, further development of the inland river courses increased their mileage to 170,000 kilometres. During the 1970s, however, many dams were built, thereby blocking the rivers, and over 4,000 sluice gates were constructed on rivers which were already open to navigation. As a result, many rivers which had been navigable in the past ceased to be so and others were only navigable in certain sections, during certain seasons, and at a reduced transport volume. Consequently, the length of the navigable inland courses was reduced by over 60,000 kilometres, totalling 107,800 kilometres in 1980. As a result of the improvements carried out and the increase in the number of motorized craft, however, the mileage of motorized craft increased as a proportion of the total mileage.

Since 1949, marine navigation has also developed rapidly. In 1980, there were 437 ocean berths (including 144 berths with a handling capacity in excess of 10,000 tonnes) and the total handling capacity of the country's harbours was 217 million tonnes (a 23-fold increase over the total in 1950). Ocean-going transport has undergone a particularly rapid development. In 1951, there were only five ocean-going liners, with a total carrying capacity of 45,560 tonnes. By 1980, the number of such liners had increased to 527, with a total carrying capacity of 9.36 million tonnes (constituting over half the total tonnage of the transport ships in the country). At present, China has contact with over 380 harbours in more than 100 countries.

The Main Navigation Networks

China's navigation network consists of four main systems: the Chang Jiang and Zhu Jiang systems, the coastal navigation lines, and the ocean-going navigation lines.

The Chang Jiang System

The longest river in China, the Chang Jiang passes through 10 provinces, municipalities, and autonomous regions (Tibet, Qinghai, Sichuan, Yunnan, Hubei, Hunan, Jiangxi, Anhui, Jiangsu, and Shanghai) before it meets the East China Sea (Fig. 25.2). It is 6,300 kilometres in length, and the mileage of its many tributaries comprises over 60 per cent of the total mileage of China's inland river navigation network. The Chang Jiang basin — consisting of a long river course, many tributaries, vast basins, and rich water resources — includes the most economically developed and most densely populated areas in China. The development of navigation along the course of the river is therefore of great significance in the development of the national economy.

The main trunk of the Chang Jiang — the 2,813 kilometres between Yibin in Sichuan and the estuary on the east coast — is navigable year-round and the section of the river between the estuary and Wuhan is navigable by 5,000-tonne ships. During the wet season, this section is navigable by 10,000-tonne ships and, during the dry season, 1,000-tonne ships can reach as far inland as Chongqing in Sichuan province. The section of the river between Chongqing and Yibin is also navigable by ships under 1,000-tonne carrying capacity. Beyond Yibin, the Jinsha Jiang is also navigable by small steamships. The ports and harbours along the Chang Jiang — including Chongqing, Yibin, Wuhan, Huangshi, Wuhu, Nanjing, and Shanghai — are China's most important inland river ports.

The conditions for navigation vary between the upper, middle, and lower reaches of the river. The upper reaches — beyond Yibin — consist of 4,500 kilometres of river course which are navigable for only part of the year. The section below Yibin is navigable year-round. The section of the Three Gorges, previously dangerous for navigation, has been improved through dredging and the improvement of navigation equipment so that the navigation capacity of this section of the river has been increased significantly. Some of the tributaries along this section are also navigable by small motorized barges. The middle reaches of the Chang Jiang — the 900 kilometres between Yibin and Hukou — are wide and smooth-flowing, thereby providing suitable conditions for navigation by large ships. The longest tributary of the Chang Jiang — the Han river — also has suitable conditions for navigation. Wooden junks can travel as far as Hanzhong, while the section downstream from Guanghua is navigable by small ships and barges. The tributaries of the Dongting lake, which forms part of the Chang Jiang system, include the

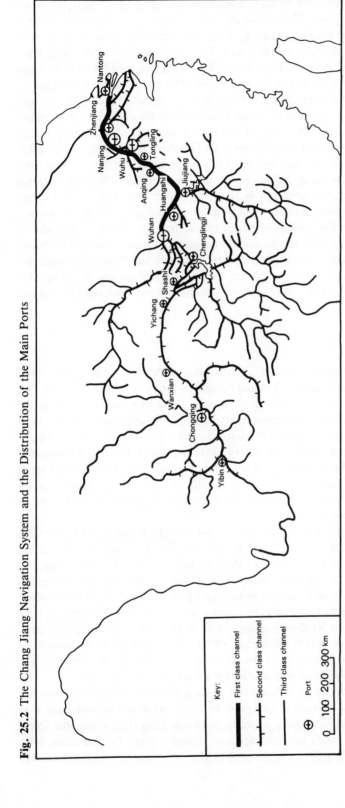

Fig. 25.2 The Chang Jiang Navigation System and the Distribution of the Main Ports

Xiang river which has suitable conditions for navigation, particularly for wooden junks. Some 95 per cent of the cities and towns in Hunan province are situated along this water system; consequently, river navigation is relatively well developed in this area. The lower reaches of the Chang Jiang — extending for over 800 kilometres between the Dongting lake and the coast — consist of a wide and deep river course which is ideal for navigation by large ships. The river is linked with the Boyang lake in Jiangxi province which has water access to 81 of the 82 counties in the province. Of the major tributaries of the Chang Jiang in this region, the Gan river is navigable by small ships and barges downstream from Ganzhou; the Fu river is navigable downstream from Fuzhou; and the Xin river is navigable downstream from Yingtan. The tributaries in Anhui province are short and of little navigational value. However, the tributaries in Jiangsu province and Shanghai, the Grand Canal, and the many harbours and ports of the Taihu lake valley criss-cross this region, forming a well-developed inland river navigation system; almost every village and town can be reached by water. The main navigation centres in southern Jiangsu province are Wuxi, Suzhou, and Shanghai, while the main centres in northern Jiangsu are Yangzhou, Huaiyin, and Nantong. This part of the Chang Jiang river system is the most closely knit river network in China.

The Zhu Jiang System

The Zhu Jiang system includes the Xi Jiang, Bei Jiang, and Dong Jiang courses. The most important inland navigation artery in south China, the Zhu Jiang system is second only to the Chang Jiang in terms of its value for navigation. The river system consist of over 300 tributaries with a total navigable length of over 30,000 kilometres and a year-round navigable length of 12,000 kilometres. Approximately 5,000 kilometres of the river's course is navigable by ships and barges. Because of its location in the subtropical zone, with its hot climate and abundant rainfall, the Zhu Jiang system has an extremely rich water volume which is favourable for the development of inland river navigation.

The Xi Jiang is the main trunk line for inland navigation along the Zhu Jiang system, measuring 2,167 kilometres. From its source in Yunnan province, the river flows eastward along the borders of Yunnan, Guizhou, and Guangxi before it eventually becomes the Xi Jiang at Wuzhou. It is navigable between Wuzhou and Guiping in Guangxi province, and is navigable year-round by ships between Wuzhou and Guangzhou. The Xi Jiang has 57 tributaries within Yunnan province, with a total navigable length of over 6,000 kilometres, 1,000 kilometres of which are navigable by motorized boats. The main tributaries of the Xi Jiang within Guangdong province are navigable only in their lower reaches for a short period of the year.

The Bei Jiang between Shaoguan in Guangdong and where it meets the Zhu Jiang delta network is navigable by ships, while above Shaoguan it is navigable by wooden junks. From its source in Jiangxi province, the Dong Jiang runs in a south-westerly direction before it joins the Zhu Jiang delta river network. Between Longchuan and Hehekou in Guangdong province, it is navigable by wooden junks, while the 400-kilometre section below Long-chuan is navigable by ships.

In addition to the Chang Jiang and Zhu Jiang navigation networks, the Grand Canal is an important inland river navigation network. With a total length of 1,794 kilometres, it links with five major river systems (the Qiantang, Chang Jiang, Huai He, Huang He, and Hai He systems) and five large lakes (the Dongping, Huishan, Hongze, Gaoyou, and Taihu lakes). It is linked through the Hangyong canal with Ningbo harbour in the south, Tianjin harbour in the north, and Shanghai and Lianyungang harbours in the east. The Grand Canal system therefore links the river systems and lakes with the sea. Following repairs which began in 1958 on the section of the canal in northern Jiangsu, the Beijing–Hangzhou Grand Canal is now basically navigable by 1,000-tonne ships; it has an annual transport volume of over 1.6 million tonnes. With the exception of the 90-kilometre section between the Huang He and Linqing in Shandong province, the Xuzhou–Tianjin section of the canal is basically navigable by 100-tonne ships, as is the 320-kilometre section south of the Chang Jiang (between Zhenjiang and Hangzhou). The canal is an important part of the network for the transportation of commodities along the Tianjin–Pukou railway line. It is particularly important for the medium- and short-distance transportation of coal, building materials, industrial products for daily use, grain, edible oil, and other farm and sideline products. It has reduced the transport volume of the Tianjin–Pukou line and strengthened the exchange of commodities between the north and the south.

The Coastal Navigation Lines

The coastal navigation lines are the main transport trunk lines between north and south China (Fig. 25.3). Dalian and Shanghai are the main centres along the northern coastal navigation area and Guangzhou is the centre of the southern coastal navigation area. In addition to the main navigation lines (which include the Shanghai–Qingdao–Dalian, Shanghai–Yantai–Tianjin, and Dalian–Tianjin lines in the north and the Guangzhou–Shantou and Guangzhou–Beihai lines in the south), many local navigation lines operate between the harbours and ports along the coast as trans-shipping lines for the large harbours and as local passenger services.

Ocean-going Navigation Lines

The development of China's ocean-going fleet dates from the establishment in 1961 of the China Ocean Shipping Company. By the end of 1980, an ocean-going shipping fleet of considerable capacity had been built up, consisting of ordinary freight carriers, modern multi-purpose ships, large oil tankers, bulk carriers, container carriers, and rolling loading freighters, which were able basically to meet the needs of developments in foreign trade.

Four main navigation lines — based around Shanghai, Dalian, Tianjin, Qinhuangdao, Qingdao, Guangzhou, and Zhanjiang — provide services to har-bours around the world. The Japan–United States–South America line is an important link in China's foreign trade network. The line to Singapore and on

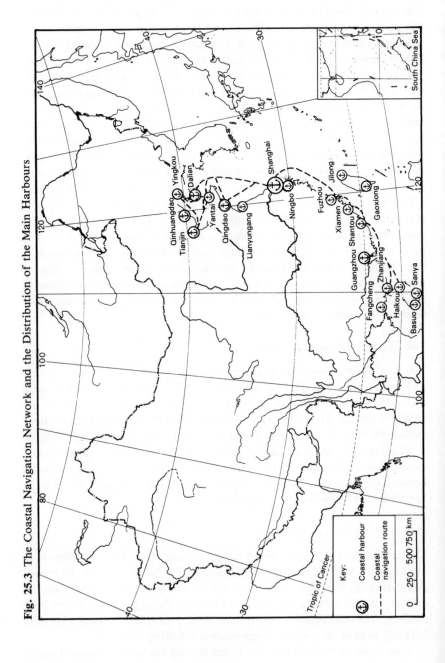

Fig. 25.3 The Coastal Navigation Network and the Distribution of the Main Harbours

to the Atlantic Ocean is the busiest ocean navigation line, providing transport to southern Asia, Africa, and Europe. The freight volume of the line which links China with South-east Asia and Oceania has also increased steadily in recent years. The northern-most navigation line links China with Korea and the east coast of the Soviet Union. With the exception of transport to Korea, this line remains undeveloped due to the current political situation.

The Development of the Main Harbours

Harbours, both river and coastal, are bases in which water transport activities are carried out. They are also transport hubs, linking other forms of transport with the inland river and ocean-going navigation systems. As such, they are important in streamlining the transportation of goods and passengers and in increasing the volume turnover of freight trains and ships.

Prior to 1949, very few harbours with suitable conditions had been fully developed. However, the number of harbours able to service the transport industry with appropriate technology has increased markedly, although China is still relatively undeveloped in terms of harbour facilities which are able to meet the needs of industrial and agricultural production and current transport requirements. In the 1950s, the harbours of Shanghai, Tianjin, and Qingdao, which had previously been used by the foreign powers to export resources and import foreign-produced goods, were upgraded and a small number of harbours with deep-water berths, such as the harbour at Zhanjiang, were built. Since the 1960s, China's ocean-going shipping volume and foreign trade have increased rapidly, however, and the coastal ports, harbours, and docks are no longer able to meet present requirements. They have become important — though weak — links in the development of the national economy.

In the early 1970s, the government decided to expand the handling capacity of the harbours and to carry out large-scale construction. As a result, a number of harbours equipped with facilities to handle bulk goods, petroleum, and passengers, as well as oil and water supply facilities, have been developed. The coastal harbours now have over 430 dock berths, 140 of which are deep-water berths which can accommodate 10,000-tonne oil tankers. There are also four harbours with dock berths able to accommodate 100,000-tonne, 50,000-tonne, and 20,000-tonne oil tankers. Their annual oil-handling capacity is 41 million tonnes. The handling capacity of the docks for coal and other bulk goods has also increased considerably. Container docks have been built at harbours in Tianjin, Qingdao, Shanghai, Dalian, and Huangpu and there are now over 40 container carriers. Of the 15 major harbours along China's coastline, 7 have an annual handling capacity of over 10 million tonnes.

In 1949, there were only 17 inland harbours and 72 docks along the Chang Jiang, with no loading or unloading equipment. In 1980, there were 25 port administration bureaux, 200 working units, and 400 docks equipped with 3,000 items of loading and unloading equipment which were either mechanized or semi-mechanized serving the majority of the inland ports and harbours. Of the 25 major inland river ports, 11 have an annual handling capacity of over 2 million tonnes. The ports of Nanjing, Nantong, Jiujiang,

Wuhu, Wuhan, Huangshi, and Chongqing on the Chang Jiang are important foreign trade shipping centres.

In spite of the progress that has been made since 1949, however, the present speed and scale of harbour construction is below the level of development of marine and inland water transport. Since 1949, the number of coastal harbour berths able to accommodate 10,000-ships has increased 2.5-fold and the handling capacity of the coastal harbours has increased 23-fold. However, the tonnage of ocean-going ships and of ships navigating in the coastal waters has increased 75-fold over the same period, thus rendering the capacity of the coastal harbours inadequate. The same situation applies with respect to the inland river ports. The development and modernization of the harbours and ports is therefore of crucial importance. In addition to improving loading and unloading facilities, container transport capacity needs to be increased if the handling capacities of the harbours are to be raised.

The Distribution of the Main Harbours

The most important harbours in China are those at Shanghai, Tianjin, Dalian, Qinhuangdao, Qingdao, Guangzhou, Zhanjiang, Nanjing, Wuhan, and Chongqing.

Shanghai Harbour

Shanghai harbour is situated at the mid-point of the continental coastline of China next to the Huangpu river, a tributary at the estuary of the Chang Jiang. The port is located 80 nautical miles from the sea. The entry navigation lines for ocean-going ships consist of the southern navigation line at the estuary of the Chang Jiang and the Huangpu river navigation line, both of which are navigable by 10,000-tonne ocean-going ships year-round. The Shanghai harbour area is distributed mainly along the banks of the Huangpu river, extending for approximately 30 kilometres from Minhang on the upper reaches to Wusongkou on the lower reaches. The harbour has more than 100 berths and a dock line 10 kilometres in length. Along the banks of the Huangpu river are more than 70 pontoons suitable for the anchorage of large ships with a draught of 10 metres. There are 13 loading and unloading zones along the banks of the river, as well as special docks with considerable handling capacity for petroleum and iron and steel products.

As China's largest hub of river, lake, and land transport, with large areas of available land, Shanghai is unmatched by other harbours in terms of its favourable conditions. Shanghai itself is the largest industrial centre in the country, and east China is one of the main industrial regions. The basin of the Chang Jiang is also the most economically advanced area in China. Navigation along the Chang Jiang system, which constitutes a large proportion of China's inland river navigation and transport network with Shanghai at the terminus, therefore connects large parts of the country with the outside world. Its adjacent areas, in particular the Chang Jiang delta and the plain on the lower reaches of the Chang Jiang, are densely populated and highly productive. The convenient water and land transport routes link these areas with the hinterland for commodity exchange. Shanghai harbour has the largest handling capacity in China; in 1980, the harbour's handling capacity of 84 million tonnes also made it one of the largest harbours in the world.

In addition to its status as China's largest harbour with multiple functions, Shanghai harbour is also of importance in international trade. Its import and export of foreign trade commodities accounts for 25 per cent of the country's total. Each year, over 3,000 foreign ships use the harbour's facilities, importing coal, petroleum, salt, iron and steel, chemical fertilizers, machinery, timber, grain, and mineral ores, much of which is trans-shipped via the Chang Jiang to Fujian, Zhejiang, and Guangdong provinces in the south. The inland river system is combined mainly with highway transport in the movement of goods from Shanghai harbour; rail transport accounts for a very small proportion of through-transport compared with the other large coastal harbours.

The main disadvantage of Shanghai harbour at present is the insufficiency of berths. Compared with the immediate post-1949 period, the total handling capacity of Shanghai harbour has increased 42-fold, whereas its handling volume in foreign trade has increased 97-fold. The number of berths has increased by only 4 per cent. In order to compensate for the lack of berths, each berth undertakes a handling volume of over 800,000 tonnes (10 times that of Hamburg and twice that of Rotterdam). Because of this insufficiency, there are also serious delays in loading and unloading. It has been estimated that 45 additional berths are required to cope with the present handling volume. As the total investment needed to construct these berths is lost each year in the delays caused by the present facilities, their construction is imperative.

The importance of Shanghai as a trans-shipment base further depletes the present handling capacity of the harbour. The expansion and development of berthing facilities at appropriate harbours and ports along the lower reaches of the Chang Jiang would therefore reduce to some extent the pressure on Shanghai's facilities. In 1980, two berths able to accommodate 10,000-tonne ships went into operation in Nantong port. These berths have diverted from Shanghai some of the commodities which previously would have been shipped to that harbour for trans-shipment. For example, ocean-going steamships carrying coal from the north can now anchor at Nantong port, and can return directly from there with cargoes of cotton for the north. In addition, barite produced in Hubei province, which in the past was transferred and shipped from Shanghai harbour, is now able to be transferred at Nantong port. Such diversion is considerably more convenient and economical than the construction of new berths in Shanghai harbour.

Tianjin Harbour

Located on the western bank of Bohai Bay and at the estuary of the Hai He, Tianjin harbour is Beijing's gateway to the sea. The harbour consists of the Tianjin, Tanggu, and Xingang harbour areas, the Tianjin harbour area being distributed along the banks of the Hai He. Due to the river's narrow course, it is able to accommodate only small ships and ocean-going vessels. The

Tanggu harbour area is located along the southern bank of the estuary of the Hai He, where 5,000-tonne ocean-going ships can be accommodated. The Xingang harbour area is located on the northern bank of the estuary, bordering on the Bohai Sea. The Xingang harbour area is the main section of Tianjin harbour as well as being a large artificial harbour. Large-scale construction and expansion since 1949 have increased the number of 10,000-tonne berths to 25, one of which was China's first container berth. It handles most of the foreign ships which enter the harbour.

Tianjin harbour is the largest hub of water and land transport in north China. It is situated on the coast of the densely populated and economically developed North China Plain and is close to the Dagang and Renqiu oilfields. The North China Plain has abundant coal and iron ore deposits and the city of Tianjin is a comprehensive large industrial city with various industrial departments manufacturing large quantities of products which are supplied to other parts of the country. The harbour's handling capacity as a result ranks sixth in the country; it is also one of the main harbours for foreign trade, handling around 1,600 foreign ships each year. The main commodities for export include grain, salt, and iron and steel. The main through-transport links from Tianjin harbour are the railways and inland river navigation, although highway transport also accounts for a considerable proportion.

Dalian Harbour

Located at the tip of Liaodong peninsula in Dalian Bay, Dalian harbour is a spacious, deep-water harbour which is ice-free during the winter and hence able to accommodate 10,000-tonne ships year-round. Large-scale reconstruction and expansion since 1949, including the construction of a number of berths and warehouses and the installation of machinery which has raised the level of mechanization of loading and unloading, have transformed this excellent natural harbour into a modern port with up-to-date equipment. At present, there are 48 berths, 28 of which can accommodate 10,000-tonne ships. The berths in the deepest areas are able to accommodate 50,000–100,000-tonne ships. The annual handling capacity of the harbour is 33 million tonnes, second only to Shanghai. It is also China's largest oil harbour; its large special docks can handle 15 million tonnes of crude oil for export each year.

Dalian harbour is closely connected with the north-east by means of the Dalian–Harbin and Daqing–Dalian oil pipelines. Adjacent to the harbour is a spacious hinterland with abundant natural resources; it is highly developed in industrial and agricultural production. Each year, large quantities of iron and steel, crude oil, timber, machinery, soya beans, and chemicals are shipped from the harbour to areas south of the Great Wall. As one of China's main harbours for international trade, it also has contacts with over 60 harbours in other countries and some 2,000 foreign ships use the harbour each year. Its export trade value is approximately US$5 billion, the highest in China; the import value is only half the value of exports. Commodities imported from other countries include iron and steel products, wheat, and flour, most of which are then trans-shipped to other parts of the country.

Qinhuangdao Harbour

Located on the western bank of Bohai Bay, Qinhuangdao harbour is strategically placed in north-east China. Spacious, protected from winds, and ice- and silt-free, this deep-water harbour can accommodate 10,000-tonne ships. As the largest natural harbour in China, with excellent conditions, it is linked with the Beijing–Shenyang railway through a branch line and it is further linked with Beijing, Tianjin, Tanggu, and the large industrial cities of the north-east. It is close to the Kailan, Fuxin, and Beipiao coal-mines, and oil pipelines run directly to the harbour.

The construction of Qinhuangdao harbour began in the early 1900s in order to export coal from the Kailuan coal-mine. After 1949, the construction of the harbour continued at the same time as docks and expansion projects were begun. At present, there are 10 berths, 9 of which have a capacity of over 10,000 tonnes (the highest capacity is 35,000 tonnes). The annual handling capacity of the harbour is over 26 million tonnes, third only to Shanghai and Dalian. The harbour specializes in the handling of coal and petroleum, exporting large quantities of coal by virtue of its being the terminus of the northern sea navigation line for the shipment of coal from Shanxi, Inner Mongolia, Ningxia, Hebei, and Beijing. Some 60 per cent of the coal produced in northern China for shipment to the south is loaded at Qinhuangdao harbour, as well as 80 per cent of the coal for export. The railways are an important transport link with the harbour, as are the pipeline; the volume of transport undertaken by highway and river transport is minimal.

In order to meet the growing needs of transporting coal from Shanxi, three 50,000-tonne-capacity berths and one 20,000-tonne-capacity berth are being constructed at the harbour. It is expected that, by the end of the 1980s when the new berths are integrated with the electric railway line between Beijing and Qinhuangdao, the gross handling capacity of the harbour will have doubled.

Qingdao Harbour

Located inside Jiaozhou Bay in the southern part of the Shandong peninsula and bordering on the Yellow Sea, Qingdao harbour faces the islets of Tuandao and Hedao across the bay, which is the sole exit channel to the sea. The harbour is spacious, deep, and ice-free in winter, thus making it navigable year-round. It is one of the best natural harbours in China. The hinterland adjacent to the harbour is also abundant in produce. The oil pipelines from Shengli oilfield run directly to the harbour. The harbour area consists of Dagang, Zhonggang, and Xiaogang. The Dagang harbour area is the main part of the harbour, with over 20 berths, 8 of which are of 10,000-tonne capacity. It services foreign ships which enter Qingdao harbour for loading and unloading. The Zhonggang harbour area specializes in the transportation of salt, while the Xiaogang harbour area is used to accommodate ships of under 200-tonne capacity. Huangdao dock, located in Jiaozhou Bay, specializes in the handling of petroleum; it has a handling capacity of 50,000 tonnes. Qingdao is one of China's main foreign trade harbours, ranking fourth in the country in handling capacity. The main commodities exported from the harbour include petroleum, chemical fertilizers, hardware, mineral ores, building materials, grain, and aquatic products.

Guangzhou Harbour

A river and ocean harbour, Guangzhou harbour consists of the inner Guangzhou harbour and Huangpu harbour at the tip of the Zhu Jiang delta where the tributaries of the Zhu Jiang (the Dong Jiang, Xi Jiang, and Bei Jiang) merge. The harbour is situated 145 kilometres from the sea. It has a narrow navigation channel suitable only for ships with a draught of six metres or less. Each year, the harbour services some 500 foreign ships. The Huangpu harbour area — the outer harbour — has favourable conditions for ships of 20,000-tonne capacity. Its 12 dock berths make it the largest harbour for export trade in south China. The main export commodities include coal, chemical fertilizers, grain, phosphate fertilizer, sugar, metals, machinery, and iron and steel products.

Zhanjiang Harbour

Located in Guangzhou Bay in the north-eastern part of the Leizhou peninsula and at the terminus of the Litang–Zhanjiang railway, Zhanjiang harbour is a modern coastal harbour, which is wide and deep, with excellent natural conditions. The harbour services Guangdong province and Guangxi, and is connected by rail with Yunnan, Guizhou, and Sichuan provinces. Bordering on the South China Sea, it is the most convenient harbour for exports in south China, with 14 dock berths, 7 of which have an accommodation capacity of 10,000 tonnes. The harbour is one of seven coastal harbours with an annual handling capacity of over 10 million tonnes. The main export commodities include iron ore, phosphate fertilizer, salt, and petroleum.

Nanjing Harbour

Located on the lower reaches of the Chang Jiang, Nanjing harbour is linked with the Tianjin–Shanghai, Shanghai–Nanjing, and Nanjing–Wuhu railways. The Chang Jiang at the harbour is wide and deep, and is able to accommodate 10,000-tonne ships year-round. The adjacent hinterland is densely populated and economically advanced. Nanjing city itself is a comprehensive large industrial city producing a great variety of goods including chemical products, machinery, and light industrial products. The harbour has a large freight and passenger volume turnover. With the exception of Shanghai, it is the largest harbour on the Chang Jiang. Its freight handling volume accounts for 37 per cent of the total handling volume of all ports and harbours along the Chang Jiang. The export volume of the harbour is almost twice the import volume. The main exports include timber, chemical fertilizers, machinery, and industrial products for daily use; the main imports include grain and mineral ores. Coal also occupies an important position in the gross handling volume. Most of the coal produced in the north and supplied to the middle and lower reaches of the Chang Jiang is transported to Pukou by rail before being transferred at Nanjing harbour. The harbour is therefore one of the most important coal transfer ports along the length of the Chang Jiang.

In association with the development of petroleum production, reconstruction of Nanjing harbour began in 1977 in order to fit it for the transfer of oil. Six docks have been built specifically to handle petroleum. The harbour is able to accommodate 20,000-tonne ships. The crude oil produced in the Renqiu and Shengli oilfields is transferred to the harbour by the Shandong–Nanjing oil pipelines where it is then loaded on barges for trans-shipment to Shanghai, Anqing, Jiujiang, and Wuhan for energy projects along the middle and lower reaches of the Chang Jiang.

Wuhan Harbour

As China's second largest river harbour, Wuhan harbour (located at the meeting point of the Chang Jiang and the Han river and the Beijing–Guangzhou railway) is one of China's main river and land communications hubs with links to nine provinces. The section of the Chang Jiang downstream from Wuhan is navigable by 5,000-tonne ships year-round; between July and September it is navigable by 10,000-tonne ships. The section of the river above Wuhan is navigable by 1,000-tonne ships. The harbour is a transfer point for goods shipped from Shanghai to the upper reaches of the Chang Jiang. The harbour has well-equipped docks and warehouses as well as highly mechanized loading and unloading facilities. The adjacent hinterland is vast and highly productive. The city of Wuhan is one of China's main iron and steel bases and an important industrial centre. As navigation has increased along the Chang Jiang, the passenger and freight handling volume of Wuhan harbour has increased rapidly; it now ranks second among the inland river ports in this respect. The handling volume of exports exceeds that of imports. The main exports shipped to Shanghai include grain, timber, mineral ores, and non-ferrous metals, while the main exports to Chongqing include iron and steel, machinery, and industrial products for daily use. The main imports are steel products, machinery, building materials, and mineral ores.

Chongqing Harbour

Located at the meeting point of the Chang Jiang and the Jialing river, Chongqing harbour is the largest harbour along the Chang Jiang. The variable water level of the river at Chongqing is compensated for by special docks, making access to the harbour possible for 500-tonne ships year-round. For many years, imports have exceeded exports. The main imports are iron and steel products, metallic mineral ores, ferrous-metal mineral ores, petroleum, salt, and building materials, while the main exports are mineral ores, grain, iron and steel products, timber, cement, and goods for daily use.

Future Development

Notwithstanding the developments in water transport which have occurred since 1949, the investment in the expansion of the country's navigation facilities is unable to meet the requirements of the present transport volume.

The total investment since 1949 is only 1.3 per cent of that invested in the development of the railways. Most rivers are still undeveloped and the lack of development has resulted in serious silting which has limited the use of ships of a high tonnage. The different river systems are unlinked for the most part, and their tributaries are accessible only indirectly. Short-distance navigation only is possible along most of the river sections, making the transfer of goods expensive and inefficient. The inland river navigation network needs to be developed further if it is to meet current requirements and become more efficient.

One of the main problems along the inland rivers is the use of sluice gates and dams which obstruct the river courses. Another problem is the under-utilization of the Chang Jiang, considering its importance in the country's inland river navigation network. The Grand Canal, running between north and south China, is also an important channel for the exchange of goods in eastern China. It is particularly important in the transportation of coal to the south from the northern coalfields and of grain to the north from the south. Its potential remains to be fully realized. Similarly, the Xi Jiang is important for the transportation to other parts of the country of coal produced in Lupanshui in Guizhou province and of the province's phosphate mine products. It, too, is under-utilized at present. In addition to the need to develop further these main river systems, the navigation conditions of the other suitable inland rivers need to be improved if a modern river navigation network based on the Chang Jiang, the Zhu Jiang, the Huai He, and the Grand Canal is to be formed. The need to link the inland rivers more closely with other forms of transport such as the lakes, seas, railways, and highways is also paramount.

At present, industrial development and the exploitation of resources along the inland rivers, particularly the Chang Jiang and the Zhu Jiang, are inadequate compared with the huge potential of the rivers for transport. In addition, the increased use of the river systems by factories, mines, and other industrial enterprises would assist in the development of the navigation systems and facilities. Wherever possible, the rivers should be utilized as the main form of transport.

There is also a need in China for additional small and medium-sized river ports with modern freight collection and distribution facilities. Co-operation between the different forms of transport and the river ports and harbours would improve freight delivery. Some harbours could also be used more efficiently and economically if they were to specialize. For example, Dalian harbour is most suited to foreign trade, while Yingkou harbour is more suited to specialization in the transfer of goods for domestic use and in the shipping of timber, steel products, and mineral ores (which is presently undertaken by Dalian harbour). Qinhuangdao should specialize in the loading and unloading of coal and petroleum; Tianjin would be better used for iron and steel products, salt, and various other commodities; and Qingdao harbour should be used to handle mainly coal, petroleum, and miscellaneous goods.

The technical and managerial levels of the water transport system in China are in need of upgrading, whilst at the same time, costs need to be reduced. (At present, the costs of water transport are about half that of railway transport.) Inland river navigation techniques are still backward, and, when combined with the low management levels, multiple transfer links, slow delivery rates, and the heavy losses suffered in transit, it is not surprising that other forms of transport are often preferred to water transport despite the excellent natural conditions and its potential for development.

26. The Road, Air, and Pipeline Networks

THE road, air, and pipeline networks in China are important in the country's overall communications and transport systems. At present, roads are the principal means of short-distance transport. Despite the low economic value of this form of transport, it has a number of advantages over other forms, including its adaptability to natural conditions, low cost, and flexibility. The rail system in China is inadequate and unevenly distributed; where railways are non-existent, roads form the main transport artery for the movement of goods and passengers. They are also necessary for the transportation of goods directly to factories and mines and in the rural and remote regions.

Air transport is costly and therefore only practical for small amounts of cargo. The cost of construction of a modern airport is equivalent to the cost of building 70 kilometres of new railway line. However, it has the advantages of speed and access to otherwise inaccessible areas. Air transport also plays a special role in long-distance and international passenger transport. However, it remains the weak link in China's transport network. Its development is an integral part of the overall development of the country's transport and communications systems, including the expansion of aircraft manufacture, improvements in air transport management, and reductions in the cost of air transport.

Pipeline transport has developed only recently in China. It is the best means of transporting gas and oil over land, being efficient, safe, suitable for different natural conditions, economical, and compact. It is less flexible than rail and road transport, however, and is suitable only for particular types of fuel.

The Distribution of the Roads Network

Roads have long been used as a means of transport in China. However, the construction of modern highways and the manufacture of motor vehicles has a more recent history. In the early 1900s, China relied entirely on the foreign powers with interests in China for road construction and the provision of facilities. In 1949, road construction began to increase. During the period 1949–52, old roads were repaired and many new roads were built. By the end of 1952, 126,700 kilometres of roads were in use (an increase of almost 60 per cent over the total length in 1949). During the 1st FYP period, roads were expanded to the interior and to the industrial and mining areas. By 1957, the total length of the country's highways was double the 1952 figure. By 1965, the figure had again doubled, and construction continued through the years of the Cultural Revolution. In 1980, there were 875,800 kilometres of roads (a nine-fold increase over the 1949 total) (Table 26.1).

The quality of roads in China has also improved since 1949. Beginning during the 1st FYP period, the existing roads were repaired and upgraded at the

Table 26.1 The Total Length of Roads, 1949–80

Year	Length (km)	Compared with Previous Period (% increase)
1949	80,654	—
1952	126,675	57.9
1957	254,624	101.0
1965	514,455	102.0
1975	783,649	52.3
1980	875,800	11.8

Source: *China's Economic Yearbook, 1981* (*Economic Management*, 1981).

same time as new roads were constructed. The discovery of the large oilfields at Daqing, Shengli, Renqiu, and Liaohe in the 1960s made available large quantities of bitumen, residual oil, and other construction materials for road building which expanded road construction and raised its quality. Some 500,000 kilometres of the present 875,800 kilometres of road are of a high standard.

China's roads are of three main types. First-grade highways (those with 70 per cent of their length of the state-required standard) total 480,000 kilometres (54.63 per cent of the country's total). Second-grade highways total 90,000 kilometres (10.13 per cent of the total); and third-grade roads measure 310,000 kilometres (35.2 per cent of the total). Of the 875,800 kilometres of highway, 650,000 have tarred surfaces. High-grade and good-quality surface roads account for 17.2 per cent of the total; those with a medium-quality surface account for 27.6 per cent; and low-grade surface roads make up 29.1 per cent of the total. Unsealed roads account for the remaining 26.1 per cent of China's roads.

In association with the expansion of industry and agriculture since 1949 and the development of the minority nationality areas, roads have been built or expanded in the industrial and mining areas, the interior, and the remote border areas. During the 1st FYP period, a number of important highways were built, including the Sichuan–Tibet, Qinghai–Tibet, Sichuan–Guizhou, Yunnan–Guizhou, Lanzhou–Ürümqi, Xinjiang–Qinghai, Yecheng–Garyarsa, and Haikou–Yulin highways. A road-building campaign in 1958 resulted in 150,000 kilometres of roads (140,000 kilometres of which were basic) being built in the rural areas during that year. This exceeded the total length of roads constructed during the whole of the 1st FYP period. Since the 1970s, road building has been an important aspect of capital construction in the rural areas, where it is often combined with the construction of dams, dykes, and farms. A comprehensive road network has begun to take shape as a result.

Despite the development of road transport since 1949, it remains a small part of China's overall transport system. In many areas, the quality of roads is very poor and motor vehicles are outdated. In addition, short-distance transport is monopolized by the railways. Distances of up to 20 kilometres account for 5–10 per cent of the total transport volume of the railways; distances of between 20 and 50 kilometres account for 13–19 per cent of the total volume; and distances of between 50 and 100 kilometres account for 23–30 per cent of the total. This reliance upon the railways for short-distance transport has hindered the development of roads, and has resulted in economic losses. Under present conditions, rail transport costs could be lowered and the burden on the railways could be eased if roads were used for the transportation of mining and building materials, industrial goods, articles for daily use, and agricultural and sideline products for distances of between 100 and 150 kilometres and under 50 kilometres. Although road transport is more expensive than rail and water transport, it is flexible and economically viable when considered in the light of the overall transport system.

The quality of roads needs to be improved if their capacity is to be utilized. New roads are also required in the remote border regions and in inaccessible mountainous areas, as well as in the forestry and pastoral areas. Roads are also important in national defence. Hence, new roads are required to link the main highways of adjoining provinces and regions.

The Distribution of the Air Transport Network

China's first airline — the China National Aviation Corporation — was established in 1929; it was followed in 1931 by the Europe–Asia Airline Company and, later, by the Southwest Airline Company. At the time, however, the aircraft in use were outdated, airport facilities were backward, and air routes were short, linking only a few large cities. Most flights ceased when the Sino-Japanese War began, with the exception of a few services in the south-west and the north-west. The development of air transport after the war was made possible only with the use of foreign equipment. In the period 1929–48, only 640,000 passengers and 54,000 tonnes of goods were transported by air.

Air transport only really began to develop after 1949, following the establishment of the national airline, CAAC (the Civil Aviation Administration of China). Air routes were opened within the next few years between Beijing, Wuhan, Chongqing, Kunming, Guangzhou, Nanjing, and Zhanjiang, and an international service to the Soviet Union was established. Additional routes were opened during the 1st FYP period, including routes to Burma, Vietnam, Japan, Korea, and the United States, as well as services to western Asia, Europe, and Africa. By 1980, CAAC had 182 air routes, totalling 190,000 kilometres. Of this number, 159 were domestic routes, totalling 110,000 kilometres and operating to 80 cities. A network has been formed linking Beijing with every provincial and regional capital as well as other main cities (Fig. 26.1). The 23 international (and regional) routes link China with 21 cities in 18 countries on four continents and CAAC enjoys professional relations with 180 countries and regions throughout the world.

Recent development of the air transport system includes the expansion, upgrading, and construction of 80 civil airports. Beijing, Hongqiao (in Shanghai), Baiyun (in Guangzhou), Di'opu (in Urumqi), Zhangguizhuang (in Tianjin), and Yanjiagang (in Harbin) airports are now able to accommodate large jet aircraft in various weather conditions. Now that Beijing and

Fig. 26.1 The Distribution of CAAC's Domestic Air Routes

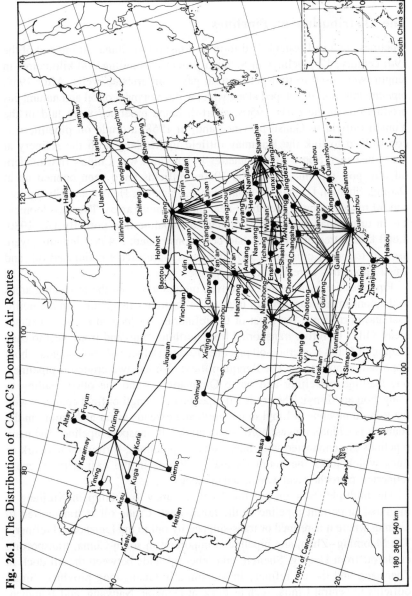

Shanghai, the country's largest modern airports, have been expanded and upgraded, they are able to accommodate the largest and most advanced aircraft in the world. China's air transport network is of major importance in promoting trade, tourism, and cultural exchanges between China and other countries.

The Distribution of Pipelines

Pipelines are a well-established form of transport in China. At the end of the 19th century, 12 pipelines in Sichuan province, totalling 300 kilometres in length, were used to transport natural gas from artesian wells. After 1949, pipeline transport developed along with the development of oil and natural gas production. in the early 1950s, short-distance pipelines were laid in the Yumen oilfield in Gansu province and, in 1958, a crude oil pipeline was constructed to link the Karamay oilfield in Xinjiang with the refinery at Wusudushanzi. Some 147 kilometres in length, it was China's first modern oil transport pipeline. Since the 1960s, oilfields have been opened up at Daqing, Shengli, Dagang, Renqiu, Liaohe, Jianghan, Henan, and Chongqing, and oil refineries have been built near the consumer areas. This development has in turn expanded the development of pipeline transport. By late 1980, 8,660 kilometres of pipelines had been constructed: 5,438 kilometres were used to transport crude oil; 560 kilometres were used for finished oil; and 2,662 kilometres were natural gas pipelines.

Pipelines are used mainly to convey oil and gas from the producing areas to the consumer areas. China's large oilfields are located mainly in the north-east and north-west, but most of the refineries are located in the consumer areas. Oil is therefore transported from north to south and from west to east. Daqing oilfield's two crude-oil pipelines lead to Dalian and Qinhuangdao, both important export ports. The Renqiu oilfield also has two crude-oil pipelines, one leading to Beijing and on to Qinhuangdao and the other leading to Cangzhou and Linyi. The crude-oil pipeline of Shengli oilfield connects with the Renqiu pipeline at Linyi in the north and extends as far as Nanjing in the south. It is China's longest north-south crude-oil transport pipeline. The main pipelines are connected with many smaller pipelines, forming a network of lines which links the country's main oilfields in the east with its main refineries, petrochemical works, and oil docks.

The multiple crude oil pipeline from Karamay to Ürümqi in Xinjiang is the most important pipeline in the north-west. Crude oil is transported to Ürümqi where it is refined or trans-shipped by rail to the Lanzhou oil refinery. The Maoming–Zhanjiang pipeline is important in south China, transporting crude oil from Daqing, Shengli, and other oilfields between the oil dock in Zhanjiang and the oil refinery in Maoming in Guangdong province. Small oilfields in central China, such as those at Dongpu, Nanyang, and Jianghan, are also linked with refineries by means of pipelines.

The transportation of refined oil in China is most often by rail and water transport; pipeline transport is of little importance once oil has been refined. The Qinghai–Tibet refined-oil transport pipeline (1,080 kilometres in length) is the longest such pipeline in China.

Natural gas production is concentrated in Sichuan province. The main pipelines constructed in Sichuan include the Bayu pipeline and that linking Dianjiang county in east Sichuan with Chongqing, Luzhou, Weiyuan, Chengdu, Deyang, and Zhongba. Together with a number of branch pipelines, they link Sichuan's large natural gas fields. Short pipelines have also been built at the Daqing, Shengli, Liaohe, Renqiu, and Dagang oilfields which also produce natural gas.

Experiments are being carried out into the transportation of coal by pipeline. Pipelines could be used to transport coal from south-eastern Shanxi — where the coal output is very large and rail transport is already over-burdened — to the eastern provinces.

27. The Distribution of Passenger and Freight Transport

COMMUNICATIONS and transport form a special sector in the national economy, linking consumers and producers and thus contributing to the development of production. The volumes of passenger and freight transport in a particular region, the form of transport, and the direction of movement are determined mainly by the industrial and agricultural production levels of the region, the transport conditions, and the distance between producers and consumers. The level of development of passenger and freight transport is a general indication of economic development both at the regional and national levels.

Passenger Transport

Passenger transport both serves and is stimulated by production. It is a means of strengthening the economic ties between the cities and the rural areas, between different regions, and between different economic sectors. In addition, it supports construction in newly developed regions, raises the standard of living, and contributes to the development of tourism.

Since 1949, passenger transport of various kinds has increased as the economy has improved, the standard of living has risen, and transport facilities have developed. In 1980, the country's total passenger transport volume was 3.418 billion persons and the passenger transit volume was 228.06 billion persons per kilometre (a 24-fold and 14-fold increase respectively over 1949 figures).

The railways are the main form of transport for long-distance and suburban short-distance passenger transport. Every province, autonomous region, and municipality administered directly by the central government is linked by express rail services with Beijing. Suburban short-distance passenger transport accounts for only a small proportion of the total railway transport. As a result, China's average annual railway passenger transport distance is over 100 kilometres, the highest in the world. Although railways account for only 30 per cent of the total passenger transport volume, passenger transit makes up 60 per cent of the country's total railway volume. The roads are used mainly for short-distance transport, their passenger transport volume constituting 65 per cent of the country's total. The average transport distance by road is only 30 kilometres, however, making it — at only 32 per cent of the country's total passenger transit volume — the smallest of all forms of transport. Limited as it is by natural conditions, the water transport distance is also short, with both passenger transport volume and transit volume occupying only a small proportion of the country's total. The average distance of the airlines, which are used mainly for long-distance transport, is around 1,000 kilometres.

The distribution of passenger transport is influenced by many factors, not least of which is population density. Those parts of the country that are densely populated also have high rates of passenger flow. China's population is unevenly distributed over its total area. As a result, the most densely populated eastern and southern parts of the country have the highest rate of passenger flow. North-east, north, and east China combined comprise one-third of China's total area, yet the rate of passenger flow in this region comprises three-quarters of the country's total. Whilst north-west China accounts for 37 per cent of the total area, its rate of passenger flow is less than 10 per cent of the total.

A second factor affecting the distribution of passenger transport is the distribution of production. Increased production and the establishment of new industrial and agricultural bases have altered the distribution of the population and the labour force, which in turn has affected the rate of passenger flow. Since 1949, both industrial and communications construction have developed rapidly in the north-west and the south-west, rapidly increasing in the process the rate of passenger flow in those regions. Their percentage of the country's total passenger transport volume has also changed dramatically.

The expansion and construction of cities have produced concentrations of people and changes in urban environments, both of which have also affected the direction and density of passenger flow. The distribution of passenger transport is influenced, too, by the expansion of the transport and communications networks and by the modernization of equipment and facilities. Areas with convenient transport services and facilities tend to have high rates of passenger transport, and developed passenger and freight transport services tend to further stimulate the development of transport and communications. Increases in the standard of living and in tourism have also affected passenger transport services and facilities.

East China has a greater passenger transport volume than west China, with Beijing being the largest rail passenger transport hub. Beijing is linked by means of the country's trunk railway lines with Tianjin, Shenyang, Harbin, Shanghai, Zhengzhou, Wuhan, Guangzhou, as well as other large passenger transport hubs. The Beijing–Shenyang, Harbin–Dalian, Beijing–Shanghai, Shanghai–Hangzhou, Hangzhou–Zhuzhou, Yingtan–Xiamen, Beijing–Guangzhou, and Beijing–Baotou rail lines have the country's greatest density of passenger flow. The density increases the closer the railways approach the large cities. For example, the density of annual passenger flow of the Shenyang–Sujiatun line is 25 million persons, 10 times the national average; the Beijing–Baoding line has an annual passenger flow density of 17 million persons, seven times the national average; and the Shanghai–Suzhou line accounts for 15.7 million persons annually, 6.4 times the national average. The density of passenger flow decreases towards the west. However, the east–west lines — such as the Lianyungang–Lanzhou, Lanzhou–Ürümqi, and Chengdu–Chongqing lines — are the busiest in the country.

Water passenger transport is concentrated in the eastern coastal areas and along the main course of the Chang Jiang. Coastal transport serves north-south traffic, although it is heaver in the north. From Shanghai, Qingdao, Dalian, and Tianjin, passenger ships sail regularly to China's other large ports. Passenger transport in the south is concentrated mainly between Guangzhou, Shantou, Haikou, and Beihai. The busiest section of the Chang Jiang is the 2,800-kilometre stretch between Yibin and Shanghai, which passes through six provinces in addition to the municipality of Shanghai and links with 17 railways, including the Shanghai–Hankou, Hankou–Chong-qing, Shanghai–Chongqing, and Hankou–Nanjing lines. The increase in water transport volume has reduced considerably the reliance upon the railways in this region.

Roads are a convenient form of short-distance passenger transport. In the north-west and south-west, where the railways are inadequate or non-existent, highways such as those linking Sichuan, Qinghai, and Xinjiang with Tibet also play an important role in long-distance transport.

Freight Transport

Freight transport prior to 1949 consisted mainly of raw materials and fuel which were transported from the interior to the ports on the east coast, or of industrial products transported from the ports and industrial centres to the inland areas. Most of the industrial products at that time were consumer products; only a small proportion consisted of production materials. The rapid expansion of the economy since 1949 has been accompanied by the opening up of resources and the construction of new transport lines. The volume and direction of flow of freight transport have also changed in a number of ways.

One of the most noticeable changes since 1949 has been the considerable increase in the volume of goods transported and the rotation volume of goods. In 1980, the country's total volume of goods transported was 2.4 billion tonnes (a 14-fold increase over the 1949 figure and an average annual increase of 9 per cent). The rotation volume of goods transported in that year was 1,151.7 billion tonne kilometres (a 44-fold increase over the 1949 figure and an average annual increase of 13 per cent). Although these increases are unprecedented in China's history, they are still lower than the rate of increase of the country's total industrial output value.

A second change since 1949 has been the fuller utilization of different forms of transport for freight transportation. The railways are the main form of long-distance freight transport. In 1980, the volume of goods transported by rail was 1.11 billion tonnes (46.3 per cent of the total national volume of goods transported and a 19-fold increase over 1949). In that year, too, the rotation volume of goods transported was 571.72 billion tonne kilometres (49.6 per cent of the national total and a 30-fold increase over 1949 figures). Roads, used mainly for short-distance freight transport, carry a rather large volume of goods (760 million tonnes in 1980, being 31.6 per cent of the national total and a 9.5-fold increase over 1949), but have a smaller rotation volume (25.506 billion tonne kilometres in 1980, only 2.2 per cent of the national total despite a 30-fold increase since 1949).

Water transport has been limited in its development by natural conditions. It is characterized by a small volume of freight transport but a large rotation volume. In 1980, for example, its freight volume was 430 million tonnes (17.7 per cent of the national total and a 16-fold increase over 1949), and its rotation volume was 505.276 billion tonne kilometres (43.9 per cent of the national total and second only to rail transport). Pipeline transport has developed from a virtually non-existent pipeline system prior to 1949. In 1979, 100 million tonnes of oil were transported by this means, reducing considerably the burden on the railways.

Major changes have occurred, too, in the composition of freight transport. Prior to 1949, the transportation of fuels constituted the bulk of the country's freight transport; industrial products and agricultural goods occupied only a small proportion of the total. This was due, for the most part, to the uneven distribution throughout the country of natural resources such as coal, oil, minerals, and timber and to the undeveloped state of industrial and agricultural production. Since 1949, as a result of the expansion of capital construction, the development of industrial and agricultural production, and the strengthening of the economic ties between different parts of the country, the volume of goods transported has increased considerably and the composition of freight transport has changed. The volume of industrial goods transported, for example, has increased significantly, especially in the case of energy and iron and steel industrial materials. Between 1952 and 1979, long-distance rail freight transportation of energy materials (coal and oil) increased from 36 to 45 per cent of the total, and iron and steel products increased from 8.5 to 18 per cent of the total. In the immediate post-1949 period, coal was the main item transported on the Chang Jiang and along the northern coastline. Oil is now the main item transported in this manner. By 1979, coal transport had declined to 30.3 per cent of the total river freight transport volume from 32.5 per cent in 1952. During the same period, oil as a percentage of the total rose from 5.7 to 38.7. Although the volume of agricultural goods transported (such as grain and cotton) increased, their percentage of the country's total freight transport decreased from 12.5 per cent in 1952 to 2.6 per cent in 1979. These changes in the composition of the volume of goods transported reflect the changes in the composition of China's total industrial and agricultural output value since 1949.

A further change in the last 30 years has been the rapid increase in freight transport volume in the western part of the country. The irrational distribution of industry prior to 1949 saw the concentration in a few large cities such as Anshan, Benxi, Dalian, and Shanghai of the country's iron and steel industry and the opening of coal mines in the more accessible eastern regions. The electric power, machinery, chemical, and textile industries were also concentrated in the coastal provinces. As a result, the economy of the inland areas was undeveloped. The flow of goods was also concentrated along the coastline, with freight transport handling mainly coal, minerals, and agricultural raw materials; only a small volume of industrial products was transported.

Since 1949, however, China's industrial centres have been expanded to the inland areas, producing a more balanced distribution of industrial production over the whole country. The increase in freight volume transport in the inland areas has exceeded that of the coastal areas, although the eastern coastal areas still account for 70 per cent of the total quantity of goods transported. The flow of goods between the north and the south also exceeds that between the west and the east, the north-south railways having a greater transport capacity. However, as coal production in Shanxi province and in western Guizhou continues to be developed, freight transport between the west and the east will also be expanded to meet the increased demand.

The Transportation of Staple Goods

The main goods transported by long-distance freight transport in China include coal, oil, iron, steel, minerals, and timber. In 1980, the transport volume of these goods made up 65 per cent of the country's total volume of rail freight transport and 80 per cent of the water freight transport of the Chang Jiang and the coastline. These staple goods constitute an even higher percentage of the country's total trunk transport volume.

Coal

Coal transportation occupies between 30 and 40 per cent of the total freight transport volume. It is also transported over the greatest distances. Coal is the principal fuel in China, accounting for over 70 per cent of the country's total energy consumption. Because it is distributed unevenly throughout the country, heavy shipments need to be transported for long distances between the producing areas and the consumer regions or the ports for export. Some 70 per cent of the coal produced is transported by rail, and water transport also plays an important role. Of the volume transported by road, 20–25 per cent is over short distances.

The largest coal-producing area is north China. From there, large quantities of coal are transported to other parts of the country. For example, coal from Shanxi and Hebei is transported to Beijing, Tianjin, and Inner Mongolia. The five main trunk coal shipment railway lines are the Beijing–Baotou, Shijiazhuang–Taiyuan, Taiyuan–Jiaozuo, Datong–Puzhouzhen, and Beijing–Taiyuan lines. However, shipments are concentrated on the Beijing–Baotou, Shijiazhuang–Taiyuan, and Taiyuan–Jiaozuo lines. Coal from the Datong area is transported by means of the Beijing–Baotou line to the north-eastern areas around Beijing and Tianjin, and from there to Qinhuangdao for transportation by coastal ships to Shanghai and the eastern coastal provinces. Coal is also transported by the Beijing–Baotou line to the Baotou iron and steel works in Inner Mongolia. Coal from central Shanxi province is transported by the Shijiazhuang–Taiyuan and Shijiazhuang–Dezhou lines to eastern China, or by the Qingdao–Jinan rail link to Qingdao, from where it is carried by coastal ships to the southern provinces. Coal is also transported south and north along the Beijing–Guangzhou line to meet the requirements of north-east and central China.

Although north-east China has a number of large coal production bases, industrial development in the southern parts of the region consumes much of the coal that is produced. Consequently, coal has to be imported from other parts of the country to meet the region's industrial requirements. Eastern China, too, imports 15 per cent of its coal requirements, mainly from the north via coastal ships and the Lanzhou–Lianyungang rail line. Within eastern China itself, coal is transported south from Shandong and Anhui provinces. The Tianjin–Shanghai line handles a large proportion of the coal transported from the north to the southern areas. Coal is also transported by ship to Shanghai from Qinhuangdao, Qingdao, and Lianyungang before being transferred by rail or inland river to southern China.

Central and southern China also depend on imported coal, their requirements being supplied by means of the Beijing–Guangzhou, Jiaozuo–Zhicheng, and Zhicheng–Liuzhou lines. Coal from Guizhou is transported east and south along the Zhuzhou–Guiyang and Guizhou–Liuzhou lines, and Henan coal is transported to provinces south of the Chang Jiang.

North-west and south-west China are basically self-sufficient in coal, and most of that produced is consumed within those regions. Only a very small volume of coal is transported from Shaanxi, Ningxia, and Guizhou to the eastern or southern provinces.

Oil

China's oil industry began to grow rapidly in the early 1960s and the volume of oil transported has now reached 140 million tonnes. Pipeline transport is the main form of transportation; oil accounts for only 6–7 per cent of the total freight volume of the railways and 30 per cent of the total freight volume of the Chang Jiang and coastal shipping in the north. It has become one of the main items transported in China. The movement of oil is mainly from north to south. Although the country's oil resources are widely scattered, the proven oil reserves and large oilfields are concentrated in the north, whereas the refineries are located close to the main consumer areas.

Pipelines account for 60 per cent of the total volume of oil transported; water transport accounts for 20 per cent and railways account for 15 per cent of the total. Oil from Daqing is transported by pipeline to refineries in the north-east and to Dalian for export overseas. Oil transported to Qinhuangdao is shipped by coastal transport to refineries in the eastern, central, and coastal areas. Oil from the north China oilfield (including the Dagang oilfield) is also transported by pipeline to refineries and petrochemical factories in Beijing, Tianjin, and Cangzhou, and to refineries in provinces along the Chang Jiang. Oil from the Shengli oilfield is transported by pipeline to Huangdao, from where it is ocean-shipped to refineries overseas or in the southern coastal areas. Some oil is also transported by pipeline to refineries along the Chang Jiang and by rail to east China. Oil from Xinjiang is carried by pipeline to the Ürümqi petrochemical works and by rail to the refinery in Lanzhou. Some 75 per cent of the total volume of refined oil is transported by rail, compared with 20 per cent transported by water and only a very small proportion transported by pipeline. Approximately one-third of the country's total oil refinery capacity is concentrated in the north-east, and its output accounts for 40 per cent of the total volume of refined oil produced. Refined oil from this area is sent to Dalian for export as well as to the eastern areas and regions south of the Great Wall.

Although east and north China have considerable processing ability, the large number of ports along the coast which consume large quantities of refined fuel necessitate the transportation of refined oil to the region by rail from the north-east. Central and south China rely mainly on imported oil, the main transport artery being the Beijing–Guangzhou rail line. Some of the refined oil transported along this line is transferred to north-west and south-west China. Although the north-west is basically self-sufficient in refined oil, certain varieties need to be imported from the north-east and the north. South-west China relies entirely on imported refined oil.

Many of the large oil refineries in China have fuel oil pipelines connected to nearby power stations or iron and steel works. Fuel oil transported in this way accounts for 60 per cent of the total volume transported, the balance being transported by rail.

Iron, Steel, and Mineral Ores

Iron, steel, and other metals and ores are staple transport goods, with iron and steel accounting for over 5 per cent of the country's total freight transport volume and metals and ores accounting for over 10 per cent of the total. China's iron and steel products are transported in large volume, over long distances, and in many directions. However, the main direction of flow is from north to south and from east to west. Pig iron is transported by rail and ocean transport from the Anshan iron and steel works and from works in Benxi, Beijing, Baotou, and Ma'anshan to steel mills in Shanghai, Tianjin, and Tangshan. Pig iron for casting is transported from north-east, north, and north-west China to the south. Steel ingots, billets, and rolled steel are transported from north to south and from east to west. North-east and north China have larger export than import volumes, whereas east and central-south China are basically balanced in terms of imports and exports and the south-west and north-west have a higher volume of imports. North-east and north China are the country's largest exporters of iron and steel products, most of which are transported by rail to the west and the south, though a small volume of goods is shipped by sea to the southern provinces from the ports of Dalian and Tianjin.

Large quantities of iron ore are shipped over long distances, mainly from the south to the north. Ore that has been imported from overseas is transported mainly to the west. For instance, iron ore imported into Shanghai is directed to the Shanghai iron and steel works and the steel works in Wuhan; ore imported into Qingdao is used in the Taiyuan iron and steel works; ore imported into Qinhuangdao is used in the Baotou iron and steel works; and that imported into Dalian is used in the Anshan iron and steel works.

Timber

Timber accounts for 4 per cent of China's total rail freight transport volume. The uneven distribution of forests over the northern part of north-east China, the south-west, and Guangdong, Guangxi, Hunan, Jiangxi, and Fujian provinces has resulted in the transportation of timber from the north and south to the country's central regions. Timber produced in the north-east is transported by the Shenyang–Beijing rail line to north China, although a small percentage is also transported by the Harbin–Dalian rail line to Dalian where it is transferred to coastal vessels for transport to the coastal areas of Shandong, Shanghai, Jiangsu, and Zhejiang. Timber produced in provinces south of but bordering the Chang Jiang is transported north to areas south of the Lanzhou–Lianyungang rail line. Fujian and Hunan provinces export large quantities of timber to Zhejiang, Shanghai, Henan, and Hubei. Timber produced in south-west China is transported to the north-west by rail and water.

Grain

Grain comprises 2–3 per cent of China's total rail freight transport volume. Short-distance transportation is mainly by road and inland rivers, and long-distance transportation is mainly by rail and trunk inland water routes. The quantity of grain transported and the direction of flow are determined by the distribution of the grain-producing and consuming areas, the grain varieties, the size of the cities, and their location. Grain is transported to other parts of the country in large quantities from the main commercial grain production bases (the Zhu Jiang delta and the Taihu, Dongting lake, Chengdu, Jianghuai, Poyang lake, Jianghan, and north-east China plains). Areas dependent mainly upon imported grain include the industrial area in the southern part of north-east China, the Beijing–Tianjin–Tangshan industrial area, the cluster of cities in the Chang Jiang delta centred around Shanghai, and the low grain-yield areas of the Huang He and Hai He basins, the Loess plateau, and the pastoral areas in the north-west. Areas south of the Qin Ling and the Huai He produce mainly rice, while in the north, wheat, corn, millet, and other crops are grown. A certain amount of grain is shipped between the two areas, for the most part from the south to the north. For instance, grain produced in the commercial grain production areas along the Chang Jiang is transported north to meet the requirements of Beijing and the north China region. A small quantity is also transported from this region to Shanghai and Guangzhou. North-east China transports its special products — wheat, soya beans, millet, and other types of grains — to the south where they are in short supply.

The harsh natural conditions in the vast area of north-west China make grain production difficult, and in the south-west, the small area of cultivated land on the Yunnan–Guizhou plateau means that the level of agricultural production is low. The increase in the non-agricultural population of these areas as a result of the rapid development of industry since the 3rd FYP period has meant that they now need to import grain, whereas in the past they were self-sufficient. In addition to the south-north transportation of grain, therefore, grain is also shipped from the east to the west.

Of the 30 or so types of staple goods transported from one part of China to another, coal accounts for the greatest percentage of the total volume. In a number of regions, inadequate transport capacity has led to problems of bottle-necks, which restrict the smooth flow of goods. For example, in Yunnan, Guizhou, Guangdong, and Guangxi, both land and water transport facilities are inadequate for the efficient transportation of phosphate ore from Yunnan and Guizhou and of coal from western Guizhou to the eastern provinces. Water transport facilities along the Chang Jiang are inadequate in

Sichuan province and rail transport facilities in the north-western areas need to be improved to facilitate the transportation of coal from Ningxia and Shaanxi to other areas. North-east and north China also require improved rail transport facilities to facilitate the movement of coal from Shanxi and southern Inner Mongolia and the flow of goods between areas north and south of the Great Wall. In the eastern parts of the country, rail and water transport need to be developed simultaneously, whilst port facilities in the coastal areas (particularly their dock loading and unloading capacity) need to be upgraded.

China's rail, water, road, air, and pipeline transport networks are based around six main east-west and six main north-south water and land transport lines. The west-east trunk lines are the Beijing–Shanhaiguan, Beijing–Baotou, and Baotou–Lanzhou rail lines; the Lanzhou–Lianyungang and Lanzhou–Ürümqi rail lines; the Shijiazhuang–Taiyuan, Dezhou–Shijiazhuang, and Qingdao–Jinan rail lines; the Chang Jiang; the Hangzhou–Zhuzhou, Zhuzhou–Guiyang, and Guiyang–Kunming rail lines; and the Xi Jiang waterway. The six main north-south trunk lines are the sea transport line; the Beijing–Hangzhou Grand Canal; the Beijing–Shanghai and Shanghai–Hangzhou rail lines; the Beijing–Guangzhou rail line; the Datong–Puzhouzhen, Taiyuan–Jiaozuo, Jiaozuo–Zhicheng, and Zhicheng–Liuzhou rail lines; and the Baotou–Lanzhou, Baoji–Chengdu, and Chengdu–Kunming rail lines. These 12 transport lines criss-cross the country, linking with 900,000 kilometres of roads, 100,000 kilometres of inland river navigation courses, 170 air routes, and 10,000 kilometres of pipelines. As such, they are the bases upon which the future development of China's transport network will be based.

Communications and transport are the weak areas in the country's economic development. The main problems requiring urgent attention are the inadequate capacity for transporting coal from north China to other areas, the low handling capacity of the coastal ports for export, and the rapid increase in passenger flow. If China's 1980 industrial and agricultural output volumes are to be quadrupled by the end of the century as planned, transport and communications facilities will have to be improved. The existing rail lines used to transport coal need to be upgraded and new lines built. Water transport — both inland river and coastal shipping — have the potential for rapid expansion, particularly in the case of the Chang Jiang and Xi Jiang systems and the Grand Canal. Additional ports need to be constructed along the rivers and on the coast. Many important railway lines need to be upgraded through the construction of multiple tracks and through electrification and renovation. New lines need to be built to supplement the existing rail network. Port construction in Shanghai, Guangzhou, Tianjin, Qingdao, and Ningbo needs to be accelerated so as to facilitate the movement in and out of the country of imports and exports. Other ports — both coastal and on the inland rivers — should be expanded and the Xi Jiang and the Grand Canal require dredging.

Communications and transport construction is costly and time-consuming. However, its importance in terms of the country's economic construction makes it a crucial consideration in any planned development and one which requires that it be given a high priority.

Part V: The Main Economic Centres and Regional Differences

28. The Main Economic Centres

The Development of China's Economic Centres

The development of cities in China during the Zhou dynasty was based on agricultural production, particularly along the lower reaches of the Huang He. As the handicraft and commercial trades developed, the number and size of cities increased as their function as economic centres emerged. Following the Southern and Northern dynasties, China's economic centre gradually shifted south from the Huang He valley to the Chang Jiang valley and southern China. By the time of the Eastern Jin dynasty, economic development had stabilized in the south, whereas frequent wars in the north had destroyed many of its large cities. The main cities in the south — Nanjing, Jiangling, Chengdu, Shouchun, Jingkou, and Yangzhou — were based on agriculture, handicrafts, and commerce. As foreign trade by sea developed, Guangzhou also developed as an important foreign trade centre. By the Tang and Song dynasties, an unprecedented boom in agricultural and handicrafts production along the Chang Jiang and in areas south of the river had led to the growth of many cities to serve the needs of the commodity economy.

During the Southern Song dynasty, Lin'an became the country's political centre and its largest commercial centre, with a population of over one million. Along the lower reaches of the Chang Jiang, Nanjing emerged as the region's principal economic centre and a city of military importance. The eastern ports of Guangzhou, Quanzhou, and Mingzhou continued to develop with the expansion of foreign trade.

Following China's defeat in the Opium War, the country's economy declined and a semi-feudal, semi-colonial society emerged. At the same time, a capitalist economy began to develop. Industrial and commercial cities serving the needs of the foreign powers grew up along the coastline, the large rivers, and the trunk railways. Shanghai became one of the world's largest cities as well as China's biggest industrial and commercial base and a hub of land and water transport and communications. Other important regional economic centres at this time included Tianjin, Dalian, Qingdao, and Guangzhou on the eastern coast; Nanjing and Wuhan on the Chang Jiang; and Shenyang, Anshan, Benxi, Fushun, and Tangshan along the trunk rail lines and in the large industrial and mining areas. The development of these economic centres was much greater than that of the country as a whole. Consequently, although their growth promoted the development of China's commodity economy, it also intensified the unbalanced economic development of the different regions and the lack of co-operation between the cities and the rural areas.

Since 1949, the number of economic centres and the urban population in China have increased significantly. In 1982, there were 236 established cities (compared with 157 in 1949) and 2,664 towns. Their total population had increased 2.6-fold from 57 million to almost 207 million, one-fifth of the country's total population, compared with one-tenth in 1949. The urbanization of China during this period has not, however, been even. During the period of the 1st FYP, when the political situation was stable and economic development was steady, the average annual increase in the population of the cities was 3.9 million (a rate of increase which far exceeded that of the previous 30 years). Between 1958 and 1960, as a result of the Great Leap Forward campaign, large numbers of people fled to the cities from the rural areas, bringing the urban population in 1960 to 19.8 per cent of the country's total population. This trend was reversed during the period of national economic adjustment between 1961 and 1965 when many people left the cities for the rural areas. By 1965, the urban population of China had dropped to 101.7 million (14 per cent of the total). The decade of the Cultural Revolution (1966–76) further depleted the population of the cities when school graduates and government cadres went in large numbers to the countryside. The rate of increase in the urban population during this period was only one million per year, compared with over 10 million per year during the period 1958–60. By 1977, however, the economy had begun to improve as government policies became more favourable to economic development and the urban population once again expanded considerably. Notwithstanding the overall urbanization of China since 1949, therefore, China's rate of urbanization and the percentage of its total population living in the cities have both at times during this period been lower than the world average.

Since 1949, the cities have also undergone changes in function which have resulted in their emergence as economic centres and industrial production bases with a strong relationship with the rural areas and agricultural production. Their distribution has been affected as changes have occurred in the distribution of production. The established cities in the coastal provinces have developed further as agriculture, industry, and transport have expanded. Shanghai, Beijing, Tianjin, Nanjing, Wuxi, Hangzhou, Qingdao, Jinan, Zibo, Shijiazhuang, Shenyang, Dalian, Anshan, Fushun, Jinzhou, and Guangzhou have all become important economic centres in this way. The inland cities and those in the border regions have expanded as a result of the construction of roads and railways. The annual industrial output value of cities such as Chengdu, Chongqing, Xi'an, Lanzhou, Wuhan, Taiyuan, Changchun, Jilin, and Harbin has increased rapidly since 1949. New cities and towns with specialized functions have also appeared. For example, Dukou is a specialized iron and steel production city, and Daqing's development has been based on oil production. Many other smaller cities have grown around coal production, forestry, hydro-power generation, and industrial production. In the early 1950s, there were only 20 cities in all of north-west and south-west China and Inner Mongolia with over 50,000 population (one-sixth of the country's total number of cities of that size). There are now more than 50 such cities in these regions, accounting for one-quarter of the country's total. The changes in the distribution of cities since 1949 has been of considerable importance in opening up the backward areas and in promoting the rational organization of the country's productive forces.

The Level of Urbanization

When compared with many foreign countries, the number of cities in China and the level of urbanization of its population are both still very low. In 1980, the average world urban population percentage was 42.2. In Great Britain, the Federal Republic of Germany, Canada, and the United States, this figure was over 80 per cent; and in France, the Soviet Union, and Japan, it was over 60 per cent. China's urban population percentage, at less than 14 per cent, was even lower than that of India, where it was 24.9 per cent. However, the proportion of large cities in the total number of cities in China was greater than that of small cities (Table 28.1)

In 1977, cities with a population of over one million comprised only 14.2 per cent of the total number of cities in China, whereas their population accounted for 48.8 per cent of the total population. Small cities with less than 0.2 million people made up 27 per cent of the total number of cities, but their population accounted for only 6.4 per cent of the total population. China's absolute number of cities with a population of over one million is higher than that of the Soviet Union, Japan, and the United States. In fact, China has the highest number of large cities of any country in the world, though it has fewer small cities than the Soviet Union, Japan, or the United States.

The large cities are China's main economic centres. Shanghai is the main economic centre of east China and is of great economic importance to the country as a whole. Tianjin, the economic centre of north China, is also of great importance in the north-east and north-west. Shenyang and Harbin are the main economic centres of north-east China; and Wuhan is the main centre in central China. Chongqing and Chengdu and Lanzhou and Xi'an are the main economic centres in south-west and north-west China respectively. Guangzhou, Qingdao, and Dalian are other centres which play an important role in the country's economic life (Table 28.2).

Of the 15 cities surveyed in Table 28.2, six (Shanghai, Beijing, Tianjin, Shenyang, Wuhan, and Guangzhou) have populations of over two million. They account for one-quarter of the country's total industrial output value and one-third of the profits and taxes paid to the state. Together with the 40 cities with populations of over 0.5 million, they account for 48 per cent of the country's total industrial output value and 58 per cent of profits and taxes paid to the state. China's large cities are concentrated for the most part in a few regions, particularly the Chang Jiang delta, central and southern Liaoning province, and the Beijing–Tianjin area. This concentration has resulted in a number of problems. As the cities have expanded, their suburbs have encroached upon cultivated land, and industry and agriculture now compete for space in which to develop. Not only has the amount of cultivated land in the suburbs of large cities decreased, but construction has also been affected. Other problems are energy and water supplies, the shortage of raw materials, transport, housing, unstable food supplies, and pollution. The growth of the large cities has also affected the growth of the small and medium-sized cities and the general distribution of industrial production.

The size of the large cities needs to be restricted and their economic

Table 28.1 The Number and Size of Large Cities in China Compared with Other Countries

City Size	China (1977)	United States (1973)	Soviet Union (1975)	Japan (1974)	France (1968)
Number of cities with over 1 million population	27	6	11	10	1
Population (10,000)	5,405	1,814	2,222	2,326	229
% of total population	48.8	29.0	26.2	39.0	23.2
Number of cities with 0.5–1 million population	33	19	30	7	2
Population (10,000)	2,422	1,234	2,128	371	142
% of total population	21.9	19.7	25.1	6.2	14.4
Number of cities with 0.5–0.2 million population	78	38	87	67	6
Population (10,000)	2,528	1,254	2,635	2,066	164
% of total population	22.9	20.0	31.0	34.7	16.7
Number of cities with under 0.2 million population	51	189	113	87	44
Population (10,000)	710	1,959	1,509	1,198	450
% of total population	6.4	31.3	17.8	20.1	45.7
Total number of cities	189	252	241	171	53
Population (10,000)	11,065	6,261	8,494	5,961	985

Source: Ma Hong and Sun Shangqing, *The Economic Structure of China* (People's Publishing House, Beijing, 1981), Vol. 2.

Table 28.2 The Relative Importance of China's 15 Main Economic Centres*

Item	Percentage of the Country's Total (%)
Land area	1.5
Population	7.8
Industrial output	37.1
Number of enterprises	11.6
Profits and taxes handed to the state	
State ownership	42.6
Collective ownership	34.3
Local revenue	36.0
Number of workers	25.3
Total workers' wages	26.5
Commodity turnover	18.7

Note: Shanghai, Beijing, Tianjin, Shenyang, Wuhan, Guangzhou, Dalian, Chongqing, Hangzhou, Qingdao, Harbin, Wuxi, Xi'an, Lanzhou, and Changchun.
Source: World Economic Herald, 25 January 1982.

functions developed more fully. If the size of cities is to be controlled, the growth of industry must also be regulated. New enterprises might be located in the outer suburbs or satellite towns of those cities which already have a population of half a million or more so as to control the growth of industry in those centres. Rural-urban migration needs to be checked and the use of land in the cities controlled. The construction of suburban towns must also be combined with the renovation of older urban areas.

Whilst the size of the large cities needs to be limited, their economic role should be expanded in accordance with local conditions and characteristics. Technology- and labour-intensive industries requiring little energy, few raw materials, a small space, and producing little pollution should have priority over other types of industry. The advanced technology and management methods of the cities are best utilized in combination with the rich resources and suitable production conditions of other provinces and regions and through strengthened economic ties with other countries.

Small and medium-sized cities and towns may also function as local economic centres. Hence, they have the potential for further development of established industries and the growth of new enterprises without the problems of over-concentration of industries and population. Large and medium-sized industrial enterprises should be set up, as far as possible, in the small cities and towns or in areas with backward industries but rich resources. In this way, the potential of smaller economic centres may be realized whilst controlling the growth of large cities.

China has 110 small cities (those with less than 0.2 million people), 3,300 county towns (including those without county administrative functions), and 53,000 commune headquarters which are also rural towns. These small cities and towns are widely scattered over the country (unlike the large and medium-sized cities) and they have considerable room for growth. They link the larger cities with the rural areas and absorb much of the surplus labour force in the countryside whilst helping to ease the over-population of the cities.

The varying natural, economic, and technological conditions of the small cities make them suitable for specialized development in fields such as foreign trade, mining, forestry, fishing, and tourism. Industrial development should not be the sole aim of development plans for such cities. Where appropriate, small industrial cities may benefit from de-emphasizing industry and emphasizing other forms of economic growth in accordance with local conditions. The growth of these small economic centres will be dependent, too, upon improved living and working conditions and improved transport, recreation, and medical facilities. As such cities prosper and grow, they will help to rationalize the distribution of industry throughout the country and to limit the growth of the large cities.

The development of small cities and towns is affected to a large extent by agricultural production. They have an important role to play in diversifying the economy of the agricultural areas and in combining industrial, commercial, and agricultural development through the promotion of sideline processing industries and the transport, storage, construction, and commercial trades.

The Main Types of Economic Centres

The main types of economic centres in China include large comprehensive centres, industrial centres, communication and transport hubs, and special economic centres.

Large Comprehensive Economic Centres

Industry accounts for a large percentage of the total output of large, multiple-function, comprehensive industrial centres. They are characterized by developed light and heavy industries and high output values of various kinds of products. Such centres usually have fairly well developed agriculture in the suburban areas; advanced public services, information channels, financial, trade, and commercial set-ups, and science and technology; and convenient transport and communications which link them with other economic areas to promote mutual economic development and the development of the country as a whole. Economic centres of this type include Shanghai, Beijing, Tianjin, Shenyang, Guangzhou, Chongqing, Chengdu, Xi'an, Lanzhou, and Wuhan. In addition to the above characteristics, these cities have particular areas of development as a result of their historical backgrounds and local conditions.

The ancient city of Beijing is the capital of China; as such, it plays a special role in the country's cultural and political life. It became a comprehensive economic centre only after the founding of the People's Republic in 1949. The country's oldest major comprehensive economic centres are Shanghai and Tianjin. Their industrial development since 1949 — when they were the country's largest industrial cities — has been less rapid than that of Beijing. Whereas Shanghai and Tianjin have focused on the renovation of existing enterprises, Beijing has expanded its industrial base, particularly in the area of heavy industry. In 1980, the city's industrial output value accounted for 4.69 per cent of the country's total, second only to Shanghai which accounted for 12.5 per cent.

Beijing, Shanghai, and Tianjin have extensive suburbs with developed agriculture. However, in each case, the industrial output exceeds agricultural output. Beijing also has a higher percentage of heavy industry than light industry (in 1980, heavy industry accounted for 60.9 per cent of the total industrial output), whereas light industry predominates in Shanghai and Tianjin. The percentage of large heavy industrial enterprises in Beijing also exceeds that of the other two main centres. In terms of economic efficiency, Shanghai's rate of profits and taxes is double that of Beijing and Tianjin. With regard to transport, Shanghai is the country's largest sea port and Beijing is the biggest railway and air transport hub.

Industrial Economic Centres

Industry, communications, and transport are the basis of production in industrial economic centres. The economic role of such centres is to supply industrial products to meet the economic development requirements of different regions and of the country as a whole. Depending on their industrial composition and the scale of production, such centres may be classified as single or multi-industrial centres.

The single industrial centre is usually small in size and often highly specialized. Most such centres developed as a result of the exploitation of natural resources such as coal (Fushun, Xuzhou, Tangshan, Fuxin, Jixi, Hegang, and so forth), oil (Daqing, Zibo, and Karamay), shale oil (Maoming), and the production of iron and steel (Anshan, Baotou, and Dukou). Other single industrial centres are based on hydroelectric power, metallurgy and mining, and forestry.

As China's national economic construction continues, most of its industrial centres have become multi-functional, with different kinds of industrial sectors occupying an important place at the regional or even national level. Multi-functional industrial centres based mainly on heavy industry have developed in areas with rich natural resources, convenient transport facilities, and sufficient supplies of raw and semi-finished materials. They are also generally located in strategically 'safe' areas. Such centres include Harbin, Changchun, Qiqihar, Jilin, Dalian, Jinzhou, Yingkou, Taiyuan, Zhangjiakou, Jinan, Nanjing, Hangzhou, Bengbu, Hefei, Nanchang, Luoyang, Huangshi, Zhuzhou, Liuzhou, Kaifeng, Baoji, Kunming, and Guiyang. Varying in size, these centres are based mainly on the machinery, chemicals, and energy industries. Taiyuan, for instance, situated in the Fen He valley in central Shanxi province and on the central Shanxi coalfields, has iron ore, plaster stone, troilite, and other resources nearby. Its main industries are coal, chemicals, electric power, iron and steel, and machinery. With a large industrial productive ability and a complete range of industrial trades, the city has become Shanxi's largest comprehensive industrial centre and also one of the country's main heavy industrial bases.

Multi-functional industrial centres based on the light and textile industries have developed in agricultural areas with abundant agricultural raw materials and large populations. The largest such centres are Mudanjiang, Dandong, Handan, Shijiazhuang, Baoding, Weifang, Wuxi, Nantong, Suzhou, Changzhou, Zhenjiang, Fuzhou, Qingdao, Anyang, and Nanning. Smaller centres are widely scattered and have close ties with the rural areas. Their industrial departments are close to the raw material-producing areas and to consumer areas, thus ensuring good economic efficiency. Such centres are important in promoting the comprehensive economic development of the region and of the nearby rural areas. Situated in the North China Plain, Shijiazhuang is close to the southern Hebei cotton-growing area and the Handan coalfield. It has well-developed rail transport facilities. Since 1949, the city has developed into a new industrial centre based on the cotton textiles, food, chemical, and machinery industries. The city is now one of north China's main cotton textile bases and it also plays an important role in promoting the rural economy.

Communications and Transport Hubs

Usually situated at the crossroads of several trunk transport lines, transport hubs are important in the movement around the country of passengers and freight. Communications and transport hubs include land, water, and air transport hubs, railway transport hubs, rail and water transport hubs, road and water transport hubs, and ports. Wuhan is a typical land, water, and air transport hub. It is situated on the middle reaches of the Chang Jiang at the junction of the Chang Jiang and the Hanshui river. It is one of China's largest inland ports. In addition, the Beijing–Guangzhou rail line and the Wuhan–Daye and Hankou–Danjiangkou rail lines meet at Wuhan, making it one of China's biggest railway transport hubs. Wuhan forms the centre of the roads network in Hubei province and is linked by air with many other large cities throughout the country.

The railways are the main form of transport in China. The main railway transport hubs are Beijing, Shenyang, Harbin, Zhengzhou, Xuzhou, Shijiazhuang, Lanzhou, Yingtan, Zhuzhou, Huaihua, Chongqing, Chengdu, Kunming, and Guiyang. Rail transport plays an extremely important role in the transport of freight within and between regions.

The rail and water transport hubs — including Chongqing, Yichang, Huangshi, Jiujiang, Wuhu, Yuxikou, and Nanjing — are concentrated on the east coast and along the Chang Jiang system. The road and water transport hubs tend to be based mainly on water transport, and they are the major form of transport where they occur. In the Chang Jiang system, such hubs include Wanxian, Shashi, Chongqing, Yangzhou, Zhenjiang, and Nantong.

The main ports in China are Shanghai, Dalian, Qinhuangdao, Xingang, Qingdao, Lianyungang, Guangzhou, Zhanjiang, and the new port of Shijiusuo. The ports are also important industrial centres and centres of foreign trade. Their industrial equipment and technology, docks, warehouses, foreign trade organizations, and communications and other facilities are important in the development of China's economic relations with other countries.

Special Economic Centres

Special economic centres include the tourist cities and special economic zones. China has many places of cultural, historical, and scenic interest which attract visitors from other parts of China and from overseas. The most well-known tourist cities are Hangzhou, Suzhou, and Guilin. However, tourism has only recently become an industry in China, and these cities developed through the establishment of heavy industries. The factories and enterprises established without due consideration of the unique landscape around Guilin, for example, have polluted the rivers, lakes, soil, and air and destroyed scenic spots. The problem — common also in Hangzhou and Suzhou — has only recently begun to be checked. The future development of scenic places as tourist centres will require that industrial production serve the needs of tourism and not pollute the environment.

The special economic zones offer favourable terms in order to attract foreign investment and technology for the development of mainly processing industries for export. The four special economic zones in China are Shenzhen, Zhuhai, and Shantou in Guangdong province and Xiamen in Fujian province. The zones have favourable conditions for the development of foreign trade. Shenzhen and Zhuhai, for example, are close to Hong Kong and Macau. Xiamen is a natural port as well as a scenic city. It is the gateway for overseas Chinese entering and leaving China. The special economic zone cities are a new form of economic centre in China's network of cities.

Shenzhen's special economic zone is developing into a multi-purpose zone, with all-round development of industry, agriculture, commerce, animal husbandry, building, tourism, and many other services and trades. Large-scale construction of industrial districts and commercial areas is progressing. The development of the sea port at Shekou has accelerated the construction of the whole economic zone and the exploitation of oil in the South China Sea offshore areas.

The construction of economic zones has promoted the economic development of these local areas and earned foreign exchange for the country. The zones have provided employment, helped accumulate experience in absorbing foreign capital and importing advanced science, technology, and management, and trained a large number of skilled workers for the country's modernization drive.

29. Regional Differences

THE vast area of China has created enormous regional differences. Excluding Taiwan, the country can be divided into three zones according to natural and social resources, historical development, and level of economic development. These zones are the developed coastal area of the 10 provinces and municipalities of Beijing, Tianjin, Shanghai, Liaoning, Hebei, Shandong, Jiangsu, Zhejiang, Fujian, and Guangdong; the seven provinces and autonomous regions in the yet to be developed border areas of Inner Mongolia, Xinjiang, Qinghai, Tibet, Yunnan, Guizhou, and Guangxi; and the 12 provinces and regions in the hinterland between them: Shanxi, Shaanxi, Gansu, Ningxia, Sichuan, Henan, Hubei, Hunan, Anhui, Jiangxi, Heilongjiang, and Jilin.

Conditions for Regional Development

Each of the three main zones in China has different conditions for the development of production. These conditions include land and population, the utilization of land resources, and mineral and energy resources.

The coastal region covers a small area of land; it accounts for only 11.1 per cent of the total land area of China. However, the population of the region accounts for over 37 per cent of the national total. In 1980, Shandong province had a population of 72.96 million, the second most populated province in the country. The population of Jiangsu, Guangdong, and Hebei provinces was 59.38 million, 57.8 million, and 51.68 million respectively and their population is the highest in the country (excluding the municipalities of Beijing, Shanghai, and Tianjin). In contrast, the border area is vast, but sparsely populated. Its population accounts for only 13.4 per cent of the total, while it occupies 57.9 per cent of the total land area. The population density of Tibet, Qinghai, Xinjiang, and Inner Mongolia in 1980 was 1.51, 5.22, 7.79, and 16.04 persons per square kilometre respectively, compared with 576.5 and 483.2 persons per square kilometre respectively in Jiangsu and Shandong provinces. Guizhou province has the highest population density in this region, with only 156.87 persons per square kilometre. The hinterland accounts for 30.9 per cent of the total land area, while its population accounts for 40.11 per cent of the total. Its population density of 162.23 persons per square kilometre is 5.83 times that of the border regions but less than half that of the coastal areas. Within the hinterland, population density varies considerably. For example, the density of population in Gansu, Ningxia, and Heilongjiang varies between 42.16 and 69 persons per square kilometre, whereas in Henan province it is 446.9 persons per square kilometre, the third highest in China. Although Sichuan has the largest population of any province in the country (98.2 million), the density is only 174.4 persons per square kilometre because of its large area.

With respect to the utilization of land resources, the index of reclamation and cultivation of land in the coastal areas is a very high 27.89 per cent.

There are large forest areas in Liaoning, Zhejiang, Fujian, and Guangdong provinces, and the percentage of forest cover is also high. In addition, there are vast areas of fresh water. China's marine breeding is also concentrated along the coast. However, in the coastal region, there are few grasslands and unused areas and most of the unused land is unsuitable for farming. The border areas have the lowest index of reclamation and cultivation (below 3 per cent). Forest cover is small, and there is only a limited supply of fresh water. However, there are vast areas of grassland (40 per cent of the national total) and unused land. The Xinjiang autonomous region alone accounts for 30 per cent of the country's unused land suitable for farming. In the hinterland, the index of reclamation and cultivation is lower than in the coastal areas, but higher than in the border areas; it is also higher than the national average. The total area under cultivation in the hinterland is larger than the sum of the cultivated areas of the coastal and border regions, accounting for over 53 per cent of the national total. Vast forests in Heilongjiang, Jilin, Hunan, and Sichuan give this area a percentage of forest cover only slightly lower than that of the coastal areas. On the other hand, the fresh water expanses in the hinterland are the largest in the country, accounting for 63.8 per cent of the national total. The region also has huge tracts of unused land. Heilongjiang province alone accounts for 21.3 per cent of the country's total. There is also much land in Heilongjiang, Sichuan, Shaanxi, Hunan, and Jiangxi provinces which is suitable for afforestation.

In terms of major mineral and energy resources, the coastal region is poor, but it has rich resources of petroleum and iron ore. Other resources in the region include coal in Liaoning and Shandong, hydroelectric resources in Fujian, copper and ferrous sulphide deposits in Guangdong, bauxite in Shandong and Hebei, tungsten in Fujian and Guangdong, and molybdenum in Liaoning. The border area has a greater variety of mineral deposits, with the richest verified resources of hydroelectric energy, molybdenum, miobium, rare earth ores, phosphorus sylvite, and lithium in the country. Deposits of coal, copper, bauxite, and ferrous sulphide are also rich, though the deposits of petroleum, iron ore, and tungsten are smaller than in the coastal region. The greatest number of rich mineral reserves are found in the hinterland areas. With the exception of a few reserves in the border areas, its proven resources of petroleum, copper, bauxite, nickel, platinum metals, vanadium, titanium, ferrous sulphide, and asbestos account for more than 50 per cent of the national total. Verified resources of coal, iron, tungsten, and antimony account for about 45 per cent of national reserves, the richest in the country, and hydroelectric resources account for 42 per cent of the national total.

China's modern industry first developed and became concentrated along the coast. As a result, transport and communications in the region are well developed, and many cities possess considerable technical know-how. The degree of intensive farming and mechanization is also comparatively high. Although the economic base of the hinterland is more developed than in the border region, it falls far short of that of the coastal region. On the whole, the coastal region has the best technical and economic conditions for development, whereas the border region has the advantage of natural resources. The hinterland is situated somewhere between the two.

Features of Regional Production

The characteristics of production in the various regions are the result of the interplay of various factors throughout their development. These characteristics in turn determine the course of future development. Since 1949, the speed and level of development of the formerly backward areas have been greater than in the coastal areas, where the level of industrial development in particular was already high. Between 1952 and 1980, the annual industrial growth rate was 13 per cent in the border region, 12 per cent in the hinterland, and about 10 per cent in the coastal region. The different level of development of particular provinces and regions is even more pronounced. For example, the annual industrial growth rate of the border area that includes Qinghai, Inner Mongolia, Guizhou, and Xinjiang was between 13 and 15.8 per cent; that of Shaanxi, Gansu, Henan, Hubei, Hunan, Anhui, Shanxi, and the Ningxia autonomous region was around 12 per cent; and that of Shanghai, Tianjin, and Liaoning in the coastal region was less than 10 per cent. This level of industrial growth has improved the industrial importance of the border and hinterland areas and corrected the over-concentration of industry in the coastal areas. Nevertheless, the gap in development of the three regions remains very large (Table 29.1).

Table 29.1 indicates that, in terms of total output value, the gap in the level of agricultural development in the three areas is comparatively narrow (especially in terms of per-capita output value), while there is a marked gap in terms of the industrial output value and the total agricultural and industrial output value between the coastal area and the other areas combined. The gap is even larger in terms of the per-capita output value and the density of output value.

Of the many indices used to indicate economic results, the most concise and comprehensive single index is the rate of profits and tax revenue. The difference between the three regions in this respect parallels their relative levels of industrial development. In 1980, the profit and tax rate of the coastal area was 35 per cent, compared with 18.02 per cent for the hinterland and 11.7 per cent for the border area. Shanghai accounted for the highest profit and tax rate, being 25 times that of Qinghai, which had the lowest. The 11 provinces and municipalities with profit and tax rates of over 23 per cent are located, with the exception of Heilongjiang province, in the coastal region. Of the five provinces with rates under 10 per cent, four (Guizhou, Inner Mongolia, Qinghai, and Tibet) are in the border region and the other, Ningxia, is in the hinterland. Most of the provinces and regions in the hinterland had a rate of profit and taxes of between 13 and 21 per cent. Economic results are determined by the standard of technology and management and the industrial structure and production composition of a region.

A third factor (in addition to the speed and level of development and economic results) determining the characteristics of production in a regio is its industrial structure. China's present industrial structure is generally weighted in favour of heavy industry. However, within the three main regions, the structure varies (Table 29.2).

Table 29.1 The Comparative Level of Development of the Coastal, Hinterland, and Border Areas, 1980

Item	National Total	Coastal Areas	Hinterland	Border Areas
1. Proportion of national total (%)				
Total output value of industry and agriculture	100.0	55.773	37.19	7.08
Output value of agriculture	100.0	42.710	46.20	11.09
Output value of light industry	100.0	63.040	31.31	5.65
Output value of heavy industry	100.0	57.170	36.97	5.86
2. Output value per capita (RMB/capita)				
Total output value of industry and agriculutre	673.7	100.0	510.7	354.3
Output value of agriculture	165.6	189.0	155.8	136.6
Output value of light industry	238.5	401.5	152.0	100.2
Output value of heavy industry	269.6	411.5	202.9	117.5
3. Density of output value (RMB10,000/ square kilometre)				
Output value of industry and agriculture	6.89	34.45	8.29	0.84
Output value of industry	5.20	27.96	5.76	0.52
Output value of agriculture	1.69	6.49	2.53	0.32
4. Proportion of total volume of goods transported in the national total (%)	100.00	47.53	44.68	7.79

Sources: The calculations are based on data selected from *China's Economic Yearbook, 1981* (*Economic Management*, 1981) and *China's Agricultural Yearbook, 1980* (Agriculture Publishing House, Beijing, 1981).

Table 29.2 The Industrial Structure of the Main Regions, 1980

Department	National Total	Coastal Areas	Hinterland	Border Areas
Agriculture : industry (1 = agriculture)	1 : 3.07	1 : 4.31	1 : 2.28	1 : 1.59
Light industry : heavy industry (1 = light industry)	1 : 1.13	1 : 1.02	1 : 1.33	1 : 1.17
Agriculture : light industry : heavy industry (1 = agriculture)	1 : 1.44 : 1.63	1 : 2.12 : 2.18	1 : 0.98 : 1.3	1 : 0.73 : 0.86

Sources: The calculations are based on data selected from *China's Economic Yearbook, 1981* (*Economic Management*, 1981) and *China's Agricultural Yearbook, 1980* (Agriculture Publishing House, Beijing, 1981).

Table 29.2 shows that the proportion of industry in each region exceeds that of agriculture; the predominance of industry is highest in the coastal region and lowest in the border areas. In the coastal areas, heavy and light industries are equally developed; heavy industry predominates in the border areas and is even more significant in the hinterland. With respect to agriculture, the level of labour productivity, per-capita output of agricultural products, and agricultural commodity rate are all low, particularly in the border areas. There are insufficient bases producing commodity grain and commodity cash crops. Insufficient support is also provided to agricultural development by heavy industry, and industrial development exceeds in all cases the capacity of regional agriculture to support it. In each of the three main regions, therefore, there is an imbalance between agricultural and industrial development.

The proportion of light and heavy industry in a region is directly related to local industrial resources. However, heavy industry generally predominates. In areas where minerals and energy resources are abundant, mining and raw and semi-finished materials industries are more developed. The proportion of light industry is greater in areas which lack mineral deposits and energy sources but possess agricultural resources and well-developed processing industries. Such areas were the earliest to experience economic development. The proportion of light and heavy industry in the coastal, border, and hinterland regions now more accurately reflects local conditions than it did in the past. Following the 1st FYP period, for example, local conditions were ignored as heavy industry was emphasized throughout China. The emphasis placed on the processing and raw materials industries led to excessive development of heavy industry and agriculture, especially in Gansu, Ningxia, Heilongjiang, Shanxi, Guizhou, and Qinghai and in the coastal areas of Liaoning and Beijing.

A further factor determining regional characteristics of production is specialization. On the whole, specialization is not well developed in any of the three main regions. However, a few areas have evolved specialized sectors and products which are peculiar to the region and which figure significantly in the regional division of labour (Table 29.3).

Table 29.3 indicates that the coastal areas produce more products of national significance — particularly technology-intensive industrial products — than do the hinterland and border areas. This pattern is consistent with the general production characteristics of the three regions.

Regional industrial networks and the concentration of industrial enterprises also affect the production profile of each of the main regions. The concentration of industrial enterprises is gauged by city density, average urban industrial production levels, and the ratio of urban industrial output value to total industrial output value in a region. In terms of city density, the coastal areas have the highest density (0.578 square kilometres), followed by the hinterland (0.337 square kilometres), and the border areas (0.049 square kilometres). The average urban production level of the coastal areas is also higher (RMB3.371 billion) than that of the hinterland (RMB0.99 billion) and the border areas (RMB0.5 billion). Of the 26 industrial centres in China with an industrial output value of over RMB3 billion, 16 are located in the coastal areas (Guangzhou, Shanghai, Nanjing, Wuxi, Hangzhou, Jinan, Qingdao,

Table 29.3 Specialized Sectors and Products in the Main Regions

Zone	Specialized Sectors and Products
Coastal areas	Steel, equipment manufacturing, electronics, machinery, salt making and salt chemistry, petroleum and petrochemicals, light-sensitive materials, basic industrial chemicals, chemicals for daily use, pharmaceuticals, textiles, sugar-cane, paper making, marine aquaculture
Hinterland	Coal and coal chemistry, petroleum, forestry, automobile industry, tractor manufacturing, non-ferrous metals, well salt, cotton and cotton textiles, tobacco curing and cigarettes, beets and sugar refining, flax and flax weaving, paper making, freshwater aquaculture, tea and tea processing
Border areas	Animal husbandry, non-ferrous metals, lake and well salt, potash fertilizer, wool and woollen textiles

Zibo, Beijing, Tianjin, Shijiazhuang, Shenyang, Dalian, Anshan, Fushun, and Jinzhou) and 10 are in the hinterland (Chengdu, Chongqing, Xi'an, Lanzhou, Wuhan, Taiyuan, Changchun, Jilin, Harbin, and Daqing). In terms of the ratio of urban industrial output value to the total value of industrial output, the coastal areas have the highest ratio (83.4 per cent), followed by 65 per cent in the hinterland, and 56.4 per cent in the border areas.

The characteristics of production of the three main regions of China generally reflect the imbalance in production in the country as a whole. The causes of this imbalance are complex, stemming from a long history of unplanned and irrational development. After 1949, the development of the backward regions emphasized industrial development to the detriment of all-round development of production. The lack of an adequate infrastructure to support the new industries exacerbated the problem of economic development of those areas. There was also a severe shortage of technology and trained personnel, and the uneven distribution of cultural, educational, and scientific research facilities inhibited the growth of technical expertise and discouraged trained personnel from the more developed regions from settling in those areas. As a result of these problems, and in spite of the heavy investment in the border regions since 1949, results have generally been poorer than expected.

Prospects for Development

The different characteristics and conditions of production in the three main areas affect their prospects for future development. The coastal region — the most developed part of China — has the most favourable conditions for further improvement of its agricultural technology and expansion of its transport facilities. A number of industrial bases are planned which will concentrate on scientific research, commodity distribution, and foreign trade. Emphasis will be placed on the technical transformation of existing enterprises, and on upgrading equipment and improving conditions with a view to raising quality, increasing variety and labour productivity, and conserving energy. Processing developments will be aimed at obtaining the highest possible economic results with the minimum of resources.

In planning production, new projects will be limited to those in short supply and those in the mining and raw materials industries which have an assured supply of natural resources. Where conditions permit, suitable industries will be moved gradually out of the large cities into the smaller cities and towns and urban expansion of the large cities will be strictly controlled. Investment in energy and transport will be increased and technology- and labour-intensive industries will be emphasized, producing an industrial structure slanted towards light and light-precision industries. Foreign trade will be developed further; imports will be aimed at expanding production capability and exports will be increased. Co-operation between cities will also be encouraged, with the large cities acting as hubs. The transfer of technology to the under-developed regions will also be increased in order to raise their technical levels.

Although undeveloped, the border regions have considerable potential for development. A number of large excavation and raw materials centres are planned and efforts will be made to raise the existing level of productivity of the established industrial centres. The new centres are planned to produce badly needed products, using the region's natural resources. Further prospecting for resources, the building and extension of existing transport routes, the development of agriculture, and the training of technical personnel will be emphasized so as to provide the necessary conditions for large-scale industrial development. Forestry and animal husbandry will also be more fully developed and industry will be based on raw materials industries, as well as processing and light industries.

Development in the border regions will also take the form of improvement of existing enterprises, supplemented by expansion into new areas and associated products where appropriate. Existing industrial centres and networks will be consolidated and the construction of coal-mines, coal-generated electricity plants, hydroelectric plants, and non-ferrous mines will be accelerated. On this basis, a number of coal-processing and large energy-consuming industrial centres are planned. The industrial structure will emphasize heavy and light industry, though heavy industry will continue to predominate. An important development will be the co-ordination of the mining, raw materials, and manufacturing industries. Agriculture will be promoted and light and textile industries will be developed on the basis of the region's agricultural and non-agricultural raw materials, with the aim of satisfying the region's own needs as well as reducing the region's reliance upon the coastal areas. However, co-operation between the coastal and border areas will be strengthened with the aim of importing advanced technology and management methods and of expanding the exploitation of resources and raising their overall utilization.

In the hinterland areas, developments in agriculture, industry, and transportation and the region's abundant natural resources have contributed to the development of a number of industrial centres. However, the region remains only moderately developed, but with enormous potential to provide support to the border areas. Together with the coastal areas, it is planned to supply products as well as material and technical assistance to the less developed areas.

At the national level, the aim of future development of production in the coastal, hinterland, and border regions is to take full advantage of local conditions whilst mutually supporting each other's development. It is hoped that in this way, the regional differences in economic development will be reduced and that the national distribution of production will be improved, thereby producing a general boost in the national economy and an increase in economic returns.

Appendix: China's Production Statistics, 1981

Table A Output Value and Industrial Structure

Department	Output Value (RMB100 m.)	Structure (%)
1. Gross output value of agriculture and industry	6,919	Taking gross output value as 100:
Agriculture	1,720	24.9
Industry	5,199	75.1
2. Of the total agricultural output value:		Taking total output value as 100:
Farming	1,103.1	64.1
Forestry	52.0	3.0
Animal husbandry	245.0	14.3
Sideline occupations	297.8	17.3
Agriculture	21.8	1.3
3. Of the total industrial output value:		Taking total output value as 100:
Light industry	2,674.7	51.5
Heavy industry	2,524.1	48.5
4. Of the total industrial output value:		Taking total output value as 100:
Metallurgy industry	415.40	8.0
Energy industry	194.09	3.7
Coal and coke	122.05	2.3
Oil industry	245.37	4.7
Chemical industry	651.28	12.5
Engineering industry	1,226.17	23.6
Building materials	180.87	3.5
Forest industry	86.16	1.7
Food industry	640.23	12.3
Textile, tailoring, and leather industries	1,079.47	20.8
Paper and stationery making	185.50	3.6

Sources: Materials for this and the following tables are from *China's Statistical Yearbook 1981* (China Statistical Publishing House, Beijing, 1982) and *China's Economic Yearbook, 1982* (*Economic Management*, 1982).

Table B The Internal Structure of the Chemical, Engineering, and Food Industries

Department	Output Value (RMB100 m.)	Structure (%)
1. Chemical industry	651.28	Taking total output value as 100:
Mining of chemical ores	4.84	0.74
Basic chemical materials	76.02	11.67
Chemical fertilizers and pesticides	123.65	18.99
Organic chemical industry	131.76	20.23
Chemicals	78.93	12.12
Chemical articles for daily use	49.00	7.52
Rubber processing	84.06	12.91
Plastics processing	103.02	15.82
2. Engineering industry	1,226.17	Taking total output value as 100:
Farm machinery	67.68	5.52
Facilities for industry	199.45	16.27
Facilities for transport	128.13	10.45
Electronics industry	229.28	18.70
Machinery for daily use	98.71	8.05
Metal articles for production	180.39	14.71
Metal articles for daily use	97.78	7.97
Repairing	66.16	5.40
3. Food industry	640.23	Taking total output value as 100:
Grain and oil processing	198.20	30.96
Salt refining	20.47	3.20
Slaughtering and meat processing	88.48	13.82
Sugar refining	35.80	5.59
Cigarettes	94.89	14.82

Table C The Output of the Main Agricultural, Livestock, and Aquatic Products
and Heads of Livestock*

Product	1981	Increase 1980–1 (%)	Increase 1978–81 (%)
Grain	32,502.0	1.4	6.6
Rice	14,396.0	2.9	5.1
Wheat	5,964.0	8.0	10.8
Potatoes	2,597.0	–9.6	–18.2
Soya beans	933.0	17.5	23.2
Cotton	296.8	9.6	37.0
Bluish dogbane and jute	126.0	14.8	15.8
Oil-bearing crops	1,020.5	32.7	95.6
Peanuts	382.6	6.3	61.0
Rape-seed	406.5	70.5	117.6
Sesame	51.0	96.9	58.4
Sugar-cane	2,966.8	30.1	40.5
Sugar-beet	636.0	0.9	135.4
Silkworm cocoons	25.2	0.1	45.7
Tea	34.3	12.8	28.0
Pork, beef, and mutton	1,260.9	4.6	47.2
Milk	129.1	13.1	
Sheep's wool	18.9	7.4	
Livestock			
Pigs	29,370.2	–3.8	–2.5
Sheep	18,773.0	0.2	10.5
Draught animals	9,764.1	2.5	4.0
Aquatic products	460.5	2.4	–1.1

Note: *The unit for livestock is 10,000 head; the unit for other products is 10,000 tonnes.

Table D The Output of the Main Light Industrial Products

Product	1981	Increase 1980–1 (%)	Increase 1978–81 (%)
Yarn	3.17 m. tonnes	8.3	33.1
Cloth	14.27 b. metres	5.9	29.4
Chemical fibres	527,300 tonnes	17.1	85.3
Synthetic fibres	384,700 tonnes	22.5	127.0
Wool fabric	113 m. metres	12.0	27.2
Silk	37,400 tonnes	5.7	29.0
Silk-knit goods	835 m. metres	9.9	36.8
Gunnysacks	429 m.	4.6	48.4
Machine-made paper and paper board	5.4 m. tonnes	0.9	23.0
Sugar	3.166 m. tonnes	23.1	39.6
Beer	910,000 tonnes	32.3	
Crude salt	18.32 m. tonnes	6.0	–6.2
Chemicals	37,300 tonnes	–7.0	–8.4
Synthetic detergent	478,000 tonnes	21.6	47.5
Bicycles	17.543 m.	34.7	105.4
Sewing-machines	10.391 m.	35.3	113.6
Wrist-watches	28.724 m.	29.7	112.6
TV sets	5.394 m.	116.5	940.0
Radios	40.572 m.	35.1	2.5
Cameras	623,000	67.1	2.5
Domestic washing machines	1.281 m.	422.9	
Domestic refrigerators	55,600	13.5	
Bulbs	966 m.	2.1	27.3

Table E The Output of the Main Heavy Industrial Products

Product	1981	Increase 1980–1 (%)	Increase 1978–81 (%)
Raw coal	620 m. tonnes	0.2	0.6
Crude oil	101.22 m. tonnes	−4.5	−2.7
Natural gas	12.74 b. cubic metres	−10.7	−7.2
Electric energy production	309.27 b. kWh	2.9	20.5
Hydraulic electro-generation	65.55 b. kWh	12.6	46.9
Rolled steel	26.701 m. tonnes	−1.7	20.9
Pig iron	34.166 m. tonnes	−10.1	−1.8
Steel	35.604 m. tonnes	−4.1	12.0
Machine-made coke	31.72 m. tonnes	−6.8	−31.9
Timber	49.423 m. cubic metres	−7.8	−4.3
Cement	82.897 m. tonnes	3.8	27.1
Plate glass	30.644 m. standard boxes	10.6	52.9
Sulphuric acid	7.807 m. tonnes	2.1	18.1
Soda ash	1.652 m. tonnes	2.4	24.3
Caustic soda	1.923 m. tonnes	no change	17.3
Chemical fertilizers	12.39 m. tonnes	0.6	42.5
Nitrogenous fertilizers	9.857 m. tonnes	−1.4	29.0
Phosphate fertilizers	2.508 m. tonnes	8.7	142.8
Potash fertilizers	20,000 tonnes	0.5	
Farm chemicals	484,000 tonnes	−9.7	−9.2
Ethylene	505,000 tonnes	3.0	32.7
Plastic	916,000 tonnes	2.0	34.9
Calcium carbide	1.513 m. tonnes	−0.4	22.2
Facilities for generating electricity	1.395 m. kW	−66.7	−71.2
Metal-cutting machine tools	103,000	−23.1	−44.0
Motor vehicles	176,000	−20.7	17.8
Tractors	53,000	−46.0	−53.5
Walking tractors	199,000	−8.7	−38.6
Internal-combustion engines	20.04 m. hp	−21.1	−28.9
Locomotives	398	−22.3	−23.6
Freight trains	8,779	−17.0	−48.2
Civil steel ships	4,983	20.4	

Table F The Structure of Transport and Communications

Item	Absolute No.	Structure (%)
Length of various transport lines (10,000 km)	141.63	Taking the length as 100:
Mileage of railways open to traffic[1]	5.23	3.69
Highways	89.75	63.37
Inland waterways	10.87	7.68
Civil airlines	34.81	24.58
Petroleum pipelines	0.97	0.68
Number of passengers transported (10,000)	384,844	Taking the number as 100:
Railways[2]	95,300	24.77
Highways	261,559	67.96
Water transport	27,584	7.17
Civil aviation	401	0.10
Passenger turnover (100 m. people/km)	2,500	Taking the turnover as 100:
Railways	1,473	58.92
Highways	839	33.56
Water transport	138	5.52
Civil aviation	50	2.00
Total volume of goods transported (10,000 tonnes)	231,605	Taking the total volume as 100:
Railways	107,673	46.49
Highways[3]	71,504	30.87
Water transport	41,490	17.91
Pipelines	10,929	4.72
Civil aviation	9.4	0.01
Turnover of goods (100 m. tonnes/km)	11,616	Taking the turnover as 100:
Railways	5,712	49.17
Highways	253	2.18
Water transport	5,150	44.34
Pipelines	499	4.30
Civil aviation	1.7	0.01

Notes: 1. Excluding 3,700 kilometres of local railways.
2. Including both central and local railways.
3. Freight and passengers and their turnover amount by highways include only that carried out by professional transport departments.

Table G The Level of Development of Production by Province (RMB100 million)

	Total Output Value of Agriculture and Industry		Total Output Value of Agriculture	
	No.	% of China's Total	No.	% of China's Total
All China	6,919	100	1,720	100
North China	1,011.63	14.62	192.91	11.22
Beijing	252.80	3.65	14.60	0.85
Tianjin	222.20	3.21	15.60	0.91
Hebei	301.46	4.36	92.10	5.35
Shanxi	149.50	2.16	40.50	2.35
Inner Mongolia	85.67	1.24	30.11	1.75
North-east China	1,001.79	14.48	189.90	11.04
Liaoning	536.70	7.76	85.30	4.96
Jilin	173.49	2.51	40.60	2.36
Heilongjiang	291.60	4.21	64.00	3.72
East China	2,598.85	37.56	604.98	35.17
Shanghai	676.10	9.77	28.60	1.66
Jiangsu	654.40	9.46	160.40	9.33
Zhejiang	308.17	4.45	91.71	5.33
Anhui	212.63	3.07	83.93	4.88
Fujian	125.32	1.81	44.12	2.57
Jiangxi	146.23	2.11	56.02	3.26
Shandong	476.00	6.88	140.20	8.15
Central-south China	1,404.37	20.30	454.99	26.45
Henan	316.70	4.58	121.30	7.05
Hubei	336.77	4.87	89.97	5.23
Hunan	273.80	3.96	98.09	5.70
Guangdong	342.84	4.96	92.94	5.40
Guangxi	134.26	1.94	52.69	3.06
South-west China	599.08	8.66	221.02	12.85
Sichuan	408.87	5.91	140.76	8.18
Guizhou	73.61	1.06	31.01	1.80
Yunnan	110.68	1.60	44.38	2.58
Tibet	5.92	0.08	4.87	0.28
North-west China	290.16	4.19	98.63	5.73
Shaanxi	143.05	2.07	36.75	2.14
Gansu	49.18	0.71	24.00	1.40
Qinghai	17.52	0.25	6.08	0.35
Ningxia	17.35	0.25	5.68	0.33
Xinjiang	63.06	0.91	26.12	1.52

Table G *continued*

	Total Output Value of Industry		Total Output Value of Light Industry		Total Output Value of Heavy Industry	
	No.	% of China's Total	No.	% of China's Total	No.	% of China's Total
All China	5,199	100	2,675	100	2,524	100
North China	818.72	15.75	393.23	14.70	425.49	16.86
Beijing	238.20	4.58	105.00	3.93	133.20	5.28
Tianjin	206.60	3.97	120.10	4.49	86.50	3.43
Hebei	209.36	4.03	104.21	3.90	105.15	4.17
Shanxi	109.00	2.10	37.90	1.42	71.10	2.82
Inner Mongolia	55.56	1.07	26.02	0.97	29.54	1.17
North-east China	811.89	15.62	303.51	11.35	508.19	20.13
Liaoning	451.40	8.68	162.70	6.08	288.70	11.44
Jilin	132.89	2.56	56.51	2.11	76.29	3.02
Heilongjiang	227.60	4.38	84.30	3.15	143.20	5.67
East China	1,993.86	38.35	1,149.63	42.98	844.20	34.81
Shanghai	647.50	12.45	361.70	13.52	285.80	11.32
Jiangsu	494.00	9.50	290.40	10.86	203.60	8.07
Zhejiang	216.46	4.16	138.03	5.16	78.43	3.11
Anhui	128.69	2.48	71.91	2.69	56.78	2.25
Fujian	81.20	1.56	51.82	1.94	29.30	1.16
Jiangxi	90.21	1.74	46.67	1.74	43.59	1.73
Shandong	335.80	6.46	189.10	7.07	146.70	5.81
Central-south China	949.38	18.26	533.79	19.95	415.95	16.47
Henan	195.40	3.76	108.20	4.04	87.20	3.45
Hubei	246.80	4.75	128.69	4.81	118.11	4.68
Hunan	175.71	3.38	81.05	3.03	94.66	3.75
Guangdong	249.90	4.81	163.04	6.09	28.76	3.44
Guangxi	81.57	1.57	52.81	1.97	86.86	1.14
South-west China	378.06	7.27	185.86	6.95	192.13	7.61
Sichuan	268.11	5.16	134.94	5.04	133.11	5.27
Guizhou	42.60	0.82	17.78	0.66	24.82	0.98
Yunnan	66.30	1.28	32.69	1.22	33.60	1.33
Tibet	1.05	0.02	0.45	0.01	0.60	0.02
North-west China	191.53	3.68	99.14	3.71	92.39	3.66
Shaanxi	106.30	2.04	56.57	2.11	49.73	1.97
Gansu	25.18	0.48	17.02	0.64	8.16	0.32
Qinghai	11.44	0.22	4.68	0.17	6.76	0.27
Ningxia	11.67	0.22	3.69	0.14	7.98	0.32
Xinjiang	36.94	0.71	17.18	0.64	19.76	0.78

Table H The Industrial Structure of Different Provinces, Municipalities, and Autonomous Regions

| | Taking the Total Output Value of Agriculture and Industry as 100 | | | | |
	Industry	Agri-culture	Agri-culture	Light Industry	Heavy Industry
All China	75.14	24.86	24.86	38.66	36.48
North China	80.93	19.07	19.07	38.87	42.06
Beijing	94.22	5.78	5.78	41.53	52.69
Tianjin	92.98	7.02	7.02	54.05	38.93
Hebei	69.45	30.55	30.55	34.57	34.88
Shanxi	72.91	27.09	27.09	25.35	47.56
Inner Mongolia	64.85	35.15	35.15	30.37	34.48
North-east China	81.04	18.96	18.96	30.30	50.74
Liaoning	84.11	15.89	15.89	30.31	53.80
Jilin	69.96	30.04	30.04	29.73	40.23
Heilongjiang	78.05	21.95	21.95	28.91	49.14
East China	76.72	23.28	23.28	44.24	32.48
Shanghai	95.77	4.23	4.23	53.50	42.27
Jiangsu	75.49	24.51	24.51	44.38	31.11
Zhejiang	70.24	29.76	29.76	44.79	25.45
Anhui	60.53	39.47	39.47	33.82	26.71
Fujian	64.79	35.21	35.21	41.35	23.44
Jiangxi	61.69	38.31	38.31	31.92	29.77
Shandong	70.55	29.45	29.45	39.73	30.82
Central-south China	67.60	32.40	32.40	38.00	29.60
Henan	61.70	38.30	38.30	34.16	27.54
Hubei	73.28	26.72	26.72	38.21	35.07
Hunan	64.17	35.83	35.83	29.60	34.57
Guangdong	72.89	27.11	27.11	47.56	25.33
Guangxi	60.76	39.24	39.24	39.33	21.43
South-west China	63.11	36.89	36.89	31.02	32.09
Sichuan	65.57	34.43	34.43	33.01	32.56
Guizhou	57.87	42.13	42.13	24.15	33.72
Yunnan	59.90	40.10	40.10	29.54	30.36
Tibet	17.74	82.26	82.26	7.60	10.14
North-west China	66.01	33.99	33.99	34.17	31.84
Shaanxi	74.31	25.69	25.69	39.55	34.76
Gansu	51.20	48.80	48.80	34.61	16.59
Qinghai	65.30	34.70	34.70	26.71	38.59
Ningxia	67.26	32.74	32.74	21.27	45.99
Xinjiang	58.58	41.42	41.42	27.24	31.34

Table H *continued*

| | Taking the Total Output Value of Industry as 100 | |
	Light Industry	Heavy Industry
All China	52.45	48.55
North China	48.03	51.97
Beijing	44.08	55.92
Tianjin	58.13	41.87
Hebei	49.78	50.22
Shanxi	34.77	65.23
Inner Mongolia	46.83	53.17
North-east China	37.38	62.62
Liaoning	36.04	63.96
Jilin	42.49	57.51
Heilongjiang	37.04	62.96
East China	57.66	42.34
Shanghai	55.86	44.14
Jiangsu	58.79	41.21
Zhejiang	63.77	36.23
Anhui	55.88	44.12
Fujian	63.82	36.18
Jiangxi	51.73	48.27
Shandong	56.31	43.69
Central-south China	56.23	43.77
Henan	55.37	44.63
Hubei	52.14	47.86
Hunan	46.13	53.87
Guangdong	65.24	34.76
Guangxi	64.74	35.26
South-west China	49.16	50.84
Sichuan	50.33	49.67
Guizhou	41.74	58.26
Yunnan	49.31	50.69
Tibet	42.86	57.14
North-west China	51.76	48.24
Shaanxi	53.22	46.78
Gansu	67.59	32.41
Qinghai	40.91	59.09
Ningxia	31.62	68.38
Xinjiang	46.51	53.49

Table I The Main Economic Targets of Different Provinces, Municipalities, and Autonomous Regions

	Population (10,000)	Workers and Staff	Total Output Value of Agriculture and Industry (RMB100 million)	Turnover Amount of of Goods[1] (100 million tonnes/km)	Output of Main Products[2]	
					Raw Coal	Generated Energy
All China	99,622	10,939.7	6,919.0	11,115	62,164	3,092.7
Beijing	902	344.4	252.8	133.5	789	99.3
Tianjin	763	253.9	222.2	150.9		73.0
Hebei	5,256	496.8	301.5	710.6	5,235	199.3
Shanxi	2,509	318.6	149.5	226.4	13,255	124.6
Inner Mongolia	1,903	270.9	85.7	244.0	2,180	54.5
Liaoning	3,535	814.5	536.7	674.3	3,371	280.0
Jilin	2,231	396.5	173.5	244.9	1,807	126.4
Heilong- jiang	3,239	672.0	291.6	435.0	4,174	135.8
Shanghai	1,163	464.5	676.1	56.7		204.7
Jiangsu	6,010	674.8	654.4	299.8	1,737	169.9
Zhejiang	3,871	380.8	308.2	181.8	133	95.8
Anhui	4,956	357.9	212.6	248.2	2,382	97.1
Fujian	2,557	242.2	125.3	85.0	417	52.5
Jiangxi	3,304	301.8	146.2	138.9	1,553	59.9
Shandong	7,395	539.6	476.0	301.5	4,131	194.5
Henan	7,397	496.4	316.7	552.0	5,825	171.2
Hubei	4,740	531.6	336.8	267.6	434	137.2
Hunan	5,360	426.9	273.8	299.3	1,994	122.4
Guangdong	5,884	678.0	342.8	133.4	723	122.4
Guangxi	3,613	260.1	134.3	165.1	561	55.8
Sichuan	9,924	744.5	408.9	222.3	3,940	164.1
Guizhou	2,827	185.7	73.6	99.2	1,416	43.6
Yunnan	3,223	235.2	110.7	67.6	1,190	59.7
Tibet	186	17.5	5.9	3.7	2.3	1.7
Shaanxi	2,865	297.0	290.2	155.4	1,845	75.1
Gansu	1,941	179.9	49.2	169.0	788	121.4
Qinghai	382	55.6	17.5	8.3	191	7.7
Ningxia	383	48.8	17.4	39.7	952	18.3
Xinjiang	1,303	253.1	63.1	57.7	1,141	25.2

Table I *continued*

				Output of Main Products[2]			
	Steel	Timber	Cloth	Grain	Cotton	Oil-bearing Crops	Pork, Beef, and Mutton
All China	3,560.4	4,942.3	142.7	6,500.4	5,935.2	20,410.4	1,260.9
Beijing	190.3	0.2	2.9	36.1	1.4	44.5	13.2
Tianjin	125.1		4.2	21.4	4.5	90.1	5.8
Hebei	182.9	10.5	10.2	315.0	443.3	928.8	47.8
Shanxi	138.5	12.0	4.0	145.0	132.0	241.9	20.5
Inner Mongolia	131.8	427.2	0.8	102.0		725.5	23.9
Liaoning	872.9	44.3	6.4	232.1	44.0	612.2	49.1
Jilin	21.0	614.4	1.6	184.4		690.4	25.1
Heilong-jiang	47.4	1,540.0	1.9	250.0		888.3	32.7
Shanghai	506.3		16.7	37.1	148.6	293.7	17.0
Jiangsu	62.1		19.2	502.3	1,126.9	1,282.1	105.9
Zhejiang	40.1	64.1	5.1	283.9	136.3	799.9	62.8
Anhui	140.1	36.0	5.3	357.5	312.8	1,986.8	48.7
Fujian	21.9	366.9	1.4	162.0		370.0	27.6
Jiangxi	42.7	269.6	3.3	253.7	93.8	396.7	39.6
Shandong	86.6	4.5	11.7	462.5	1,350.0	2,842.8	96.3
Henan	55.7	11.4	9.9	462.9	710.1	1,119.8	48.2
Hubei	342.3	64.5	11.4	341.4	705.4	785.8	54.0
Hunan	73.1	207.8	4.2	434.1	187.6	715.1	99.7
Guangdong	39.9	327.0	2.7	331.1		1,220.3	74.8
Guangxi	22.8	159.7	1.5	229.9	1.3	284.7	43.3
Sichuan	302.5	344.1	6.7	693.1	173.4	1,950.1	189.0
Guizhou	8.6	83.1	0.7	113.5	1.2	679.3	31.6
Yunnan	41.4	199.8	1.5	183.4	2.4	214.2	35.2
Tibet		18.8		9.7		23.8	5.7
Shaanxi	21.4	33.2	6.8	150.0	125.0	336.1	25.7
Gansu	15.0	45.0	0.7	87.0	8.0	263.7	14.1
Qinghai	17.3	5.6	0.2	16.0		126.9	8.4
Ningxia	0.4	0.8	0.1	25.3		75.5	2.0
Xinjiang	10.3	51.9	1.8	78.0	227.2	421.4	13.2

Notes: 1. The figures show only the turnover amount of goods transported by rail, road, and water.

2. The unit for raw coal, steel, pork, beef, and mutton is 10,000 tonnes; the unit for generated energy is 100 million kWh; the unit for timber is 10,000 cubic metres; the unit for cloth is 100 million metres; the unit for grain is 100 million *jin*; and the unit for cotton and oil crops is 10,000 *dan*.

Bibliography

Books

Atlas of the People's Republic of China (Atlas Publishing House, Beijing, 1979).

Chen Hui, *The Railways of China* (Sanlian Bookstore, Beijing, 1955).

Chen Zhen and Yao Luo, *A History of China's Modern Industry* (Sanlian Bookstore, Beijing, 1957), Vols. 1–4.

China's Agricultural Yearbook, 1980 (Agriculture Publishing House, Beijing, 1981).

China's Economic Yearbook, 1981 (*Economic Management*, 1981).

China's Economic Yearbook, 1982 (*Economic Management*, 1982).

Chinese Academy of Social Sciences, *The World Economic Statistics Handbook* (Chinese Academy of Social Sciences, Beijing, 1981).

Directory of China's Industrial and Commercial Enterprises (Xinhua Publishing House, Beijing, 1981).

Li Changnian, *A History of Agriculture* (Shanghai Science and Technology Publishing House, Shanghai, 1981).

Li Rui, *The Hydropower Industry and the Long-term Planning of the Rivers* (Water Conservation and Hydropower Industry Publishing House, 1982).

Liu Zhongyi et al., *Research on the Issues of Agricultural Economy in China* (People's Publishing House, Beijing, 1981).

Ma Hong and Sun Shangqing, *The Economic Structure of China* (People's Publishing House, Beijing, 1981), Vols. 1 and 2.

Policy Research Office of the Ministry of Agriculture, *An Outline of China's Agricultural Economy* (Agriculture Publishing House, 1981).

Research Office on Economic Geography of the Geography Research Institute of the Chinese Academy of Social Sciences, *An Outline of the Agricultural Geography of China* (Science Publishing House, 1980).

China's Statistical Yearbook, 1981 (China Statistical Publishing House, 1982).

State Statistical Bureau, *The Great Decade* (People's Publishing House, Beijing, 1959).

Sun Yutang and Wang Jingyu, *References on the History of China's Modern Industry* (Science Publishing House, 1957).

Tu Guangzhi and Ye Lianjun, *China's Natural Resources and their Rational Utilization* (Knowledge Publishing House, 1980).

Wu Zhonghua, *The Way out of the Energy Crisis in View of Energy Science Techniques* (Knowledge Publishing House, 1980).

Yan Zhongping, *A Selection of Material on China's Modern Industrial History* (Science Publishing House, 1955).

Zhang Youyi, *References on the History of China's Modern Agriculture* (Sanlian Bookstore, 1957), Vol. 3.

Articles

An Zuoxiang, 'Issues on China's Oil Energy', *Energy*, 1981, No. 2.

Cai Xuelin, 'Problems in China's Aviation Transport', *Comprehensive Transport*, 1979, No. 2.

Chen Dongsheng, 'An Analysis of the Historical Experience of Industrial Distribution in China', *Research on Financial and Economic Issues*, 1982, No. 3.

Chen Yun, 'Major Issues in Present Capital Construction', *Red Flag*, 1959, No. 5.

Chen Zhikai, 'China's Water Resources', *Guangming Daily*, 9 October 1981.

Chen Zugong, 'How Will the Distribution of the Textile Industry be Rationalized?', *Textile Industry of China*, 1985, No. 10.

'Understanding the Second Part of the Report Made by Hu Yaobang at the 12th Congress of the Communist Party of China', *Economic Weekly*, 1982, Nos. 41–3.

Feng Weiran, 'On Rational Transport', *Comprehensive Transport*, 1979, No. 1.

Gao Shangquan, 'On the Problem of "Working According to the Local Conditions and Appropriate Concentration" in Agricultural Production', *People's Daily*, 16 November 1978.

Gao Yuan, 'On Problems Concerning the Economy of Water and Highway Transport', *Comprehensive Transport*, 1979, No. 2.

General Construction Bureau of the Ministry of Water Conservancy and Hydropower Industry, 'New Prospects and Achievements in China's Hydropower Energy', *Hydropower Industry*, 1981, No. 2.

Guo Hongtao, 'The Present Situation of China's Transport and Communications and Prospects for the Near Future', *People's Daily*, 28 July 1982.

Hou Xueyu, 'Opinions on the Development of Agriculture in China', *Guangming Daily*, 25 July 1979.

——, 'On the Problems in the Development of Agriculture, Forestry, Animal Husbandry, Sideline Occupations, and Aquaculture from the Viewpoint of the Ecological System', *Issues of Agricultural Economy*, 1980, No. 2.

Hu Zhaoliang, 'Initial Analysis on the Returns of the Iron and Steel Industry', *On Economic Returns* (Henan People's Publishing House, 1982).

Hua Shiqian, 'The Distribution Characteristics of China's Water Resources and Problems in Exploitation', *Natural Resources*, 1979, No. 2.

Huang Rongsheng, 'Division of Work in Economic Regions to Achieve Economic Superiority', *Dongyue Thesis*, 1981, No. 4.

——, 'Theory and Methods for Research on the Regional Economic Structure', *Exploration*, 1982, No. 1.

Ke Ziyuan, 'Agricultural Natural Resources and their Rational Utilization', *Natural Resources*, 1977, No. 2.

'The Construction of Grasslands to Develop Animal Husbandry', *People's Daily*, 15 October 1978.

'Formation of the Nationwide Comprehensive River and Land Network', *World Economic Herald*, 6 September 1982.

Li Dazhong, 'Expanding the Exploitation of Coal to Meet the Requirements of the Four Modernizations', *Energy*, 1981, No. 2.

Li Fuchun, 'The Correct Handling of the Achievement of Economic Superiority in the Ethnic Minority Regions', *Academic Forum*, 1982, No. 1.

Liang Xizhang, 'Accelerating the Development of Pipeline Transport', *Comprehensive Transport*, 1979, No. 2.

Liu Baitao, 'A Study of the Issues Concerning the Distribution of Farm Crops', *Research on the Economy*, 1963, No. 7.

Liu Shaobo, 'Problems in the Development of Animal Husbandry', *Guangming Daily*, 11 November 1979.

Liu Wenlin, 'Brief Notes on the Correct Handling of the Contradiction between the Farm and Sideline Raw Materials-producing Bases and the Industrial Processing Regions', *Study and Thought*, 1982, No. 1.

Liu Yuren, 'Exploitation and Utilization of Manpower Resources, Land Resources, and Other Economic Resources', *Economic Weekly*, 9 July 1982.

Liu Zaixing, 'Issues Concerning the Distribution of the Exploitation of Coal Resources in China', *Teaching and Research*, 1979, No. 6.

——, 'Problems Concerning the Construction and Distribution of the Iron and Steel Bases in China', *Correspondence on the Technical Economy and Modernization of Management*, 10 November 1980.

——, 'The Necessity of Readjustment of Industrial Distribution in the Establishment of a Rational Economic Structure', *Jinyang Academic Journal*, 1982, No. 3.

——, 'How to Evaluate the Distribution of the Construction of Railways since the Third Five-year Plan', *Theory of the Economy and Economic Management*, 1982, No. 2.

Luo Anren, 'On the Necessity of the Development of Nuclear Energy for Civil Purposes in China', *Energy*, 1980, No. 1.

Luo Yuchuan, 'A Major Development is Imperative for the Forestry Industry in China', *Guangming Daily*, 12 December 1979.

Ma Ye et al., 'The Role of Economic Centres', *Guangming Daily*, 21 February 1980.

Meng Guizhi, 'The Iron Ore Deposits of China and their Future Prospects', *Correspondence on the Technical Economy and Modernization of Management*, 10 May 1981.

Sai Feng, 'Prospects and the Task of Prospecting for Oil Energy in China', *People's Daily*, 16 April 1982.

Science and Technology Committee of the Ministry of Water Conservation and the Hydropower Industry, 'The Position of Hydropower Energy in China's Energy Industry and Policies Concerning its Exploitation', *Hydropower Industry*, 1982, Nos. 1–3.

Sun Han, 'Basic Features of the Natural Conditions and Environments of Agriculture in China', *Beijing Science and Technology Paper*, 26 October 1979.

Sun Xiangjian, 'On the Regional Division of Work in China's Economy', *Study and Thought*, 1981, No. 4.

Tian Ban et al., 'The Importance of the Formation of the Railway Network in the Four Modernizations', *Railway Transport and Economy*, 1981, No. 2.

Wei Fengyan et al., 'Acceleration of the Development of Aquaculture', *Guangming Daily*, 24 April 1979.

Wu Peiru, 'The Position and Role of Coal in the Energy Structure of China', *Energy*, 1981, No. 1.

Xue Muqiao et al., 'Economists on the Central Cities and the Economic Centres', *World Economic Herald*, 25 January 1982.

Yang Hongnian et al., 'On the Problems of Development of Transport and Communications in China', *Comprehensive Transport*, 1979, No. 1.

Yang Zibin et al., 'Views on Increasing the Economic Returns of the Non-ferrous Metals Industry', *On Economic Returns* (Henan People's Publishing House, 1982).

Yu Guoyao, 'Problems Concerning the Inner Structure of Agriculture in China', *Problems of Agricultural Economy*, 1980, No. 5.

Yu Zhenhan, 'Industrial Distribution and Environmental Protection', *Environmental Protection*, 1979, No. 1.

Zhou Lisan et al., 'Realization of the Regionalization and Specialization of Agricultural Production According to Local Conditions', *Beijing Daily*, 7 May. 1979.

Zhu Pirong, 'The Distribution of Agriculture According to Objective Rules', *Correspondence on the Technical Economy and Modernization of Management* (Publishing House of the Chinese Academy of Social Sciences, 1979).

Zhong Han, 'On the Urbanization of Roads in China', *Exploration*, 1982, No. 1.